W9-BZB-653

JEB

America's Next Bush

JEB

America's Next Bush

S. V. DÁTE

JEREMY P. TARCHER / PENGUIN

A MEMBER OF PENGUIN GROUP (USA) INC.

NEW YORK

JEREMY P. TARCHER/PENGUIN
Published by the Penguin Group
Penguin Group (USA) Inc., 375 Hudson Street, New York, New York 10014, USA •
Penguin Group (Canada), 90 Eglinton Avenue East, Suite 700, Toronto, Ontario M4P 2Y3, Canada
(a division of Pearson Penguin Canada Inc.) • Penguin Books Ltd, 80 Strand, London WC2R 0RL,
England • Penguin Ireland, 25 St Stephen's Green, Dublin 2, Ireland (a division of Penguin
Books Ltd) • Penguin Group (Australia), 250 Camberwell Road, Camberwell, Victoria 3124,
Australia (a division of Pearson Australia Group Pty Ltd) • Penguin Books India Pvt Ltd,
11 Community Centre, Panchsheel Park, New Delhi–110 017, India • Penguin Group (NZ),
67 Apollo Drive, Mairangi Bay, Auckland 1311, New Zealand (a division of
Pearson New Zealand Ltd) • Penguin Books (South Africa) (Pty) Ltd, 24 Sturdee Avenue,
Rosebank, Johannesburg 2196, South Africa

Penguin Books Ltd, Registered Offices:
80 Strand, London WC2R 0RL, England

Most Tarcher/Penguin books are available at special quantity discounts for bulk purchase for sales
promotions, premiums, fund-raising, and educational needs. Special books or book excerpts also
can be created to fit specific needs. For details, write Penguin Group (USA) Inc. Special Markets, 375 Hudson Street, New York, NY 10014.

Library of Congress Cataloging-in-Publication Data

Dáte, S. V. (Shirish V.)
Jeb : America's next Bush / S. V. Dáte.
p.   cm.
ISBN 978-1-58542-548-8
1. Bush, Jeb.   2. Governors—Florida—Biography.   3. Florida—Politics and
government—1951–   4. Bush family.   I. Title.
F316.23.B87D38   2007   2006037106
975.9'063092—dc22
[B]

Printed in the United States of America
1 3 5 7 9 10 8 6 4 2

Book design by Lovedog Studio

While the author has made every effort to provide accurate telephone numbers and Internet
addresses at the time of publication, neither the publisher nor the author assumes any responsibility for errors, or for changes that occur after publication. Further, the publisher does not have
any control over and does not assume any responsibility for author or third-party websites or
their content.

For the many good people
in and around Jeb's orbit who risked
their jobs and careers to point me toward the truth

CONTENTS

PREFACE

Jeb Bush is going to hate this book.

Yes, *hate* is a strong word, but I do not use it lightly. Jeb does not *kind of dislike* things; he isn't *not crazy about* them. You're either with him or against him, and this book clearly is not with him.

I know Jeb. I know how he thinks. And what he thinks is that an independent, unauthorized biography of his Florida tenure written by the guy who had become the biggest journalistic thorn in his side cannot possibly be a good thing, particularly when, sooner or later, he runs for president.

Now, I can completely appreciate Jeb's irritation and displeasure with me over the years. I was one of the handful of reporters in Tallahassee who would go deep into the internal documents and statistics of *his own* agencies to compare his rhetoric against the facts. I was the only one who did it so regularly that Jeb felt compelled to punish me and my employer, the *Palm Beach Post*, by restricting our access to him and his staff.

When Jeb claimed, for example, that students in his voucher program for disabled children were getting educations superior to those in the public schools, I found out that 77 percent of the schools in that program did not even have any teachers trained to teach disabled children. When Jeb claimed his massive tax cuts on the state's wealthiest residents had produced new jobs, I wrote how his own employment agency's records showed that Jeb had the lowest job creation rate of any governor going back to 1970. When Jeb claimed that "rounding down" the fractional cent part of a drink tax would save restaurateurs accounting headaches, I pointed out that according to his own Department of Business and Professional Regulation, the drink tax was actually paid by the gallon, and that the "rounding down" would simply not make anyone's math in the least bit easier.

And so it went, on and on, for eight years.

If the Bush family's past is prologue, at first the Jeb machine will ignore this book—might even pretend that no one among them has cared enough to read it—in the belief that any comment will only serve to enhance its "buzz." If, by chance, it nevertheless finds a growing audience, then Jeb and his people, or more likely, just his people, will explain why my deep-seated "bias" against Jeb should render all of my conclusions suspect.

So let me state my bias as a journalist:

I have a bias in favor of the truth. I believe that reporters generally, but particularly political and government reporters, have a responsibility to gain the expertise necessary so that they can make an informed quest for the truth in matters on which they write, and then convey that truth, or as close to it as they can possibly get, in their reports.

If a source lies to you—that is, utters something that is provably false—then you as a journalist have a responsibility either not to print the statement or, if for some reason you do print it, to make sure that you immediately follow it with the correct information that belies it. Why not just print everything, and let the reader sort it out? Because I am not a stenographer, whose job it is merely to take down what I hear and transcribe it. If, after two decades in this business, I have not acquired the ability to separate actual facts from PR "spin" and deal with them accordingly, then I am offering no added value to my readers and would do everyone a favor by retreating to my workshop and taking up cabinetry or some other honest craft.

The fact of it is, I came upon Jeb as a complete blank slate. I had covered NASA for the *Orlando Sentinel* for four years, and then had taken a sailing sabbatical with my wife. When we returned to the States, Jeb had lost his first bid for governor and was regrouping for his second run. I began covering the statehouse for the Associated Press by the time he was again in full campaign mode. I saw him as a high-energy, intelligent individual who had obviously spent a lot of time studying the issues. I personally disagreed with some of his stands on those issues, but in general I had a neutral to favorable impression of him by the time he took office.

Not terribly long into that first term, though, Jeb's relationship with the press, and with me in particular, began to deteriorate. It became abundantly clear that Jeb was not remotely interested in adhering to the spirit of Florida's "Government in the Sunshine" laws as he set about recasting state government according to his own vision.

I think his particular displeasure with me was based at least in part on my peculiar style of reporting, which is heavily based on public records. As I will happily tell cantankerous sources: I do not care if they want to talk to me or not. As long as I have access to those documents to which I have a legal right, I can go ahead and report and write the quantitative analyses that I enjoy doing whether a dozen sources give me interviews, or no sources. I would prefer, for the sake of thoroughness, that politicians and government officials *did* choose to talk to me. But if they do not, it's no great loss, and the paycheck comes on Friday either way.

This style generated instant conflicts with Jeb and his staff for two reasons: first, Jeb Bush has no use for public scrutiny, and his administration went out of its way to devise new and ingenious methods for withholding what historically had been public records. And second, Jeb's press office used as its primary means of manipulation—of which they developed a good many—a carrot-and-stick approach that rewarded good media behavior with improved "access."

I wasn't remotely interested in access to Jeb or his minions. I only wanted full access to public records, as Florida law permitted. Jeb wasn't remotely interested in giving full access to public records. He only wanted to "work" with reporters who would "work" with him—meaning trading favorable or toned-down articles in return for "face time" with Jeb or off-the-record tips for upcoming news.

You see now the basis of the irreconcilable differences.

What's important here is that my impression of Jeb, my *entire* impression of Jeb, is based on my daily coverage of him through his two terms. It is not based on any dislike of his father when he was president—in fact, I rather liked his father when he was president. It is not based on ideas fed to me by Democrats or other Bush haters. It is based on what I've seen of Jeb with my own two eyes, and what I've heard with my own two ears during his eight years in office.

It is, obviously, my point of view—but I will respectfully submit that, given my background, it is an informed point of view.

. . .

If and when the Bushies *really* want to get nasty with me, they will no doubt call me a liberal—the vilest epithet in the family lexicon going back five decades.

Naturally enough, a book—as opposed to a newspaper article—is told through the prism of the author's worldview. Readers will certainly discern mine in these pages, but let me just state them briefly up front: I believe government should provide a *real* quality education to all children, and that the wealthiest nation on the planet can afford to make sure that its poorest and unluckiest have decent medical care. I do not believe any taxpayer should have to subsidize anybody else's religion. I believe that everyone in government, local, state, and federal, works for *us*, and that we have a complete right to know what they are doing on our dime. I believe in the New Testament idea that to whom much is given, much is expected—even in the area of tax policy. I do not believe winning an election gives you the right to rule as a despot. And I believe that our nation should treat other nations the way we would have them treat us. Finally, in all of these things, I believe in facts, and the idea that humans can improve themselves through the study of history and the natural world.

If these views make me a *liberal*—well, okay, as my ten-year-old would say: what-*ever*.

Full disclosure: in December 2003, Jeb banished me and my *Palm Beach Post* colleagues from a round of year-end interviews with him in the governor's office. This action, my editors and I believed, was in retaliation for a long series of articles a colleague and I had written exposing fraud, abuse, and a complete lack of oversight in Jeb's beloved school voucher programs.

Jeb insisted that my articles had nothing to do with it, and that it was because I had offended his press office spokeswoman by using the word "goddamned" in an argument over their stonewalling the *Post* on the release of various documents. Never mind that I had immediately apologized months earlier, when the incident had taken place. What made the whole thing more than a little ridiculous was Jeb's own penchant for cursing a blue streak, when that seemed the most effective means of bullying a hesitant legislator. (Indeed, a decade and a half earlier, he had bragged to a *Miami Herald* reporter how he and his brothers could beat the Kennedy kids in baseball, football, "any goddamn sport" they wished to play.)

That year and also in coming years, Jeb's press office also let it be known to other reporters at the *Post* that it wasn't the newspaper per se they had a problem with, but me personally. And if only *Post* management could do *something* about their staffing in Tallahassee. . . .

In spite of all this, I must confess that I do not dislike him personally. To the contrary, and somewhat inexplicably, I find myself empathizing with his frustrations in dealing with a world that does not agree with his vision, that does not reward his intellect and his hard work by handing over the keys to the kingdom and making him benevolent despot for life.

As much as my personal interpretation of history and human nature and justice differ from his, I nonetheless admire his seemingly inexhaustible energy and intensity. A look at a day's worth of his e-mails tells the story. He got hundreds of them, from a broad cross section of humanity, and did a yeoman's job of reading pretty much all of them. Many he answered personally. Many more he directed to his staff to deal with. Still others, those from his staff to him seeking guidance, showed his level of involvement in the minute details of his administration—whether the Department of Education, for example, should move "Fred" from the graphic design office to a community college position. "Fred has been approached about his interest—and is very interested. He would get to travel more," Jeb was informed in an e-mail seeking his permission. Then there were the many other queries he directed to his staff based on something he had read, either in the stacks of policy notebooks he took home with him at night, or—perish the thought—in the newspapers that day.

We can debate the wisdom of this micromanagement style. If you are paying someone a quarter million dollars a year to run the education shop, surely that person should be entrusted to hire a $40,000-a-year employee.

Still, his dedication to the job was phenomenal. He was not afraid of hard work, and he was not afraid to get into the muddy details of an issue to understand it properly. He is conversant on a wide variety of topics, and can even be thought of as an expert in a few.

This is a person who has done a lot with what was given to him, and that deserves respect.

Part of my affection for him, I think, is also that I see in Jeb some of the qualities I see in myself, both the good and the bad. I like to think I work hard. I like to think I'm reasonably bright. Yet I know I can be impatient, and sometimes I can be frustrated by lack of progress or setbacks.

Jeb also has a biting, at times sarcastic sense of humor, which, as a writer of biting, at times sarcastic novels, I can appreciate. Perhaps naively, I believe that under different circumstances he and I might have been friends—strangely competitive friends, perhaps, but friends nonetheless. (This is, of course, absurd. Jeb has little use for any journalist. We are no more than mosquitos, bothersome irritants that, because of the *liberal* EPA, cannot be exterminated with good ol' DDT.)

A quick note of explanation regarding the lack of "dirt" about Jeb's immediate family: Jeb's wife, Columba, did not run for office. Nor did their children. In Florida they had no role in setting state policy, and therefore I could not see why it was any of my readers' business what problems any of them might have been having. Columba, as First Lady of Florida, had a quasi-public role, and so I touched briefly on that, as well as the conventional wisdom about her desire for, and value in, a presidential run.

Finally, throughout this book, I refer to members of the Bush family by their first names. This is not in keeping with the conventions of journalism, where it is normal to refer to a person by surname on second reference, unless you are the *New York Times*, in which case it is Mr. Surname. I do not do this to suggest some easy familiarity with Jeb—during his entire time as governor, I never called him anything other than "Governor"—but because of the confusion calling him "Bush" would create in a book that frequently mentions George W. Bush, George H.W. Bush, Barbara Bush, and Prescott Bush, among others.

This is what happens when your family is bent on global domination.

Readers may note that this work is somewhat different from the typical political book in that it focuses on actual public policy and governance style, rather than personality and election strategy. There are a couple of reasons for this. One is that there are only a handful of journalists who have had the honor and privilege of covering both Jeb's successful run in 1998 as well as his full two terms in office. I have seen how he works and what he has done, and that is what I can bring to the national conversation about the man.

Second, and more important: unlike many politicians, who want to rule primarily for the sake of ruling (Jeb's father is a good example), Jeb will seek the presidency with a forceful and clear agenda. If we learned anything in Florida, it is that he is relentless, and will not stop until that agenda is accomplished or he is forced out of office.

And if you want to see what he would do with the nation, take a good look at what he did here in Florida. It's important.

It probably goes without saying that Jeb chose not to cooperate with the writing of this book. Not only did he not want to sit for interviews, he generally put out the word to his allies that they also should not talk to me. Because of this, all of my interviews with his current and former staff had to be done on a not-for-attribution basis.

When I asked him questions for articles for the newspaper, he was—except for those occasions when he was particularly mad about something I had written—generally civil about answering them. But when I asked for time with him specifically for the book, he declined. He told me in an e-mail that he might have considered doing so had he thought I would be fair, but that I had proven myself to be "the least fair" of all Tallahassee journalists.

I would respectfully suggest that his and my views on what's a "fair" journalist are substantially different, and would further suggest that my definition is correct and his is not. Based on how he dealt with the media during his campaigns for governor and then during his two terms, I would suggest that his idea of a fair newspaper article is one that showcases his side of the story—notwithstanding whatever the actual facts of the case might be.

Beyond that, though, I believe that Jeb would not have given extensive interviews to any journalist with the possible exception of the few who accepted a symbiotic relationship with him and his press office. Jeb is above all a control freak. He would lash out at his staff in e-mails when articles appeared in newspapers quoting actual employees of his agencies, rather than the designated spokespeople. Given that the only real campaigns left in his life are ones for the presidency or vice presidency—John McCain approached him in December 2005 about serving as his running mate in 2008—Jeb had absolutely nothing to gain and a lot to lose by lending any sort of legitimacy to any sort of book other than a glowing hagiography.

I think it is important to note that Jeb's ostensible reason for not cooperating with me was my lack of fairness, not my lack of accuracy. I work hard to get it right, and over the years have made very few mistakes in my reporting about him and his administration. When I erred, my newspaper and I acted quickly to correct the record.

Finally, I will point out that this volume is not merely my idle musings. It is based on the underlying research that produced for the *Palm Beach Post* a body of work about Jeb's elections and administration that topped eight hundred articles in over a decade. I have read tens of thousands of pages of original government documents about Jeb's policies, and many thousands more pages of e-mail messages to and from Jeb and his top aides. I have conducted hundreds of interviews with both Jeb lovers and Jeb haters. I have participated, cumulatively, in hundreds of hours of formal and informal news conferences in which Jeb has answered thousands of questions.

And so, yes: Jeb Bush is going to hate this book.

But as I hope I will show in these pages, he is going to hate this book not because it is inaccurate, but because it is not.

JEB

America's Next Bush

Chapter One

PRINCE JEB

"Making a bunch of money didn't excite me. Politics is a contact sport, it's ugly. But I think I can do something. My father saw politics as service. You can be far more effective if you view it as a mission, like a religion."

—JEB BUSH, 1994

"If he has been so devoted to this state, why hasn't he run for his local school board, mayor, or even dogcatcher? His decision to seek the governor's office to begin his rise through politics speaks volumes for his ego."

—LETTER-TO-THE-EDITOR
WRITER SHERRY FOSTER, 1994

"Dynasty, shmynasty."

—JEB BUSH, 1998

November 8, 1994. Mark it down, the worst day in young Jeb Bush's life. For it was on that election night that Jeb understood that his best-laid plans had suffered a serious, perhaps catastrophic setback.

He was supposed to win, by God. . . .

On the Tuesday that Newt Gingrich's Republicans took over the U.S.

House and GOP candidates all over the country stormed the barricades, Jeb Bush, a Republican's Republican, a son who would restore the family honor after the Great Usurpation of 1992, had lost. Walkin' Lawton Chiles, a Florida legend, had come from behind in the closing weeks and eked out a 63,940-vote victory—which, in those pre–Katherine Harris days, was actually considered a razor-thin margin.

It had all been planned so beautifully, each item with a little box beside it for checking off, all the way from Andover to Pennsylvania Avenue: Graduate college. Check. Get a job. Check. Get married and start a family. Check. Make millions. Check. Take over local party apparatus. Check. Become governor. . . .

And so, there sat Jeb on the bed in his room in downtown Miami's Crowne Plaza, thinking about his life as he smoked his first cigarette in years. Now what? He'd invested eighteen months, put a serious strain on his marriage, beaten a half-dozen Republican rivals for the nomination, only to fall to a guy who called himself the He-Coon, whatever the hell that meant. *Now what?*

Meanwhile, a thousand miles to the west, on the far side of the Gulf of Mexico, fate had delivered a perverse twist. For just as Jeb was supposed to beat Lawton Chiles in Florida, big brother George W. was supposed to get his clock cleaned by Texas governor Ann Richards.

So guess what?

At first, there was little to this beyond a cruel joke. Big brother George, who had coasted through life until age forty, would get to be governor of a major state, and Jeb would not. Jeb—hardworking, industrious, took-himself-seriously-when-he-was-a-lad Jeb—would return to his real estate development business. George W. would call a legislature into session, deliver state-of-the-state speeches, live in a governor's mansion. Even their own mother couldn't help but remark on the irony.

But it wasn't until four years later that the full implications of that 1994 election night became clear. By election night 1998, Jeb had remade himself. He had worked to repair his marriage, made a point of spending more time with his children, and then consciously built an image playing up the compassionate and playing down the conservative. He won easily, becoming only the third Republican governor in Florida since Reconstruction.

Meaning, in the end, he had only lost four years off his schedule. Right?

Well, not exactly. Because in Austin, George W. won a landslide reelection, this time with a huge chunk of the Hispanic vote. And when the national GOP money guys started casting about for a candidate to take on

Vice President Al Gore two years later, guess which Bush brother was at the top of the list?

IN JEB, Bush watchers should take care not to see merely a younger, taller version of his brother, for he is not. Far from it.

This is a man with the brainpower to be an intellectual—but with enough empathy for the GOP's core constituency to be scornful of the title. Jeb Bush is smart enough to delve deep into the intricacies of government policies—yet often chooses not to, dealing instead with complicated issues wearing a pair of ideological blinders and brandishing a right-wing think tank's white paper.

This is a man, even those who hate all things Bush must agree, who appears to feel a sense of noblesse oblige, however silly that might sound, in seeking high political office. His opponents call it the height of arrogance—someone who, because of his family, believed it was his destiny and obligation to be governor of the fourth-largest state without having served even one day in lesser office. Still, they cannot quarrel with this: Jeb's personal motives in pursuing leadership are not in any way venal. He honestly believes that his vision and skills are necessary for a better state and a better nation. He did not get into politics to make money. To the contrary—given his family and his work ethic, Jeb Bush probably could have been a billionaire, if that's what he had wanted.

And so, America, here he is: the great-grandson of a wheeler-dealer investment banker who made the family fortune during the Depression, the grandson of a United States senator, the son of a one-term president, the younger brother of a two-term president.

He was a millionaire by the time he was thirty-five, but he doesn't much care about money except for its ability to bring him the two things he does crave: power, and the thrill of winning it. He opposed the Vietnam War, to the point that he seriously considered registering as a conscientious objector rather than submitting to the draft—but nevertheless has received the same electoral support of the active and retired military traditionally enjoyed by his family.

He dallied with the Socialist Club at his elite boarding school, Phillips Academy, in Andover, Massachusetts. Yet as an adult, he pushed a tax policy in Florida that exceeded even his brother's in its generosity to the wealthiest citizens at the expense of the state's poorest.

He is a born introvert, who as a younger man was content to melt into

1964: A family portrait of the Bushes the year George H.W. first ran (and lost) for the U.S. Senate in Texas. Everyone else is doing what the photographer asked while Jeb, age eleven, looks at the camera. Standing: Neil, Jeb, and George W. Seated: George H.W., Doro, Barbara, and Marvin.

the walls at large gatherings. "I am kind of antisocial," he told a writer for *Women's Wear Daily* in 1988, blaming it on his mother. "I learned that from her. She dislikes phony formalities." Yet by the time of his second run for Florida governor in his midforties, he had become a polished candidate and far-and-away the best extemporaneous speaker of his family.

He claims as his major legacy the very transformation of the public educational system in Florida, and can quote dozens of statistics to make you believe him. Yet by the time he left office, his biggest education legacy was having spent his entire second term trying to repeal a costly constitutional amendment that really did hold the potential to transform Florida's dismal public schools.

He tried his best to privatize Florida's state government, outsourcing huge swaths of work to for-profit companies, often based outside of Florida. He tried his best to voucher-ize the public schools, sending hundreds of millions of dollars to mainly religious schools, despite a state constitution that said he couldn't.

He did his best to hide all of this from public view, except for those bits that made him or his policies appear successful. He bullied and cajoled legislators, judges, and journalists who questioned him, flouted Florida's tradition of open government, and otherwise took his electoral mandate to lead as a license to rule.

He was charming. He was vicious. He was brilliant. He was dogmatic. He was reading, learning, prying—always on the move, never resting.

And most important of all: he was always, always playing for keeps.

To UNDERSTAND this juggernaut of a man, it is necessary to appreciate the aura he generates whenever he enters a room. All side conversations cease as all eyes move to the new focal point. It becomes, for however long he chooses to hold it, all about Jeb.

Whatever combination of intelligence, charm, self-confidence, ruthlessness, and wit it is that gives some politicians that magnetism, that presence, that sense of command to take and hold the spotlight in whatever situation they find themselves in, Jeb possesses it in spades. And the response of most Floridians to this man—well, it really had to be seen to be believed.

This was not the mere wonder of seeing a famous or powerful figure in person, as is the case with most politicians. This was something more akin to the adulation shown by preadolescent teens to the newest pop star. Wherever Jeb went, be it a shopping mall or a college or a county government center—the faces of those around him more often than not would wear shining eyes and ecstatic smiles, as if merely being in his presence brought sublime joy. This phenomenon surfaced first during his 1994 run for governor, and only grew more pervasive over the next dozen years.

Perhaps it's easy for a conservative Republican from a prominent family to wow the chamber of commerce set, to have community leaders falling over each other to be near him, to get a smile or a nod from him, maybe even touch him. Perhaps it's easy for any major politician to win the fawning admiration of his base of supporters.

What makes Jeb such a force is his ability to win if not the approval, then at least the respect of people who might reasonably have cause to dislike or distrust him. A perfect example of this is Jeb's ability to charm the journalists who covered him in Tallahassee—even after eight years of wearing his utter contempt for those same journalists as a badge of honor.

For two full terms, reporters who would among themselves describe Jeb as an arrogant megalomaniac would turn meek as mice during his press conferences. All the bluster would disappear, and Jeb would typically get softball questions on the approved topic of the day. This is partly based on fear. Jeb is a daunting presence—both tall, at six feet four, and large, well north of two hundred pounds, and with a great, enormous head. He has a well-practiced glower to make that head seem even bigger, and a willingness to snap back at unprepared reporters with retorts designed to embarrass them into silence.

Yet the deference he received from the news media went beyond mere conflict avoidance. Government reporters as a group run across their fair share of abusive personalities. Generally they manage this without falling into some bizarre Stockholm syndrome–type deal where they wind up wanting, more than anything else, for the person they cover to *like* them.

For that, right there, is what sets Jeb apart. Such is his command of policy details, his ability to think on his feet, his willingness to utterly *destroy* a challenger, that it brings a sense of quiet accomplishment, even joy, when he acknowledges with a nod, a smile, and—best of all—an actual attaboy, that your query had merit. Even I, who, because of the articles I wrote about him and, later, because of this book, had earned more of Jeb's abuse than any other Florida journalist, will confess my satisfaction at the thought that, despite everything, he somehow liked and respected me.

Remember here that we're talking about reporters—the one group of people with whom Jeb had to interact regularly whose careers and day-to-day lives he could affect the least. If Jeb could still manage to use *their* desire for his approval to his benefit, just imagine what he was able to accomplish with legislators, lobbyists, bureaucrats, local government officials, and all the other satellites in his orbit.

The best example of this is probably Tom Lee, who over his career as a Republican state senator from Tampa had become the biggest impediment to Jeb's agenda. Lee blocked Jeb's attempt to deregulate electricity California style, and had forced him to accept a watered down version of medical malpractice "reform"—and that was all before Lee ascended to the Senate presidency. And yet, in his final year in that position, Lee did an about-face on a number of issues critical to Jeb, most notably school vouchers. The simple explanation would have been Lee's campaign for statewide Cabinet office that year, and his desire for Jeb's endorsement.

The fact that an endorsement was given just days after the legislative session ended lends credence to that theory—but it falls short. In fact, the co-opting of Lee was a more subtle thing. Of all the Tallahassee establishment, Tom Lee was probably the closest thing Jeb had to a match, both in intellect and stubbornness. In the spring session of 2005, Lee warned Jeb to stay out of his Senate, because he had "no role" there. In the spring session of 2006, Lee was calling Bush "my governor" as he explained his willingness to push Jeb's agenda.

Why the change? The two had grown closer in the intervening year, Lee explained. "I think he respects me," Lee said.

It should come as little surprise, then, that Jeb was able to maintain rock-star popularity, leaving office with nearly as high approval ratings as when he had entered it eight years earlier, even as Floridians remained dubious about his signature issues. Poll after poll showed that voters did not believe the schools were getting significantly better, even though Jeb repeatedly claimed that they were, and did not believe that they had received much of a tax cut, even though Jeb repeatedly claimed that he had given them a huge one. It didn't matter. Floridians loved him anyway.

Like the journalists, like Tom Lee, they just wanted him to like them.

JOHN ELLIS BUSH was born February 11, 1953, in Midland, Texas—the place his older brother, the president, who is actually a native of New Haven, Connecticut, likes to call his hometown. It would be a big mistake, though, to think of Jeb as a Texan, just as it is a mistake to think of him as a Floridian.

Jeb Bush is a Bush, first, last, and always. True, his first sentient visions may well have been the pan-flat landscapes of West Texas, just as, as Florida's governor, he has learned to talk Florida's talk about safeguarding natural resources like the beaches and the Everglades. In reality, these other milieus have been little more than stage scenery. Like his elder brother and a long line of their forebears, Jeb is a product of Andover—although, following prep school, he forsook his father's, grandfather's, great-great-grandfather's, and older brother's Yale for the University of Texas in Austin, so as to be closer to the Mexican girl who would become his wife within days of his graduation.

Bush has lived in Florida since 1981, a year and a half after he came back to the States to work on his father's presidential campaign following a brief stint as a bank officer in Venezuela. His dad's moderate brand of Republicanism didn't play well in the primaries (George H.W. famously called the front-runner's vision of massive tax cuts "voodoo economics"), but Ronald Reagan chose him as his running mate anyway en route to sweeping Jimmy Carter back to Plains, Georgia.

With his father the sitting vice president, Jeb's future was suddenly much brighter. He was not yet thirty years old, but his relative lack of experience in life or much of anything else, for that matter, did not prove much of a hindrance. A wealthy Miami real estate developer made Bush a 40-percent partner in his business. Jeb insists it happened because Armando Codina valued Jeb's acumen and work ethic. Skeptics suggest it might have had a little more to do with his last name.

Whatever the reason, the Codina Bush Group and its related entities quickly made young Jeb a rich man. Other business opportunities provided similar windfalls. Jeb allied himself with an HMO owner who later fled the country after being charged with defrauding Medicare. He did land deals with a former CIA operative, netting him hundreds of thousands of dollars in a series of complicated transactions. Jeb, by then a self-described "head-banging" conservative who opposed government handouts, nonetheless availed himself of the opportunity to sell water pumps in Nigeria in a deal that soon afterward won $74 million in loans guarantees from the federal Export-Import Bank. As perennially corrupt Nigeria defaults on the note—many of the pumps ended up rusting in the fields, unused—U.S. taxpayers have wound up picking up the tab. Jeb claimed, however, that none of the $600,000 he made from the pump venture came from the Nigeria deal. He also refused to detail what exactly those payments were for, telling journalists prior to his 1998 election: "You either trust me, or you don't."

These and similar businesses were what Jeb mainly did in the early and mid-1980s. Note there was no real pattern to Jeb's business interests, save for the fact that he made money. Jeb has no specific training as an accountant or an engineer or, God forbid, a lawyer. This seems to be a family trait shared by older brother George W. and younger brother Neil. All three were "businessmen." Doing a little of this, a little of that—and getting spectacularly rich.

IN FAIRNESS, Jeb Bush is an extremely intelligent man, and has worked hard at everything he has done. Had he been born John Doe, chances are good that he still would have been financially successful. No, the criticism here is one of philosophy. Jeb Bush was born with the mind and the family name that would enable him to do anything he wanted. And given that, what did he choose to do? Sell real estate in South Florida and subsidized water pumps in Nigeria. Given the world spread before him, could he possibly have aimed any lower?

In these choices, Jeb betrays telling hints into his worldview. One that emerges later in his years as governor is the core belief that a wealthy person is, until proven otherwise, of high moral character. It is a curious but perhaps uniquely American yardstick. For Jeb, the question is not: has this person used his or her God-given talents to full potential? Or: has this person contributed to society? But rather: in the jungle of competition out there, did this person come out on top?

Another conclusion that emerges is that Jeb had neither time nor interest in acquiring expertise in any particular sphere of human understanding—the law, for instance, or medicine—because he knew that whatever he did in his twenties and thirties, it was merely a way station to bigger and better things.

He was a Bush, and Bushes were born to rule.

In any event, his own easy road to financial security has bred in him a sincere lack of patience with those who have a tough time simply getting through life. He doesn't understand poor people, and cannot relate to their existence. In Jeb Bush's America, an adult who cannot make it almost certainly sowed the seeds to this condition in his or her past, either by a failure to pay attention during school, or a drug or alcohol addiction, or an even more fundamental character flaw. After all, he was a millionaire when he was still a young man, and he wasn't even trying all that hard, what with devoting so much of his time to politics. Surely a modicum of effort by the average American should produce similarly fruitful results.

A corollary to this is Jeb's angry rejection of critics' complaints that his policies too often have benefited the wealthy. These criticisms typically include the insinuation that Jeb helps out his rich friends so that they will give him campaign money. Nothing, in Jeb's mind, could be further from the truth, for two reasons. First, he promotes policies advanced by rich people because, to him, it makes total sense to do so. If someone is rich, it means he or a recent ancestor has proven himself on this Earth, and his opinion is therefore on its face more valuable than that of a poor person. And second, Jeb promotes the interests of the rich not because they give him money and support, but because he truly believes that doing so is in the nation's best interest.

In this, Jeb knows, he is being neither hypocritical nor craven, and he is probably right. His motives are, more or less, pure. A bit odd, perhaps, and on the face of it more than a little self-serving, but pure.

Nonetheless, this is his worldview, and given the success it has brought him thus far, it is not likely to change.

AFTER HIS FATHER became vice president, Jeb rose to chairman of the Dade County Republican Committee, but did not seek elected office. In 1987, upon the election of Tampa Republican Bob Martinez to the Governor's Mansion, Jeb took his first (and, prior to becoming governor himself in 1998, only) job in government as Martinez's secretary of commerce. It was not a high-level post, and Jeb was not happy there. He lasted a year and a half before returning to Miami, his dad's successful 1988 presidential campaign, and, after the election, his various business enterprises. He and wife Columba lived in an upper-middle-class suburb with their three children: elder son George P. (whom Bush aficionados are already pegging as the next generation's shining star), daughter Noelle, and younger son Jebbie.

In 1992, his father was evicted from the White House—a stunning blow to the clan, particularly in the wake of the Gulf War, when reelection seemed a near certainty. Work to start rebuilding the dynasty, however, began within weeks, both in Florida and Texas. In Florida, Governor Lawton Chiles had inherited a deep recession when he took office in 1991. The massive budget cuts he was forced to make had driven down his popularity ratings, which by early 1993 had yet to recover. Chiles was beatable, and everyone knew it. Jeb, as well as a handful of established Republicans, two of them statewide officeholders already, jumped into the race. In Texas, in contrast, Democrat Ann Richards appeared to be in good shape. Few serious candidates wanted to take her on. Into that breach stepped George W. Bush—evidently still plenty angry at Richards for ridiculing his father during the 1992 Democratic convention as having been born with a silver foot in his mouth.

The two races seemed mirror images of each other. George W., in Texas, was well behind in Labor Day weekend polls. Jeb, in Florida, had put together a national-campaign caliber political machine for a statewide race that caught Chiles's staff sleeping. In early September, after handily dispatching the more established Republicans in the primary, Jeb was leading the incumbent by double digits. In the final two months, though, George W. beat Richards over the head with "God, gays, and guns"—and pulled off a stunning upset. And in Florida, it was Walkin' Lawton who came from behind, delivering in the campaign's final debate the famous warning: "The He-Coon walks just before the light of day." The crackerism appeared to throw Jeb back on his heels, and he never regained his momentum.

JEB RETREATED to Miami and his lucrative businesses. Quickly enough, 1994 was let go. While continuing his work with Codina Bush, Jeb quietly set up the Foundation for Florida's Future, a think tank ostensibly designed to ponder the weighty issues facing the state. Pundits quickly dubbed it the Foundation for Jeb's Future—its staff was the core of the Bush campaign team. Using corporate donations from the usual suspects, Jeb kept his machine together until the next governor's race, in 1998. He also remained *the* Republican star of Florida, serving as the head of the state delegation to the 1996 Republican convention, even though there was an incumbent Republican United States senator and a dozen Republican congressmen. So it was little surprise to anyone when he announced he would run again. This time, there was no Republican opposition, and Jeb beat the sitting lieutenant governor, a nice, smart guy but a hapless campaigner, by ten points.

Much to his critics' surprise, his first year showed a governor with an outsider's attitude and little concern for Tallahassee's ways. He vetoed pork barrel projects by the hundreds and, to the surprise of many Democrats, increased spending for such things as programs for the developmentally disabled and for abused children. That first year, of course, also saw a billion dollars in tax cuts and the first statewide school voucher program in the country. Because the economy was roaring along and Governor Chiles's landmark lawsuit against Big Tobacco had brought in so many extra billions, there was money to burn. Who could mind if a big chunk of it went back to taxpayers, even if the cuts were disproportionately skewed toward the richest five percent of Floridians?

Then came 2000 and his brother's bid for the presidency. It was as if a light switch had been thrown. Gone was the reasonable-sounding Jeb Bush who actually seemed like he was trying to forge a consensus, and back came the win-at-any-cost politician.

That year, Jeb's second as governor, started with a sit-in by two black lawmakers in the office of Jeb's lieutenant governor to protest his unilateral dismantling of Florida's affirmative action programs—designed, in part, to thwart a petition drive by California activist Ward Connerly to put the question on the November ballot. Brother George W. was running as a compassionate conservative. The last thing Jeb wanted was a divisive, hot-button question like that on the Florida ballot. Jeb handled the situation poorly—at one point being caught on video telling his staff to "kick their asses out." (Jeb clarified later that he meant kick out the asses of the journalists who were with the black lawmakers, not the asses of the black lawmakers themselves.)

Two months later, ten thousand black protesters descended on the Capitol on the opening day of the legislative session, the largest such demonstration in decades. One of the sit-in legislators, Kendrick Meek, made it his personal mission to avenge Jeb's affirmative action decision with a voter registration drive to turn out the black vote against George W. Now, most voter registration drives end in failure. Signing up new voters is one thing. Getting them to actually show up is another. Meek delivered, and the 280,000 extra black voters who cast ballots over and beyond the 1996 turnout rate gave Al Gore a virtual tie, broken a month later by the United States Supreme Court.

Which is a long way of saying that if election night 1994 was the worst in Jeb's life, election night 2000 was a close second.

After all, what kind of brother are you if, as governor, you can't even deliver your own state in a presidential election? And yet, that's exactly what appeared to have happened as he, George W., and their parents ate dinner at an Austin restaurant. The food had not yet arrived when the television announced that Florida had been called for Al Gore. Jeb reportedly apologized in tears. (Other reports had the two brothers quarreling through the meal, to the point where George H.W. Bush had to make them stop.)

By the time the long night was over, a thirty-six-day ordeal had begun. Comedians had a field day. Fidel Castro offered to send election observers. Jeb, who always figured he would be the one to follow in his dad's footsteps, instead publicly claimed neutrality while, behind the scenes, did what he could to preserve a small-and-dwindling lead so his brother could be president.

The most telling moment probably came after it was all over, the following January. Jeb had an informal discussion with the Tallahassee capital press corps. The reporters danced around the subject for a while, until finally someone asked him: what's it like to be brother of the president rather than president yourself?

How do you answer a question like that?

This is how Jeb answered it: President? Who wants to be president? You can't change anything in Washington. A governor can change things. A president can't. That's why I like being governor.

So you don't want to be president?

Nope.

No one in the room believed him, not for a minute. Not even, I am convinced, Jeb.

JEB—THE NAME, incidentally, is an acronym of his initials, John Ellis Bush; a fact which never got in the way of his frequent public ridicule of bureaucrats who used acronyms in their speech—is a complicated man, no question. Far more nuanced and capable of seeing nuance than his brother.

Yet his all-consuming drive to become our leader and impose his view of the world upon us has entangled him in a variety of contradictions and hypocrisies through the years that seem all the more stark precisely because he can be such a thoughtful man.

For example, during his 1994 run, he made welfare a main issue in his campaign, vowing to get tough on recipients of public assistance—even if it meant, he said at one point, having the state take away the children of parents who were too lazy to find a job. At event after event, Jeb talked about the welfare mom who, given all the various freebies available to her like Aid to Families with Dependent Children and Medicaid and so forth, was pulling down an extravagant $15,000 a year in benefits. Jeb could only shake his head in disbelief at this travesty—even though, just six years earlier, Jeb and his partner Armando Codina had walked away with $4 *million* in public assistance, thanks to the forgiving manner that savings and loan regulators dealt with a note a business associate of theirs had defaulted on. Jeb's welfare queen would have needed 267 years to get as much from the public dole as Jeb and Codina managed with a few signatures.

In 2002, Jeb worked mightily to defeat a ballot initiative sponsored by confirmed foe Kendrick Meek that sought to put in the state constitution the requirement that Florida's public schools reduce their class sizes by two children each year until they reached the goal of no more than eighteen, twenty-two, and twenty-five, depending on the grade level. A reasonable enough idea, it would seem, to a man who had paid many tens of thousands of dollars to ensure that his own children attended private schools that advertised small classes. But no, to Jeb the plan was mere political treachery, designed to saddle his second term with an expensive mandate that would make further large tax cuts impossible. He campaigned his heart out against the measure, lashing out against it, in fact, with more enthusiasm than he did against his Democratic opponent that year. By election day, he drove the favorable ratings of the amendment down from the mid-sixties to a mere 52.4 percent passing margin, setting up a repeal of the amendment as his top legislative priority for his second term. Again, given the schools he himself attended and the schools he chose for his children, what was most amazing about all of this is that, through it all, he managed to keep a straight face.

And his work against the class-size amendment in 2002 serves as a nice contrast to Jeb's work against a slot-machine gambling amendment in 2004. Jeb, as a good Christian conservative, has long opposed gambling as emblematic of the "something for nothing" culture that afflicts America. And so when the gambling interests put on the ballot an initiative to allow slot machines at pari-mutuels in Miami-Dade and Broward counties by local referendum, one would have expected Jeb to fight it tooth and nail, right? At least as hard as he fought the class-size amendment, right?

Wrong. In fact, Jeb barely lifted a finger, leaving it to the usual antigambling groups to fight millions of dollars in dog- and horse-track money. The consequence: the pro-slots initiative passed, leaving the question of slots in those two counties to the local voters in early 2005. Jeb mobilized his people to defeat it in Miami-Dade, but could not stop it in Broward. But why so little effort, so late in the game? Why not a full-bore campaign against the statewide ballot question in 2004?

"I was busy," he said in February 2005. "I was trying to be a good governor, and the other priorities were important. The reelection of the president, and election of a United States senator. I would have preferred that it not win."

Translation: my brother was facing a tight race again, and I needed every Republican and independent vote I could get, including the libertarians who have no problem with gambling.

And so, Florida in 2006, with a conservative Republican governor, finally got the casino-style gambling that Democratic governors Reubin Askew, Bob Graham, and Lawton Chiles had successfully staved off in 1978, 1986, and 1994.

SOME OF THIS hypocrisy, I have come to understand, is not necessarily intentional, but more a function of his upbringing, which was so absurdly unlike the rest of ours that he simply cannot relate to the lives of typical Americans.

Like any politician, Jeb tries to talk as if he's a just a normal, down-to-earth guy with his head on straight and his feet on the ground. Of course, though, he is not. He has grown up in the world of ridiculously expensive boarding schools, of houses with servants, of acquaintances who can write six-figure checks to their favorite political party. He has an uncle (his namesake, actually, Jonathan Bush) who once said that, growing up during the Depression, he never thought of his family as rich, even though they had a cook, a maid, and chauffer because: "Other kids had more." He has an aunt who described how strict and frugal their mother was by recounting how she made them *bring their own tennis rackets in out of the rain*. He has a mother who noted, as one of her chief complaints about Watergate in 1973, how difficult all the unpleasantness was making it to find a tennis partner who did not believe Richard Nixon was lying. He has an older brother who once told one of his Harvard Business School professors: "Look. People are poor because they are lazy." He has a father who, as president, once asked an aide who wanted time off so he could pay his bills, wash his clothes, and so forth: "Don't you have people to do those things for you?"

In 1994, as a first-time candidate for governor, Jeb kept telling everyone how "independent" he was, how much of a "self-made man." And yet his own entry to Miami a decade earlier, at age twenty-eight, was eased with a $20,000 loan from his father to buy a $175,000 house—figures that inflate, by the way, to $43,500 and $380,000 in 2006 dollars. Also during that 1994 campaign, his personal contribution to the horror stories of Florida's never-ending crime wave was a burglary at his home in which thieves stole a diamond necklace worth $25,000—a figure that significantly exceeded the per capita income in the state at the time.

In 1998, on the final day of his second try for governor, the same day the state Democratic Party chartered an American Eagle turboprop for its "fly around" of the major media markets, Jeb's entourage and traveling press were split between two Gulfstream 4 business jets owned by billionaire Wayne Huizenga.

So it was a bit of a comedown when he took office and won access to the pride of the state of Florida air fleet—a 1984 Beechcraft King Air B100, a six-seat turboprop.

"That stupid little plane," he called it.

Well, that stupid little plane, at the time, was worth some $2 million. As small planes went, it had an excellent safety record, it was fuel-efficient, and it was fully capable of ferrying Jeb and needed staff from Tallahassee to any city in Florida and back. In fact, given that the absolute longest flying distance in Florida—Pensacola to Miami—is 462 nautical miles, the difference between the King Air and a jet amounted to thirty-three minutes. This was the reason that a previous governor had unloaded a jet the state once owned and replaced it with the King Air.

None of this logic mattered. Jeb as a young man had grown accustomed to flying around with his dad aboard the brand-new 747 that became the primary *Air Force One*. That plane could cross the Pacific, with his father asleep in a full-size bed, at a steady 500 knots. The King Air could only hit 265 knots.

And so, in his second term, Jeb quietly dumped the King Air. Instead, the state leased a Cessna Citation that can fly at 385 knots. The irony is that the Citation is considerably smaller than the King Air, meaning that six-feet-four Jeb has to squeeze into a smaller space, albeit for several fewer minutes on each trip.

Of course, by then, George W. had already gotten the keys to *Air Force One*, enabling him to fly around the country and the world, taking along such comforts as his treadmill.

It's of note that Florida did not purchase the Cessna, which would have made more sense economically, but leased it. Why? Because the state was in a recession. It would have *looked bad*, buying a new jet for Jeb when the state's school budgets had only recently been slashed. Then again, even more economical than buying a jet was to have bought another turboprop.

But that was never really on the table. Turboprops, recall, are both "stupid" and "little."

JEB'S TASTE for the more extravagant comforts in life is not unexpected, given his background and expectations. More of a surprise is his solitude.

For although the phrase Prince Jeb is meant partly in jest—here, the next Bush in the long line of family members who think they should be president—in some ways Jeb really has come into the life of a prince, and not in a good way.

Because to be a prince, a true heir apparent, in an Old World monarchy was to be alone. You couldn't have real friends, because you were the prince, someday to be the king, and it was just not right to treat commoners as equals and vice versa. It upset the natural order. Instead of friends and playmates, a prince had tutors and regents. Most of all, a prince had people who kowtowed to his every wish, and showered him with sycophantic praise. A prince was, really, all alone.

Somehow, amazingly, this was the life that Jeb created for himself. In his Capitol suite, he was surrounded almost exclusively by admirers who did not like to disagree with him, let alone tell him when he was wrong. Most were vastly younger than he, without families or outside responsibilities. However demanding he was of them, they remained ever obliging. And after longtime campaign manager and closest confidante Sally Bradsaw left, there was really no one left who had the gumption to challenge him. Once, at a Capitol news conference, Jeb asked his ideological soul mate and aide Brian Yablonski who had come up with a particular idea. Yablonski, who is at least Jeb's intellectual match, felt compelled to offer a worshipful smile, a thumbs-up, and a "You did, sir."

When he was campaigning, he immersed himself into a different world of admirers—the kind with money, and who wanted something, and who believed that their check or envelope full of checks would mean something when they had some pressing need at some point in the future.

And yet . . . these were aides and supporters, not friends. In fact, he had no close friends at all.

This was partly because he was too busy with Important Things. When he played golf, he was in a hurry to finish. When he went to a football game (Florida governors have to do this; it is one of the few things we, as a state, do well), he cut out at halftime to get some work done. When he sat down to watch sports on television, he did this not with a pal or two and a beer, but with his laptop, so he could get some work done at the same time.

He is, obviously, a workaholic to make ordinary workaholics look like slackers. A first-rate type A. But even workaholics have friends. Jeb's solitude goes beyond that—something more akin to the adolescent monarch, getting ever closer to the coronation where he will accept the crown and the scepter.

THAT GIVES us a good way to understand Jeb, in fact, which is to picture him as the brooding child-king, going through life with twin angels on his shoulders. On one side one says: "Do what's right." On the other, the one with the horns and the wicked grin whispers: "Make sure you win!"

What chronic Bush haters will find surprising is how often Jeb does try to listen to the good angel. Maybe it's his father's insistence in following the forms and manners of good breeding. Maybe it really is an honest desire to obey the "moral compass" he's always talking about.

In any event, it's been there a while, the good angel. In 1988, when the state Republican establishment was lining up behind congressman Connie Mack as their Senate candidate, it was Jeb who went across the room to shake the hand of Robert Merkle. Mad Dog Merkle, as he was known, was a no-holds-barred federal prosecutor who had earned the party's wrath by letting a Tampa corruption case veer dangerously close to newly elected Republican governor Bob Martinez. Everybody else in the place shunned Merkle at a GOP soiree. Jeb went out of his way to welcome him.

Six years later, the morning after Democrat Lawton Chiles had come from behind in the polls to beat Jeb in the governor's race, Jeb saw his opponent standing on a street corner in Miami waving a thank-you sign to motorists. Jeb stopped his car and got out to congratulate Lawton before heading on home.

Even with reporters he does not like—even with me, whom he cheerfully described as the "least fair" journalist in Tallahassee—Jeb usually had a tough time not taking their questions and generally answering them in a civil manner.

Of course, the good angel did not always win. Within days of going out of his way to congratulate Chiles, Jeb was approached on an airplane by the eldest daughter of then-senator Bob Graham. Gwen Graham offered her condolences, telling him that she knew how hard it must have been for him to lose. Jeb bawled her out, telling her that he might not have lost if her father had not cut television ads, helping Chiles in the campaign's final days.

And as civil as Jeb tries to remain during news conferences, there were too many times over his eight years in office when Jeb would deflect a question he deemed as unfriendly by challenging, intimidating, or even be-littling the questioner. It was the schoolyard bully in him. Given his phys-ical size and his stature, it did not become him.

Interestingly, for the first year of his governorship, Jeb frequently, per-haps even mainly, listened to his good angel. He appeared to be trying so hard to remember that he was governor of all Floridians, not just those who had voted for him or given him campaign money. He tried to give a fair hearing to policy arguments that countered his intuition. He even vetoed the pet budget projects of his legislative allies because he thought that giv-ing legislators hometown "turkeys"—Tallahassee lingo for "pork"—to brag about come election time was not an appropriate use of tax money.

All that came to a crashing end in early 2000. His brother was the pre-sumptive Republican candidate for president, and Jeb was watching in dis-may as two black legislators successfully put an end to his rapprochement with the black community over his proposal to restructure affirmative ac-tion. It was like watching a machine being flipped into its reverse gear, as Jeb realized that two back-bench Democrats had outmaneuvered him and were trying to cost his brother the election.

And at that moment, the dark angel decided his time had come, and he took a pike and smote the good angel, knocking him off his perch entirely. We haven't really seen much of him since.

TO A LARGE EXTENT, the story of this generation of political Bushes is the story of two bullies—one who cannot admit error for fear of being found out as an indolent imposter; the other who does not admit error be-cause, well, he is simply never wrong.

George W. has governed from the outset as if he knew that his presi-dency was a total fraud, and had to compensate with an exaggerated sense of self-assurance. By fraud, I do not mean in the literal sense of the elec-tion process, but in the psychological sense. Nothing in his life had re-motely prepared him to lead the world's only superpower. And like the corporate overachiever who shoots for the promotion for which he is un-qualified but which he wins anyway, once in the Oval Office, he had to fake his way through it.

This is not meant to be as harsh a criticism as it might seem. The American presidency now carries such absurdly immense responsibilities that it is hard to imagine that any new president does not sit at the Oval Office desk for the first time and wonder exactly what he has gotten himself into—let alone somebody who has won the election despite getting fewer votes than his opponent.

Of course, there is one person, should he ever find himself behind that desk, who would not doubt for even a moment that he, more so than any other American of his generation and perhaps even the one previous, was absolutely the most qualified to be there. And that would be brother Jeb.

For this is the Curse of Being Jeb. Ever since he was eight years old, there stood the White House as the ultimate goal. Not a fantastic dream, like a trip to the moon or Mars might have been for other children grow-ing up in Houston in that era, but a concrete destination, achievable by hard work and steady, quantifiable steps.

Forty-six years later, he has taken most of the steps. Only a few, the steepest, remain.

Pop singer Jimmy Buffett, campaigning in 1998 for Jeb's opponent, Democrat Buddy MacKay, told an airport rally in Titusville that if Jeb's last name were Smith, you wouldn't make him manager of an Ace Hardware store, let alone governor of the fourth largest state in the country. The crowd—it wasn't big, maybe a few dozen people—ate it up.

The fact of it is, though, that Buffett got it wrong. That fact is, Jeb would make an excellent manager of an Ace Hardware store. And chances are, if his last name had been Smith and he'd gone to public schools and, like the rest of us, had no connections, he would have wound up doing something very much like running an Ace Hardware store.

Jeb is smart, fast on his feet, and has a head for numbers. He is consci-entious and takes his work home with him. He would keep the books ac-curately. He would keep a firm hand on the sales staff, would make sure everyone who needed to be trained on the key-duplicating machine got trained, and would only courier things overnight that absolutely had to get there the next day. He would make sure to keep the higher profit margin

models of Weedwhackers in stock come spring and would add a good rope
and stainless-steel fasteners section when a new marina opened up down
the street.

After a few years, or five, or ten under his belt, he might even make regional manager. But . . . that probably would be it. In all likelihood, that's
the point where the opportunity and ability curves would intersect, and
he would plateau. He would pay his dues at the Chamber, maybe join the
Kiwanis, but it would never cross Jeb Smith's mind that he should run for
the city commission, let alone something like governor.

But Jeb's last name is not Smith, and it probably never crossed his mind
that he should run any sort of retail establishment, let alone a hardware
store.

For Jeb Bush, the destination was clear from the time he was a grade-
schooler and told everyone he wanted to be president someday. His grandfather was a United States senator for the first ten years of his life. His father
ran for the Senate at age forty, when Jeb was eleven. By the time Jeb
started his own run for Florida governor (on the cusp of his fortieth birthday), his dad been vice president, and then president.

Interestingly enough, though, it was a task in many ways as basic and
as based on common sense as running a hardware store that Jeb drew
almost universal praise from all Floridians: handling the spate of hurricanes that hit Florida in the late summer of 2004. Jeb was fast. He was
efficient. He got things done. All the traits that make him such a scary
leader in other areas actually work to good effect, when it comes to managing disasters. One of his top emergency management people put it this
way: Jeb is good at this "because he won't take no for an answer. He tells
you what he wants done, and if you can't get it done, he'll find someone
who will."

Jeb didn't sit there dreaming up ways to give all the hurricane victims
private school vouchers for their children. He didn't scheme to privatize
disaster response and direct the contracts to Aramark or Halliburton or
some such. He didn't make the top hurricane priority a tax cut.

No, he used common sense and hard work to do those things everyone
agrees should happen when a storm strikes. Implement an effective, thorough evacuation. And, afterward, come in quickly with massive quantities
of help: search and rescue teams, water, ice, food, law enforcement—in
more or less that order.

Now, granted, a skeptical view might see this as pure political survival.

After all, unlike most of the right-wing-think-tank experimentation Jeb did with government services that affected primarily the poor and disaffected, the Florida hurricanes struck a broad cross section of constituents, many if not most of them white, middle class, and Republican—charter members of the Bush base. And the four storms in Florida's 2004 Hurricane Season from Hell did take place as his brother was in a tough fight for reelection.

This view, though, misses a key component of Jeb's personality, which is that he loves a tough challenge. He loves to compete, and in a perverse way, standing up to a category four or five Gulf storm is the ultimate challenge a Florida governor can face. Get the number of deaths as close to zero as possible. Rebuild to status-quo-ante in as few months as possible. Those are the metrics, and Jeb wants to show that nobody has ever done it better. So bring 'em on.

In the state-of-the-art Emergency Operations Center on the southern edge of Tallahassee, with its giant, Mission Control–type display screens and dozens of computers, Jeb was in his element. There, walking around getting status reports about how many shelters were open, and was the convoy of ice and water trucks in position yet, and why the hell not—there, effortlessly giving commands without having to worry about recalcitrant state legislators or obstructionist judges, Jeb was the man.

So the argument that Jeb responded well to hurricanes because they were hurting his supporters misses the point. "I have learned a lot during my tenure as governor," Jeb told the *Pensacola News Journal* that storm season. "One is when to be partisan and when not to be. Storms don't hit just R's and D's or Independents. They're all Floridians. As governor, it is essential that I respond in the same way."

Jeb, I believe, was being candid. He really would have responded just as vigorously if the storm had struck a predominantly black, entirely Democratic town as he did when it hit Republican-rich cities like Punta Gorda, Stuart, and Pensacola. Because a black, Democratic Florida city is still a Florida city, and to let a hurricane kill hundreds in one, or to allow it to destroy a town without quickly rebuilding is to let the hurricane defeat him. As we will see, Jeb doesn't do defeat.

KATRINA, that great, awful, killer storm of 2005, in fact, serves as the perfect illustration of the difference between Jeb and Big Brother.

Even after a term and a half in the White House, George W. seems al-

most proud of his lack of knowledge about public policy. As Texas governor, he kept banker's hours, if that, with plenty of time carved out in the
middle of the day for exercise and naps. As president, the schedule has been
busier, but still nothing back-breaking. It is a rare day when the president's
head isn't on his favorite pillow by ten each night. That work ethic, such
as it is, is touted as a good thing—Reagan-esque, almost. George W. knows
how to delegate, the line goes. He wants to stay up at thirty thousand
feet and see the big picture. He doesn't want to get down and muddy in
the details.

Jeb is happy to get muddy. This is not to suggest that he misses the for-
est for the trees, because he does not. Jeb wants both the big picture and,
for a shocking number of things, also the minutiae.

In practice, this means that had Jeb been president in the days before
Katrina made landfall, he likely would have known precisely the catastro-
phe that such a huge storm threatened as it aimed directly at New Orleans.
He would have called up the FEMA analyses about what such a hurricane
would do. He would have sat down at his computer and, within a few minutes, found the New Orleans newspaper's five-part report detailing exactly
what even a category three storm would do to the city.

In short, Jeb would have known that the levees could break—and he
would have *unleashed Chiang*, as the Bushes like to say (echoing the ex-
hortation of right-wing nuts in the 1950s who wanted a war with Mao's
China), making sure that the city and state government got all the help they
needed to go house to house, if necessary, dragging people out and sticking them on buses to evacuate.

George W. did none of these things. Three days after the storm, he
claimed on a national television interview that nobody could have foreseen the levees breaking, when, in fact, emergency planners and the *New
Orleans Times-Picayune*'s series had foreseen exactly that.

After criticism of his response grew even among Republicans, the president swooped in for an inspection. The television pictures showed him listening to the governors of Alabama and Mississippi explaining the damage.
You could almost see the thought bubble: *I had to give up my vacation at the
ranch for this?* Then, later, at the New Orleans airport, he fondly recalled
the great times he'd had as a young man living in Houston and driving over
to the Big Easy for some fun—perhaps, he allowed with a laugh, a little
too much fun.

It seemed terribly callous, and, even in retrospect, it was. But terribly surprising? Not really. After a shaky first day, George W. found his voice after

September 11 because the terrorists had challenged his Texas machismo, and he was going to give it right back to them. He likes a fight, and this would be a big one. But a hurricane? That couldn't possibly be laid at the feet of Osama bin Laden, Saddam Hussein, the French, or even the Democrats. Consequently, George W. couldn't get himself engaged. It took him two days just to abandon the remainder of his five-week vacation—a striking contrast to the night six months earlier that he managed to fly back to Washington to sign the Terri Schiavo bill, even though it made him stay up way past his bedtime.

He didn't want to deal with Katrina, and it showed. Overseeing FEMA, coordinating National Guard deployments into the stricken area, untangling bureaucratic formalities—all of that stuff is boring. And, after years of speaking only to friendly audiences and meeting only those who already agree with you, dealing with mad local officials and even madder hurricane victims just did not seem like much fun. George W. even said as much as he arrived at the first stop on his tour in Alabama: "I'm not looking forward to this trip."

The contrast between the two brothers can further be seen in their respective choices to lead their disaster agencies. In Florida, Jeb had the ability to put in whomever he wanted as director of the state Division of Emergency Management. There were plenty of brothers and uncles and children of Republican donors looking for six-figure government jobs, and Jeb easily could have stuck one in that role. But he didn't. Instead, he promoted a longtime department insider, Craig Fugate, even though he had come in under a Democratic governor. Fugate was supremely competent and, in a life-and-death agency, Jeb valued competence.

Turn now to the Federal Emergency Management Agency, which George W. initially entrusted to Joe Allbaugh, who had helped run his presidential campaign. Allbaugh hired as his deputy an old college buddy, Michael Brown, who had recently been forced out of his job in charge of judging for the International Arabian Horse Association. When Allbaugh quit in 2003 to work for George W.'s reelection, Brown moved up to the top spot. Three days after Katrina had struck, Brown told a national television audience that he was unaware that thousands of victims were stranded at the convention center. The following morning, he was on TV again, this time claiming that everyone in that convention center had been getting at least one meal a day. The *Times-Picayune*, in an open letter to George W., wrote: "Lies don't get more bald-faced than that, Mr. President," and called for the firing of "every official" at FEMA, but "Director Michael Brown, especially."

This is not to say that Jeb did not install cronies and political hacks into important positions. He did. But there seemed to be a heavy line drawn around certain core functions of government in which competence seemed to matter. It's not clear whether any similar politics-free zone exists under George W.

THAT WAS a major, perhaps the key difference between the two brothers. There are however, many more similarities between them than differences—chief among them their sense of entitlement to leadership.

It seems something has happened to the vaunted Bush family sense of public service these past couple of generations. Prescott Bush, by all accounts, took political leadership seriously. He served as moderator of his town meeting in Connecticut for seventeen years before he ran for higher office. Granted, the office he ran for (and lost the first time) was United States Senate—a quantum leap, but perhaps explainable given the size of the state. Prescott thought in later years that he had waited too long to get into politics, and that if he'd started sooner, he might have been president.

Sure, that reflects sort of a large ego, but, again, not unexplainable. What United States senator, a member of the most exclusive club in the world, has not thought about being president?

Still, Prescott's accomplishments were his own. His father held no helpful influence. Yes, his father-in-law afforded him the wealth that made such an adventure possible, but it was clear that being the son-in-law of Bert Walker meant very little to Connecticut voters.

Move down a generation, and we find George H.W., even as a young man back from the war in the Pacific, already laying out a life's roadmap to let him not only match his father's political accomplishments, but surpass them. As far back as the early 1960s, George H.W., without anything to his political resume but the chairmanship of the county Republican Party in Houston, had in mind a career ladder to take him all the way to the White House.

He, too, made the leap from local level politics to the statewide stage, running for Senate in Texas in 1964. In both that unsuccessful run as well as his successful 1966 bid for a seat in the U.S. House of Representatives, the name of Prescott Bush loomed large. When it was time for committee assignments, for example, George became the first freshman in sixty years to get on the powerful Ways and Means Committee. Prescott made the necessary phone calls to chairman Wilbur Mills and ranking Republican Gerald Ford.

But as a mere congressman, and then as vice president and finally president, George H. W. Bush was unfailingly polite and genteel to the public. You could disagree with what he thought was best for the country, but it was plain that he wanted to please his constituents with his leadership, that he wanted them to see that he meant well. He deserved to be president, in his view, because he was the best man for the job, with the most experience in the broadest areas and the best temperament.

He felt it was his duty to lead, yes, and that he was eminently qualified to do so, but also that if he failed to sell himself and his qualities to the American public, the fault lay in himself, not with the people.

Move down to the next generation, and things have changed dramatically.

George W. and Jeb, by 1993, had decided it was their turn. Like their dad and granddad, they saw no need to climb any sort of ladder. Jeb, like his father, had run a county Republican Party, only in Miami, not Houston. George W. had zero experience, having lost his only political race in 1978 in a try for a congressional seat in Midland.

Somehow Prescott Bush's duty to lead has, through a new combination of chromosomes, mutated into the right to rule.

Indeed, Jeb once let slip a fascinating insight into his views of the importance of breeding in human affairs, and how it can be that certain people are born to rule and others—most others—are born to follow. It came out in that other arena of Bushly prowess, sports—the day that Celtics legend Larry Bird announced his retirement.

It was amid his 1994 campaign, and Jeb decided this was an occasion momentous enough for him to offer tribute: "That's a tragedy. We're going to miss the deft passing and all that," Jeb opined. "How old is Larry's son? That's the only question—that's how long we're going to have to wait to see another Larry Bird in the NBA."

At the risk of reading too much into what was meant as idle chitchat about the news of the day, Jeb's view of primogeniture and basketball prowess can't help but require a double take. Was he suggesting that Larry Bird's son would, by dint of his birth, have the athletic skills, the drive, the freakish height to match his father's name on the court? Sure, granting that any Bird child would have a pretty decent coach growing up, aren't there nevertheless a great number of variables that are beyond either the child's or the father's control in terms of reaching the National Basketball Association, let alone shining as a star?

Or is it that Larry Bird's child *should*, because of that lineage, be afforded the benefit of the doubt whenever possible in his youth and collegiate career?

IN TERMS of his own genes, Jeb is a curious mix of his parent's traits. He has his father's ability to sympathize with society's less fortunate, breaking into tears at public events. He keeps in touch with parents of developmentally disabled children he has met on the campaign trail or who once wrote to him for help—not because he is building a public image, but because he cares about their troubles. At the same time, Jeb also has his mother's mean streak, and will bully or humiliate a staffer, a reporter, a legislator, or even an ordinary citizen who gets in his way.

With Jeb, Floridians in 1994 and 1998 were told they were getting a Bush who, despite his family, was his own man. He was a thinker, a "searcher," Jeb told us. Someone who would *think outside the box*. Someone who would puzzle through a problem and come to his own conclusion. Should he run for the presidency, this idea will become a major theme for his campaign, the number one talking point, at least at first, to open as much space as possible between the Jeb the Serious and Curious Grown-up and George W. the Perpetual Frat-boy Adolescent.

A decade and a half after his first appearance in statewide politics, it became clear that there was some truth to the original sales pitch. Jeb does seem more thoughtful and analytical than his father had been, and is obviously much more so than his older brother. But to focus on these differences downplays a far more important truth: that Jeb's agenda and his views on most major topics are virtually identical to that of his father and brother, with at best minor refinements.

In the area of tax policy, George H.W. and George W. both believed that America is served best by taxing the wealthiest Americans the least. So did Jeb.

In the courthouse, George H.W. and George W. both made minor careers of trying to limit Americans' ability to sue corporations. So did Jeb. George H.W. and George W. made major careers attacking "activist" judges. So did Jeb.

In schools, George W. built his educational credentials on the idea of requiring more and more standardized tests and pushing private school vouchers. So did Jeb. Regarding church and state issues, George H.W. and George W. both supported sending more government money to religious groups, even if some of it helped them proselytize. So did Jeb. Regarding the environment, George H.W. and George W.—more so George W.— paid lip service to clean air and water and protecting wilderness but actually undermined environmental laws. So did Jeb.

Where George H.W. may have read the executive summary of a report and schmoozed with the people who wrote it, and George W. may ask for a one-sentence synopsis and then snap at the aide for giving him too much information, Jeb will actually take the briefing book home and read it. In a press conference, Jeb will far more articulately explain the report and the policy than either his father or brother. In the end, though, the result is likely to be the same: a set of policies that in most cases only hard-core economic and cultural conservatives can support.

So Jeb, despite all the hype, does not really think outside the box as much as he thinks inside a different box—the Heritage Foundation box, where he was once on the board, for example. By and large, it's the same box in which his family has dwelt quite comfortably for years.

THAT JEB decided to follow in his father's footsteps at all is testament to a strength of will that does not bow to minor impediments like, say, an incompatible personality.

Unlike his father, the natural extrovert who over the decades has tried to befriend nearly everyone he meets, Jeb is actually an introvert, for whom human interactions require effort. A psychological screening that his secretary of Children and Families got him to take once indicated this, to the great surprise of some on his staff.

In reality, though, his relationships with others make a lot more sense viewed through this prism. Jeb is not a chatty guy. His own mother has remarked that a typical telephone conversation with her second son is a short one, and typically ends when Jeb has said his piece and hangs up.

So a guy who would just as soon be around only a few people he already knows, or around no one at all, instead thrusts himself into a world in which the normal course of action is to meet as many people as possible and act like you want to be the best friend of each of them? What kind of a man would do something like this? Well, the same kind who, despite being right-handed, as a child would go out of his way to become a left-handed hitter in baseball—a skill that, in Jeb's youth as now, is considered a much more valuable asset than hitting right-handed.

Even Jeb's most severe critics would have to agree: he has rarely shied away from challenges because they were too hard.

AT THE same time, even Jeb's staunchest defenders would have to allow that one of his most difficult traits is his stubbornness. It would be cheap and easy to call Jeb as stubborn as a mule, except that to do so would impugn any number of more reasonable, open-minded pack animals.

Once Jeb has decided on something, that's it. End of discussion.

Now sometimes, perhaps even many times, stubbornness can be a good thing. Persistence in the pursuit of a difficult but worthy goal, for instance, is an admirable trait, and certainly Jeb's hardheadedness has helped him overcome problems that might have stymied lesser men. Unfortunately, Jeb does not appear to have control over this particular gift, especially when the subject of his certainty is his own judgment.

In other words: if you think he made a mistake, well, he doesn't want to hear about it—particularly if the mistake in question is the competence or rectitude of one of his appointees. He will cross his arms, purse his lips, and dig in his heels, defending his decision to the point of embarrassment before he will concede an error. And if the error has been discovered by an avowed enemy like a Democrat or the news media, so much more the resolve to hang in there and lead with his chin.

Maybe this is considered a virtue in some circles. That it is better to be wrong and "resolute" than to be seen as "vacillating." Some have even described it as the familiar Bush loyalty, made famous by his father. Jeb, in this view, is merely extending to the members of his team the same undying support that they provide him. This interpretation, though, misses a key point: Jeb, while publicly loyal, is privately seething. He sees the screw-up or the malfeasance as a direct embarrassment of him personally, and is mad at hell at the person who has created it. The reason for the charade of public support is that, in his eyes, to fire someone is to admit defeat—defeat at the hands of the enemy. This is far worse than having incompetence or even crookedness committed on his watch.

In any event, what all this has meant for Floridians is having to watch Jeb stick with a policy or a person long after enough facts have come out for most reasonable people to agree that a mistake was made and that it was time to fix it and move on.

For Jeb, this evidently was not possible, particularly if others were pressing for some sort of change. If the mistake was so egregious that it simply could not be allowed to persist, what Jeb would do was to wait some weeks or months until the political furor or the media attention had died down, and then quietly change the bad policy or have the offending employee leave to "spend more time with the family" or "explore new opportunities."

This frequently created situations that would seem funny if there hadn't been such serious public policy consequences.

When a colleague and I began writing articles about the complete lack of oversight in Jeb's prized school voucher programs, he could have responded like a normal leader—that he was unaware the problem was as bad as it was, that he would look into how it had gotten to that point, and he would make it right. Instead, he claimed that the articles were completely wrong and that his office was in fact keeping track of the programs as it was required to. It was only when further articles detailed the allegations of an in-house whistle-blower that Jeb started to realize he had to do something other than just stonewall. And it was only after even more articles described how a school founded by an accused terrorist was getting voucher money that Jeb belatedly rolled out an oversight plan.

Jeb's political friend in charge of the education department, Jim Horne, hung onto his quarter-million-a-year job for another year, despite a steady stream of revelations—not just by the press but by the state's independently elected treasurer—that showed his incompetence. Horne finally left to pursue other opportunities *and* spend more time with his family, both, but only after the elections campaigns of 2004 had revved up, diverting the reporters who had been writing the voucher stories.

This pattern repeated itself with the dismissal of other top appointees. The press hounded Cynthia Henderson almost from the start of Jeb's administration for her questionable ethics and cozy relationships with those she was supposed to be regulating. She laid waste to two different departments before leaving to pursue other opportunities. And Jeb's fundamentalist Christian choice for Children and Families secretary hung on through a slew of negative articles about his views on corporal punishment and a stinging internal report on his taking gifts from lobbyists seeking contracts. Only when the furor died down somewhat did Jerry Regier decide that he, too, needed to spend more time with his family.

To Jeb, this issue became a matter of winning, and, recall, winning is everything to Jeb. In fact, on one occasion, I asked Jeb to comment on the state Democratic Party chairman's belief that Horne should be fired. Jeb turned to me and said: "So do you."

Horne stayed put, for another six months and another $120,000 in state salary.

GIVEN JEB'S lack of cooperation in the writing of this book, there is probably a heightened level of contrast in his depiction that his participation might have softened somewhat. I say *might have* because I believe that this is a fair and, even more important, an accurate portrait of the First Brother.

Nonetheless, there is the danger that those new to Florida politics or Bush family politics may come away with the idea that Jeb is an unmitigated ogre. This is not the case. He is human, with human desires, dreams, and dreads. He is a husband—a husband of uncommon duration, given his relative youth—and a father of three, whom no one can suggest he does not love and fear for like any father would.

One of two times daughter Noelle saw her dad cry, she explained once, was on a trip to Dadeland Mall, a terrifying Miami bazaar, when older brother George got separated from them. To put this in context: it happened not long after six-year-old Adam Walsh was kidnapped from another South Florida mall and murdered. "It scared the . . . wits out of me," Jeb recalled softly after a missing children's ceremony in the Capitol courtyard, an event he institutionalized after taking office.

We all want to look at ourselves in the mirror and believe we are honest and decent and doing good on this planet, and Jeb is no exception. When he's not in win-at-any-cost mode, Jeb can be warm, engaging, personable, even self-deprecating—really self-deprecating, that is, not the fake self-deprecating he uses in campaign appearances to emphasize his strengths. He can spend long stretches chatting with other people's young children, taking actual delight in their whims and worldviews—to the point that he almost seems wistful at having missed so much of his own children's youth to his business career and his family's various political campaigns.

If and when he chooses to take his career national, Jeb will charm voters in Iowa and New Hampshire and even New Jersey and California like he charmed voters in Florida in 1998.

Which makes this as good a time as any to get this on the record: Jeb is not a bad man, in the sense that, in ordinary human intercourse, he would think to cheat you or harm you.

To the contrary, if you had to be marooned on a deserted island, and you couldn't have your fantasy film star for a companion, Jeb would not be a bad second choice. He would help build a lean-to, gather coconuts, catch crabs, and so on with energy and optimism. He would stand his fair share of the night watches to keep an eye out for passing ships. If a bottle of single malt whiskey were to wash ashore, he would cheerfully share it with you.

Just don't bring up the idea of forming any kind of island government, and everything ought to be just fine.

If all this leads to the conclusion that there is more than a little bit of Jekyll-and-Hyde to Jeb, then you're on the right track. There is the friendly, considerate Jeb, to those he is meeting for the first time or to those he genuinely likes or cares about. This is the Jeb we see on the campaign commercials and at visits to inner city schools and nursing homes. But there is also the cold, manipulative, vindictive, and downright mean Jeb—the one who once cautioned *Doonesbury* cartoonist Garry Trudeau to "walk softly" for making fun of his dad. This is the Jeb the public rarely sees, but the one that legislators, staff, lobbyists, and journalists who have crossed him know only too well.

It is important for America to bear this in mind: both manifestations are real, sometimes within minutes of each other.

ALL OF WHICH brings us to the inevitable question: is he smarter than his brother?

To be fair: this query almost always comes from those who dislike, usually intensely dislike, the president. Second, those asking the question generally are working from the assumption that a Jeb presidency is a dreadful inevitability, and are seeking some assurance that he won't be as bad as they perceive George W. to have been.

That said, it is a tough comparison to make, for a number of reasons.

First, George W. is seven years older than Jeb, and there is the notion that with age comes a measure of wisdom, although I'm fairly certain that those asking the "which one's smarter" question are not ready to concede that point in this instance.

Second, and more important, there are different kinds of smart.

There is book smart, there is street smart, there is people smart. There is intelligence as measured by standardized tests. There is intelligence as measured by quickness, a gleam in the eye, a ready wit.

Which of these is important in a president? All of them, obviously. Which of them are necessary to become president? Obviously, not as many.

Let's start with George W. Contrary to what many of those who hate him believe, George W. is not a moron and he is not stupid. He is, in fact, quite clever and can, when he believes he needs to, think on his feet. A perfect example was the South Carolina Republican debate in 2000, broadcast nationally on *Larry King Live*. On the issue of gays, and why he had declined to meet with the Log Cabin Republicans, George W. lost neither a beat nor the twinkle in his eye: "Well, they had made a commitment to John McCain."

It was truly brilliant, if something mean-spirited and devious can be called that. He got his message across to the Republican "base" that was already suspicious of McCain thanks to a nasty, under-the-radar e-mail and anonymous flyer campaign: gay people liked John McCain and did not like George W. The best McCain could do was splutter a minute later that there had been no such endorsement, but he couldn't even press that very forcefully and still keep his moral high ground.

It was a verbal stiletto, delivered with precision. Morons and stupid people cannot do that.

At the same time, it is obvious that George W. has not taken the sort of interest in national and world affairs that one might think is important for the chief executive of the world's preeminent power. By all accounts, he coasted into and out of Yale on the strength of his legacy, and in subsequent years made it clear that he had no use for many of the Ivy League's intellectual traditions. He later was turned down by the University of Texas law school, but then got into and attended Harvard Business School. It's not clear that he applied himself there, either—but even if he had, graduate schools of business are not places where one gets a grasp of general knowledge and how to analyze it. Rather, they are places that teach that the running of a business is a discipline separate and apart from the specific concerns of any given business. It's more important to know the principles of running a profitable widget factory than anything about that particular widget—a concept contrary to the general idea that people in charge ought to know facts and details about the thing of which they are in charge.

As a "businessman," George W. relied on family friends to help him get into various oil-industry concerns, and then again and again to bail him out when things went bad. Those family friends once more were there when he positioned himself as the deal-maker and public spokesman of the Texas Rangers. The Rangers became profitable under his watch, but almost entirely because of a new, government-funded stadium (read: corporate welfare) he pushed for.

As governor of Texas, George W. took this management style to an extreme, enjoying long, exercise-filled lunch breaks and priding himself on not knowing details of his own policies. Not that any of this apparently mattered. He defeated a popular incumbent in 1994, and then crushed the Democratic sacrificial lamb in 1998 before quickly making himself the front-runner for the GOP presidential nomination in 2000.

In fact, throughout his history, it seems clear that knowledge as a useful commodity was not part of George W.'s value structure. All except for one particular type of knowledge: how to win political campaigns.

In that small area, George W. Bush knows a lot. A lot more than any of his political opponents have given him credit for. With the exception of his very first campaign, back in 1978, against a popular Democrat in a yellow-dog district, he has won every time. But for Jeb's mismanagement of the affirmative action issue in Florida in 2000 that wound up sparking a massive black voter turnout, George W. would likely have taken the state by nearly 300,000 votes.

Which goes to prove the point that knowledge does not always equate with intelligence, although the two traits generally have a positive correlation. In George W.'s case, we have an intelligent person who, for a variety of reasons, decided long ago that he would be willfully ignorant. He wouldn't know, and he wouldn't care. And then, later, that person decided he would deal with his self-esteem issues vis-à-vis the man against whom he had always been compared and had always come up short by matching and besting his greatest accomplishment: the winning of the presidency twice, compared to his father's mere once.

Jeb has a far more traditional brand of intelligence. He does know a lot about a lot of different things, and is not shy about showing off when given the opportunity. He was known to take home thick notebooks from his office in the Capitol back to the Governor's Mansion at night. And night meant night. He came to work early and typically left late. He took little time off. He was a workaholic and seemed genuinely to have loved being governor, digging down into the nitty-gritty details about any number of state policies. (As discussed above, however, he will not let facts get in the way of conservative Republican orthodoxy.)

George W. is the clever but unmotivated frat boy we all knew in college, who would party until the night before the final, and then cram just enough to pull out a C. That, naturally, was the whole point—to prove that he was smart enough to beat the system. To have a great time and still manage to get by.

Jeb is more like the rest of us were in school—trying hard to play by the rules, diligently studying, doing all the reading, even if it meant missing the football game . . . and then, in the end, wondering what the hell kind of world it was where the frat boy could end up getting the better job after graduation.

One thing neither Bush brother seems to have much of is self-awareness, which certainly explains the to-the-victor-go-the-spoils attitude that George W. showed after the 2000 election, despite having pulled half a million fewer votes. A more thoughtful person may have approached the presidency after such a "victory" with a dose of humility.

Not George W. Bush. No, whatever doubts he might have had in his anti–intellectualism were certainly washed away by his defeat of Al Gore in 2000. *If Al Gore is so freakin' smart, how come I live in the White House and he's all fat and has a funny beard. . . .*

It must have made poor Jeb crazy.

Can you imagine? Complete, total, and depressing proof of the maxim that it is better to be lucky than good proved right before your very eyes?

NOT THAT Jeb's all *that* brainy. He's not an intellectual, in the sense that he seeks knowledge for knowledge's sake. Rather, he wants to know enough on a subject to be able to argue persuasively about making radical changes to it so that it conforms with his worldview.

There's a significant difference there. Jeb and education is a perfect example. Jeb thinks he knows about schools. He's visited a lot of them, sure, running for office and then being governor. He even cofounded a charter school in Liberty City, a blighted section of Miami. In 2005, he was appointed to the National Assessment Governing Board by his brother's secretary of education, Margaret Spellings. Presumably this was in recognition of his philosophy that schoolchildren should be tested as much as possible, as often as possible.

But is he interested in really learning about education? That's not clear. He doesn't have much rapport with teachers, except with those who happen to agree with his ideas about schooling. He knows that *all children can learn*, and that *no child should be left behind*, but doesn't want to hear from people who might agree with those noble concepts yet who believe that schools need more money and more teachers to accomplish them. And he definitely does not want to hear that an annual high-stakes test that consumes weeks if not months of a school's effort is not the best thing for actual learning.

No, in the area of education, Jeb has an extremely selective interest in facts. If it fits with his ideology, great. If it runs contrary to his preconceived notion, forget it. In that case it's not actually a fact at all, but merely liberal dogma.

Education, in fact, serves as a good reminder to the strange, impermeable barrier in Jeb's mind between the need for facts in some areas and the aversion to them in others. Here is the distinction: if there is an accepted, conservative, Heritage Foundation–type orthodoxy on a particular matter, then no facts from the real world are required; ideology will see you through. If, on the other hand, there is no prefabricated, conservative viewpoint on a given matter to which he must conform, then, by all means, bring on the facts. The more the better.

This is an oversimplification, yes, but only a minor one.

Private school vouchers, the benefits of "outsourcing" state work, shifting Medicaid over to the insurance companies and HMOs—the list goes on and on. It is taken on faith that all of these are not only good ideas to try, but that they work. When evidence is presented that perhaps they do not work, or do not work to the extent advertised, Jeb doesn't want to hear it.

Contrast this to Jeb's performance in dealing with Florida's four hurricanes in 2004. In this area, there is no Cato Institute white paper for handling natural disasters caused by tropical revolving storms.

The result: Jeb made normal, rational, smart decisions to help protect Floridians from getting killed and, afterward, helping those who were hurt get on their feet again as quickly as possible.

GIVEN ALL THAT, it would be tempting for Bush haters to hope for a measure of symmetry with Jeb and his brother. That if Jeb has more of a thirst for knowledge, then maybe he is wanting in his older brother's forte, the will to win. It might be tempting for them to think that, but it would be a serious mistake.

For Jeb is every bit as competitive, every bit as ruthless when it comes to winning as his older brother. He, too, will do what it takes—and not just to his opponents in a campaign, but to anyone who poses a threat. Jeb, like his brother, is big on behavior modification to make sure he gets what he wants. He destroyed the careers of state workers who went public with their criticisms of his policies and attempted to ruin the reputations of journalists who have been tough in their coverage. After Michael Schiavo succeeded over Jeb's vociferous opposition in letting his wife die after fifteen years in a vegetative state, Jeb used his office to brand him a murderer.

Perhaps the only trait George W. possesses that Jeb lacks is the instant ability to connect at a human level. Jeb does not memorize names and faces and assign nicknames to everyone. One of his biggest political disasters, in fact, was when he failed to memorize the face of one of his own staffers' wife—who happened to be a reporter and recorded a candid remark that was not meant for the public.

Jeb can, when he wants, seem warm and caring. He can turn on the charm. His problem is that he doesn't like to turn it on. Making nice and meeting and greeting and doing all the little things that politicians need to do is not, amazingly enough, one of his natural strengths. He was known to walk into major fund-raising events, surrounded by five- and six-figure donors, and instead spend much of his time chatting up someone's child, or a disabled person. On the surface this is a way of showing where his real interests lie—children, and society's most unlucky and vulnerable. But on a deeper level, it has more to do with Jeb's resentment at having to ask, and then to thank, donors for their political contributions. In his view, people should support him because he is so obviously the best possible candidate. Indeed, they should be thanking him for so graciously agreeing to be their leader.

But this is a minor flaw. The vast majority of voters in a statewide race and especially a national race never meet a candidate, but form their impression based on what they see on television. So far, voters have loved what they see on television, and he's always had plenty of money on hand to get that message out in sufficient quantity. Rich Republican political donors are smart enough to understand that Jeb's worldview is far more in line with their bottom lines than that of any Democrat. They also know that Jeb is vindictive enough to hold it against them, should they support any Republican other than a Bush in a primary.

In other words, what we have in Jeb is a Bush who represents, easily, the best synthesis of all the winning qualities his family has had to offer. He is physically attractive, taller even than this father—a trait, any political consultant will tell you, that actually matters to many voters. Like his brother, he is a quick wit. Unlike his brother, he can think policy on his feet, and instantly pull out a fact or a statistic to support his position. Like his brother, he can raise a lot of money. In fact, given the record he set in Florida during his 2002 reelection—at least $35 million, including "soft money" funneled through the state party, for a mere statewide race—he would likely be able to beat his brother's 2004 mark, in a national run.

Unlike his father and his brother, Jeb does not thread his way through candidate debates like they were minefields, but actually uses them to his advantage. In 2002, he sealed his victory by thrashing his Democratic opponent in the prime-time, televised debate. Jeb is articulate and passionate in speeches, all the more so when he is speaking without notes. Unlike his brother, he doesn't shy away from press conferences, but actually enjoys sparring with reporters and getting the better of them.

Finally, and perhaps most significantly, in a national race Jeb would be coming from a key swing state and essentially lock it down. Were he to run for president—or even vice president, as Arizona Senator John McCain asked him to consider during a late 2005 meeting—Jeb would win Florida. Period. End of story. Florida has never had a president before, and the novelty value alone would push aside any ill will that Jeb accumulated among independent voters and moderate Republicans over his eight years.

That done, and with his native Texas in the bag and the Solid South too, Jeb would be well over halfway home. Now toss in his fluent Spanish and his Mexican-born wife, and Jeb could very easily force the Democrats to play defense in California, as well. As a Catholic, Jeb might also keep Pennsylvania in play, and even Michigan, while likely holding Ohio.

In short, Jeb would merge his brother's relentless juggernaut of a permanent candidacy, with its take-no-prisoners, win-at-any-cost style, with an actual interest and competence in governance that his brother lacks.

What one thinks of this über-Bush depends on where one sits. Economic and social conservatives would see him as a once-in-a-lifetime candidate who would not only win elections but then have the wherewithal to push their agenda after taking office. It's one thing to have a president jet around the country campaigning to privatize social security for a couple of months but then get bored of it. It's quite another to have somebody so dogged about an issue that he will not rest until it is accomplished—as Jeb was with the privatization of Florida's Medicaid system.

In contrast, liberals and moderates will see realized their greatest nightmare: a Bush, with the keys to the vaunted family fund-raising machine, who has not only his brother's relentless will to power, but also the attention span to ram his vision down the nation's throat long after election night is over.

In fact, given the realities of the Electoral College and the Bush family's dominance of the Republican Party's grassroots machinery, liberals' best hope is that Jeb's sibling rivalry gets the better of him, and that he decides that the only way to be certain not to come up short against George W.'s accomplishments is not even to try.

THERE ARE, of course, good reasons for Jeb not to run for president.

He has articulated some of these himself, while his surrogates have put forward others. In 2001, Jeb himself took to explaining how he didn't really want to be president, how he just wanted to get things done in Florida, and how being governor was about the best job anyone could ever imagine, and why would he want to go to Washington and get himself mired in that gridlock? Later, after his brother had safely won reelection in 2004, Jeb continued to insist that he wasn't interested in succeeding George W., and that all he wanted to do was go back to Miami and get on with his life.

Jeb's surrogates and allies, including some in the media, have built on this theme, adding into the mix the idea that Jeb, after eight years of public service, simply cannot afford another period of years when he is not making any money, "any" being defined as substantially more than the $120,000 per year he averaged as governor. There was also the excuse that Columba has had it with public life, and that she would not permit him to run for president.

Simply put: these are rationales, not reasons. Sure, there are a few real reasons Jeb may not want to run in 2008 or 2012 or even 2016, for that matter. Running for the presidency is an all-consuming thing, an ordeal that will make his runs for governor seem like Sunday strolls. If by early or mid-2007 other Republicans are running away from his brother and not with him, obviously Jeb likely will not run in 2008. If in 2010 young American men and women in Iraq are still getting regularly blown up by roadside bombs, then that would make a run in 2012 more difficult.

And yet . . . and yet these are all external things, outside factors that mere mortals might consider enormously important when deciding whether to spend years of their lives on a difficult and painful quest.

But Jeb is not a mere mortal. While it is true that most, if not all, politicians have big egos—the very nature of the political process makes one a prerequisite for success—Jeb's ego knows no bounds. If and when he decides he needs to be president, outside factors will not matter. He will be incapable of accepting the possibility that winning could be beyond his control. It is this self-assurance—some would say arrogance—that makes him such a powerful candidate.

So if, somehow, Jeb does not run for the presidency, it will be because he himself, and no one else, has decided that he does not want it. And that in turn leads to the scenario of a hyperactive governor going from a pinnacle of power and prestige to near-ordinariness, and realizing that he cannot bear it.

This is a hard enough transition for normal people. It cannot have been easy for former governor Bob Martinez to go from the power suite in the Capitol to walking the halls of the state House Office Building as a lobbyist, briefcase in hand, to pitch his client's views to freshman lawmakers who might have been too young to vote for him.

In the case of Jeb, it defies the imagination to see him peddling anyone's ideas other than his own, for any amount of money. The thought of him back in the business world, hustling various and sundry deals to make a quick buck, like he did prior to running for governor, seems similarly unlikely.

But here's something that is plausible:

Jeb Bush, back in Miami several months after his successor has taken office. His phone no longer rings all the time. His laptop doesn't interrupt him with constant reminders of new mail. It has slowly dawned on him that not that many people really care to talk to or correspond with a former governor. His children are grown and have moved on with their lives. And so, there he sits on his couch, eating his Swanson Select, clicking between the basketball playoffs and C-SPAN, his laptop beside him—when a "Road to the White House 2008" comes on, featuring some likely Republican candidates for president. Names like Bill Frist or George Allen or even Mitt Romney or George Pataki.

Jeb stops chewing and listens to them answer a few questions. And he stares down at his dinner in its plastic tray and over at his laptop and back to the TV. And he listens to their answers and he stares some more. And he thinks about his various job possibilities—commercial real estate, policy director at an education think tank, speechifying for the Heritage Foundation. And he listens to another couple of questions and answers. And he thinks to himself how, without breaking a sweat, he could blow away each and every one of the guys on his TV screen in the southern primaries. . . .

Jeb's analysis of the political climate may, in the end, lead him back to flogging office towers and shopping malls to big investors. It's just hard to imagine him remotely happy about it.

WHAT JEB does in the future, of course, cannot be known, and after some amount of discussion, the speculation begins to encroach upon the silly.

What Jeb has done in the past, though, is already known, and it offers a portrait that Americans can study today.

That portrait shows policy objectives that, as already suggested, will either be loved or hated depending on the observer's own philosophical and religious values. Far more interesting, though, is the leadership style that really transcends Republican-versus-Democrat, liberal-versus-conservative divisions.

Because in his two terms as Florida governor, it was not so much the content of the policies that he pushed that created most of the problems, but the manner in which he pushed them. Republican legislators were expected, by virtue of his role as party leader, to muzzle any objections they might have had to his ideas and to get with the program. Democrats were given even less deference. The entire court system, but especially the judges who challenged his laws, quickly earned his undying contempt.

Even lower in his esteem than the other two branches of government, though, were the members of the press and the public who attempted to obtain information about his administration that he did not wish to be generally known. He built new barriers to the state's public records law, forcing requesters to wait weeks or months, and then pay hundreds and thousands of dollars, to obtain information that should have been theirs for the asking. He instituted a regime of message control—rewarding journalists who carried his official line, punishing those who did not, but also attempting to censor outside entities, like a chamber of commerce study group that found far less than advertised in his touted educational gains.

This was a man with the benefit of as exclusive, as elite a private school education as can be imagined. During his years at the Kinkaid School in Houston and at Phillips Academy in Andover, Jeb was certainly taught the fundamental concepts of a pluralistic republic with three distinct branches of government and the open exchange of information and ideas. He must have learned about Benjamin Franklin and Thomas Jefferson and Alexander Hamilton, and why it enhanced freedom to have separation of powers and checks and balances.

He must have learned all this stuff, but then at some point decided that it was all obsolete, goody-two-shoes, fuzzy-headed, liberal dogma for which he had less than no use. He ran his administration with all the openness and transparency of the Politburo, and tried to run Florida like it was Soviet Russia.

This is a harsh indictment. I understand this, and I do not make it lightly. Jeb is so smart, so quick, so well-spoken, and, when he wants to be, so charming that those seeing him not just for the first time, but for the fiftieth time will find it hard to be skeptical, find it hard not to like him, and not to want him to like them back. Florida is full of these people. Poll results that consistently showed dismal regard for his policies but high personal approval bear this out.

But facts, like John Adams said, are stubborn things. And the facts of Jeb's years in the Governor's Mansion paint a portrait of a leader who would have been much happier born to a European monarch of old—a true prince who, at the appropriate time, would have effortlessly slipped into the mantle of rule, his every word a command, his every thought a divine revelation. Sure, he would have been benevolent to all his subjects, even the downtrodden and the unlucky—unless, of course, they ticked him off.

America today is so big, with so many divergent interests, and so bound by her own inertia—an enormous supertanker of a society—that a mere president can really only change course a few degrees, even after eight full years.

Still and all, the president of the United States is a powerful person, constitutionally a far more powerful executive at the federal level than the Florida governor is at this state level. Yet even down here, Jeb maximized every bit of the power constitutionally available to him, and then tried to grab some that was not. Should he one day wind up in the White House, there is no evidence to suggest that he would behave any differently in Washington than he did in Tallahassee.

So if and when the day comes that John Ellis Bush decides to follow the family destiny and put himself forward as our leader, that is when those who might agree with his goals or admire his intellect and tenacity will have to decide: is it worth it? Is it, weighing everything, good for a country that prides itself for its openness and its participatory government to have a leader who fundamentally believes in neither?

And if the American people decide that the answer is yes, they should do so with eyes wide open. Jeb behaved as if the people of Florida had elected him king, rather than governor. We can only imagine how he might interpret being elected president.

Chapter Two

BORN TO RULE

"I respect very much your father and I like your mother. I just have found no reason from their past service to see where it gives them the opportunity to give one of their sons Texas and the other Florida."
—FLORIDA GOVERNOR LAWTON CHILES, 1994

"We didn't talk politics or duty and destiny at the dinner table. Everything was sublimated. We talked about tennis or ball games. We were taught to be doers."
—JEB BUSH, 1994

"These people are nasty, and they have very long memory."
—FORMER TREASURY SECRETARY
PAUL O'NEILL, 2003

The most exclusive tennis court in the world is tucked away on the fifth floor of the Hart Senate Office Building, behind two locked doors. It was finished in 1987 thanks to the budgetary influence of former Louisiana Democrat Bennett Johnson, an accomplished player who felt that members of the most exclusive club in the world should be able to hit a few, between and after Senate business.

On May 16, 1989, this most unusual court became the setting for a most unusual doubles match—in which not one of the players was a United States senator, normally one of the ground rules. Instead, two adult boys of the president of the United States were taking on two women professionals. It wasn't for publicity. It wasn't for charity. It was . . . to win.

For two and a half hours, the players went at it, hitting hard, sweating hard. . . . When it was over, Jeb and his younger brother Marvin had come through with a convincing, 6–3, 1–6, 6–4 victory. Their victims? Only the former pros Chris Evert and Pam Shriver, occasional partners with various Bushes during charity tournaments over the years.

Now, granted, the ladies were not at the top of their game—and the Bush boys were not your typical weekend hacks. Jeb walked onto the University of Texas team as a student there in the early 1970s, and Marvin had since overtaken him as the Bush family's strongest player.

Still, for complete amateurs to have defeated two professionals who were once top ranked in the *world* was a big deal. Jeb could not contain his glee. When they all got back to the White House and he was asked who won, he responded with a big grin and a thumbs-up. His father, the president, couldn't help but brag how Jeb had practiced for the event back home in Miami to the point of getting blisters, and how, years earlier, he had put up outdoor lights so young Marvin could practice his shots even after it got dark.

SPORTS AS a metaphor for life.

It's not a new idea, and it's certainly not unique to the Bush family. Parents and high school coaches the world over have looked to games and sports as tools to teach life skills like perseverance, teamwork, and winning and losing with grace.

What we see in Jeb and his clan, though, is this idea taken to an extreme, with perhaps a de-emphasis of the "teamwork" and "losing" parts. Rather, it is the winning that matters, both in sports, and in life. When George H.W. Bush was a boy, summering at his maternal grandfather's estate in Maine, there was another young lad who was an exceptional sailor and who typically won the youth races the town enjoyed. One year, George decided that the champion's string had run its course. Young Poppy, as he was known (his grandfather and namesake, George Herbert Walker, was known as Pop—hence, little Pop, or Poppy) knew he was not likely to out-tack and out-jibe Bill Truesdale. And so, he cheated, diving under his foe's boat

1991: Jeb, age thirty-eight, teams up with his father during a doubles match at Kennebunkport. Jeb was a walk-on tennis player at the University of Texas. Two years before this photo, Jeb and brother Marvin defeated former pros Chris Evert and Pam Shriver.

and tying a bucket to the centerboard. The next day, Truesdale's boat moved like a slug. When he finally realized what had happened, he was furious. Poppy thought it was hilarious.

Yes, it was a prank, and relatively harmless, apart from being mean and unsportsmanlike. But understand the psyche that would go to the trouble of carrying out such a thing, and suddenly it all makes sense, when you fast-forward five decades and watch as Poppy and his crew tie a large, murderous black man named Willie Horton to Michael Dukakis's campaign and laugh as the Duke sits helpless, dead in the water.

It was not just George H.W. who was bred to play hard. His mother, Dorothy, was possibly even more competitive. Family legend has her hitting a home run when she was pregnant with Prescott Jr., George H.W.'s older brother, and rounding the bases at Kennebunkport before continuing straight off the field to go give birth. And Dorothy's father, Bert Walker, forced her four brothers to settle disputes by climbing into a boxing ring he fashioned in his house. As the boys got older, Bert himself would put on his gloves and go at it with his sons. Whoever was left standing was deemed to have been correct.

All the Bush children of George H.W.'s generation, and the next, were taught to excel in all games, from tennis to tiddlywinks, with the parents keeping careful track of who could defeat whom at what. Jeb, George W., Neil, and Marvin were taught to catch pop-ups with a tennis ball by competing for dimes. Later, when traditional sports were not enough, the boys became enthusiasts of a particularly violent cross of volleyball and racquetball called "wallyball," which they played at Camp David when their father was president. When Jeb decided to set his mind to golf, he dropped has handicap from twenty-two to nine in a single year.

There is a point to both sports and life, and that point is to win. The Bushes understandably are quite proud of their ability to do so—a pride that gushes forth even as family members deny ambitions of dynasty.

In a 1986 article, for example, journalist Joel Achenbach was making the inevitable comparisons between the Bushes and the Kennedys—both clans breeding well-do-to, politically ambitious youth with all-American good looks. It is a comparison that makes the Bushes crazy. They cannot see the least resemblance. Besides, the Kennedys are *liberals* from *Massachusetts*. But when the comparison turned to the love of sports—memories of the Kennedy clan touch football games on the Hyannis Port lawn—Jeb just about lost it.

"I think we could probably beat the Kennedys in touch football, we could beat them in basketball, baseball, any goddamn sport they want to play," Jeb declared.

Everyday Americans could not have cared less if all the Bushes were about was winning in sports, or even succeeding in the business world. But what has made the family a matter of national, even worldwide, interest and concern is their generation-to-generation compulsion to run for president of the United States.

This started with Prescott Bush, George H.W.'s father and a two-term senator from Connecticut. He retired because of failing health, and later conceded that, had he not waited until his fifties to run for Senate, he would have liked to have run for the presidency.

From that point forward, it seems, Bushes have grown up with the idea not only that they *could* be president, but that they *should* be president.

George H.W. in 1975, as he was seeking Senate confirmation for the director of Central Intelligence post, was put off when he was asked to agree not to seek the vice presidency the following year. "To my knowledge no one in the history of the Republic has been asked to renounce his political birthright as the price of confirmation for any office."

Political birthright? He tried explaining to an interviewer a few years later: "I want to score and then be captain, get promoted and then be boss, achieve something and then get elected to something else." But he probably said it best to the *Washington Post* in 1979, as he put the finishing touches on a decades-long plan to run for the White House. "I know that it's tough. I never thought it would be easy. But the reason that I'm going to win the nomination is that I really want to be president." The following year, he told *The New Yorker*: "I started thinking a long time ago—I mean, like, hasn't everybody thought about being president for years?"

That explanation, to his credit, illustrates that George H.W. still held the idea that while he was seeking the Leadership of the Free World, others could also legitimately pursue this prize. That humility appears not to have survived the reshuffling of chromosomes into this current generation.

This happens in rich families all the time—the children of wealth too often come to think of their privileges as entitlements, as things they somehow deserve—and now it has happened in the nation's premier political family. For despite the ability of both George H.W. and his political children to connect with middle America—pork rinds, country music, evangelical Christianity, and so on—this new generation embodied by George W. and Jeb has little in common with the rest of us.

They were born comfortable and remained comfortable as young adults, thanks to the generosity of their father's friends and supporters. When they decided in their forties that their life experiences qualified them to run for the top political job in two of the nation's four largest states, their parents were right there, opening doors.

As car dealer Harold Wells said at a Florida visit by then former president George H.W. Bush for Jeb's 1994 campaign: "He's doing what you or I would do—he's helping his son get into the family business."

Jeb was born to rule, and he is proud of it.

HISTORIES IN most patriarchal societies, including ours, tend to go right up the father's side of the family tree to demonstrate lineage. In the case of the Bushes, this takes us back to Samuel P. Bush, born in 1863 as the son of an Episcopal minister who settled in Columbus, Ohio, in the 1890s from New Jersey, where he had grown up.

But to look there for the roots of this current Bush generation would be a mistake, for the traits that have manifested themselves most loudly in George W. and his next-younger brother Jeb really have nothing to do with Samuel P. Bush, but rather their father's *maternal* grandfather—George Herbert Walker, known to most as Bert Walker and, in his family, Pop.

Bert Walker was born in 1874, the fifth of six children of a prominent St. Louis family in the dry goods business. His mother named him after the English metaphysical poet, which—given his nature and the nature of the many Bushes who have had the name handed down to them through the generations—was possibly the least appropriate name she could have chosen.

Think about it: the metaphysical poets and George Herbert Walker. Somehow the image just doesn't work. He no doubt realized that himself, which explains his preference for the more masculine "Bert."

Bert was raised Catholic, and evidently St. Louis's brand of Catholicism was too German for his mother's tastes, so Bert was sent off to boarding school in Scotland. It probably was not as daunting an experience as it sounds, given that his valet went with him. But, from a historical standpoint, the setting became enormously significant. Bert, always an athlete, happened upon a sport that wasn't widely played in America and made it his own, eventually making the Walker's Cup a major prize in the golfing world.

The pastime also came to hold an important spot in the lives of Bushes through the years. When Prescott Bush wooed Bert's daughter Dorothy, the old man wasn't so much impressed with the lad's social standing as his golf game. George H.W. and Barbara turned to it the afternoon following the funeral of their daughter Robin. Five decades later, not knowing what else to do in a strange city with all air travel grounded, they sought refuge in a round of golf on the afternoon of September 11. Jeb plays the game feverishly, and to win. And who can forget George W. warning terrorists with one breath, and urging reporters to watch his drive off the tee with his next?

INTERESTINGLY, given where the family is today, Bert Walker had no interest in politics and had outright contempt for politicians, particularly those who tried to get involved in his business. His reaction to congressional concern about his brokerage's investments in Bolshevik Russia is typical. While partner Averell Harriman tried to explain that dealing with the communists was an important part of moderating their behavior and their ideology (shades of President George H.W. and China's Tiananmen Square in 1989?), Bert Walker was offended that politicians were even asking the question. His Brown Brothers Harriman investment house was again criticized after Adolf Hitler seized power for working closely with Fritz Thyssen, a vocal supporter of Hitler whose factories helped arm the dictator.

Walker was in it for one thing—the money. He pushed hard to get it, and played hard and lived well once he'd acquired it. On Long Island, Bert Walker had a manse with two Rolls-Royces and two butlers—one as his personal valet and the other to polish the silver. It was he who bought up eleven acres on a rocky Kennebunkport promontory, earning it the name Walker's Point.

To afford all this, Bert Walker was not shy about pushing the edges of the envelope to amass the money he believed he deserved and needed. In his Brown Brothers days, he tried to get a partner to call in loans and cash in treasury notes for a big financing deal Walker was putting together—money that he would vouch for with an IOU. Colleague Knight Woolley refused to help Walker, calling the proposition too risky, and the dispute led to Walker leaving the brokerage to return to his own, G.H. Walker and Company. In 1937, Bert Walker was hauled before Harry Truman's Senate committee to explain his role as a banker in the sale of a railroad that wound up going bankrupt. Of the $518,681 net profit, he personally had received $173,388. His brokerage had gotten another

$72,245, while a third brokerage of which he was president received $43,347. The numbers sound much more impressive when it is remembered that his and his companies' net haul inflates to $3.97 million in 2006 dollars. A committee lawyer pointed out that his compensation exceeded the salaries and expenses of all the railroad's employees. Bert Walker made no apologies, declaring that he had worked on the project for a decade and deserved the money.

IN CONTRAST to Bert Walker's aggressive capitalism, the Bush family at the time was positively docile. Which is not to say that Samuel P. Bush was by any means poor. Both his father and grandfather had attended Yale, but Samuel instead headed to Hoboken to study mathematics and engineering at Stevens Institute of Technology. He worked with the Pennsylvania Railroad, and then moved on to the Buckeye Malleable Iron and Coupler Company in Columbus, Ohio. His big break came when Franklin Rockefeller, brother of John D., bought part of the company and in 1907 turned it over to Samuel to run for $25,000. That may not sound like much, but it equals more than $800,000 in 2006 dollars, and was two and a half times what chief executives of similar companies were making at the time.

Sports also played a big part in Samuel Bush's life. He is credited, in fact, with helping bring football to the Buckeye State by serving as one of the first assistant coaches for the game at Ohio State University. That love for sports was passed along to his son, Prescott, who was a star athlete in high school and, eventually, at Yale, where he played baseball and golf.

As Prescott neared graduation, the United States was entering World War I, and he joined a battalion made up of Yale grads, winding up in France. His service was a matter of great pride for Samuel and Flora Bush in Columbus, Ohio. So much so that when Prescott wrote home with a fantastic story about how he had deflected an artillery shell in midair with his Bowie knife, thus saving the top Allied generals and earning the top medals from three different countries, Flora immediately passed it along to the local newspaper. Only afterward did she stop to wonder whether it might all have been Prescott's idea of a joke.

The retraction printed a month later was an enormous embarrassment to Samuel, and started a strain in the father-son relationship that continued until Samuel's death in 1948, when Prescott made a point of passing his share of the inheritance to his sisters, so that he could continue to claim that he'd never gotten a penny from the old man.

This estrangement actually caused Prescott considerable discomfort, after his return from the war. Instead of a cushy job with Buckeye Steel, as it had become known, or with one of his father's friends, Prescott was on his own. He started by selling hardware, and then floor coverings, which is what he was doing in Milton, Massachusetts, when his second son, George Herbert Walker Bush, was born. It was not until 1926, when his father-in-law, Bert Walker, got him into the investment banking business that he began making serious money.

WITH THIS current generation of Bushes, it cannot be forgotten that Jeb and George W. also have a parent who was neither Walker nor Bush.

Barbara was the third of four children born to Marvin and Pauline Pierce of Rye, New York. Her father was in publishing, rising to the top position at McCall's, which published the magazine *Redbook*, by the time Barbara had grown. Her mother was the daughter of an Ohio Supreme Court justice but also an injudicious spendthrift. So much so, in fact, that she hid receipts and debt notices from her husband, who found them tucked in a drawer after her death in a car accident in 1949. To that, Barbara has attributed her own frugality—she bought a $29 pair of shoes for George H.W.'s inaugural in 1989, on the theory that she would only wear them once and she could not stomach paying any more. They left her feet sore and stained blue from the dye.

It may surprise voters who have always thought of her as "America's grandmother," but she was a beauty in her youth, despite a weight problem that won her constant criticism from her mother, who at the same time had to urge her skinnier older daughter to put on more pounds: "I spent all my life with my mother saying, 'Eat up, Martha' to my older sister, and 'Not you, Barbara.'"

She and George H.W. met at the Round Hill Country Club dance over the Christmas holidays in 1941. He was home from Phillips Academy in Andover. She was back from Ashley Hall, a boarding school for girls in Charleston, South Carolina. They were informally—but secretly, since they hadn't technically told their parents—engaged by the time George graduated high school and, against his parents' wishes, enlisted in the Navy to fly planes.

By the time he came home, a war hero, she had dropped out of Smith College, a decision she later regretted but made at the time because academics held no interest for her. They married on January 6, 1945, fully expecting that George would be rotated back into the fighting in time for the final push to the Japanese main islands—a push that was made unnecessary by Truman's dropping of atomic bombs that August.

They moved to New Haven that fall as George H.W. became one of five thousand veterans out of the eight thousand freshmen that autumn in Yale's incoming class, sharing a large Victorian house subdivided into a rabbit's warren of student apartments. Barbara kept score in the bleachers while George played first base for the Yale squad, and on July 6, 1946, she became a young mother with the birth of George Walker Bush.

LIFE SINCE then has had its ups and downs for Barbara.

She has been First Lady of the United States of the America, and wealthier than her wildest dreams from when she was growing up in Rye and cutting out paper patterns from old issues of *Redbook*. She has written four books—two memoirs, and two from the point of view of her pet dogs—that have been best sellers. In one of those books, she writes with wonderment about living in the White House, and how, on a rainy morning when she fully expected she would have to cancel a tennis date, she awoke to find that groundskeepers had sponged and blown-dry the court for her. One of her sons is now president, and another could well follow. She is the matriarch of America's foremost political family.

And yet, she will be remembered as the helpmate of a president, not as a historic figure in her own right. Her accomplishment in life was that she partnered with a man who would become Leader of the Free World. There are, of course, innumerable women who would die to have found such a man, and Barbara makes a great show about having had a great life, and not having traded any of it. . . .

Still, there were times when it was oppressive, being the 1950s housewife while George H.W. traveled the country and the globe to pitch his oil businesses. Barbara, like George, considered herself a good conservative, which meant that she, as a woman, was supposed to devote herself to hearth and home and like it. So it was all the more unsettling when the 1960s brought women's "liberation," and she watched women a decade younger than herself insisting on opportunities and responsibilities that had not been available to her.

"I had moments where I was jealous of attractive young women out in

1967: George H.W. Bush, now a member of the House of Representatives from a newly carved Republican district in Houston. The children are in order of youngest to oldest: Doro, Marvin, Neil, Jeb, George W.

a man's world," she allowed. "I would think, well, George is off on a trip doing all these exciting things and I'm sitting home with these absolutely brilliant children who say one thing a week of interest."

George lost his second run at the Senate in 1970. He had only gotten in the race at the urging of President Richard Nixon, who persuaded him to give up a safe congressional seat. Nixon made up for it by making George ambassador to the United Nations, which Barbara thought was an okay reward, and then chairman of the Republican National Committee, which she didn't think was any reward at all.

Similarly, Gerald Ford did not choose George H.W. as his vice president upon taking office, and instead gave him the new diplomatic post in Beijing. After a year there, Ford then moved George into the directorship of the CIA, which many insiders saw as an attempt by Ford staffers Dick Cheney and Donald Rumsfeld to kill his political career.

Whatever the motive, Barbara saw each assignment as worse than the last, and her periods of unhappiness over the years deepened into a dark depression. "Night after night, George held me weeping in his arms while I tried to explain my feelings. I almost wonder why he didn't leave me," she wrote in her memoir. "Sometimes the pain was so great, I felt the urge to drive into a tree or an oncoming car. When that happened, I would pull over to the side of the road until I felt okay."

BARBARA GOT over that bad spell, and emerged as a tough woman ready to follow her husband on the mind-boggling leap from being a former congressman, diplomat, party chief, and spy chief right to the presidency itself.

They made a good team, she learning to go off on her own campaign swings to talk about her man. She started out nervous when speaking to crowds, and got over it by narrating slide shows of their time in China to give her something easy to talk about. By the time George H.W. had been chosen by Ronald Reagan as his running mate, Barbara was ready and willing to travel the country, talking up the Republican ticket and trashing incumbent Jimmy Carter at every turn. "I was asked over and over again about what Reagan felt about this or that. Since I really did not know the governor, this was difficult for me. But it was fairly easy to talk about Jimmy Carter's inflation, Jimmy Carter's interest rates, Jimmy Carter's unemployment, Jimmy Carter's failed foreign policy."

It should be noted here how willing she was to make the negative case against Carter—including blaming him for the economy (she perhaps had a different view of a president's ability to control the American economy during the election of 1992). The conventional wisdom about Jeb and George W. is that George looks more like their father and Jeb favors their mother. A more important take is that both of them have inherited her temper, and her ability to use hurtful words to exact revenge.

For this, more than any other single attribute, appears to be the defining characteristic that the two political Bush brothers of this generation have gotten from their mom: the ability, when necessary, to be as mean as a snake.

That's a hard thing to say about anybody's mother, let alone one who so many Americans regard as the idealized parent and grandparent. But nonetheless, there it is. Even Richard Nixon, an appreciative admirer of humanity's darker side, was keen on Barbara's ability to go for the jugular. Nixon, over lunch with columnist Murray Kempton, dismissed George H.W. as a "lightweight," the "sort of person you appoint to things."

"But now that Barbara, she's something else again!" Nixon added. "She's really vindictive!"

The tendency was there as a child, as Barbara Bush biographer Pamela Kilian found from interviewing friends who recalled a bully who, for fun, would call the clique to announce which of them would be humiliated for the day by being frozen out of the group. Kilian found another childhood friend who grew up with a speech impediment. "She could make fun of you and, since I stammered, that was one of her delights," said June Biedler. "She was sort of the leader bully. We were all pretty afraid of her because she could be sarcastic and mean. She was clever, never at a loss for what to say—or what not to say."

The first public sign of this probably was her calling Democratic vice presidential nominee Geraldine Ferraro a "word that rhymes with rich" during the 1984 reelection campaign. Yes, she apologized for it—but she said it behind Ferraro's back, and apologized only after what she thought was an "off the record" remark appeared the next day in print.

In 1988, when George H.W. was fending off a stronger-than-expected challenge from Kansas senator Bob Dole—no slouch himself, in the mean-when-he-needed-to-be department—it was Barbara who chimed in about a strong negative ad against Dole, telling George H.W.: "I don't think ours is that bad" and persuading him to use it.

Then, after they had won that November, Barbara seemingly took every chance she could to toss backhanded darts at her predecessor, Nancy Reagan, but never seemed to earn the reputation that might have accompanied such behavior. Maybe it was that comparison with Nancy Reagan that worked so much to Barbara's advantage. Nancy just *looked* mean, and with all the information that had emerged about her extravagant tastes and her pettiness, in contrast Barbara seemed both more down to earth and a nicer person. Okay, she was a bit heavy and dowdy, with the fake-pearl thing, but many if not most Americans are heavy and dowdy. Barbara seemed to be someone we could relate to.

THIS IS NOT to suggest that George H.W. was incapable of spitefulness. The conventional portrait of him is of someone who believed that he could befriend literally everybody, and in so doing lead the nation and do great things and be remembered as *a good man*. And for the most part this thumbnail is accurate. Through his tens of thousands of handwritten notes and phone calls and tennis matches and invitations to ride on his speedboat and to throw horseshoes—George H.W. Bush believed in improving the world through the force of his charm.

Most of the time.

But once in a while, even in the province of governing, which he held to be a wholly different realm than campaigning, George H.W. gave in to his dark angel. In 1989, when he named disabilities activist Justin Dart to chair the Committee on Employment of People with Disabilities, his White House declined to invite former Connecticut senator Lowell Weicker, even though he was a friend of Dart and had been the longtime champion of the Americans with Disabilities Act when he had been in the Senate. Why the slight? Well, Weicker had once backed a challenger to Prescott Bush. Three decades later, George H.W. was still settling the score.

An even more telling example was George H.W.'s confidante, secretary of state and campaign manager James Baker, who during the interregnum was moved off the "friends" list because of his inability to get his boss re-elected. So at the dedication of the George H.W. Bush Presidential Library in 1997, all the VIPs got limos to take them to the ceremony. Baker rode the bus, with the peons.

Whatever the exact genetic combination that was passed down from George H.W. and Barbara to the next generation, it is clear that George W. and Jeb have taken the *get-even* trait to new levels. Not that George W.

and Jeb enjoy hurting people for its own sake, although the family's authorized biographers did report that George W. would, as a child, blow up frogs by sticking firecrackers into them and lighting them.

But in the retribution area, their actions speak for themselves. They have shown that they will come down on those they consider inimical to their interests without hesitation and with overwhelming force. *New York Times* columnist Maureen Dowd has satirized the family over the years as Mafia-like, in their obsession for revenge. Apart from the implied use of violence, the analogy actually seems apt. If you cross George W. or Jeb, you must be punished. You *will* be punished.

GEORGE W. ACKNOWLEDGES that his role in the 1988 presidential run was that of the family "loyalty enforcer" at campaign headquarters. The classic example in his own administration, of course, is Valerie Plame, the CIA undercover agent whose cover was blown—and her career ruined—in order to get back at her husband, diplomat Joseph Wilson, who had had the unmitigated gall to question George W.'s reasons for going to war against Iraq.

To appreciate the magnitude of this act, remember that George H.W. had once been director of Central Intelligence, and had often criticized journalists, congressmen and anybody else who, through their work, identified an intelligence agent and thereby jeopardized not only that life, but the lives of countless others who had worked with them over the years. Barbara Bush in her memoirs accused—incorrectly—a former CIA agent of having written a "traitorous tell-all" book that got the agency's station chief in Athens murdered. She was sued, (she called it a "costly nuisance suit"), and had to delete that reference in the paperback edition—but it illustrates how sacrosanct the family held American intelligence agents. Until, of course, the husband of one of them was deemed an enemy and a threat.

In Florida, Jeb has been, if anything, an even bigger believer in the big stick.

In the weeks preceding his 2002 reelection he talked in an unguarded moment about finding ways "to whack the trial lawyers," a group that historically had backed Democrats and that year was supporting Jeb's opponent, Bill McBride.

Jeb's administration fired people—people who should have been lauded as whistle-blowers—when they brought to light information that embarrassed Jeb by revealing flaws in his policies. Robert Metty was a manager in the education department office that was supposed to oversee Jeb's prized school voucher programs. Metty made the mistake of pointing out serious gaps in that oversight to his supervisors, and then compounded the error by talking to the press about it. He was initially transferred to a do-nothing job, and some months later "downsized."

Jeb's efforts to wreck people's careers did not end with those who worked within his agencies. After the Florida Catholic Conference came out in support of tough regulations cracking down on abuses in those voucher programs, Jeb's staff tried to get the group's Tallahassee lobby-ist fired.

People he could not get fired, he got back at in other ways.

In the spring of 2005, the Republican majority leader of the state Sen-ate, Alex Villalobos, became the lead voice against repealing the class-size amendment voters passed in 2002. Jeb hated the amendment, because it required that he increase spending on schools and because the teachers union had supported it—and he hated the teachers union because they had backed his opponents. In any event, Villalobos represented Miami, and Miami stood to lose hundreds of millions of dollars in education money if the class-size amendment was repealed. Villalobos was the first to speak on the Senate floor against the repeal, and probably swayed at least a few other Republicans. The Senate that morning voted down Jeb's repeal 19–21, when Jeb had needed twenty-four votes to put the issue back be-fore voters.

Weeks later, Jeb included in his list of vetoed budget items $926,000 for spinal cord research at the University of Miami, a top priority through the years for Villalobos. Jeb denied, naturally, that he had done it to get even. He even said it with a straight face: "There is no retribution. There is nothing punitive to what we do."

But the state senator wasn't buying it. Jeb had approved money for the program in previous years, and had in fact requested that same amount in his own budget proposal five months earlier. "Incomprehensible," Villalo-bos said, unable to fathom how Jeb could take his anger out on something like medical research for paralyzed people in order to get back at a legis-lator. "I understand why he's upset with me. He wanted the repeal, and I wouldn't go along with the repeal."

A year later, in Jeb's final legislative session, Villalobos again was pivotal in killing both a class-size repeal as well as Jeb's push to enshrine school vouchers in the state constitution. Weeks after session ended, a Jeb ally in

Miami had jumped in with a well-funded challenge to Villalobos in the Republican primary. Before the summer was over, Jeb had actually endorsed this ally against Villalobos, the incumbent from his own party.

Finally, and most famously, was Michael Schiavo, the husband of Terri, who fell into a vegetative state in 1990, and who became the center of first a family, then a state, and finally a national dispute over her right to die with dignity. Jeb did all he could do to keep her hooked up to the feeding tube—in fact, he even tried to do what he legally could *not* do with an aborted attempt to override a judge's order and take her into custody. In the end, Jeb lost. So he got even with Michael Schiavo by trying to launch a criminal investigation into her collapse fifteen years earlier—essentially using his office to accuse Michael Schiavo of murdering his wife.

If you're not with the Bushes, you're against them.

"LOYALTY ENFORCEMENT," naturally, is not part of the Bush family marketing campaign. That, rather, has centered on the importance of succeeding in business—in *pulling yourself up by your bootstraps* and making your own way in the world as a qualification to run for office.

Nowhere in the story line is there acknowledgment of the importance of good, old-fashioned luck.

Sure, there is the general gratitude of being "blessed" in having such wonderful parents or children or having been born in such a wonderful country and so forth, but all of that comes in the goody bag they give you the first time you sign up to run for dogcatcher.

What's missing is a more intellectually honest appraisal of the role chance played in their family fortunes. George W. and Jeb certainly were lucky to have George H.W.'s name opening doors for them, both in the business world and in politics. George W. is lucky that former Palm Beach County elections supervisor Theresa LePore designed such a confusing ballot.

But even more fundamentally, no one seems to appreciate the enormous strokes of luck that put George H.W. Bush in a position of national prominence to start with.

The first took place back in 1953, in the dusty flats of west Texas about seventy miles east of Midland. George H.W. had three years earlier set out on his own, albeit with some serious financial backing from his main benefactor, Herbert Walker, or Uncle Herbie, as George called him. The first business was relatively risk-free, by oil business standards. That, in fact, was the reason he and his partner John Overbey had chosen it. The Bush-Overbey Oil Development Company bought and sold oil rights on land *adjacent* to tracts where someone was planning to drill. The idea was to make money on the anticipated increase in land values without actually doing any drilling of their own.

There was not that much money to be made that way, however, and George H.W. was impatient. So in 1953 he started Zapata Petroleum Corp. with Hugh Liedtke, later of Pennzoil fame. (An odd name, sure, for a company created by dedicated capitalists. A Brando film about the Mexican revolutionary had come out the year before, and they liked the sound of it.) This new outfit would purchase actual leases in the hopes of finding oil. George H.W. and his partner had found what appeared to be a promising opportunity in the West Jameson Field, and decided to put everything on a single roll of the dice.

A total of $850,000, nearly half of it from Uncle Herbie, went to secure and drill on eight thousand acres. A year later, they had sunk seventy-one wells, and not a single one had come up dry. Zapata, and George H.W., had struck it rich, and there was no turning back.

Bush lore invests much in this tale. Here is proof that George H.W. had the pluck to leave a comfortable future at either his father's or his uncle's brokerage houses, to head west with nothing but his car, his wife, and his new baby and to make his name in the world. Everything else that followed, from his great wealth to his rise to the presidency, occurred because he had done this brilliant thing and earned his success.

There are only a couple of minor glitches in that theory. First, although it was admirable that he wanted to strike out on his own—and on his own, it pretty much was; he and Barbara lived in a couple of low-rent places in the late 1940s, including a one-bathroom shack they shared with a mother-daughter prostitute team—it was more an adventure than a necessity. Had things not worked out, well, his mother's family had plenty of money.

Barbara has recognized this part herself in a moment of candor: "We both knew that if we got into trouble someone would help us. . . . And so to say we knew what it was like to be poor is ridiculous."

But an even bigger flaw is that George H.W. could just as easily have gone broke with his gamble on that single oil field as have gotten rich. Yes, there was basic, hard, grunt work involved in researching the land, in studying geological surveys, lining up financing, and so on. But in the end, the success of the venture was a matter of good fortune. It could have gone the other way. It *did* go the other way for countless others in the oil business in the years before and since—including for one George W. Bush, who lost quite a bit of other people's money in oil before turning to baseball.

George W. explained it to fraternity brother Bob Reisner who by 1976 was working for federal regulators: "Let me tell you, Bobby, how you do quantitative analysis. You do all your analysis, you do all your statistics, and then you punch a hole in the ground. And if there's no oil there, you just lost five million bucks."

Such a huge part of the Bush family mythology is the self-made, rags-to-riches stuff (although, in truth, it was more of a riches-to-even-more-riches tale; not quite Horatio Alger material). Where would George H.W. have been if, after spending all his uncle's and his uncle's friends' money, he had struck out and been forced to run back to Connecticut with his tail between his legs?

But for a lucky bet on the West Jameson field, the Bush saga would have read completely differently.

THIS IS NOT to say that the Bushes have led a completely charmed existence, for they have not. George H.W. and Barbara were touched by the thing that all parents fear the most, the loss of a young child.

Pauline Robinson, their little girl born three years after George W., was three and a half when Barbara took her to the pediatrician one day after discovering that little Robin had strange bruises, and was constantly listless. The doctor called back and insisted on a face-to-face meeting with both parents to talk about the test results.

As a parent, you never want that from a pediatrician. You want a slightly harried, slightly bored, maybe even a slightly condescending "she's doing fine" or "I wouldn't worry about it" in response to your concerns.

When Barbara and George H.W. went back to the office, Dr. Dorothy Wyvell was on the verge of tears as she explained that Robin had childhood leukemia, that it was in its advanced stages, and that the best they could do would be to let it run its course and to keep her happy and comfortable until it was over.

They reacted to the news as any parents would—shock, and a refusal to accept the idea that there was nothing they could do. George got on the phone with an uncle, Dr. John Walker, a cancer specialist who recommended they bring Robin right away to Memorial Sloan-Kettering in New York City, where he was president.

And so began the most painful months in George and Barbara's lives, watching their little girl under the experimental treatments—the only types available in 1953. George had just started his new oil business, and had to be on the road almost constantly to keep it on track. So it was left to Barbara to stay with Robin, and she made a temporary home of Walker's Sutton Place apartment a few blocks from the hospital.

Meanwhile, back in Midland, George W. and Jeb were left in the care of the housekeeper and family friends. George W. was six years old when his little sister fell ill, and Jeb was not much more than a newborn—barely a month old when Robin was diagnosed.

For the next six months, until Robin eventually succumbed to the disease and its harsh treatments in October, baby Jeb had only limited contact with either parent—essentially those times his dad could drop in for a visit or in those rare periods when Robin was well enough to travel. This is not to blame Barbara or George H. W.—they behaved like any us would have, had it been our little girl. They did what they had to do to try to save their daughter.

Nonetheless, it could not have been easy for Jeb. Babies thrive on emotional contact, but from age two months to eight months, he saw his mother only briefly, and when he did, she was understandably preoccupied with Robin. And then, when his mother did return, she was distraught and in mourning for some time to come.

It cannot be known what long-term effect this had on Jeb, and it's probably not worth speculating. Some babies who grew up with parents doting on their every smile nevertheless end up as aloof and distant adults. And some children raised in crowded orphanages grow up happy and well adjusted. Jeb, who scoffs at self-reflection as "psychobabble" and a waste of time, would certainly laugh at the idea that his parents' long absence during his first year hurt him or even affected him in any way.

WHICH BRINGS us to the more general issue of family—which, in the context of the Bush family, inevitably means *family values*.

Approximately every election cycle from 1964 forward, there has been a great celebration in this country of the Bush family. First George H. W. and Barbara, and then George W. and Laura in Texas and Jeb and Columba in Florida—all of them are blessed, the campaign machinery explains, to have had such wonderful, loving parents, and wonderful, loving children.

Children are great. Family is great. Faith is great. Isn't America a great nation to let people have children and family and faith?

It has been a major campaign strength, through the decades. The comparison was obvious, in 1980, between the Bush children who all loved
their parents and the Reagan children who did not. It was even more obvious in 1992 and 2000, when the Bush candidate was a faithful husband
and William Jefferson Clinton (even though he technically was not on the
ballot in 2000) was not.

When George W. and Jeb ran in 1994 for governor in their respective
states, many voters said they didn't know much about the candidates, but
that they loved their parents, and figured therefore that the children could
not be so bad.

Since Jeb has been governor and George W. president, the rest of us are
frequently lectured about how important it is to love our children, and how
we are their first and best teachers. Barbara Bush, in 1984, scolded parents
to spend more time at home. "You can't, in my opinion, be a bank president and a full-time father." Six years later, during a 1990 commencement
address at Wellesley College, she told the graduating seniors: "Fathers and
mothers, if you have children, they must come first. You must read to your
children and must hug your children and you must love your children. Your
success as a family, our success as a society, depends not on what happens
in the White House but on what happens inside your home."

It is a case, it seems, of do as we say, not as we do.

Because the Bush grown-ups, through the decades, have frequently led
lifestyles and taken on career and political commitments that have left their
children to be raised primarily by one partner, instead of two, or even in
the care of family friends and boarding school staffs.

Perhaps to deflect possible criticism, the notion of "quality time" has frequently crept into Jeb's discussions of his relationship with his father as he
explained how George H.W. was such a loving dad despite having been
on the road so much for business and political campaigns. When George
H.W. *was* home, he and Jeb did really meaningful, really important things,
we're told. Jeb has also explained that the relationship served as a model
for how he spent time with his own young children, back when he was
balancing family with running his businesses and running various political campaigns.

This is interesting because the notion of "quality time," that the nature of
shared time with one's children is far more important than the total amount,

has long been blasted by many Christian conservatives as a liberal invention to justify the use of day care in families where both parents work full time.

Jeb himself, in other, more candid interviews, has acknowledged that his father wasn't there for vast stretches. "Even when we were growing up in Houston, Dad wasn't home at night to play catch. But if anything ever went wrong in my life, Dad would be right there to help," Jeb said in 1980. "Mom was always the one to hand out the goodies and the discipline. In a sense, it was a matriarchal family."

Another time he joked: "At least we weren't put in a kennel."

THE BUSH family's child-rearing methods certainly are not unique. It has been something rich people have done for generations—hire nannies to feed, bathe, and tutor their children, and then farm them out to boarding schools when they enter their teens.

For the rest of us, this lifestyle has always been a bit mystifying. Boarding schools, for one, are more an abstract threat than a real possibility— the punishment of last resort. Keep it up, young man, and you're on your way to military school. More generally, the question arises: if you cannot be bothered with caring for your children, then why have them? The world is plenty crowded as it is.

It's important, here, to distinguish the inability to spend time with one's children because of a greater good. Certainly, men and women who serve in the military and are called away for weeks or months are leaving their families behind because they believe that their service is important to the nation, and we honor them for it. Same thing in the case of Barbara and George H.W. leaving Jeb in the care of others so that they could care for his dying sister—that is completely understandable.

But this is not what we're talking about. Generally with the Bushes, the outsourcing of the children has been a matter of choice, not necessity.

Prescott and Dorothy Bush, in the 1930s and 1940s, sent Prescott Jr. and George—or Pressy and Poppy, as they were called—off to Andover for high school, this after having had plenty of household help to get them through Greenwich Country Day School. And once up in Massachusetts, they were expected to stay there until school vacation. No coming home for the weekends, even though it was no great distance.

George W. and Jeb, in turn, got the boarding school treatment when they were sent off to Andover in 1960 and 1967, respectively. In fact, Jeb left his parents' home six months early, as he was turning fourteen, when his father won a newly drawn congressional seat in Houston in 1966. George H.W., Barbara, and younger siblings Neil, Marvin, and Dorothy moved to Washington, D.C., in January. Jeb stayed with the parents of one of his best friends, Rob Kerr, to finish out his ninth grade at Kinkaid. Some summers were also time away from home, as George H.W. would seek out camps and employment opportunities for the boys. Even daughter Doro, the youngest, was put up at Miss Porter's, a girls school in Connecticut, when George H.W. took the China liaison office posting in 1974.

Jeb's older children were spared the Andover experience—probably because Jeb has come to hate his own time there. George P. and Noelle attended prep schools in Miami, where the family lived from 1981 through 1998, with the exception of a year and a half in Tallahassee in 1987 and 1988. But youngest son, Jeb Jr., attended high school at Bolles, a Jacksonville boarding school.

This was done, according to Columba, because of the all-consuming nature of a statewide political campaign in 1998. "It's not fair to the kids when you're gone so much of the time and they're home alone," Columba told the *St. Petersburg Times.* "I feel very responsible. So does Jeb. I want to have Jebbie under very strong supervision."

Not to question how much Jeb loves his son . . . but wouldn't a "responsible" parent who really wanted to ensure that his child got strong supervision have put off a governor's race for four years rather than sticking his child in a boarding school four hundred miles away? Yet perhaps the even more telling detail came after Jeb's successful election. Instead of transferring Jebbie to a school in Tallahassee, Jeb left him at Bolles—180 miles away.

The do-as-I-say, not-as-I-do irony of this was obvious in 2005, when Jeb hosted "Family Day" in the Capitol courtyard to encourage parents to have supper together with their children as a way to stay close and help keep them away from drugs and booze. Family Day took place barely a week after young Jebbie was arrested for public intoxication in Austin, where he was a senior at the University of Texas.

"Families are the first line of offense and the first line of defense in providing support for children," explained Jeb to a pretty television reporter. "It's common sense. I think everybody would understand how strong, wholesome family life really matters, but there is really data, real research that suggests that families that are united, families that eat together, just have dinner together will have a better chance of their children being drug free and alcohol free."

So I asked Jeb if he wished he had spent more time with his own children when they were growing up. He walked away without saying a word.

Do as we say, not as we do. *Watch* what we say, not what we do.

Between the last Bush generation and this one, the family has not been shy about telling the rest of us how to live. Yet they themselves frequently have failed to live by those rules. Amazingly, this hypocrisy has not seemed to hurt them, with the public indeed listening to what they say, rather than watching what they do.

The incessant lecturing about how to raise our children is just one example and probably the least offensive one. We all make mistakes, and if we can help others avoid them, that's probably a good thing.

More interesting are the vast gulfs between other of their public pronouncements and their own behavior.

In the area of military service, for instance, both George W. and Jeb are proud hawks, explaining how it is necessary to use American might in the defense of our ideals and our strategic interests. This tough talk offers a striking contrast with the actions of their youth. Jeb, when the opportunity arrived to enlist in the Army and fight communism firsthand in the jungles of Vietnam, seriously considered registering as a conscientious objector. He ultimately did not do so—but he also did not voluntarily join the fight, choosing instead to head off to college. His older brother was even worse. George W. openly defended the war during his Yale years and ridiculed those who did not want to fight. Yet he opted to defend the skies over east Texas in an obsolete jet fighter rather than trudge through rice paddies and shoot and got shot at by Viet Cong guerrillas. Today, the two brothers have five children of prime military service age, but have persuaded none of them to wear the uniform. Despite this, both proudly defend the sending of other people's children to Iraq.

The Bush leaders, both of this generation and the last, also have been strong opponents of welfare, of government assistance, of the "something for nothing" society.

Yet when George H.W. Bush settled in Midland and bought his first home for $7,500 ($67,230, in 2006 dollars), he did so thanks to a loan subsidized by the Federal Housing Administration. True, George H.W. *had* put his life on the line during wartime, and if anybody deserved government help, it was World War II vets.

But his political sons, who were considerably more strident in their anti-welfare views, benefited even more from government largesse.

George W. was able to sell his $500,000 stake in the Texas Rangers for a $15 million profit thanks largely to a new ballpark that was built for the team by the taxpayers of Arlington—a ballpark that brandished the much-reviled power of eminent domain, in fact, to get unwilling sellers off their property.

And Jeb and his partner Armando Codina were relieved of a $4 million loan obligation during the savings and loan bailout in 1988. Yes, that is correct: Jeb Bush, who a few short years later was blasting welfare moms who received all of $15,000 a year in food, medical, and housing subsidies, with his partner shared a $4 million benefit thanks to American taxpayers.

THIS BELIEF that their pronouncements are more worthy of our attentions than their actions—perhaps it makes sense, in the context of a central belief the family has worked under these past two generations, that it is their destiny to rule the rest of us.

Recall the much-publicized story about the prayer service at George W.'s second inaugural in 1999. The Reverend Mark Craig spoke about Moses' reluctance to take on the role that God had given him, but how it was Moses' responsibility and the rest of our responsibilities to fulfill the mission God had in mind for us. Generic enough, right? Be all you can be? Do what's right?

Not to the Bushes, who read into it a message from God that George W. should be president. Barbara leaned forward and told him: "He's speaking to you."

Barbara also offers the flip side of the notion of being born to rule, which is that the rest of us are clearly *not* born to do so. In her memoirs, she expresses some rare sympathy for Michael Dukakis and the Democrats for having to deal with Jesse Jackson in 1988. The preacher and civil rights leader had run up impressive numbers in the Democratic primaries, so much so that Dukakis was forced to pretend to consider him for the running-mate slot.

Here's Barbara's take on Jackson's presidential run: "He must be a chore for the Democrats. He has his own agenda and has never missed a funeral, a strike or a march," she wrote in her first memoir. "And it always saddened me that Jesse did not get out of politics and use his charismatic talents to turn kids off drugs and into school."

So Jackson didn't have the qualifications to be president and therefore shouldn't have run. Okay. But how much thinner was Jackson's resume than, say, George W.'s, who in 2000 had a checkered business history and all of six years in elective office, and that as governor in a weak-governor state?

More to the point, how would Barbara feel if that question were turned on her husband or on George W. and Jeb? Imagine all the *good* they could have accomplished, if they weren't such megalomaniacs. Jeb in particular— if he truly wanted to be a public servant, he would be angling to run FEMA. His experience in Florida suggests he would be good at it, and God knows, the nation needs someone good in that job, as Hurricane Katrina showed in 2005. In fact, he was specifically asked about the possibility of taking over as New Orleans reconstruction "czar" when some Republicans were suggesting that George W. appoint one. Jeb said he was not remotely interested.

Of course not. Because the possibility of real "service" does not occur to the Bushes. Not to Barbara, not to George W. and certainly not to Jeb. They're not a particularly self-reflective clan—Jeb wears this as a badge of honor—but there's no evidence to suggest that even if they were, they would have behaved any differently.

The Bushes *were* born to rule. The rest of us had just better get used to it.

Chapter Three

MIAMI

"I want to be very wealthy, and I'll be glad to tell you when I've accomplished that goal."
—Jeb Bush, Miami, 1983

"When I see the kind of people who Jeb Bush hangs out with, I can't decide if he is very naïve or very cynical."
—A South Florida law
enforcement official, 1991

"The only documented allegations come down to the fact that he did business with people that turned out later to be deadbeats or crooks."
—Jeb's 1994 running mate,
Tom Feeney, July 1994

"You either trust me or you don't."
—Jeb Bush, 1998, declining to give details
about one of his business deals

As a not-so-young man, Jeb Bush sold shoes. He bought and sold office buildings. He became part owner of a new National Football League franchise. He helped market water pumps to Third World countries.

He didn't do these things because he was an expert in crop irrigation, or held a master's in sports marketing, or had a background in civil engineering, or even knew anything about footwear. He did these things for one reason, and one reason only: to make money. Preferably a lot of it. Preferably quickly.

With brains, with a willingness to learn and to work hard, and—most important—with a dad who was vice president, and then president of the United States, Jeb accomplished this goal and did so handily. Between 1980 and 1993, Jeb went from having no savings and tens of thousands of dollars in credit card debt to a net worth of $2.2 million.

The whole point of this accumulation of wealth, naturally, was to be financially secure enough to enter politics at a relatively young age. This was something the political Bushes had already done for two generations, and if their mere example wasn't enough, George H. W. Bush made sure to instill the message into his second son loud and clear when Jeb briefly considered running for Congress in the early 1980s.

How Jeb went from having no money when he arrived in Miami to run his father's presidential campaign in 1980 to an impressive nest egg by the time he was ready to run for governor is important. So are Jeb's choices of business associates, which even his 1994 running mate conceded had included in their number "crooks and deadbeats," as are Jeb's explanations of why none of that should matter to the public.

First, let's state right up front that Jeb's ultimate goal was not just money. Had it been so, he would have made a lot more of it than he did. A *lot* more. With his drive and acumen and ability to grasp both the big picture and small details instantly, Jeb could have built himself an obscene fortune, if that had been his only goal.

Second, let's emphasize, again, that while Jeb got a lot of breaks and open doors that the rest of us do not get, he did in fact work extremely hard to make the most of them. For proof that help from your daddy's friends and political sycophants in and of itself does not spell success, just take a look at the business careers of George W. and Neil Bush.

Much more important to the debate is the fact that Jeb was able to build a pile of money without benefit of any advanced academic degree or even any specific knowledge about the businesses he engaged in. This shaped his worldview in profound ways and has important implications for his rule in Florida and, possibly, beyond.

First and most obvious, Jeb has little respect for traditional measures of expertise. In Jeb's view, teachers and principals do not necessarily know how best to educate children. Doctors don't always know what's best for their patients. Even scientists are not to be trusted on scientific matters. And lawyers and judges . . . well, in Jeb's view, they are the cause of many of society's problems.

Jeb spent only two and a half years in an institution of higher learning, in his case, the University of Texas in Austin. Nonetheless, he considers himself, and in some cases rightfully so, to be close to an expert on a wide range of topics. If he has been able to achieve this level of functioning without a string of letters after his name, then what good is the string of letters?

This attitude in Florida created a limitless supply of ill will among people whose knowledge and experience was simply overruled by Jeb and his people in their quest for some particular political outcome. In some cases Jeb was correct—that he was fighting an obstinate bureaucracy bent on preserving its turf. But in many cases Jeb was wrong, and his poorly thought-out ideas resulted in messes that others were left to clean up. We'll explore this area in greater detail in the "King of Florida" chapter.

But a more general consequence of Jeb's successful Miami years was the impression they left with him that given hard work, one can achieve just about anything in this world. That the only limits are of our own imaginations. That anyone who puts his mind to it can replicate his accomplishments.

It is an incredibly romantic ideal, and a peculiarly American one. Unfortunately, it is simply neither true nor practical. Not all of us can be millionaires. Not all of us will overcome adversity to achieve our dreams. Not all of us can transform ourselves into *knowledge-based workers of the twenty-first century* to free ourselves from the tyranny of a thankless job. This is not pessimism, this is just reality. There is not enough of a "pie," and nor can the pie be "grown" enough, for everyone on this planet to live the fulfilling and secure life that Jeb Bush enjoys.

A leader who does not understand this reality could well be doing us more harm than good.

NOT GRAVITATING toward one of the "professions" or advanced schooling, certainly, was not unique to Jeb among the Bush clan.

Recall that great-grandfather Samuel P. Bush was an engineer, but from that point forward the idea of acquiring expertise in any particular field diminished in importance within the high-profile, political wing of the family. Prescott Bush, Jeb's paternal grandfather, returned from France after World War I and, having alienated his parents but possessing a Yale degree, took a job selling hardware parts. It was that job, in fact, that took him to St. Louis where he met Bert Walker's daughter, Dorothy. From there, Prescott moved to the floor-covering business in Massachusetts and, eventually, in Greenwich, Connecticut.

It was only there that he moved into his father-in-law's line of work, investment banking, where he started earning the kind of money that his children and grandchildren later came to see as a birthright. Even here, though, Prescott did not have an advanced degree in finance or account-ing or any such. It was family that brought him into one of the most pres-tigious brokerage firms on Wall Street, not any particular expertise.

The pattern continued with Jeb's father. George H.W. knew nothing about the oil equipment business, other than that one of his dad's best friends, Neil Mallon, had a company that sold and serviced drilling rigs. Mallon—after whom George H.W. and Barbara named their third son, Neil—brought George H.W. in with the idea of letting him learn the business from the ground up. George H.W., seeing all the oil wealth sur-rounding him in west Texas, lost patience and, using family money, jumped into the oil side himself. He struck it rich, reinforcing the idea again that actual expertise is unimportant.

There is considerable irony in that the political Bush who has gone the furthest academically to date is the one who appears to be the least intel-lectually curious: George W. The president, not his father, not Jeb, applied to law school. He was turned down by the University of Texas, but was later accepted by Harvard for its MBA program. Now, granted, a master's in business administration is not medieval philosophy and it is not astro-physics, but rather is about as practical and as make-more-money-in-the-real-world a degree as there is. And, true, George W. appeared to use the MBA program as a way to reorient his life after a period of drifting—a problem Jeb never had to confront.

Jeb, in terms of work ethic and focus, is much more like his father than George W. has been, even though George W. tried to mimic his father's life story in seemingly every way possible.

George W. went to Yale, got into the oil business, became a military pilot—just like his dad. In every respect, though, he could not measure up. He was not a good student. His oil ventures all flopped. He flew obsolete fighters for the Texas Air National Guard. Even in sports: his dad played first base for Yale, but the best George W. could manage was cheerleading at Andover and later becoming a part owner of the Texas Rangers. George W. bettered his father only in the realm of politics, first by winning a statewide office—whereas George H.W. twice lost bids for United States Senate seats in Texas—and then by winning a second term in the White House.

Jeb, in contrast, actively chose a different path than his father, just as George H.W. chose to strike out in a different direction from Prescott. After Andover, which he disliked because of the Vietnam-era campus turmoil that marked his time there, Jeb went to the University of Texas for college, ostensibly to be closer to the Mexican girl he had met during an Andover program his senior year. Upon graduating, Jeb chose the banking business, spending five years at Texas Commerce Bank, including two in the bank's Venezuela branch in Caracas. After coming home in 1979 to work on his dad's unsuccessful run for president, Jeb settled in Miami—again, to escape his father's shadow in Texas—and got into real estate, a business his father had never entered.

Ironically, the very process of trying to chart a different course from his father led Jeb to parallel George H.W.'s life to a greater degree even than this brother did.

George H.W. Bush graduated from college in two and a half years with Phi Beta Kappa honors. So did Jeb. George H.W. Bush married young, at age twenty, and had his first child, George Walker, eighteen months later. Jeb married within days of turning twenty-one and had his first child, George Prescott, two years later.

George H.W. struck off into waters uncharted by the family—oil—but got that first job thanks to one of father's closest friends, Neil Mallon. Jeb struck off into new grounds—banking—but got a job thanks to one of his father's closest friends, James Baker. George H.W. left New England to settle someplace far from his own father, Texas. Jeb left Texas to settle someplace far from his own dad, Florida.

Even their political trajectories are similar. George H.W.'s first elected post was the chairmanship of the Harris County Republican Party in Houston, his adopted hometown. And from that mighty perch, at age forty he ran for a statewide office in Texas, a United States Senate seat, and lost.

Similarly, Jeb's first elected post was chairman of the Dade County Republican Party in Miami. When he won, his father even sent him the gavel he had used in Harris County. And from that slot, at age forty-one, Jeb ran for a statewide office, governor of Florida, and lost.

. . .

LET'S GIVE credit where it is due. Jeb is not one to shrink from work, nor from the need of doing one's homework.

View Jeb's mission through the 1980s and early 1990s with the sole criterion of making money, and it is undeniable that Jeb was a phenomenal success. No, he did not take care to remain, like Caesar's wife, completely beyond reproach. As his own 1994 running mate correctly noted, Jeb in his haste associated with all sorts of bottom feeders.

However, it is important to bear in mind that doing so did not appreciably add to his wealth. Yes, those particular enterprises made him richer— in the case of his partnership with J. Edward Houston, significantly richer, thanks to the largesse of American taxpayers. But did he truly need them to achieve his goal? Not really. Jeb made the vast majority of his net worth partnering with completely legitimate business partners with no criminal record whatsoever. He did not choose the various and sundry crooks and deadbeats to associate with *because* they were crooks and deadbeats. Rather, he hooked up with them because he was in too big a rush to care.

Unyielding Bush critics are not willing to acknowledge that there is a difference. To them, Jeb is as bad as Miguel Recarey or Camilo Padreda or J. Edward Houston. Given all his advantages, they argue, that he would stoop to join up with the likes of these people to make a buck is all the proof that is necessary to reveal Jeb for the sleazeball that he is. And, give these folks their due, Jeb exhibited exceptionally lousy judgment in getting involved with some of these people, and it belies his claims that he always acted honorably and with constant vigilance against those who might have been more interested in the marketability of his last name than his business acumen.

Even by the time of his 1994 run for governor, Jeb still had a hard time admitting a lack of judgment. "If I knew what I know now—which is impossible so I shouldn't even say this—if I went back and relived my life, would I be more cautious, even more cautious than I was? The answer is, yes," Jeb told the *Palm Beach Post*. "Now, did I do anything wrong? I don't believe so. Did I lack judgment? I don't believe so. Would I like to do some things over again? Absolutely."

All of that notwithstanding, clearly Jeb could have been more careful as he set about making his fortune. It might have slowed him down a wee bit, here and there, not cutting those corners. Yet what the critics fail to understand in Jeb's peculiar worldview is what made these shortcuts seem perfectly reasonable in the first place: to Jeb, making gobs of money comes about as close to godliness as you can get on this Earth.

Again, this is not to say that money drives Jeb. Even his famous remark captured by the *Miami News* about wanting to be "very wealthy" gives only half the story. Yes, he wanted to be "very wealthy," and he wanted to do it quickly—but only because he had a state, a country, and a planet to run, and he couldn't get to those more important chores until he got the "make a million dollars" box checked off on his list.

This gets us back, in a way, to Jimmy Buffett's entertaining but inaccurate Ace Hardware store analogy about Jeb. Perhaps the best way to explain this is to compare him to his other brothers with political ambitions, George W. and Neil. The latter's name seems absurdly out of place in this context, but that's only because it came to evoke Silverado Savings and Loan and, later, anonymous Asian hookers. But in the early 1980s, some actually considered Neil the most natural politician of the brood. "If you just observed their personalities, you'd say Neil," said family friend Doug Wead, who at George W.'s request researched and wrote a report on presidential children. "He's relaxed, he's funny, he's a better speaker than anybody in the family." Barbara publicly talked about having three of her sons governing different states: George W. in Texas, Jeb in Florida, and Neil in Colorado.

Bush family critics are quick to point out that the actions of George W. in his Texas "oil tycoon" phase and Neil in his role as a bank director, had they been committed by ordinary mortals and not the sons of a sitting vice president and president, would have led to some Hard Time in the Big House. This is probably true. The Securities and Exchange Commission often takes a dim view of insider trading, which is what a reasonable person might conclude that George W. engaged in when, despite his position on Harken board's audit committee, he unloaded $835,000 worth of stock just weeks before it dropped in value and then did not file the required disclosure forms until eight months later. And banking regulators have taken more hard-line stances against other directors who approved loans to business partners, although, in Neil's case, the partners were more like sugar daddies. In fact, in the case of Neil, an intriguing tidbit that faded harmlessly away after George H.W. was not reelected in 1992 was that pressure was applied from Washington, D.C., in October 1988 to hold off on an investigation of Silverado until after the November 1988 election.

Those who dislike all things Bush point to these instances on their long lists of scams and rackets this generation of the family has gotten away with over the years. George H.W., Barbara, and Bush loyalists point out that despite all the smoke, no one has proven the fire—the hard evidence that government officials altered their handling of these cases because of the Bush name. Of course, as anyone who has even a vague idea of how large organizations work, this defense is beyond silly. No one *has* to tell an investigator or a regulator to lay off the vice president's kid, because any investigator or regulator with half a brain knows that doing so is a career-ending move. Consider it also from the point of view of the bureaucrat looking for the path of least resistance: does your life become easier, or more difficult, if you choose to put the vice president's child under investigation? An analogous incident comes from Jeb's Miami years, when he visited Nigeria as a water pump salesman after his father had become president. He informed the State Department that he wanted no special treatment during his visit, that he was just another American businessman. Did it come as a big surprise to him that his message pretty much ensured he got the red carpet treatment upon his arrival? This is sort of like the boss calling to say he'll be coming to visit you in the field office the next day, but that you should do nothing special for the occasion. So, what do you think? Do you actually do nothing special? Or do you spend the rest of the day cleaning up and ironing your best suit?

But this question of whether George W. and Neil got kid-glove treatment by federal authorities in the 1980s and early 1990s misses a more fundamental point, which is this: if their father had not held a White House office, neither of them would have *needed* kid-glove treatment by federal authorities. Does anybody seriously believe that George W. would have been bailed out by rich benefactors as his business ventures invariably tanked, time after time, if his last name had not been Bush? He never would have *had* the $800,000 worth of stock, nor the insider knowledge of when to dump it, had his name been George W. Doe. And to think that Neil Doe, based on his own academic and business track record, would have been made responsible for hundreds of millions of dollars in loans is similarly preposterous. Nothing against either man personally—and being fully aware of Neil's dyslexia as a child—but the trajectories of their youths suggest that without the family name, a middle- to lower-middle class existence might have been their lot in life. George W. particularly, with his addictive personality and his affinity for alcohol and good times, might have wound up in considerably more desperate straits. Consider what he once said of his first real position after college, a position he only got because the boss had once worked for his father and was returning the favor: "A stupid coat-and-tie job."

With these two, managing the Ace Hardware store really *might* have been a stretch.

JEB'S YEARS as a young adult in Florida are nothing short of puritanical virtue.

He woke up early, was thinking and planning deals before most people have had their second cup of coffee, and was running full speed all day and into the night. Given his role in his father's 1980 run for president, when Jeb based himself in Miami in an effort to win the state's Republican primary, it is no surprise that he was from his arrival in South Florida instantly a Republican player. In December 1983, he formally became Dade County's most influential Republican player, beating out for the county party chairmanship the wife of Watergate conspirator E. Howard Hunt and a Cuban-American who claimed Fidel Castro was behind Jeb's candidacy.

Now, a county chair in politics is somewhat like a college education—it is what you make of it. Jeb made a lot of it, putting in place a recruitment program to boost the party's registered voter roll in Dade County. Between December 1983 and December 1986, the number of Republicans climbed from 150,651 to 238,520, a 58 percent increase, while the number of registered Democrats actually declined from 425,559 to 422,205. Certainly, this was to an extent just taking advantage of existing conditions. Miami Cubans had been angry at the Democratic Party ever since President Kennedy had opted not to provide American air support during the disastrous Bay of Pigs invasion. Still, Jeb deserves credit for following through with the grunt work part of the operation. His goal was to register all newly naturalized Hispanics, not just Cubans, as Republicans, and he was extraordinarily successful in this. His influence, helped by his by-then fluent Spanish, grew to the point that his support of Tampa mayor Bob Martinez in the 1986 governor's race helped him win the nomination, even though he was a recently converted Democrat.

Martinez then went on to win the general election against a Democrat weakened by a fratricidal primary and runoff, which then led to Jeb's brief and only tenure in government prior to his election as governor in 1998. For twenty months in 1987 and 1988, Jeb moved to Tallahassee to serve as Martinez' secretary of commerce.

It was not a particularly memorable stint—then again, it was not a particularly memorable job, consisting largely of being a booster for the state to entice businesses to expand or relocate there. Jeb foreshadowed his priorities as governor by closing down the department's six regional offices and consolidating the work in Tallahassee, a move that he bragged would save the state $585,000. The local county administrators who liked having state tourism officials in their region to help pitch their areas to businesses opposed the plan, but Jeb proceeded anyway. This dynamic was writ large starting in 1999 when Jeb, despite a campaign that promised to "devolve" power from "Mount Tallahassee" because the best ideas came from local governments and community-based groups and so on, nonetheless consolidated an unprecedented amount of power within the agencies under his control at the expense of local governments and, especially, local school districts.

In 1988, though, Jeb was in charge of only a small, thin slice of state government, and it was clear that he wasn't particularly enjoying it. Jeb traveled on behalf of the state all over the world, not only trying to drum up business for Florida but also making the contacts that he was able to exploit when he returned to his career as a "Miami businessman" and, later, when he needed to raise money for his political campaigns. He put out press releases about how wonderful Florida's economy was, and how the following year would bring more vacationers by automobile to the Sunshine State than ever before. He shilled for rich, would-be sports team owners trying to bring Major League Baseball to Florida. The state subsidy designed to bring the Chicago White Sox to St. Petersburg? That was Jeb.

Perhaps his most memorable episode as a Martinez aide was his public support for the issue that proved to be Martinez' undoing: an expansion of the sales tax onto services, rather than just goods. Martinez originally endorsed the plan and then—months after its passage but under pressure from service providers, especially advertisers—called a special session for its repeal. The governor was never able to recover from this phenomenal flip-flop, and was easily defeated by Lawton Chiles in 1990. Jeb's role in the services tax debacle was minor, but fascinating, given the subject. In early 1987, Jeb came out solidly behind his boss: "If this is a way to broaden taxation and at the same time lower the rate, I think a lot of people would really go for it."

That actually should have been a fairly enlightened, logical position, except for the fact that by the mid-1990s, any type of tax "reform" such as this had been branded by the Grover Norquist wing of the Republican Party as a tax increase. No worries, though, for Jeb had thought ahead. Even as he was publicly supporting the services tax, he had privately sent Martinez a letter telling him it was a bad idea. And in 1998, Jeb was able to produce the letter when Democratic opponent Buddy MacKay started talking about the services tax and how Jeb had once supported it.

Five years later, when state Senate president John McKay pushed the idea of an expanded services tax that at the outset would be "revenue neutral" through a reduced tax rate, Jeb didn't need to think twice. This was, somehow, a tax increase, and he opposed it.

BY EARLY 1988, Jeb had already made it clear that he needed to work for his father's presidential campaign, and the short, not necessarily happy life of Jeb Bush, government bureaucrat, was soon over.

As expected, he performed well on that campaign—the last one in Florida where the Republican could count on winning without much of a fight. Dukakis's team pretty much conceded the state early on, pulling people and money to use in places where there was more of a chance, and that freed Jeb to spend much of his time in California, where his Spanish and his Mexican wife helped make inroads into the largely Democratic Mexican-American vote. Perhaps coincidentally, that election was the last time California has supported the Republican in a presidential race.

Back in Miami after his dad was safely in the White House, Jeb was back to his familiar occupation of getting rich. Only this time, things were even more lucrative than when he was only the son of the vice president.

Which really gets to the basic point of this chapter, which is not to begrudge the money Jeb made in his Miami years or to belittle how hard he worked. As already mentioned, Jeb worked extremely hard to succeed. and wasn't making money for the sake of money.

Rather, what remains astonishing more than a dozen years after he turned his sights away from acquiring wealth and toward the governorship is his continuing insistence that he would have succeeded regardless of his situation in life, and even that his family name was actually more of a hindrance.

In both his 1994 and 1998 runs, Jeb made it clear: not only was he not apologizing for his background, he was proud of where he was financially, and certain that it was the result of his own pluck and work ethic. "I've worked real hard for what I've achieved and I'm quite proud of it," he told the *St. Petersburg Times* in 1993. "I have no sense of guilt, no sense of wrongdoing."

The attitude was much the same as he had expressed on CNN's *Larry King Live* in 1992: "I think, overall, it's a disadvantage," he said of being the president's son when it came to his business opportunities. "Because you're restricted in what you can do."

This thinking cannot be described as anything other than delusional.

IMAGINE YOU are twenty-eight years old, with five years of experience in one field, followed by two years on a totally unrelated project. What do you suppose the odds are that an extremely wealthy, extremely successful businessman will come and offer to make you a full partner, with a 40 percent share of the profits, in a completely unrelated third enterprise, in which you have not one iota of knowledge?

Slim and none, right? That's probably correct for the vast majority of us. Fortunately for Jeb, he is not among our vast majority. Which is why, in Miami, Florida, in 1981, those were the precise circumstances Jeb found himself in.

Seven years earlier he had breezed through college in just five semesters, earning his degree from the University of Texas in Latin American studies. As usual, he'd been in a great rush. "'I wanted to get it over, get on, get married," was how he remembered it later.

His bride to be was Columba Garnica, the young girl he'd met during his senior year at Andover, when he took a course called Man and Society, which started with some Outward Bound–type camp time but then finished with half the class heading to South Boston to work with the poor, and the other half heading to Leon, a town in the Mexican state of Guanajuato, to help build a school. Jeb was among the ten who went to Mexico, and that is where he met Columba, the younger sister of a girl dating one of the other Andover boys.

"Boom! I was gone," he told the *Washington Post* as his father moved into the White House in 1989. "She was the first girl I ever loved, and the last."

To understand this, you have to appreciate Jeb as the young romantic who questioned authority, questioned the Vietnam war, took part in campus debates about political issues of the day—while at the same time idolizing his father and the way he lived his life. Here, with this seventeen-year-old Mexican girl, was a chance for Jeb to both prove his ideals as well as emulate his dad.

The official explanation for Jeb's sprint through college is that he knew what he wanted—a life with Columba—and that his bachelor's degree was his last hurdle. There is, I think, more to it. George H.W. had also gotten through college in two and a half years. Of course, that was the accelerated program Yale was offering to servicemen back from the war, but no matter. His father had done it, and Jeb would do it. His father had married and started a family young, and so would Jeb.

Jeb and Columba wed at the University of Texas chapel on February 23, 1974, all of two months after Jeb had informed his parents of the event. It was a small ceremony: Jeb's immediate family, plus his parents' housekeeper, and Columba's sister and mother, but not her father, who had abandoned them when Columba was three.

Jeb had also just graduated, and he moved on to his first job with Texas Commerce Bank, an institution founded by the family of his father's close friend, James Baker. They lived in Houston, where he had grown up, and two years later had their first child, George Prescott. Daughter Noelle followed fifteen months later.

But Houston was not a friendly place for Columba. Discrimination against Mexicans was rampant, so when an opportunity came in 1977 to open a Caracas branch office, Jeb grabbed it. They were living in a twelfth-story apartment, in a country that Jeb later reported was not particularly "warm and friendly" to foreigners, when he got a phone call from his father in the spring of 1978 to let him know of his decision to run for president. Jeb responded with the obligatory *president of what?* wisecrack, but by the end of the phone conversation had decided to return home and work on the campaign.

By May 1979, Columba and the kids were back in Houston, and Jeb became a full-time operative of the George H.W. Bush for President campaign. His father took full advantage of his second son's linguistic abilities, dispatching him to Puerto Rico, where Jeb was able to win the island's fourteen delegates for his father nine days before the New Hampshire primary that saw the momentum George H.W. had won with his stunning Iowa caucuses victory shift for good to Ronald Reagan. But Jeb also spent much of his time in Florida, and that is where he befriended a big supporter of his father, Cuban refugee Armando Codina, who had made millions though a computerized accounting business, and had since turned his attention to what would remain the next big thing in South Florida for decades to come, real estate.

Which brings us back to How Jeb Became a Millionaire.

. . .

CODINA MADE Jeb an offer the young man had no possible reason to refuse: become my partner in the real estate business, keep a large percentage of all the commissions you earn, and have the opportunity to participate in some of the deals as an investor. Codina Bush Group would be the name of the company, and it would soon cover a healthy family of subsidiaries: Bush Realty, Bush Real Estate Management, Codina Construction, Codina Development, and so forth.

Again, there is no question that Jeb is a quick study and worked hard. There is no question that South Florida real estate in the early 1980s was booming, and anyone willing to work could have made some money.

At issue, though, is Jeb's claim that his success was *entirely* due to that hard work, and not at all to the sweetheart deal that Codina had given him. "I learned the job the hard way: on the job," Jeb said once. In 1992, he told the *Los Angeles Times*: "I wasn't using him, and he wasn't using me."

Well, no, they did not "use" each other in the sense of some addict-enabler relationship. But was Jeb seriously suggesting that it did not help Codina financially to include the name of the vice president of the United States in the name of his business? Or that Jeb did not, in turn, benefit immensely from that dynamic?

To suggest that this opportunity could have fallen into just anyone's lap is to inhabit some parallel universe. Armando Codina would not have restructured his business to accommodate Jeb Doe. There would have been no Codina Doe Group, no partnership with a twenty-eight-year-old Doe who had *no experience whatsoever in the business*.

This, again, is not to diminish Jeb's talents and work ethic. One can only imagine the future of a Codina Bush Group had the "Bush" been referring to George W. or Neil. One can imagine the always courteous Codina, having to find some way to end the financially disastrous relationship before it put him in the poorhouse.

And this is not merely to prick the ego of someone lucky enough—as Ann Richards once said about Jeb's father—to have been born on third base yet who continues to believe he hit a stand-up triple. Jeb is someone who well could have hit that triple on his own, or at least a single or a double. More important is the incorrect life lesson that Jeb evidently drew from his own experience: that *anyone*, if he or she tried hard enough, could not only financially succeed in this life, but succeed wildly. The logical contrapositive of that—that if you do not succeed, it is because you are not really trying—was even more of a menace, when it became the underpinning to Jeb's punitive welfare "reform" proposals in his 1994 campaign for governor.

Even four years later, when Jeb had dropped some of the strident rhetoric that came off sounding more than a little antiblack and antipoor, he was still insisting that his path to success was a model available to anyone. "The American dream is shattered for far too many people," he explained to a group of alumni from Florida A&M University, the state's historically black university. "Too few people have confidence in capitalism."

ACTUALLY, it is probably a good thing that welfare recipients trying to get off the dole do not, as a rule, have the ruthless drive to be wealthy that Jeb did in the 1980s.

Filling every available square inch of land in South Florida with pavement, buildings, and golf courses was, in the long run, a questionable objective. But Jeb and his colleagues at Codina Bush were hardly alone in that regard. Florida was then and is now pretty much hell-bent to "build out" as quickly as possible, quality of life and the environment be damned.

If that was the worst that could be said about Jeb's rush to get rich, that he was part of the pervasive, mindless, strip-mall-and-condo culture that helped ruin so much of Florida—well, that would be one thing. There are a great many people both in Florida and the rest of the nation who would happily trade rapid "growth" for the promise of an *expanded tax base* and *more jobs*. Certainly, the evidence in Florida suggests that their economic theories are at best wishful thinking and at worst a con job. That's a different debate for a different book. What's important here is that Jeb's path to wealth would have been considered squarely in the mainstream of the Florida experience, if all he had done was to wheel and deal commercial real estate and build high-end waterfront homes on Biscayne Bay.

That, unfortunately, was not all. What made Jeb's years in Miami the centerpiece of his political opponents' campaigns against him was his puzzling tendency to hook up with people who would end up in jail or on the lam.

Puzzling not because Miami was not chock-full of this subspecies. It most definitely was and still is. It's puzzling because Jeb was making *plenty* of money through Codina Bush's legitimate clients. After starting out at $44,000 a year in 1981—that's $96,000 in 2006 dollars; again, not bad for a twenty-eight-year-old with no real estate experience—Jeb pulled down

$1.2 million in 1990 ($1.8 million in 2006 dollars). Here's just one example of how he managed that: for a $1,000 investment in the Museum Tower office building in 1984, Jeb cleared $345,000 in profit six years later. What possible need was there to look beyond deals like that?

This goes back to the "businessman" discussion. Jeb never really considered his occupation "real estate" or "developer" or "home builder" or even "strip-mall designer." His occupation was making money, and he evidently did it whenever, and with whomever, possible.

"There was quite an array of characters who tried to get close to Jeb," Codina told the *St. Petersburg Times* in 1998. "This is a frontier town."

Carol Wilkinson, a federal prosecutor during Jeb's Miami heydays, put it another way: "If you want to make money in the Southern District of Florida, what you do is, you see no evil, hear no evil, and speak no evil."

WHEN JEB was chairman of the county Republican party between 1984 and 1986, his finance chairman was Camilo Padreda, a former counterintelligence officer for Cuban dictator Fulgencio Batista in the 1950s. Padreda was indicted for embezzling $500,000 from a Texas savings and loan in 1982, but the case was dropped when the CIA intervened to protect one of its "assets" from the failed Bay of Pigs invasion. Jeb also came to handle the real estate business for a housing partnership that Padreda owned— which was the business that ultimately got him convicted for violating federal Department of Housing and Urban Development laws in an apartment complex deal. He was given house arrest in return for his cooperation with a larger investigation into Dade County corruption.

Even though Padreda's name was spread all over the *Miami Herald* in 1985 for a deal he worked with the Miami city manager to get a zoning change on a piece of property, Jeb could at least make the argument that his financial dealings with Padreda were limited to Jeb's role as a leasing agent for one of Padreda's buildings.

This was not the case with Jeb's relationship with a Padreda associate, Miguel Recarey, who in the mid-1980s was a luminary in Miami society as head of the International Medical Centers health maintenance organization, one of the largest in the country. Recarey, who called himself *Pluma Blanca*—"white feather"—in his secretive business dealings, drove a Maserati, lived in a waterfront mansion, ran his 42-foot yacht across the Gulf Stream to private Cat Cay in the Bahamas. He was also a major Republican donor, and in 1984, he needed a favor from Jeb.

IMC wanted to keep its waiver with the federal Department of Health and Human Services that let it have as much as 80 percent of its patients on Medicare, rather than the 50–50 ratio the agency had adopted. The rule was to make sure that participating HMOs were financially healthy, and not overly reliant on federal money.

In fact, IMC was already a house of cards. In 1981, the state of Florida had canceled its contract with the company for treating Cuban and Haitian refugees because of numerous complaints about its poor service and shaky finances. One of the complaints, for example, was that its clinic in Little Haiti did not even have drapes to shield gynecological patients during exams. Jeb evidently did not know about this or about Recarey's 1973 conviction for tax evasion, for which he served a month in jail, or about his habit of bragging about his association with mob boss Santos Trafficante. He did not know these things or, if he did know them, he did not care. At Recarey's behest, the second son of the vice president of the United States picked up the phone and called Washington.

After the whole thing had collapsed and Recarey had fled and Congress got around to holding hearings, former HHS chief of staff C. McClain Haddow testified that his boss, Margaret Heckler, had held a "dim view" of Recarey and IMC, but changed her mind after Jeb's phone calls. Haddow explained to *Newsday* in 1988 that Jeb told him that "contrary to any rumors that were floating around concerning Mr. Recarcy, that he was a solid citizen from Mr. Bush's perspective down there [in Miami], that he was a good community citizen and a good supporter of the Republican Party."

In 1986, Recarey hired Jeb's real estate company to find him office space for a new headquarters. Jeb never did come up with an agreeable building, but wound up getting $75,809 from Recarey anyway over three years. Jeb said the fees were more than justified, given how much effort he had put into the project, and that, besides, he personally only received $5,000 out of that amount.

As to the phone calls in 1984 and 1985, Jeb initially denied making any. After the congressional testimony made it clear that he had, he explained it like this: "I asked that they be given a fair hearing. That's not lobbying."

Ultimately, as the questions started coming faster as he ran for governor, he explained his involvement like this: "If I had any reason to believe that Recarey was anything other than the legitimate businessman he appeared to be, I would have had nothing to do with him," he wrote to the *South Florida Sun-Sentinel* in 1993. "Any attempt to imply that I knew of

Recarey's illegal activity or that I and my company were paid to exert improper influence in Washington on Recarey's behalf is absolutely false and an attempt to imply guilt by association."

Certainly, Jeb was not the only Republican of that period to have cozied up to this spectacular felon. Records that become public after his escape to Venezuela show that a low-level HHS investigator had wanted to go after Recarey as early as 1983 based on suspicions of fraud and embezzlement, but that his superiors were not interested. It was only in 1986, after other federal investigators were already on Recarey's trail—he was indicted for bribing union officials to put their retirees in his HMO—that a formal HHS probe began.

Even this, though, appears to have been done with kid gloves. Recarey was next indicted on federal wiretapping charges based on his efforts to cover up the bribery scandal, and finally indicted for Medicare fraud. Usually, people indicted on federal charges have to surrender their passports and have their accounts frozen. Not so with Recarey, who instead got a $2.2 million tax refund from the Internal Revenue Service in August 1987. The last thing he did before skipping town was to wire $30,000 to Nick Panuzio, chairman of the board of the Washington, D.C., lobbying firm that included Lee Atwater, the top strategist of the George H.W. Bush presidential campaign.

The $200 million that Recarey appeared to have stolen was gone forever. And, as far as anyone knows, he continues to live the life of a wealthy fugitive—Spain was his last known domicile.

WHILE PADREDA and Recarey show that Jeb did not particularly care whom he associated with when it came to making money, the amounts of arguably "ill-gotten" gains he reaped were relatively small, compared to his staggering take-home pay in those years.

There were other examples of these, during Jeb's Miami years. In 1995, Jeb was invited to join the board of directors of Ideon Corp., a Jacksonville company that sold credit card protection services. A quick read of Ideon's Securities and Exchange Commission filings should have warned Jeb that the company was bad news. It had taken a big write-off in 1994, and its chief executive allowed close ties between the company and its directors through consulting contracts. Jeb didn't know or didn't care or both. Now, directorships of companies are a well-known perk available to already rich people: attend a few meetings a year, all expenses paid, and in return make tens of thousands of dollars. Even by this standard, a directorship for Ideon—which, among other things, marketed insurance to parents offering private investigative services in the event their children were kidnapped, presumably believing this to be a growth market—was a scam and a half. Jeb's take was $50,000 a year, plus stock options. It was soon mired in a class-action shareholder lawsuit, and Jeb was lucky to get out unscathed when the company was purchased.

No matter, the same Jacksonville friend and political supporter who turned him on to Ideon let Jeb in on the group seeking an NFL franchise for that city. Tom Petway—who by late 2005 was on the board of Jeb's revived "Foundation for Florida's Future," a nonprofit Jeb originally set up in 1995 to keep his name in the media and his campaign team together for a second run in 1998—in 1989 got Jeb to join the "Touchdown Jacksonville" investors to bring football to the northeast Florida city with the dismal self-esteem problem. Jeb borrowed the $450,000 for his 1 percent and later sold it for a $58,000 profit. But the more interesting story here was the $121 *million* that Jacksonville taxpayers agreed to put up to prettify the old Gator Bowl so as to help Jeb's rich friends get even richer. Jeb, so offended by welfare for poor people, evidently had no trouble with welfare of the corporate kind.

Jeb also managed to get on the $1,200-a-year board of The Private Bank and Trust, an operation that was opened on Miami's Brickell Avenue by the Bank Oppenheim Pierson, of Switzerland. It did not take deposits or make loans. In fact, if you called its office, the receptionist would answer: "4643," the last four digits of the phone number. It was designed, as might be guessed, to manage the investments of clients, mainly Latin American, who did not want a lot of attention. It was shut down in 1991—five years after Jeb had resigned to become secretary of commerce under Governor Martinez—by federal regulators for making investments against the clients' wishes and using inappropriate, bank-managed vehicles. Jeb later told reporters: "There were no financial problems for me to be aware of when I was a director."

His involvement in a marketing firm for water pumps was similarly curious. Again, the business opportunity came from a Republican donor and friend, Jeff Eller, who together with Jeb in 1988 created the Bush-El Corp., to sell the pumps made by Eller's other business, M&W Pumps, a Broward County company that sought business all over the world. Jeb traveled to promote the irrigation pumps, both big and small, but the most attention came with his 1989 efforts to sell them in Nigeria.

Set aside for a moment the royal treatment he got from military dictator Ibrahim Babangida—Jeb made the national news every night, was treated to a rare pageant of 1,300 war horses, and at one point drew a crowd of 100,000. Also set aside whether a Nigerian cohort in the enterprise paid cash bribes to officials to grease the deal, like a U.S. government lawsuit later alleged. A more important detail is that the $74 million deal's private financing fell through, and Nigeria eventually sought and received taxpayer-financed loans through the Export-Import Bank. Which means that when Nigeria defaulted on the loans, as a country ruled by a parade of corrupt officials was wont to do, we the people of the United States were on the hook. Hence the lawsuit by the U.S. Justice Department to recover $28 million that supposedly went for bribes from Eller and his pump company. Jeb claims he personally did not benefit from any Export-Import backed transactions, but would not break down exactly which deals netted him the $196,000 in commissions and $452,000 he received for selling his share back to Eller before he first ran for governor. A lawsuit against Jeb and Eller by a former M&W employee was settled four days before Jeb was supposed to give a sworn deposition that might have shed light on the matter. The settlement terms of the suit—which had alleged that Jeb and Eller had improperly diverted M&W profits to their marketing company—required that details remain secret.

EVEN FLYING around an African dictatorship selling pumps, though, paled before a single real-estate deal in the mid-1980s: 1390 Brickell Avenue, the crown jewel of Jeb's Miami years escapades.

It started out as a relatively run-of-the-mill desire by Jeb and Codina to purchase a downtown office building in 1984. The two found an insurance company to lend them $7 million, and came up with a third party, J. Edward Houston, to put up another $4.56 million. That total was to purchase the building for $9 million and have $1.7 million left to renovate it and a nearly $1 million reserve. Houston, though, did not have the cash, and instead borrowed it from Broward Federal Savings and Loan, where one of his law partners was a director. Houston lent Jeb and Codina the money in exchange for a note promising repayment using lease proceeds. He turned that note over to the thrift as collateral.

All this took place against the backdrop of an amazing office space glut in Miami and other cities. When lease income dropped, Jeb and Codina stopped making payments to Houston, as their agreement with him stipulated. Houston stopped making payments to Broward Federal, and Broward Federal, having made a number of these sweetheart loans, collapsed in the national savings and loan crisis.

When federal regulators came to clean up the mess, they eventually negotiated a deal that let Jeb and Codina keep the building by closing out the $4.56 million Broward Federal liability for a mere $505,000 and calling it even. The two partners had to pay $1.3 million in income tax on the forgiven loan.

Let us grant here that Jeb's culpability in this is nothing on the order of brother Neil's adventures with Silverado Savings and Loan, where he was actually a director helping dole out questionable loans to the men who had made him a millionaire. Let us also accept that, accusations by Bush haters to the contrary notwithstanding, federal regulators all around the nation were liquidating bad loans for a dime on the dollar in an attempt to salvage at least *some* value in what would wind up a $500 billion bailout of the industry.

Jeb's explanation of why this was not a big deal is nothing short of astonishing. He claimed, after accounting for the expenses he and Codina incurred, that he at best broke even on the project or even lost money. It is a testament to the inability of too many political reporters to do simple arithmetic that, as a group, they let Jeb get away with such nonsense during his 1994 run for governor.

The question here is not whether Jeb turned a profit. The question is the *seven-figure* contribution that U.S. taxpayers made to Jeb's net worth. How do we know there was a seven-figure contribution? Because Jeb and Armando Codina *paid $1.3 million* in income tax on it. Certainly, they did not do this out of pure love for the Internal Revenue Service.

Imagine, for example, that regulators had not been in a hurry to close the books on 1390 Brickell and had remained part owners of that building. When the time came to sell, the U.S. government would still have held a note that would have required Jeb and Codina to pay it—well, *us*—$4.5 million. So instead of breaking even on the project, they would have *lost* approximately $3 million.

As the industry publication *National Mortgage News* said in 1992, "This use of a 'straw borrower' has been viewed in numerous thrift cases as a felony and has been prosecuted aggressively when little-known miscreants were involved."

Even accepting Jeb's claim that he had no idea that Houston intended to borrow the money from Broward Federal, and therefore he was not trying to use a "straw borrower," his indignant defense of the deal, and his protestations that he did not benefit from taxpayer funds, are, at the very least, telling.

Here is how Jeff Gerth, the *New York Times* investigative reporter who broke the original story, phrased it in 1990: "Both Mr. Bush and Mr. Codina expressed surprise that the settlement of the loan could be interpreted as the use of taxpayers' money to make good a loan whose proceeds went for their building. Asked if they were aware that the funds for the repayment of the Broward Federal loan came from the taxpayers, both men said no."

This is how Jeb, when asked the same question by the *St. Petersburg Times*, phrased it three years later: "*Hellllll*, no. Absolutely not."

THE FLORIDA legislature every two years publishes a clerk's manual with all manner of little facts about the House members and senators. Education, previous government experience, name of spouse, district office and Capitol phone numbers—and then one that Tallahassee journalists look at very closely: occupation. Almost all Florida legislators have one, given that the legislative salary is $30,000 a year.

In most cases this is pretty straightforward. A schoolteacher would put "teacher." A doctor might list "physician," or perhaps the specialty. A stockbroker might put "stockbroker." And then there are those who list simply "businessman," and it is those entries that set off warning bells in the heads of political reporters who have spent any time at all covering the legislature.

Sometimes "businessman" is simply shorthand for "business owner." A personnel-services business, or a printing business, or a restaurant business. But far, far too often, "businessman" as used by a Florida legislator means: a little of this, and a little of that, and maybe some of this other thing on the side. Usually this means that the legislator's "day job" is working deals— getting in on a new apartment complex here, while doing some "consulting" for a developer there. Usually the legislator's "business" success is tied directly to his or her influence in the Capitol. Usually the "business" benefit was the reason the legislator ran for office in the first place. It is pathetic, particularly when this type of legislator rises through the ranks and enjoys sudden wealth as lobbyists and their clients who need a favorable tweak in a particular law find reason to steer "business" their way.

These are, however, merely Florida legislators, and no one really expects much from them. Here is something far more pathetic: Jeb was a "businessman," in the exact style of the weaselly, low-rent Florida lawmaker, and nothing more.

In defense of many of the legislative weasels, going from one questionable moneymaking deal to the next is about the limit of their abilities. Some only have high-school educations, or GEDs. Many are not necessarily the sharpest knives in the drawer—not university material, as it were.

What was Jeb's excuse?

Jeb had the benefit of an elite private school education, not to mention a keen intellect and an incredible work ethic. And so for the better part of two decades, he directed all of those advantages toward flogging luxury condos on Biscayne Bay and water pumps to Third-World dictators.

Therein lies the great shame of John Ellis Bush: the breathtaking waste of potential. As mentioned earlier, he really had the entire world before him. No possibility was too remote. All he had to do was choose something, anything, onto which he could focus that intellect and acquire the expertise to make a real contribution to humankind's progress. Heart surgeon, solar energy engineer, prosecutor—the list is endless.

It's important to note here that acquiring this expertise would not necessarily have slowed him down on his quest to rule the state, and then the world. Not only would humanity have received a greater benefit from his drive and intellect than it wound up getting from him during those dozen years, but such experience in any of those fields would have given him a measure of maturity that he clearly did not have in 1994. It certainly would have given him an appreciation for the notion that some people, by dint of their extensive education and training, ought to be afforded a measure of respect for their views in a particular area, something he lacked even toward the end of his second term in 2006.

Rather, Jeb reveled in his ability to speak knowledgeably on a wide range of subjects. That is not something to be dismissed in a political leader—and certainly the comparison can be made with his elder brother, who seemingly has difficulty speaking knowledgably on even one subject. And yet, there is a difference, a *consequential* difference, between being able to speak knowledgably on something, and truly knowing it. And too often as Florida's governor, Jeb exhibited the former, and not the latter. Even worse, this tendency was combined with a stubborn refusal to listen to experts who did know the subject at hand but who did not share his ideology.

Alas, this was a predictable result of the inordinate worth Jeb placed on getting rich, by any convenient means at one's disposal: he came to value that as a respectable and admirable goal, much as the rest of us might respect a college professor or a brain surgeon or even an appellate court judge.

Not Jeb. For better or worse, Jeb puts "businessman" at the top of the worthiness pyramid. In an undereducated yet rapaciously materialistic society such as Florida's, Jeb's encouragements further in that direction, as we will see, were at best misguided and at worst disastrous.

Chapter Four

ELECTIONS ARE A CONTACT SPORT

"If I can make Willie Horton a household name, we'll win the election."
—LEE ATWATER, 1988

"I love competition. The feeling is almost identical in sports and politics. The adrenaline gets flowing."
—GEORGE H.W. BUSH, 1988

"Hit 'em again. Hit 'em again. Harder! Harder!"
—THE CROWD OF DELEGATES AT THE
REPUBLICAN NATIONAL CONVENTION, 1992

The scene is the Midland airport in West Texas in the autumn of 1952. California senator Richard Nixon, Ike's running mate, has flown in for a rally organized by the son of Connecticut Republican Prescott Bush, who that November will become elected to the United States Senate on his second try.

Prescott's son, George H. W., is a New Englander who has gone west to seek his fortune, and only recently has set up shop with a neighbor in an oil-rights leasing company designed to piggyback on the success of real oil companies. So far it hasn't made much money, but it's a start. His work on the rally is also the twenty-eight-year-old's first involvement in a national campaign, and he is eager to see it go off smoothly.

But no sooner has Nixon started to speak than a couple of "seedy-looking guys," in the view of George H. W.'s partner John Overbey, hold up insulting signs and start heckling the candidate. George H. W. Bush is not pleased. He races over, grabs their signs, rips them up, and tells the gentlemen to get the hell out.

As Overbey explained it to a reporter thirty-six years later: "He can be a pretty aggressive guy, you know."

Like father, like sons, as America has come to see in recent years.

Jeb does not like dissent, and George W. took "message control" at public events to a new level, allowing into his audiences only those who already agreed with him and tracking down and kicking out potential troublemakers, at least in one case, based on the bumper stickers on their cars.

Representative democracy and electioneering might be a messy thing, in the vision of our Founding Fathers, with raucous debate and battling viewpoints. This is not necessarily the vision of the Bush family, particularly when it comes to their own elections. The rules they seem to favor are simple enough to understand: their side can do pretty much anything they want, while their opponents should pretty much just grin and bear it.

Elections, like everything else the Bushes engage in, are a contact sport, only without an umpire or any sense of fair play or sportsmanship.

The most instructive thing about the above example is that its protagonist was George H. W., a man whose graciousness has been his defining characteristic even according to many Democrats whose main purpose through the 1980s and early 1990s was to defeat him. He is and was, by all accounts, a nice and decent guy—yet that didn't stop him, borrowing the title of writer Richard Ben Cramer's narrative of George H. W.'s 1988 presidential victory, from doing *whatever it took* to win.

Neither of the political Bushes of this generation has seen any similar need to temper his ambitions or behavior. The lessons they have taken to heart from their father, rather, were those drawn from the things he did not do in 1992. He did not turn his undivided attention to his reelection early enough. He did not hit Democrat Bill Clinton hard enough. The boys' six subsequent victories in 1994, 1998, 2000, 2002, and 2004—against only Jeb's one loss in 1994—suggest that they learned those lessons well. Just ask Ann Richards, Buddy MacKay, Al Gore, Bill McBride, and John Kerry.

Just as one wouldn't get between a hungry polar bear and an Arctic seal, so it is unwise to get between a Bush and electoral victory. Those guys, and gal, should have known better.

IT IS NOT fair to blame the Bush family for the condition that American campaigns and elections find themselves today. In a government of and by the people, that fault must fall squarely on Americans. If we, collectively, paid more attention to government and elections, there would be less stupid stuff going on and more smart, competent people serving in office.

Still, it is fair to point out that Bush family members over the last several decades have made little effort to increase the caliber of this nation's discourse in the area of choosing leaders. From Willie Horton to questioning John McCain's sanity to denigrating the patriotism of political opponents to the Swift Boat attacks, George H.W., and then George W. and Jeb have used the same "divide and conquer" strategy that Great Britain once used to rule much of the world.

George W., who told everyone that he was a "uniter, not a divider" turned around and ruled by consciously dividing, and not uniting. Then he used the 50-percent-plus-one nation he had helped create to win a spectacularly cynical reelection in which he cast himself as the only one moral enough to protect the nation from its enemies.

Lee Atwater, an attentive student of the Southern Strategy first consciously used by Republicans in 1968, put this down for posterity in 1984, when he was preparing the playbook for the Reagan-Bush reelection campaign: "We'd like to win the country, but we only have to win a little over half of it. Indeed, given the vagaries of the Electoral College, we can win with a minority of the popular vote. Therefore we shouldn't hesitate to polarize, play the South against the North, the West against the East, and so on," Atwater wrote.

This was quality advice, for Republicans interested in winning and not terribly bothered by pandering to closet racists, and Jeb was only too willing to take it.

In 1994, Jeb played two favorite gambits from the Atwater, us-against-them strategy, welfare and crime. When these topics are brought up with

1964: George H.W., candidate for U.S. Senate, yucks it up with a living version of his party's mascot. From left: Barbara, Doro, Marvin, Neil, Jeb, and George H.W. Eldest son George W. was off at school.

members of the Republican "base" in the South, it's understood what's really meant. Welfare and crime are code for: blacks are destroying our society.

The most pathetic thing about this was that Jeb understood exactly what he was doing as he was doing it. With crime, for example, statistics showed that the problem was on the decline by the mid-1990s with the improvement in the economy, and that if people were increasingly terrified, that was at least in part a function of the proliferation of microwave trucks at local television stations, making "live" reports from crime scenes the latest fad.

"People's fear is heightened beyond what is reasonable," Jeb told the *St. Petersburg Times* in November 1993. So did that keep him from using that fear to his advantage? Not hardly.

"The simple fact is we are not safe. Not in our homes . . . not anywhere," Jeb said in the speech officially kicking off his campaign a month earlier. And in December, he would tell campaign audiences: "People now cannot walk on their streets without fear of crime!"

In 1989, Jeb was proud to stand by Lee Atwater, just a couple of years after questioning whether he would be loyal enough to his father. "Atwater could go to hell tomorrow and I'd be a supporter. He has proved himself with our family," Jeb declared.

Ironically enough, if there was any single reason that George H.W. lost his reelection bid in 1992, it was because Lee Atwater had died, and that no one could take his place.

As history has proven, though, he was not needed by either of George H.W.'s political sons. They were both astute enough to internalize his lessons.

ANOTHER LESSON that this generation of Bushes has taken to heart is that politics is marketing—nothing more, and nothing less. And in marketing, what you say about your product is far more important than any of your product's actual attributes.

In other words: calling something "new and improved" will persuade an astonishing number of people that the particular something really is new and improved, even if, in reality, it is neither. (By the by, calling yourself "fair" and "balanced," when you are neither, apparently works, too.)

It is tradecraft they watched up close with their father, who in 1988 repackaged himself as the populist who understood and empathized with average Americans. He was a New England WASP with a prep school, Ivy League education and an oceanfront mansion in Maine, but Michael Dukakis, the son of Greek immigrants, *he* was the elitist. To help prove this, George H.W. told everyone he drank beer and ate pork rinds—even though his favorite snack was actually popcorn and his favorite drink a stiff vodka martini. People believed him. Why? Because he said so.

His boys, in 1994 and 1998, both borrowed a phrase from their father's campaign, and explained how they were "compassionate conservatives" as they ran for governor. People believed them. Why? Because they said so.

And after September 11, George W.'s spinners sold America on the idea that he was "resolute." Hundreds of times, they told us this. Thousands of times. Americans believed this, too. In fact, it's amazing how thoroughly this particular "word of the day" permeated throughout the political world, including political journalism. In the on-deadline crunch following his first debate with John Kerry, for example, news organizations from CNN to the *New York Times* to the *Miami Herald* all described George W. as "resolute"—even though, after a day or two of reflection, it became clear that the president actually had been peevish and whiny, and that Kerry had stomped him.

Perhaps this is self-evident, to those whose business is advertising and public relations. But to many Americans—particularly those who consider themselves educated and sophisticated—it's still a strange concept that with mere repetition something that may not be true, or even something provably untrue, will eventually be accepted as conventional wisdom.

George W. has thus far exhibited the most prowess in this area of all his family members, and the tactics that vanquished two genuine Vietnam War heroes are the best proof.

This is important because Vietnam should have been George W.'s Achilles' heel. True, America had already shown by electing Bill Clinton that it would forgive somebody who opposed the war and avoided service. But George W. had not opposed the war. To the contrary, he had vocally supported it—but then had finagled his way out of getting shot at and into the Texas National Guard.

This could have been his undoing, in South Carolina in February of 2000. The guy who had come out of nowhere and slapped him down in New Hampshire was now in a state where his war record should have been a big plus. So what did George W. do? He and his allies managed to turn John McCain's time as a POW against him, is all. The fact McCain had spent five and a half years in Hanoi prison camps made him unstable, dangerous . . . and then he had *abandoned his fellow vets!*

It defied any rational explanation. It was so outlandish that McCain couldn't believe it was happening to him. And that was his big mistake. He let patently absurd accusations go answered, assuming that anyone with a small fraction of a brain would see them as patently absurd.

Four years later, John Kerry failed to learn from McCain's mistake, and reacted with disbelief as George W.'s people unleashed their Swift Boat attacks—essentially accusing Kerry of lying about the injuries behind his medals. In terms of pure chutzpah, this one put even the sliming of McCain to shame. As Kerry sat on his hands, the charge, ridiculous as it was, was repeated enough times so that enough people came to believe it. Once again, George W., who had avoided any confrontation with actual armed North Vietnamese, was able to successfully denigrate a guy who had led others into firefights with them.

Sure, embellishing one's own accomplishments and strengths while denigrating the other guy's has always been a part of American electioneering. And given the Bush family's six-decade history in that electioneering, it's possible to trace the improvements in the various candidates' efficiency at massaging the truth over the years.

Prescott Bush, running for the Senate the first time in 1950, was hammered late in the campaign by accusations that he supported the use of birth control. The charge was made during a popular radio show on a Sunday night, and Catholic voters in Connecticut—of which there were many in 1950—were urged to tune in via anonymous flyers passed out during church services that morning. The charge had the virtue of being largely true—Prescott was treasurer of Planned Parenthood, a successor organization to the Birth Control League, the group mentioned in the flyers. Prescott nonetheless tried to deny it, but to no avail. He wound up losing that election by a thousand votes out of 862,000 cast.

There were several lessons that not just Prescott but also his progeny drew from that experience. The first was that attacks had to be answered immediately, if not sooner. And the second was: do unto the other guy before he does unto you. In short, politics was a blood sport, and you had to be ready to do whatever it took to win.

JEB, of course, was not running in 1950s New England, but in 1990s Florida, which gets to an important and easily misunderstood point. Too often, political analyses of Florida talk about a sea change that supposedly started in the 1980s and finished in the 1990s, as Florida's state government shifted from domination by the Democratic Party to the Republican Party.

Superficially, this is indeed true. Democrats controlled the governor's office, the Cabinet, and the legislature in the mid-1980s. With the election of Jeb in 1998, control of all three institutions had switched to Republicans. But there is much less to this than meets the eye. To understand why, take a look at how the state has voted in presidential races—the races that attract the highest turnouts and are therefore the most representative of voter sentiment—over the past hundred years.

For the first five decades of the twentieth century, with the memory of Union troops still fresh, Florida went Democratic all but once, from William Jennings Bryan in 1900 to Harry Truman in 1948. Republicans were the guys who freed the slaves, and during Reconstruction actually let black people vote and get elected to office. In those years, there were no blocs of New York liberals in Miami Beach and Fort Lauderdale. Florida was the Deep South. Period. Only in 1928, when the Democrat was Catholic Al Smith, did voters go with the Republican.

With the end of World War II, though, the national Democratic Party began to change. Emboldened by how well integration had served the armed forces during the war, Democrats in the north started talking about ending segregation and extending civil rights, including real, enforceable voting rights, to black Americans everywhere, including the South. Naturally, this did not go over too well anywhere in the region, including Florida. In 1952 and 1956, war hero Republican Dwight Eisenhower trounced Democrat Adlai Stevenson. In 1960, Richard Nixon narrowly lost the national election but narrowly won in Florida. In 1968, 1972, 1980, 1984, and 1988, the Republican candidate won Florida easily. True, Lyndon Johnson won Florida in 1964, but only by two percentage points against a candidate who was getting destroyed just about everywhere else. And in 1976, Florida supported Jimmy Carter by five points, but Carter was a neighboring Southerner in the post-Watergate catharsis.

The point here is that even before the Republicans formally settled on the not-so-subtly racist "Southern Strategy" in 1968, Florida voters—still overwhelmingly Democratic by registration and still largely voting for Democrats at the state and local levels—were overwhelmingly supporting presidential candidates who appealed to their darker instincts. In 1968, for example, Florida voters gave Nixon 40.5 percent, Hubert Humphrey 30.9 percent, and segregationist George Wallace 28.5 percent.

So what really changed in the 1980s and early 1990s was not the nature of the electorate—Florida voters did not become more conservative. Rather, the state Republican Party was able to sell itself to that large slice of conservative Democrats and persuade them that just as the national Democratic Party had long ago sided with blacks rather than middle-class whites, so the state Democratic Party had now come under the spell of blacks, radical feminists, gays, and Jews from South Florida. And once those voters started switching, so did candidates and officeholders.

It was, given the history of the place, a natural realignment, with the state party finally following the lead of Nixon, Reagan, and George H. W. Bush in their cultivation of the Southern White Man.

BECAUSE, really, that is the key to American politics generally and Florida politics in particular in the last third of the twentieth century and thus far in the twenty-first: the Southern White Man.

It is his alienation, his sense that the world is out of whack and out to screw him, and the Republican Party's willingness to stroke his ego from Richard Nixon forward, that has—with a couple of exceptions—created and maintained that party's lock on the Solid South.

It's hard not to empathize to some degree, even when one finds the bigotry abhorrent.

Consider: Southern culture places great stock on military service. I do not necessarily mean to put a positive value judgment on this—after all, it might reasonably be argued that if more would-be soldiers stopped to consider the morality of some aspects of our foreign policy, the resulting diminishment of the armed services would force political leaders to consider our military deployments more carefully. Nonetheless, regardless of what one thinks of Vietnam, Grenada, Iraq I, or Iraq II, the fact of it is that the Southern White Man is disproportionately represented among the young men sent abroad and put in harm's way.

And then, when they come home, they are put back into a workforce that has less and less use for them. All too often they lack the college degree or the technical training that is the key to a living wage, particularly in the "right-to-work" South.

In the meantime, blacks and Hispanics, while still behind—in the case of blacks, abysmally behind—are nonetheless catching up, both economically and socially. White women have already caught up in the South and in areas have even moved ahead.

There is naturally some bitterness here, directed primarily (but not justifiably) at blacks. The Southern White Man sees affirmative action and other programs invented by Northerners and liberals as taking away what was rightfully his and giving it—*giving* it—to an undeserving group.

And so, from the civil rights struggles of the 1960s forward to this day, the Southern White Man has been deeply resentful. And what the Republican Party has done, starting with Nixon in 1968, was pander to this resentment masterfully.

Sure, it was couched in other language. Nixon's law-and-order plank, for instance, technically was race neutral. But everyone in the South just *knew* that it was blacks who were committing most of these crimes. They understood what Nixon was getting at. If they wanted someone to stand up to those rioters making crazy demands, and those hippies egging them on, then Republican Richard Nixon was their man, not an unreconstructed Minnesota liberal like Hubert Humphrey.

Every successful Republican presidential campaign since then has employed similar tactics, to varying degrees. Ronald Reagan had his apocryphal welfare queen, driving a Cadillac and taking food off the Southern White Man's table. George W. Bush spoke against affirmative action and supported South Carolina's Confederacy-honoring state flag. And George H.W. Bush's campaign took the strategy to breathtaking heights, coming up with the infamous Willie Horton theme. Its message was clear: if you want a large black man to rape and kill your wife, then vote for Michael Dukakis. If anyone doubts how well George H.W. sold himself to that target group, just look back at a poll commissioned by the *New York Times* in 1991, which found that *100* percent of Southern white males between the ages of eighteen and twenty-four approved of his performance. The following September, when he was going down against Bill Clinton, Southern white males and white Protestants were the only two groups still supporting George H.W., according to a Times-Mirror poll.

In recent years, this strategy—what former Nixon aide Kevin Phillips described in *The Emerging Republican Majority*—has been merged with a related GOP plank, the appeal to the Christian Right. In many areas of the South, including much of rural Florida, these two groups have significant overlap. Bubba doesn't always go to church, but his wife usually does. It's a strange phenomenon, and more than a little creepy, particularly since the roots of the abolitionist movement were in churches. But in the South, evangelical Christianity is too often allied with the Confederate flag. Bob Jones University is the perfect example. God wants to keep the races separate. Or at least He did until the 2000 Republican primaries, when George W.'s visit there raised a national ruckus about the school's ban on interracial dating and then-president Bob Jones III announced that he'd had an epiphany and learned that God had changed His mind.

In any event, between the Southern White Man, angry at the world in general and black people in particular, and the hard core evangelical Christian, determined to make the Bible the law of the land, you have two of the three supporting legs Republicans have used to rule the South. The third leg is the traditional Republican, the economic conservative—the quasi-libertarian most concerned about keeping government small and taxes low.

These three groups have much that separates them. Economic conservatives, for example, generally are not interested in the social agenda of the evangelicals. Religious conservatives are much more interested in laws ending abortion than they are in a balanced budget. The one thing they all have in common, and what loyally keeps them in the Republican fold: they always know that no matter how weak the Republican candidate is on any one of their particular issues, the Democrat can only be worse. Bubba knows that a modern Florida Democrat, even a moderate Democrat, will owe his election to blacks and liberals. The evangelicals know that a Democrat will be unlikely to put biblical creationism back in the public schools. And the country-club retiree knows that a Democrat is far more likely to raise taxes to build new schools.

These three groups in total account for and have accounted for between 40 and 45 percent of the electorate. The difference was, by the late 1980s, all three were voting, for the first time, in lockstep with the Republicans.

AND SO it was that by 1993, Florida was primed for a Republican to return to the Governor's Mansion. In a last gasp, Democrats in the legislature had tried to cling to power in the redistricting of 1992, despite their wholesale losses of conservative voters who were switching their allegiance to Republican candidates. Predictably, they overreached, trying to keep more incumbents in office than they reasonably could have and thereby creating far too many marginal seats. Republicans lawmakers shrewdly encouraged this by allying themselves with both blacks and Hispanics in an effort to create as many minority seats as possible. They knew that the blacks who won would be Democrats, but understood that the squabbles between white Democrats who had to compete for fewer seats would only help their cause. The Cuban-Americans who got elected, they knew, would be Republicans.

So by the time Jeb formally announced his candidacy for governor in February 1993, things were looking good for his party. Incumbent Democrat Lawton Chiles seemed adrift, and polls showed him plummeting. He had been unable to get either his health-care plan or his tax reform plan through the legislature. Republicans had successfully labeled the first as yet more welfare, and the second as a major tax increase.

Chiles had won in 1990 both because he was a Florida legend returning as a conquering hero and because incumbent Republican Bob Martinez—Jeb's former boss—had been mortally wounded by his handling of the services tax. Martinez had first embraced the idea of expanding the sales tax to cover most services, but then, after a lobbying and publicity blitz by those newly affected by the tax, had led the call to repeal it. He succeeded, but only after agreeing to another increase in the sales tax, from 5 percent to 6 percent. Martinez never recovered, and Chiles beat him easily.

Unfortunately for ol' Walkin' Lawton—so named for the gimmick he used to rise from obscure state senator to a United States senator in 1970, walking the length of Florida from Pensacola to the Keys to start his campaign—he took office in 1991 just in time for the "Bush" recession to clobber the state. All his big plans to improve health insurance and schools and so forth flew out the window as Chiles was forced to call special sessions instead to cut the existing budget.

A poll in 1993 showed Chiles's unfavorable ratings at 71 percent. It was so bad that certain tax proposals actually polled worse when respondents learned that they were ideas pushed by Chiles.

That year, there was actually considerable question whether Chiles would even run for reelection. Many Democrats wanted former governor and then U.S. senator Bob Graham to come back and run for the job, and he gave the idea serious thought when it seemed that Chiles might not run.

Republicans, naturally, were giddy at the prospects of winning back the Governor's Mansion. State insurance commissioner Tom Gallagher was running, as was secretary of state Jim Smith, Senate president Ander Crenshaw, and antiabortion lawyer Ken Connor. All four, but particularly the three elected officials, were openly miffed not only that Jeb was running, but that he had pretty much become the front-runner the day he announced his candidacy.

In reality, it was no surprise at all that Jeb ran that year. He had actually considered running for Congress a decade earlier, taking on a Miami Democrat, but had been talked out of it by his father, who asked him what he would do financially were he to win, with three young children in Miami while maintaining a second household in Washington on a congressional salary. Jeb took his father's advice, but others in his party continued trying to get him in the ring. As early as 1986, when incumbent Republican senator Paula Hawkins was looking vulnerable against retiring Governor Bob Graham, some tried to talk Jeb into a primary challenge. In late 1987, Jeb considered but then rejected the idea of running for the Senate seat being left by Lawton Chiles. In 1990, there were rumors that Republican governor Bob Martinez would make Jeb his running mate. In 1992, party leaders tried recruiting Jeb to take on Graham in his first re-election.

Through all of this Jeb stayed put, save for the twenty-month stint in Tallahassee as Martinez's commerce secretary. But with his father's reelection campaign headed for near-certain disaster by late 1992, Jeb was already thinking about 1994. Just weeks after George H.W. had lost to Bill Clinton, Jeb told the world that he was running for governor.

And once he was in, it was never really a fair fight, in terms of his Republican opponents. In March 1994, in a three-day swing, George H.W. and Barbara raised $1.1 million for their son—which was about what his two nearest contenders had each raised in the previous fifteen months. A luncheon ticket at the Boca Raton Resort and Club cost $250. A photo with mama and papa Bush cost an extra $250. And so it went, across the state, at events in ten different cities.

"I knew Jeb Bush was going to be running for governor," Jim Smith told supporters a few weeks later. "I didn't know his mom and dad would be, too."

Smith later talked about a poll his campaign had conducted, which asked Jeb's self-described "strong supporters" what they liked in him. "It's frustrating, frankly," Smith said. "They either said 'Daddy was a great president' or 'I really liked his mother.'"

Of all Jeb's opponents, Smith had the longest resume and probably the best chance of winning, had Jeb not run. As the state's elected attorney general, Smith ran as a Democrat in 1986 to replace Bob Graham, but lost to liberal Democrat Steve Pajcic in a primary runoff. He became a Republican not long after that and had been waiting for another chance to run, only to see Jeb muscle in.

Among Smith's campaign team was Paul Bradshaw, a lawyer and former Department of Community Affairs staffer under Republican Bob Martinez, who would later, ironically, marry Jeb's closest confidante, Sally Harrell, and become the guy Jeb would turn to for all his major speeches. But in 1994, Bradshaw concocted a David Letterman–style "Top Ten" list of ways Jeb got rich while his dad was president. Among them: "Didn't invest in Silverado," and "had the 'Magic Fingers' concession in the Lincoln Bedroom," and "cashed in Miguel Recarey's frequent flyer coupons." But the number one reason? "Had great foresight in selecting his parents."

JEB WAS even more thin-skinned then than he is today. Questions about his parents' assistance angered him, even when the evidence overwhelmingly showed this was the case—such as with the Honolulu orthodontist who sent both Jeb and George W. thirty dollars for their respective campaigns that year. "I think she's a wonderful lady. Any of her kids would be good," said Lloyd Kobayashi.

Kobayashi was by no means an anomaly. Donations streamed in from fans of Barbara and George H.W. in all fifty states, the District of Columbia, Puerto Rico, Guam, and American Samoa. One contribution for fifteen dollars came from an address in Scotland.

Jeb would treat questions about this with a long silence and a "so?" Then he would icily point to the long hours he was out campaigning, all the small lunches and dinners he had done since the summer of 1993, long before the other contenders were spending serious time on the road. And, true enough, Jeb did work hard on his 1994 election, just as he does for every election. On one summer trip in 1994, he hit fifty different events in twenty-eight cities in six days. Apart from his legwork, he had put together a national-caliber campaign for use in a single state—something admittedly easier when he had $4 million to spend before the September primary.

His four Republican competitors probably never understood the buzz saw they had run into. While some of them made do with two or three paid staff, the Jeb for Governor Machine had fifteen, spread among Tallahassee, Orlando, and Miami. On September 8, 1994, Jeb very nearly won an outright majority in the Republican primary. His 46 percent of the vote was 28 points better than the next finisher, Jim Smith, who, realizing the futility of further resistance, bowed out three days later rather than face a runoff.

It was only then, with the Republican nomination sewn up, that Jeb had to confront the reality that his "head-banging conservative" views that had played so well in his party's primary now had to be sold to, or toned down for, the rest of Florida. And probably the first thing that needed explaining was the guy Jeb had so unwisely chosen as his running mate.

IT's BECOME a cliché in presidential politics that the first real measure of a candidate is the person he picks for a running mate. All manner of things are read into the choice, possibly because it's done in the doldrums before the conventions. The choice of a running mate can show boldness or timidity. Courage or conformity. Wimpiness or wisdom.

Some of these things are debatable, but here are two clear things that the running mate choice does show: maturity, and the candidate's level of respect for the voters. Because forget geographic balance and diversity and sucking up to powerful constituencies. What's important here is how the candidate considered the question: if, God forbid, something should happen to me, this is the person I'm inflicting on the electorate.

In 1994, making his first run for any sort of government office, Jeb Bush chose as his running mate a man who openly hated government even more than Jeb did: Tom Feeney.

Feeney could merit a chapter to himself, for sheer entertainment value, but to do so would be to cross that fine line between historical context and gratuitous piñata-bashing. So I'll attempt here a balance that conveys a sense of why Lawton Chiles and his strategists experienced such joy when Jeb chose the thirty-six-year-old, two-term state legislator from an Orlando suburb.

The single most insightful fact about Tom Feeney is the one he pointed out to Florida reporters several years later: in 1975, as a high-school hockey player, he had won the honor of racking up the most penalty minutes. Keep that in mind, and most else about Feeney falls right into place. Because despite all his talk about the Founding Fathers and the Constitution, Feeney's demeanor makes it clear that, rather than debate you, he would just as soon check you into the boards and then punch you in the kidney for good measure.

Feeney, in short, is a goon. Think the Robert De Niro character from *Goodfellas*, except maybe a touch less violent. Feeney believes in winning, even if it means playing dirty. He showed that as House speaker—a position he won largely from the name he made for himself among conservative Republicans in 1994. Whenever Democrats interrupted the steamrolling they normally took in the course of business in Feeney's House by coming up with a procedural tactic, Feeney would simply call a brief recess and schedule a Rules and Calendar Committee meeting to change the rule the Democrats were using. Then it was back into session to continue the steam-rolling.

(On a side note, and in the interest of full disclosure, Feeney took par-ticular umbrage at this writer in 2002. He had hired a former Hooters wait-ress as one of his top aides, even though she had no college degree and no legislative experience. She accompanied him everywhere, so naturally the rumors in the Capitol were in full flow. I wrote a story—not about the ru-mors, but about the fact that she was doing fund-raising for his run for Congress, from the speaker's suite in the Capitol. Lobbyists were com-plaining privately that she was shaking them down for campaign contri-butions and implying that the success of legislation depended on a healthy donation. Feeney retaliated by banning me from the House on the grounds that I was physically dangerous. I had never previously in my life been ac-cused of being intimidating—particularly by someone whose job it had been to skate into people and hurt them.)

Feeney in 2002 won a congressional seat that he carved for himself during the redistricting that year. Alert readers of congressional news will no doubt recognize his name as author of the so-called Feeney Amend-ment, which limits the ability of federal judges to depart from congres-sionally written sentencing guidelines—yet another skirmish in the jihad conservative Republicans have declared against the judiciary.

In 1994, of course, Feeney's eventual rise could not be guessed. Back then, he was merely a brash, young, wing-nut who sat in the back rows and tossed his bombs without much consequence or accountability. In 1991 and 1992, as Chiles dealt with a terrible recession that cut state rev-enues, Feeney and his allies countered Chiles's tax reform plan with a pro-posed budget that would have slashed the jobs of thousands of social workers, teachers, and prison guards. In 1994, Feeney posited that yoga was a dangerous, anti-Christian religious expression, and that children should be required to get parental permission slips before being allowed to learn about it in public schools. That same legislative session, Feeney backed a resolution urging Florida to secede from the United States if the national debt ever exceeded $6 trillion.

Once on the campaign trail that summer, Feeney accused Chiles of being among those "who will be trying to execute as many unborn as you can get away with and, in case they're viable, surround them by HRS [the state's social services agency] for the rest of their lives, make them feel good about themselves, never punish, never discipline. I believe failure to discipline is a form of child abuse in itself."

YOU CAN see now why Chiles's campaign guys got so giddy when Bush announced it was Feeney. Even Republicans were left scratching their heads. Here is what a running mate pick is supposed to say: "This is the person who I feel is, apart from myself, best qualified to govern this state." Honestly now. Jeb was telling us that, after himself, Tom Feeney was the next best leader of America's fourth-largest state?

The choice was simply breathtaking in its callowness, and fairly trumpeted Jeb's disdain for the idea that governing was a serious thing. He was lucky that, in the end, people barely pay passing attention to running mates. Otherwise, Chiles would have clobbered him.

Interestingly, Jeb's choice immediately brought back visions of Dan Quayle, the not-quite-ready-for-prime-time pick his father made, and got away with, in 1988. (The most intriguing explanation of Quayle comes from Jeb cousin John Ellis, who told the family's authorized biographers that George H.W. had chosen the Indiana youngster after seeing how Congress had taken down Nixon, knowing that Gerald Ford was fully competent to step in. Quayle, in Ellis's view, would have forced Congress to think twice before going after George H.W. over the Iran-Contra Affair. "Impeachment insurance," Ellis called it.) Even more interestingly, Jeb had opposed his father's choice in 1988, and was a charter member of the dump Quayle movement four years later when that seemed to offer the best chance of turning around the reelection campaign's dismal prospects.

Years later, it's still unclear what motivated Jeb. He had a stable of rising GOP stars to choose from. He could have picked a Miami Cuban, a Tampa Bay moderate, a woman, or a combination thereof. Instead he picked a bomb-thrower from Orlando, possibly the most strident nutball in the Florida legislature while simultaneously the least interested in actual governing.

It was as if to say to his critics: *Ha! You think I'm bad, wait till you get a load of my running mate.*

Give Jeb this: he appeared to learn from at least this part of his history. Four years later he picked Sandra Mortham, a longtime legislator who in 1994 successfully ran for secretary of state. She was a pro-choice moderate, who in the years after her election won praise for putting the state campaign finance records into a user-friendly database on the state Web site.

Unfortunately for Jeb, she'd also had a weakness for soliciting big donations from corporations for programs that seemed more about self-aggrandizement than public service. Tens of thousands of dollars from Philip Morris tobacco were meant for a historical museum but instead paid for Sandra Mortham golf balls and Sandra Mortham fans and Sandra Mortham paperweights. Also unfortunately for Jeb, state party chief Tom Slade had never much liked Mortham, and sped her downfall with such helpful remarks as: "If I were Sandy, I would be getting tired of this crap," which he cheerfully gave to any reporter who asked.

She withdrew from the ticket not long afterward, and Jeb ultimately went with Frank Brogan, the sitting education commissioner who superficially resembled Jeb (both Catholic white guys who opposed abortion and favored school vouchers) but in tone and personal history was about as different as can be imagined.

Brogan was a nice guy with a sharp wit and a self-deprecating sense of humor who helped immensely both during the 1998 campaign as well as the first term by softening Jeb's hard edge. In the end, he predictably had little influence on Jeb's policies. Jeb is such a domineering personality, it was hard to imagine otherwise. Jeb's much-vaunted "A-plus" education plan is a perfect example. Brogan, a former teacher, a former school administrator, a former education commissioner, had drawn up the first draft. Jeb rejected it out of hand because it wasn't punitive enough and didn't generate a sufficient number of school vouchers quickly enough. Jeb's eventual proposal was instead drafted by Paul Bradshaw, the husband of his campaign manager, first chief of staff and closest confidante, Sally Bradshaw.

Brogan lost his wife of twenty years to breast cancer not long into the first term, but he stuck with Jeb through the reelection. But with a new bride and the chance to start a family as president of Florida Atlantic University, few were surprised when he jumped at the opportunity to escape Jeb's shadow.

Jeb's second-term lieutenant governor was former state Senate president Toni Jennings, who like Brogan served to soften Jeb's public image but otherwise had little effect on the administration. That also was predictable. Her brand of Republicanism is much less confrontational than Jeb's—the two had never seen eye to eye when she had run the Senate. And, because she replaced Brogan after the 2002 reelection campaign, she never appeared with Jeb on a statewide ticket—a factor that led her, in 2005, to abandon her own brief quest for the governorship to succeed Jeb.

Which, in 2006, led to the odd irony of Jeb leaving office in an election in which he had no real interest at all. Jeb didn't like one of the two Republican candidates running to replace him and didn't respect the other, which meant that for the first time since 1996 and only the third time since 1980, the Florida election would not involve either Jeb personally as a candidate or campaign chairman, or one of his blood relatives.

It was very un-Jeb-like, the quietness with which his era would end.

A DOZEN years earlier, though, all these other people were the ghosts of elections still to come, and it was still Tom Feeney tied around Jeb's neck. And it was a testament to the political trends nationally that year as well as just how low Chiles was that Jeb's choice of Feeney did not, by itself, doom his candidacy.

The story line favored by many of Florida's political journalists is that Chiles's use of an Old Florida crackerism during the televised debate with Jeb—"The old He-coon walks just before the light of day"—became the turning point in the election, that the momentum shifted at that moment and started Chiles on an upward trajectory that put him over the top.

That version certainly has its charm and its magic—there on the ropes, the old man reaches back and pulls out a trick that baffles the uppity youngster and leads to his eventual triumph. Under closer examination, though, it does not seem to hold up. In reality, Jeb's demise actually started about ten days earlier, when his team taped a television commercial designed to hit Chiles on the issue of crime.

The theme was all the rage for Republicans back in 1994, when they had successfully pushed the idea that they stood for law-abiding citizens and crime victims while their Democratic opponents supported criminals' rights. Jeb's new spot would feature the mother of a murdered child who had reached out to Jeb because of his desire to shorten the appeals process for condemned killers. She offered to tape a commercial, and Jeb's people were happy to take her up on it.

From the outset, the idea edged toward the boundaries of bad taste. No matter what the spot said, it would appear unseemly at best to take advantage of a mother's grief. Nonetheless, Jeb's team thought they had a tough but fair ad—all except for Mac Stipanovich, the grizzled veteran of the bunch, who thought it was too soft.

Stipanovich had worked on both Martinez campaigns and had served as his chief of staff for a time, as well, and the rest of Jeb's people usually deferred to him. Mac took the script outside, did some quick edits and they reshot the commercial. His changes essentially accused Lawton Chiles of not doing enough to send the killer of Wendy Nelson's daughter to the electric chair. The others on Jeb's staff were a little uneasy about the new script—but when Jeb polled them on a conference call, none of them objected.

It was, in retrospect, a disastrous reticence.

As in most states, capital punishment in Florida is governed by a rigid, arcane body of law that gives the various players certain specific roles at certain specific times. One thing that a Florida governor cannot do is order a prisoner's death until his automatic appeal has been rejected by the Florida Supreme Court. Signing a warrant in such a circumstance would result in an automatic stay by the courts. It would be a public relations exercise and nothing more.

When Lawton Chiles's people heard of the ad, they howled, and rightfully so. By that point in his term, Chiles's had put to death exactly as many murderers as his Republican predecessor Martinez had. Chiles publicly supported the death penalty. He correctly pointed out—as Stipanovich should have known—that there was absolutely nothing more he could do in the Nelson case until it had moved through the courts.

Jeb, who had been leading in the polls by as much as ten points in September, suddenly found himself on the defensive. At first he and his people stood by the ad, arguing that if Chiles didn't like it, then he should have done more to bring justice to Elisa Nelson's killer.

Within days, though, Jeb had to concede that there was nothing Chiles could have done to expedite Larry Eugene Mann's death sentence. (In fact, at the time this book went to press, Jeb, during his two terms, also had been unable to bring about Mann's demise. The killer was alive and well on Death Row.)

Chiles had already started to eat into Jeb's early lead with a series of television ads questioning the various business deals that had made the president's son a millionaire in the 1980s. The ads had been part of the Chiles campaign's effort to sow seeds of doubt about Jeb in voters' minds. His questionable ethics and his lack of governing experience, their argument went, made for a dangerous mix in the state's chief executive. When Jeb overreached with the Wendy Nelson ad, and then had to admit that he was mistaken, that gave voters who may have been supporting Jeb reason to pause. Maybe Chiles was right. Maybe Jeb wasn't quite ready for this.

So a few days later, in the final debate, when Chiles let loose his he-coon remark, undecided voters may have been as perplexed as Jeb clearly was. South Florida liberal Democrats—who typically don't see many raccoons wandering around their condo complexes—also may have been confused. It didn't matter. Chiles's people correctly saw it as a rallying cry and used it to successfully build momentum, boosting turnout in strongly Democratic South Florida counties to presidential election year levels. A last-minute round of "scare" phone calls also helped, telling elderly voters that Jeb's even brasher, even younger running mate had once called for the abolition of the federal government, including Social Security, if the national debt got too big.

On November 8, 1994, Chiles pulled out a 63,940-vote win—a margin that back then was considered razor thin. That same night, a thousand miles to the west, Texas Democrat Ann Richards lost to Jeb's older brother.

The die determining the future of the Bush family, and of America, had been cast. And Jeb had lost.

EVEN THOSE who intensely dislike Jeb must have felt for him, at least a little, after that loss. He went out to Austin like a good brother to watch George W. take the oath of office to become governor of Texas. George W., on the other hand, made sure everybody understood which brother had won and which one had not.

"Jeb would have been a great governor," George W. told reporters. "But such is life in the political world. You cannot go into politics fearing failure." At his inauguration in Austin, George W. pointed out Jeb again, and the shame of his losing in Florida, in case anyone had missed his earlier remarks.

Jeb went home to Miami. His wife was disgusted with him, blaming him for putting his political ambition ahead of his family and his marriage. And Jeb's children—well, they had problems typical among the offspring of parents with plenty of money but not enough time to pay attention to their families. Jeb vowed to make things right at home, and as part of that, he explained later, he converted to Columba's Catholic faith. (It was, as we will explore in more detail in a subsequent chapter, at least his second, and possibly his third such conversion, but who's counting?)

In relatively short order, he collected himself sufficiently to make a clear-eyed analysis of what had gone wrong—how was it that an incumbent with a 71 percent disapproval rating just eighteen months earlier . . .

in an election year that had produced seismic wins for Republicans all over the nation . . . how with all of that could he still have lost?

Republicans in the state legislature soon discovered that the Chiles campaign had secretly made tens of thousands of the deceptive, last-minute phone calls to senior citizens that claimed Jeb and Feeney would, if elected, do horrible things to Social Security. It was a fairly big deal in Florida, and Chiles had to apologize—but Jeb knew that the "scare calls" had not been decisive. In any event, the claims made in the calls would not have had any effect on voters, without the kernel of truth that sprang from both Jeb's statements and Feeney's far nuttier remarks through the years.

Jeb quickly put together his Foundation for Florida's Future because, he claimed then and still claims today, he wanted to remain active in public policy and to advance conservative, free-market concepts. "It was my idea to take the enthusiasm and the passion for my candidacy, which I believed was based on some ideas that I consistently advocated, and stay involved in the political process to allow their voices to be heard and those ideas to be heard," he told the *St. Petersburg Times* in 1998.

The money for the group, $1.7 million in 1995 and 1996, coincidentally enough came from all the familiar stable of big donors—Big Sugar, the owner of the Outback Steakhouse chain, billionaire Wayne Huizenga, gambling giant GTECH, utility companies, Philip Morris tobacco. All the usual suspects.

That the foundation happened to employ the core of his campaign team, so they would remain together and remain loyal to him, was, again, the merest coincidence. That it gave him the justification and financing for travel, thereby keeping him "in play" for the next governor's race, was also coincidental. As was the name of his outfit itself, just a word and two syllables off from his father's Fund for America's Future, which George H.W. had used to pay his pre-campaign travel expenses in 1978.

Jeb also teamed up with the head of the local Urban League, T. Willard Fair, to start a "charter" school in Liberty City, a poor, black section of Miami. Ostensibly this was to give him an understanding of the challenges facing the state education system, although it is not clear exactly what lessons Jeb took away from the experience. For example, Jeb claimed in 1997 that he had come to appreciate that smaller schools, in which the principal could know every student, were better schools. Yet as governor for two full terms, Jeb did absolutely zero to reduce the size of schools built in Florida because, frankly, smaller schools are also more expensive schools on a per-student basis—and Jeb was far more interested in tax cuts for the wealthy than he was in public education for the masses.

Through all of this, Jeb came to understand that what had scared voters in 1994 was the very essence of what Jeb is all about. Republican donors and primary voters loved his "hang 'em by the neck" conservatism, but mainstream Floridians found it more than a little disconcerting.

And so, his strategy for the 1998 election became . . . to hide his true beliefs.

He talked about the need for helping juvenile delinquents. He said he respected people who opposed capital punishment and would not use it against them in a campaign. He even became a godfather to the child of a black woman who had voted against him in 1994, before the charter school and before they had met. He became a *compassionate conservative*, just as his brother had done in Texas.

Mind, his real values and beliefs did not change much at all. In fact, if you want to see a list of all the things Jeb pushed hard for once he became governor—faster death penalty appeals, private school vouchers, privatized Medicaid—just look at what he said he would do in 1994.

On election night, 1998, the new branding worked like a charm. Jeb won by ten points, and he has not looked back since.

ANOTHER IN the long list of lessons the Bush boys learned from father was how not to lose focus once elected. That is to say: never forget that a prime goal, if not *the* prime goal, of your first term in office . . . is to get a second term in office.

This is an interesting point, because the definitive analysis of the George H.W. Bush presidency, *Marching in Place*, by Michael Duffy and Dan Goodgame, charged that George H.W.'s reelection was really the only tangible goal of the White House team during the first term. That sounds harsh, at first blush, but when it is put in the context of his personality, it actually makes sense.

George H.W. never really had a big agenda that he wanted to accomplish as chief executive of the United States. Rather, he wanted to be president for the sake of being president. It was the ultimate prize in American politics, and he wanted to win it. Besides, he was a damn nice guy—surely everybody could agree on that—and would do a fine job. And, compared to the others who were running, certainly he deserved it the most. At least, that's the way he saw it.

Once he was in the White House, he'd accomplished his mission. Unlike Reagan, he didn't feel compelled to slam through tax cuts or rewrite federal regulations or change the course of the Supreme Court or any of those things. He believed the nation was more or less doing okay, and his job was merely to be a good steward of that condition.

As his staff saw it, then, the answer to that pesky "vision" thing was actually quite simple: "The image Bush saw when he imagined a better future for America was . . . himself in the Oval Office through January 1997! Silly as it might sound, this revelation proved useful as 'an organizing principle,' in the recollection of one senior official present at the meeting, and 'gave us a quiet, internal coherence' that had been missing until then."

His handlers picked and chose small, easy-to-advertise goals, like "clean air" and "crime control," legislation on which would serve as the reelection platform. What ended up being a relatively trouble-free military excursion in Kuwait seemed to make a second term that much more certain.

The only trouble was, George H.W. let the burden of the presidency grow on him. He came to believe that cutting the federal deficit was actually important, and essentially went back on his own memorable campaign promise to accomplish it. He wrote in his diary on July 24, 1990: "If I didn't have this budget deficit problem hanging over my head, I would be loving this job. . . ."

More to the point, George H.W. believed that governing was more important than campaigning, and that the two were completely separate things. Just days after his 1988 election, in fact, he was asked about the tone of his campaign, and what it might signify for his administration. His response made it clear that he did not believe the campaign was any longer relevant. "That's history," he said just before his inauguration. "That doesn't mean anything anymore."

Later, as his advisers and his hyperpolitical sons worried that he wasn't paying enough attention to his reelection campaign, George H.W. made clear in his diary and his letters to friends that they were correct. In a footnote he added later to his compilation of papers, *All the Best, George Bush*, he wrote: "Part of the problem was I was too darn busy trying to be President."

NOT TO LEARN your family's campaign mistakes is to repeat them, and George W. learned those mistakes well. It was he who was on the phone, calling his dad's campaign headquarters to tell them of what he was seeing through his Dallas window in 1992: a line of cars waiting at Ross Perot's headquarters to get signs.

And so, after finding among the U.S. Supreme Court the majority vote that he could not find among the nation's electorate, George W. upon taking office January 20, 2001, set about making his top priority his own reelection three years and nine months later. His political director, Karl Rove, was assigned the task of finding those voters whose failure to appear at the polls the previous November had nearly cost him the presidency.

It came to be accepted that the number in question was four million— four million men and women who had sat on their hands and let Al Gore run up a popular vote victory of 500,000. It was also determined that these four million were largely evangelical Christians, led to abstain that year, perhaps because of the final-weekend revelations about George W.'s drunken driving conviction twenty-four years earlier.

From that point onward, the Christian Right was given special attention, from giving federal money to "faith-based" programs in the social services to suspending aid to foreign family planning clinics that provided abortions to finding suitably conservative lawyers to appoint to the federal bench.

In that regard, the terrorist attacks of September 11 were a political godsend, particularly among "the base" who saw them quite clearly as Islam attacking Christianity. In that context, George W.'s use of the word *crusade* to describe the nation's response may have been seen as unfortunate in much of the world, but he was singing from the Christian Right's hymnal.

When by the summer of 2002 Republicans were starting to get nervous about the coming midterm elections, there came the fortuitous beating of the war drums again, this time foretelling the long-sought attack on Iraq. There is no need to be so cynical as to postulate that the Iraq invasion took place because of sliding poll numbers heading into those elections. We can accept at face value that George W. and his inner circle truly did believe those various reasons offered for the war, both before and after: Saddam had hidden biological and chemical weapons; Saddam was an evil man who tortured his own people; Saddam had to go to let democracy take root in the Middle East.

But we need not let a benefit of the doubt for his motives prior to the 2002 midterms cloud our judgment as to his use of terrorism and Iraq to maintain his office subsequent to those elections and heading into his own reelection campaign. George W. and Rove could see from the 2002 results that fear-mongering and shrill patriotism were not only effective, they were incredibly effective in a nervous nation with a cowed opposition party.

From that point clear up until Election Day 2004, George W. rarely had a public utterance that did not include the words *terror* or *evildoers* or *war* or, about himself, *resolute*. Those who opposed George W. were, by dint of that opposition, supportive of the nation's enemies—a startling tactic, from the offspring of one of the first senators to denounce Joseph McCarthy. (Prescott Bush said: "Either you must follow Senator McCarthy blindly, not daring to express any doubts or disagreements about any of his actions, or in his eyes you must be a communist, a communist sympathizer, or a fool who has been duped by the communist line." Replace *communist* with *terrorist*, and Prescott could have been referring to his grandson a half a century later.) A message-control team that had already been zealous became ruthlessly so, essentially ending George W.'s press conferences and other unscripted exchanges. His departments bought good press coverage, literally, with paid columnists and propaganda video pieces disguised as news segments.

It was the 24/7/365 campaign, always political, all the time. And on November 2, 2004, it worked, by 3,012,171 votes.

COMPARED TO the tactics used by George W. in both his presidential elections, Jeb's strategies throughout his three elections in Florida have been positively mild.

The negative ad campaigns against Lawton Chiles in 1994, Buddy MacKay in 1998, and Bill McBride in 2002 were sharp, sure; misleading, absolutely; mean, perhaps. But they never completely twisted reality around to where black was white, like the George W. campaigns successfully did in both 2000 and 2004.

It should be remembered, though, that Jeb never needed to do this— or, more accurately in the case of 1994, did not believe he needed to do this. Buddy MacKay, certainly, and even Bill McBride never represented the threat to Jeb that John McCain and John Kerry's Vietnam records presented to George W. In Jeb's Florida, there was never any need to "Swift Boat" his opponents.

Perhaps more alarming than how Jeb ran his election campaigns is how he essentially transplanted election campaign tactics directly into his style of governance—something George W. also did as president. Loyalty was all, message was all. Competence meant little, and facts, when inconvenient, meant nothing. From January 2000 forward, with rare exceptions, everything was political. Everything was about winning.

These issues will be dealt with in greater detail in the coming chapters, but it is important to note here how dangerous this has become for government generally.

There is no truth. There is only spin.

This is where we end up, when elections become a contact sport.

And yet . . . there *is* truth. Everything is *not* spin. And insofar that these electioneering rules became the standard in Jeb's Capitol, Florida paid a heavy price in the quality of its public policies, as we will see.

ON NOVEMBER 8, 2000, Jeb with convincing sincerity kept a straight face as he announced how he would thereafter recuse himself from his role in the election certification because of the obvious conflict of interest.

It was the biggest slice of nonsense Jeb has uttered during his entire governorship.

For starters, the guy he appointed to replace him, then-agriculture commissioner Bob Crawford, was the highest-ranking Democrat to have endorsed him during the 1998 election. Crawford endorsed Jeb, and the Republican Party made no effort to run a credible candidate against him. That was the deal. Within a couple of years, Jeb appointed Crawford to an even more lucrative job running the Citrus Commission, which also allowed him to move back home to Lakeland.

Maybe the rest of the country was fooled, but no one who followed Florida politics believed for a minute that Bob Crawford was going to take any action regarding the election that Jeb Bush did not want him want to take.

To complaints that he hadn't really stayed out of the maneuvering, Jeb had this response: "I recused myself as the chairman of the canvassing board. But I was not going to recuse myself as governor or from being my brother's brother." That was comforting, no doubt, to the 50 percent of Floridians who had cast ballots against his brother and for Al Gore in that election.

Nonetheless, no one really believed that Jeb was staying out of the machinations that November and December. And, as the e-mails and other public records started trickling out in the months to follow, they proved that people were correct in their skepticism.

Phone records from Jeb's office in the Capitol showed that he and his direct employees in the Executive Office of the Governor called his brother's campaign, its lawyers, and advisers ninety-five times during the 36-day recount period, according to a review by the *Los Angeles Times*. Ten calls went from the line in Jeb's office that he uses the most to a private line in Governor George W. Bush's office. Another call from Jeb's line went to Karl Rove. Still other calls from Jeb's people went to the cell phones of George W.'s campaign advisers in Florida for the recount.

When the *Times* asked Jeb about them in July 2001, Jeb claimed he couldn't recall. "I have no clue what these calls were about. . . . They most likely were return phone calls," Jeb wrote. "In the alternative, they could have been my assistant passing on a request for an invitation to speak or an autographed picture. They might have been answering a request on where to eat in Tallahassee for the hoards [sic] of Austin folks that made their way here. They could have been for many reasons. I don't remember."

Jeb's acting general counsel, the brutally hard-right Frank Jimenez who had written an e-mail suggesting ways of recruiting more reliably conservative judges for Jeb to appoint, meanwhile made it his mission to let the state's major law firms know that signing on to the Gore legal team would be a seriously bad political mistake.

Years later, details were still coming to light. When George W., for example, nominated Judge John Roberts to replace Sandra Day O'Connor on the Supreme Court, it turned out that Roberts, a private Washington lawyer at the time in the politically connected Hogan & Hartson firm, had—what else?—come down to Tallahassee during the recount.

Roberts, Jeb's press office confirmed after the story broke, had come on his own dime and met with him to offer his advice on how Jeb needed to carry out his duty regarding the slate of presidential electors. Beyond that, it seemed that Jeb couldn't actually remember meeting with him, or recall what exactly was discussed because, after all, it had been so long ago.

"It was not related to politics. It was related to my official duties," he told the *Miami Herald* the summer his brother nominated Roberts.

The *Herald*, though, was able to turn up a couple of folks with somewhat better long-term memory. They remembered a thirty- to forty-minute meeting in which Roberts helped develop a strategy to counter an expected Democratic move to physically stop the slate of electors from reaching the National Archives by subpoenaing it. That way, Gore would win because he had a majority of votes from the other forty-nine states.

So, in other words, here was Jeb, squarely in the middle of intense strategizing to make sure his brother won the White House, not terribly long after he'd promised to stay out of it.

Jim Baker, George H.W.'s former top right-hand man who served as George W.'s master of ceremonies during the recount, described Jeb's involvement this way: "Jeb did whatever we asked of him. He never looked at the political cost to himself."

As THE legal battles progressed in November, George W.'s and Jeb's people quickly figured out that the United States Constitution gave each state legislature the sole power to decide how to determine which candidate would receive that state's electoral votes. So where was it written that the rules in place for the allocation of those votes *before* the election could not be changed to suit one's needs *after* the election?

And so, with Jeb's old running mate Tom Feeney leading the charge as the newly minted House speaker, the postelection scene in the Florida Capitol became a breathtakingly brazen display of might-makes-right thuggery.

Here was the logic Feeney and his allies put forward: we the Florida legislature need to get involved and pass a law giving the state's electoral votes to George W. Bush because otherwise all these lawsuits could wind up disenfranchising Florida's voters by not getting the state's totals up to Washington in time.

It was another of those moments that gives credence to the idea of the Almighty as a watchmaker who wound up the universe and then let it do its thing, rather than a micromanager who watches over the smallest sparrow. Because if God were the latter, surely a bolt of lightning would have come down and smote Feeney and the others the moment they opened their mouths to utter the word *disenfranchise*.

Because despite some 2,600 voters in Palm Beach County effectively disenfranchised by one confusing ballot design, and another 25,000 mainly black voters in Duval County disenfranchised because of another confusing ballot—a ballot so badly drawn, by the way, that had you followed the printed instructions to the letter, your vote would have been discarded—not one Republican in Tallahassee thought these 27,600 lost votes were of any consequence at all. Tough luck. Should have known how to cast a ballot properly. Should have been smarter.

Gore's only hope was the courts, as Jeb and his allies in the Capitol were ready and willing to play their usual hardball in the other two branches of state government. The Gore team's main problem was that it didn't early in the game take the high road and ask for a statewide manual recount— the only fair way to settle the election. No, check that: the Gore team's *real* problem was that they didn't want to win badly enough. They weren't ready to do whatever it took. Like send in squads of goons from D.C., say, to intimidate a county canvassing board from conducting a lawful recount. Like filing lawsuits to the stop the counting of some votes while filing others to make sure other votes, such as overseas military ballots, were counted no matter when they were cast, including after the election. While the Bushies raised and spent $13.8 million on lawyers, staffers, protest participants, travel (including the corporate jets of Enron and others), and hotels, Gore's people came up with a mere $3.2 million—better than a four-to-one spread. In other words, Gore and his supporters just weren't ready, in the parlance of a younger Tom Feeney, to take a hockey stick to the other guy's head.

WHAT THE whole episode made clear was that winning is so ingrained in the Bush brothers that elections are treated not as solemn governmental responsibilities, but as merely another venue in a partisan street fight. The only rules are the ones the likely losers are sissy enough to accept.

Going into the 2004 election, for example, Jeb had full control of the election machinery that once had been in the hands of an elected secretary of state. He had nothing to do with the constitutional change that made that occur—voters approved it in 1998, as part of a raft of "reforms"—but, once it had happened, he was not at all shy about using that advantage to help his brother.

Just as he had in 2000, he pushed ahead with an aggressive scrubbing of the voter registration rolls to eliminate felons, who under a dated, Jim Crow–era state law cannot regain their right to vote unless they first undergo a tedious clemency process through the Governor's Office and the elected Cabinet. Needless to say, a disproportionate number of the felons are black, and blacks disproportionately vote for Democrats.

Jeb not only defended the creation of the list—done, naturally, through an outsourced $2.2 million contract to the firm Accenture—but also the clearly unconstitutional law that prevented the list from being released as a public record. It took a lawsuit by CNN and some Florida newspapers to get the matter before a judge—who needed about five seconds to declare the law unconstitutional and ordered Jeb's handpicked secretary of state to turn over the list and the master voter roll to anybody who wanted it. And it took about five days for a pair of reporters at the *Sarasota Herald-Tribune* to notice that there was something unusual about the felon list: it included virtually no Hispanics. In fact, Hispanics, who made up 17 percent of Florida's population in 2004, were represented by a mere 61 people on a felon list that was 47,763 names long—less than one-tenth of one percent. Of course, Florida Hispanics tend to vote disproportionately for Republicans, but Jeb and his people said that that had nothing to do with the glitch, which they blamed on a database mismatch between the way that election supervisors and the Florida Department of Law Enforcement treated Hispanic ethnicity.

Within days, Jeb was shamed into dropping the scrub list. That October, the same paper obtained an e-mail through the public records law that Division of Elections experts had advised Jeb back in May to abandon the felon list because they weren't comfortable with its accuracy, but that Jeb insisted they proceed. Jeb, naturally, denied getting any such warning from his elections experts.

IF JEB learned any lessons about meddling in election administration from the felon-list debacle, he ignored them. Because within weeks, Jeb's Division of Elections was once again hip-deep in the politics of the presidential race, this time over the candidacy of Ralph Nader.

Nader, recall, had won Republican fans all over the country in 2004—not for his anticapitalist views, but for the damage his candidacy was likely to do to Democrat John Kerry that November. In Florida alone, Nader's 97,000 votes had likely cost Al Gore the election in 2000. Exit polls showed that of Nader's supporters who would have considered another candidate had Nader not been running, two-thirds said they would have voted for Gore.

But trouble was brewing in Tallahassee, where a circuit judge declared Nader's Florida candidacy "a sham" because the Reform Party that put him on the ballot, thereby letting him avoid the time and expense of gathering 90,000 signatures, had only eighteen dollars and eighteen cents to its name, had nominated him via a conference call, and then had staged a "convention" by recruiting college students to attend.

Now, certainly—it was the Democrats who were doing the complaining and who were working to get Nader off the ballot because they, too, saw the threat he posed to their candidate. And they were using the Democratic Party apparatus to persuade Circuit Judge Kevin Davey that Nader should be tossed from the ballot. And, just as certainly, the Republican Party apparatus, including lawyers associated with the party, helped Nader stay on. No question that neither side particularly cared for the integrity of the nomination process and the ballot or any such. They wanted to win, and Nader was a pawn.

This behavior, we expect from political parties. We do not expect it from the government—yet there was Jeb, his secretary of state instantly countermanding the judge's order by appealing the case. For that was the critical requirement. Had Nader sought the appeal, that by itself would not have undone Davey's order barring him from the November ballot. But when the *state* appealed, Florida law automatically put Davey's order on ice until the appeal was decided.

In the end, the appeals and counter-appeals landed before the Florida Supreme Court, which ruled in Nader's favor—not because it thought much of the Reform Party's organization in Florida, but because it found the law regarding "national" party status hopelessly vague and therefore unenforceable.

Once again, Jeb did not care how bad it looked. And, once again, Jeb had won.

ALL OF this notwithstanding, it is not an easy thing that the Bushes do, winning elections.

Anyone familiar with the nuts-and-bolts process of it will appreciate the family's mastery of two mind-numbingly boring but crucial aspects of electioneering. The first is organization—do you have contacts in every county? In every city commission district? In every precinct? Do you have enough volunteers to canvass neighborhoods? Do you have enough coordinators to organize the volunteers? Have the proofs for the door-hangers gone back to the printer yet? When will they be delivered?

Note that none of this has anything to do with whether the candidate has the temperament to be a good leader or even if the all-important "message" is any good. Yet this is the stuff that builds a solid campaign, and George H.W. Bush and his children worked—and, yes, it was *work*, insofar as it in no way can be considered fun—to build it in state after state, starting back in 1978 and 1979. It was George H.W.'s superior organization in Iowa that won him his out-of-the-blue victory in the caucuses there. And had Ronald Reagan not successfully snookered him at the Nashua debate several weeks later in New Hampshire, making George H.W. look like the poor sport for wanting to freeze out the second-tier candidates . . . well, who knows how far his candidacy might have gone in 1980?

In this area, Jeb has been working tirelessly for decades. As commerce secretary in 1988 in Tallahassee, Jeb helped raise money for a Republican city commission candidate. In the 1990s, he walked neighborhoods for county commission candidates, and campaigned with state House candidates. During all of this he was building up his own network, collecting his own chits. It's grunt work, but Jeb has done it diligently and cheerfully.

The second tedious part of campaigning, naturally, is the campaigning itself. You get up at oh-dark-thirty, make a breakfast speech at some Rotary Club, then stop by two retirement homes en route to a luncheon fundraiser, followed by three visits to local party committees in various people's houses, followed by a chicken-dinner speech at which you have to sound interested in the nine other candidates who are running for various local and legislative positions who are scheduled to speak before it's your turn. When you finish shaking the last hand, you get in the van to be driven three hours to get to a motel, where you can get a few hours sleep before starting all over.

For nearly a year and a half in 1993 and 1994, and then for another year in 1998, Jeb did this, day in and day out. It must have stopped being fun after about, oh, the first couple of hours, but he stuck with it. Just as his father stuck with barnstorming the country in 1979, flying coach with a friend from Jeb's childhood as his travel aide, in a seemingly impossible quest to win the White House despite having only 38 percent "name ID" and 3 percent support. Things were so grim, in fact, that he was running third in his adopted home state of Texas, behind Ronald Reagan and John Connally.

The tenacity and work ethic needed for this are admirable. These qualities, merged with the by-now legendary Bush family fund-raising apparatus, gave Jeb a national-caliber campaign machine in Florida—one that gave him such an advantage over his opponents, that it is still a wonder that Chiles managed to hold onto his job in 1994.

Still, there ought to be more to becoming a political dynasty than merely being good at winning. Yet, sadly, that is where the nation finds itself with the Bushes. George H. W. had the most ambivalent view about it, wanting desperately to separate the obvious lowness of campaigning from what he considered the higher art of governing.

George W. has made it plain that while he loves campaigning, he has little interest in governing. Recall how he set about trying to sell his Social Security privatization plan just after winning reelection, racing from city to city in carefully stage-managed "meetings" with real citizens. It was as if he wished the campaign never had to end.

Jeb has been more of a mixture of those two. Unlike his brother, he does enjoy governing as well as campaigning. But like his brother, and unlike his father, he has seen the advantages of governing as if he were campaigning.

There are real public policy consequences for this style of leadership, not the least of which is an enervating unease for everyone around him, including even the leaders of the legislative and judicial branches. Everything is a fight—with us, or against us. Everything is a crisis.

At least in Florida, very little good came of this.

Chapter Five

THE KING OF FLORIDA

"What we will do is club this government into submission—let the people in Tallahassee know that they are the servants, not the masters."

—JEB BUSH, 1994

"If you become too popular, it probably means you're not expending political capital properly. This is a really cushy job. It wouldn't be my nature, but I could do little, and I might be popular. Or I could try to do the things that I was elected to do, and try to make a difference in the lives of Floridians."

—JEB BUSH, 2001,
STARTING HIS THIRD YEAR AS GOVERNOR

"I hate whiners."

—JEB BUSH, REGARDING OPPONENTS
OF HIS EDUCATION PROGRAM, AT AN
ORLANDO HIGH SCHOOL VISIT, 2005

It was mid-August of 2003 in Tallahassee, a steamy, nasty hot place for wearing coats and ties by that time of year, which is why calling special legislative sessions during the summer is considered truly bad manners.

Finally, though, after two summer sessions Jeb had already called had blown up in his face without any legislation, he stood in the Capitol rotunda, a pained smile on his face, explaining how he was glad that he and lawmakers were able to come to a reasonable compromise on his plan to limit pain and suffering jury awards to medical malpractice victims.

Jeb was saying this, but it was obvious that he wasn't enjoying it, probably because everyone knew it wasn't true. The "compromise" was hardly that—more like a near-total capitulation on Jeb's part. Behind him, state senators stood in the familiar semicircle of solidarity, but they were scarcely able to contain their glee.

Then, after hands were shaken and the senators had withdrawn to their private offices, there were laughs and high fives all around. "This is probably the first time he's ever been spanked," crowed one. Said another: "I don't want to gloat. Well, yes I do."

A pretty normal dynamic, right? Lawmakers from the opposite party celebrating after beating a governor? Yes, except for one little thing: these legislators were all Republicans.

For five years, they had been whipped and beaten by a fellow Republican with a famous name and a domineering personality, divided and conquered, ridiculed and marginalized, until finally they rose up and stared Jeb in the eye on an issue that both he and his presidential brother were making a top priority. Jeb huffed and puffed and threatened and pouted . . . and then he blinked. And then there was much joy in the Florida Senate, where some of the leaders had been involved in state GOP politics long before Jeb even moved to Florida, and were tired of being treated like chess pieces in his grand game.

How did it get to this? How did it happen that the first Republican governor ever reelected in Florida had alienated a legislative chamber run by his own party to the point where they took childlike glee in beating him?

Looking back, taking into account his upbringing, his family, his energy, his impatience, his certitude, his intolerance for dissent . . . well, actually, in this light, it actually does not seem remarkable at all. The Kinkaid School in Houston and Phillips Academy in Andover no doubt did a yeoman's job, teaching young Jeb the basics of American civics and the separation of powers. It's not the fault of those fine institutions that Jeb learned more about politics and government from his family than his teachers and his schoolbooks. In fact, given who he is, Jeb's testy relationship with Republican legislators was probably inevitable.

Jeb came into office with a plan, and he expected to carry it out, in its entirety, *exactly* the way he envisioned it, by the time he left. And not judges, not the press, and certainly not state legislators were going to stand in his way.

Jeb ran Florida like he owned the place. It's a wonder that he left Tallahassee with any friends at all.

GIVE JEB his due: on the campaign trail, neither in 1994 nor in the kinder, gentler 1998 version, did he ever promise he was going to make friends.

The politicians who talk about understanding the art of politics, about giving and taking, about working together in a bipartisan manner for the good of all Floridians—well, Jeb never claimed he would be one of those. No, he came to kick butt and take names, and he did. Like his presidential brother (but not like his presidential father), Jeb governed on the 50-percent-plus-one rule—if he had a bare majority, there was no need to give even one inch more.

His signature "A-plus" education plan is a perfect example. It was Jeb's main issue in the 1998 campaign—Florida's schoolchildren would be tested every year, with good schools getting bonus money and failing schools having to offer private-school vouchers. The first draft was written by Frank Brogan, Jeb's lieutenant governor who had been a teacher, school principal, district superintendent, and elected education commissioner prior to running with Jeb. His version was something that would have gotten wide support from both moderate Republicans as well as some Democrats. Jeb had no use for it. Instead, he assigned the task to the husband of his chief of staff—a lawyer who, like Jeb, had served in former governor Bob Martinez's administration—and got a properly confrontational draft to take to the legislature.

Getting it through the House was no problem. It was run by his buddy John Thrasher. The more moderate Senate was another matter, and Jeb gave just enough on issues of oversight to satisfy twenty-one of the forty senators—50 percent plus one. So when moderate Jim King gave an impassioned speech about why he was voting for the bill despite his misgivings, he didn't know that Jeb was watching him on a television in his office. He was talking back to the TV, telling King: "Don't vote for it, then. I don't need your vote."

. . .

WITHIN A FEW months of taking office, Jeb delighted good-government types and ticked off the legislative establishment by vetoing hundreds of pork barrel projects, or, in Tallahassee parlance: budget "turkeys." He reversed some fifteen years of state policy by canceling, on his own, Florida's high-speed rail project. He capped his first year in office with a special session to speed up Florida's use of the electric chair in death penalty cases, even though lawyer after lawyer warned him that the law would be ruled unconstitutional because it ran roughshod over the separation of powers doctrine. Jeb rammed through his law. The Florida Supreme Court promptly ruled it unconstitutional.

On issue after issue, Jeb decided on a course of action, announced it to the world, and then ordered, cajoled, threatened, and browbeat others to get his way. He insisted on a private school voucher program with minimal standards or accountability and dragged moderate Republicans down to his office and cussed a blue streak to get their votes. When he miscalculated on how many votes were necessary to rewrite rules for the court system in the death penalty special session, he turned to the Republican Party's stable of rich donors to send private planes out to retrieve missing GOP legislators. One was dragged away from a pregnant wife on the brink of childbirth, another from his sister's funeral.

The reaction to this style of leadership varied, and was not always predictable.

To many, even in the much-reviled press, Jeb was a breath of fresh air. He said what he was going to do, and then he did it, without the mealy-mouthed games that are so common among elected officials. The budget vetoes particularly found unlikely allies. For years, powerful lawmakers had used their control of the state budgeting process to reward allies and hand out chits by sticking hometown projects into the spending plan. This was not done according to any objective needs assessment, but on the basis of raw political power. If you had risen to a position of influence, your community or your alma mater benefited. If you were a nobody, and weren't pals with a somebody, your community did without.

An exhaustive *Palm Beach Post* analysis of all the turkeys showed—to no one's surprise—that on a dollar value basis, 54 percent of the $690 million in hometown projects was funneled to just fourteen of the 160 state legislators—the most powerful fourteen. Jeb, to his credit, vetoed a large percentage of these goodies, $264 million in all, because of that lack of fairness. Even more to his credit: when I matched the projects vetoed against the legislators' vote that first spring on Jeb's main issue—his education plan, including school vouchers—I found little correlation. The median House member who voted for his plan saw 62 percent of his or her project dollars whacked. The median House member who voted against his plan lost 64 percent. Most telling: Jeb's strongest ally in the legislature, House Speaker John Thrasher, lost $15 million he'd set aside for his "legacy" project, the start of a new medical school at his alma mater, Florida State University.

REPUBLICAN LEGISLATORS, not surprisingly, felt betrayed. They believed that Jeb's success was a reflection of their long work to make theirs the majority party in Florida, and they felt that work should have been rewarded. Moderate Republicans particularly, who had enjoyed the support of teachers unions over the years, believed they had cast a tough vote for Jeb by supporting his school vouchers, one that could cost them in coming elections. And so, in return, Jeb slashes the $50,000 for an exercise trail in their hometown park? Or the $100,000 for an elderly community center? If Jeb was not going to bend on those issues because of his principles, they felt, then he should not have forced them to vote against their principles for his priorities.

Jeb professed to feel their pain, but it's doubtful he had much empathy. In his view, he was doing the right thing in both instances. He was bringing forward a bold and moral experiment in school choice, and if he had to twist arms and use foul language . . . well, he was doing God's work. And then, in the matter of the budget turkeys—he had a responsibility to all the residents of Florida, and if money was being allocated arbitrarily or according to pure politics, that was worse than not allocating that money at all.

The vetoed millions returned to the state's general fund, unspent. In a single stroke, Jeb was both acting as a budget referee and saving for a rainy day.

Besides, and more to the point, somehow equating the needs and goals of state legislators with the needs and goals of Jeb was more than a little silly. Jeb was the son of a president. His brother was governor of Texas. He had Big Ideas (or "big hairy audacious goals," as he modestly called them).

He was going places. He was supposed to make compromises and bend to the desire of some yocal from Yulee or Yeehaw Junction?

The idea was preposterous. In fact, not only did Jeb not accept the other two branches of government as his equal, but he actively pushed the boundaries of his own power, both through dint of his strong personality as well as a string of legislation designed to transfer and consolidate power within the office of the governor.

In the spring of 2001, Jeb and his conservative GOP allies in the legislature pushed through changes to the way judges are nominated for appointment, giving the governor far more power in picking the panels that pick the judges. Jeb, over dinner one night with House Speaker Thrasher, cooked up the plan to eliminate the long-standing Board of Regents that oversaw the state universities. In its stead came individual boards of trustees for each of the schools—boards that Jeb promptly stacked with Republican donors.

This is not to suggest that Jeb always got what he wanted. When he tried to deregulate electricity production, for example, back before Enron's market-fixing schemes had come to light, Jeb was blocked by the only state senator who was as smart and as strong-willed as he was. Fellow Republican Tom Lee's subsequent rise to senate president, in fact, effectively put a damper on Jeb's final two years as governor. And Jeb's tampering with the higher education system so ticked off Bob Graham, then a United States senator and a former governor himself, that Graham led a petition drive that successfully pushed a constitutional amendment essentially recreating the Board of Regents under a new name.

Still, especially in the first six years of Jeb's tenure, these setbacks were the exceptions that proved the rule. Generally what Jeb wanted, Jeb got, both in terms of actual policy objectives as well as the expansion of his own power. These changes, particularly when added to the new powers granted his office by voters through a 1998 constitutional amendment, by 2003 had made Jeb the most powerful governor the state had since Andrew Jackson ruled Florida, the newly acquired territory, by military fiat in 1821.

ONE OF the cosponsors of the "Cabinet reform" idea was then-treasurer (now U.S. senator) Bill Nelson, a Democrat. One of the biggest proponents of the plan was Democratic Governor Lawton Chiles's chief lawyer and friend. Obviously, a majority of Democratic voters supported the change.

It probably didn't occur to them, at the time, the practical effects of the new structure. In part, that was because of the personalities of the previous four or five governors, who all preferred, whenever possible, to build a consensus with legislators and others before trying anything big. They couldn't have known that Jeb would not be remotely interested in a consensus, that he had his ideas and plans, and that he would push them full-bore until he got what he wanted.

They couldn't have anticipated this, but they learned it soon enough. Jeb rammed his first school voucher plan through the legislature within months of taking office. Then, after two more voucher plans were put on the books, Jeb was able to appoint a political crony as the state's top education official, whereas before it had been an independently elected Cabinet officer.

This, arguably, was the point of the constitutional amendment: that the state's public schools should be the responsibility of the top executive branch official, not the shared responsibility of seven elected officials, jointly led by a governor as well as an education commissioner. And if voters were so offended by a particular governor's handling of education, they could express that disagreement in the next election.

Jeb's education policies and his voucher laws, under this view, were a logical and defensible consequence of his defeat of Democrat Buddy MacKay in November 1998. Even the most hard-core Democratic voters would probably agree that the winner of an election gets a chance to implement his policies.

What Democrats probably did not foresee, until Katherine Harris's behavior during the 2000 election illustrated the point, was that being in charge of the elections machinery meant having the ability to influence the outcome of those elections.

It was, prior to 2000, something so completely beyond the pale that it wasn't even considered. Elections were seen as sacrosanct, and notions that a statewide elections official would even try to put a thumb on the scale seemed far-fetched. But when Harris, who had been honorary cochair of George W.'s Florida campaign, systematically and unapologetically used the power of her office to give him the benefit of every discretionary call she was allowed to make, it suddenly dawned on Democrats how completely they had empowered Jeb with that 1998 Cabinet "reform" amendment.

Because Katherine Harris was actually an exception to the rule, which had been secretaries of state running elections with little fuss or controversy. There had been close elections before (admittedly, none as close as the 2000 presidential election), and there had been disputed elections before, but never a situation like Harris, whose state-paid cell phone was used to place a call late that election night to the George W. campaign in Texas. She explained afterward that she hadn't made the call, but that she had lent the phone to the state Republican chairman, and *he* had called.

But starting in 2003, it would no longer be an independently elected Cabinet member who ran statewide elections. Rather, it would be a political appointee who served entirely at Jeb's pleasure.

AS DETAILED EARLIER, Jeb made the most of this power in 2004 when his brother stood for reelection. His appointed secretary of state, former Orlando mayor Glenda Hood, just like Harris, used the discretion within her office to make decisions that, coincidentally enough, helped George W. and hurt John Kerry.

Which gets to an important point about Jeb and his modus operandi, one that distinguishes him from his brother. While it is true that Glenda Hood was nominally the one in charge of elections issues, in reality it was Jeb. Yes, all directives about election matters, all memos to county election supervisors, all of that went out above Hood's signature. But nothing of any consequence went out at all until it was fully vetted by Jeb's office. In case there was any question on this, it was made crystal clear when Jeb's number two press officer at the time was transferred over to serve as Hood's spokeswoman during the election season. Just to help out.

The secretary of state's office, of course, is just one example. All education decisions of any consequence also were made in Jeb's ground-floor suite of offices in the Capitol, not a quarter mile away at the Department of Education. Same with the decisions made by the Department of Environmental Protection, the Department of Business and Professional Regulation, the Department of Children and Families, and on and on. No, Jeb did not personally oversee every single purchasing contract, every single temporary office staff hire and every single travel voucher. But more so than any previous governor in modern times, Jeb involved himself in policy evaluations and decisions at an extraordinary level of detail.

E-mails obtained from Jeb's office under Florida's public records law show that Jeb personally, his chief of staff, his deputy chiefs of staff, his general counsel, and, occasionally, his budget officers made up the core group that handled most of the decision-making for the governor's agencies.

Policies were crafted within that small circle—sometimes with the involvement of the leadership of the affected agency; sometimes not—and then presented to agency managers to implement.

Proposed rules regarding school voucher oversight, for example, were written by Jeb's education policy staffer, Patricia Levesque, with the help of a home-schooling lobbyist—even though staff within the education department had been looking at the problem for over a year. And a tax cut benefiting restaurants and bars was cooked up by Jeb and his budget director, using language submitted by restaurants lobbyist and friend of Jeb Carol Dover. The proposal was then sent over to the Department of Business and Professional Regulation for them to implement. (Jeb was forced to swallow a rare policy reversal in this case after the Senate, reacting to a *Palm Beach Post* article, asked Jeb what legal basis he believed he had to implement a tax law change without the legislature's approval.)

The practical effect of this was that it did not really matter who held the top jobs at the various agencies, as they had very little autonomy. They could not implement policy changes without the approval of Jeb's office. They could not hire top deputies without the approval of Jeb's office. They could not even field questions from the media—indeed, their press officers could not even handle press queries—without the approval of Jeb's office.

Jeb was, as might have been predicted, a control freak to make ordinary control freaks seem like attention-deficit cases.

THE ONLY two sorts of people who could thrive in this environment, naturally, were total zealots, with a burning need to serve and advance All Things Bush, and total political hacks, happy for a government job paying far more than they were likely to find in the private sector.

Jeb's top leadership—with the aforementioned, bright, shining exception at the Division of Emergency Management—had plenty of examples of both. Jeb's first secretary of Business and Professional Regulation was a Tampa lawyer who in her earliest months on the job transformed an audit of a politically connected Tampa restaurant from a $184,000 bill for back taxes into a $6,263 refund. Then she took a junket to the Kentucky Derby, courtesy of restaurant and gambling interests—both of which groups she happened to regulate. Jeb then rewarded this performance by shifting her over to run the Department of Management Services, where she oversaw the letting of botched contract after botched contract as part of Jeb's outsourcing and privatization initiative. Her qualifications? She was a top fund-raiser for the Bush family. (She also had worked briefly as a Playboy bunny in college; Jeb in 2001 held a press conference to announce that he was not having an affair with her.) In 2005, the environmental group Public Employees for Environmental Responsibility released a sheet detailing the political campaign contributions of a Department of Environmental Protection employee who had won a big promotion two years earlier. Where had they dug it up? From his personnel file.

Even Jeb's supposed top priority, education, saw political loyalty trump knowledge and competence. He could have picked someone with teaching experience, or a former school principal, or a university administrator, when he had the chance to name the head of the state's education bureaucracy. Instead he chose a Republican state senator, whose only experience with schools—apart from having attended them as a child—was his private accounting business in which he sold charter schools in Jacksonville both consulting services as well as the "independent" audits required by state law. It was an obvious conflict of interest—the sort later made illegal by the Sarbanes-Oxley Act—but Jeb had no problem with it. In fact, he paid his friend $225,000, twice what the governor and elected Cabinet members made, and far more than his friend had ever made before in the private sector.

At times, the emphasis on loyalty at the expense of experience crossed over into the realm of the absurd. In 2001, for example, Florida had more than 60,000 licensed lawyers. Apparently not one of them was capable of taking on the duties of general counsel in the Department of Management Services, requiring the hiring for that position of a thirty-year-old lady, who at that point had not yet passed the Florida Bar exam. Her qualification? She was the fiancée of one of Jeb's occasional golf partners.

NOT ALL of Jeb's agency heads were incompetent.

Again, the promotion of Craig Fugate to lead the Division of Emergency Management, where he had been a bureau chief for four years, is the proof that Jeb is smart enough to appreciate competence when he sees it, and also smart enough to understand its value in an area of government where incompetence can get a lot of your supporters killed.

Eventually, the same realizations must have come to Jeb regarding other departments, too. After crony Jim Horne finally left the education job to slide over and lobby for slot-machine gambling at dog tracks and horse tracks, Jeb replaced him with longtime education technocrat John Winn.

Winn, though he had to defer to Jeb and top educational aide Patricia Levesque on their perennially nutty policy goals, nonetheless did bring some expertise and organizational skills necessary to run a large bureaucracy that Horne lacked. And after former Playboy bunny Cynthia Henderson finished wreaking havoc in the Department of Management Services, Jeb replaced her with first William Simon and then Tom Lewis. Both were eminently qualified. Simon had been a regional executive of liquor giant Diageo. Lewis had been former governor Bob Graham's community affairs secretary two decades earlier. Both men found themselves spending much of their time doing damage control—which is to say, dealing with the consequences of the disastrous privatization contracts let during Henderson's tenure. The department also found itself the depository of failed experiments from other of Jeb's agencies. When the State Technology Office—Jeb's plan to consolidate all computer purchasing in one agency—went through a string of embarrassing screw-ups, it was eventually eliminated, with the functions put under Simon's shop. Same thing with the Correction Privatization Commission, the entity charged with overseeing the state's five privately operated prisons. It, too, was abolished (and its director ultimately indicted for embezzling) and its tasks transferred to Management Services.

In his second term, Jeb also seemed to throw his hands up in frustration that, in some agencies, no matter how hard he tried, nothing could be done, and he appointed a caretaker bureaucrat to finish things out. Both the Department of Children and Families and the Department of Corrections followed this formula. Lucy Hadi, a longtime bureaucrat and confidante of second-term lieutenant governor Toni Jennings, was brought in to run scandal-plagued Children and Families, while prison system good-ole-boy and goon James Crosby was allowed to take over Corrections. Hadi did a passable job, given the inherent constraints of a boss who would have preferred to turn over her entire department to the evangelical churches. Crosby ran Florida prisons like Florida prisons have been run for decades—like a five-family fiefdom based in the North Florida hinterlands of Starke and Raiford. By late 2005, state and federal prosecutors had broken up a steroid and theft ring based—ridiculously enough—on Crosby's singular obsession of prison softball. In February 2006, Jeb finally asked Crosby to resign as a federal criminal probe closed in on a prison privatazation contract from which Crosby and a top crony were taking $12,000 a month in kickbacks. (Both Crosby and the crony pleaded guilty that July.) Jeb replaced with him his "drug czar," James McDonough. By then, with only ten months left, Jeb had lost all interest in prisons.

2005: Lt. Governor Toni Jennings looks over Jeb's shoulder as he works on his laptop in his inner office. Jeb was known for reading and sending hundreds of e-mails a day, at all hours of the day, from his personal account, jeb@jeb.org. Visible on the top, left-hand corner of his desk is the small digital countdown clock that showed him how many days, hours, minutes, and seconds were left before he had to step down on January 2, 2007, because of term limits. The clock was a second-term gift from his secretary of Environmental Protection.

. . .

UNFORTUNATELY FOR Florida during the Jeb years, such appointees like Simon and Lewis or even Hadi were the exceptions, not the rule. This is what happens when the top requirement for any job is pure and undying devotion to Jeb Bush.

Again, this is pretty much par for the course, within the Bush family. Similar demands were made of federal appointees during George W.'s years in the White House. And Jeb and George W. famously insisted on it from Republican consultant Lee Atwater during the 1988 race. Jeb informed Atwater that if a grenade were tossed at their dad, he expected Atwater to jump on it.

What person with any level of experience or competency wants to live under that kind of attitude in a boss? The sort that either pretty much agreed with everything Jeb was saying to start with, or were so starstruck with the thought of working with this shining, young Bush that they internalized his worldview, top to bottom.

Jeb's hard-charging, always-in-a-hurry personality created still another hurdle to recruiting and, more important, retaining qualified staff. Jeb the workaholic goes from before dawn through midnight, and he expects his top advisers to work that hard, too. One staffer, early in his tenure, worked past nine one evening and decided not to call Jeb to give him his nightly update. The next day, Jeb wanted to know why he'd not gotten his call. He reiterated that, no matter how late, he wanted a call every night.

Another time, a dedicated and behind-on-his-chores staff member dragged himself to the office on Thanksgiving. Jeb caught up with him that afternoon to berate him for leaving his family on that holiday, but then added: "Don't you have a home office?"

It comes as little surprise, then, that with precious few exceptions, Jeb built for himself an inner circle that was not only utterly devoted to their leader, but also had no life or major responsibilities outside of the workplace. Which is to say: lots of young, childless men and women, with little in the way of real life experience.

This hyperenthusiastic acolyte was the sort that, upon reading Jeb's company handbook, *A Message to Garcia*—an 1899 tract that glorifies the virtues of doing what you are told and not asking any questions—rather than shaking his or her head sadly at what a loon the boss was, instead believed it was simply brilliant, and tried to get his or her own friends to read it.

Little wonder that when Jeb really needed the people around him to tell him, *Governor, this is a really stupid idea you have,* all he heard instead was, *How high?*

Florida was not well served by this—a fact that even Jeb, in a rare moment of candor six and a half years into his tenure, seemed to recognize. "Sometimes, if you don't always focus on creating a climate on where staff members' opinions are valued, you don't get them. That's a weakness I think I've gotten significantly better on, but it continues to be a weakness."

Truly great leaders co-opt their opponents, and respect those who are smarter than they are. Jeb instead saw opponents as enemies, and seemed threatened by those who could challenge him intellectually.

LOOKING BACK after two terms, however, it becomes obvious that much of the irritation and anger that Jeb engendered was due to the content of his agenda as well as the style. True, a less obstinate and more congenial personality might have accomplished as much or even more of that agenda without having ticked off everyone who disagreed with him. But it is also fair that some of that opposition would have been every bit as vociferous regardless of Jeb's methods, so long as he insisted on his peculiar vision. It's hard to believe that the teachers unions, for example, would have been amenable to *any* form of school vouchers, even if Jeb had invited their input on his program, rather than slamming the door in their face.

What's important to note is that Jeb's leadership style created problems for himself even when the actual goal in question was roundly lauded. A perfect example was what should have been—and despite everything could still be—one of Jeb's lasting legacies: Scripps.

In 2003, freshly off reelection, Jeb got wind that the Scripps Research Institute was looking to expand. With an initiative and an energy that maybe only Jeb could have mustered, he decided that Florida would be the place where it would come, and he went about making it happen.

The sheer chutzpah alone is admirable. Florida, unlike California or Massachusetts, is not known for its institutions of higher learning, apart from their hosting some really good football teams. Yet Jeb, who in his life had never shown any major interest in science or research, saw opportunity where others might not have even thought to look.

He personally courted the director and the board of Scripps and sold them on the virtues of a Florida campus, way back before they had officially decided whether and how much to expand. By taking—in bad, PR lingo—such a *proactive* approach, Jeb essentially prevented a bidding war with other locations by preempting them.

To pay for it all, Jeb suggested a big chunk of the nearly $1 billion in "economic stimulus" money Florida got as part of his brother's attempts to curry favor with state governments in 2003, in preparation for what was already looking like a tough reelection campaign the following year. Even here, Jeb thought big: $310 million—nearly a full third of what Florida would get for the whole state. Some in the legislature suggested that such an amount going to a single location was excessive, that the money was to benefit all Floridians, and should therefore have been allocated to various "economic development" projects around the state. There is some validity to that argument, but in the grand scheme, Jeb was probably correct that there was more real benefit to spending it all on a single big project, with potentially huge rewards, than on dozens of smaller enterprises, in which some or many were bound to fail and much of the money would get wasted in the myriad little ways that "economic development" money is always wasted.

There was also a more general criticism of giving the money to an already successful entity like Scripps, but that too appeared misplaced. Unlike other states and communities that put together nine-figure inducement packages for such entities like for-profit, luxury automobile makers, Scripps was essentially in the business of doing scientific research. Granted, much of the research was directed toward the pharmaceutical industry, but that's true of most universities nowadays. In fact, that's probably the most appropriate comparison: going after Scripps was like sinking a big chunk of money into a new university—a new, graduate-level, research-oriented university that already had a sterling name around the world. It's hard to make a straight-faced argument that such a thing is bad use of public money, particularly when it offered to bring a clean, high-tech dimension to an economy far too reliant on jobs changing bed linens at hotels or running the cash register at the newest Wal-Mart. The goal was not just the five hundred jobs Scripps itself would create, but several thousand more generated by bio-tech firms that would want to locate in a science village Scripps would anchor.

Jeb dubbed his idea "Project Air Conditioning," on the premise that the endeavor would bring as much long-term benefit to the state as the invention of air-conditioning had done. When Jeb held a press conference to make the announcement—naturally, carried live over the Internet—in October 2003, he proclaimed: "Scripps is the brand name for biomedical research, and its decision to build a sister research facility in Florida is a seminal moment in our state's history."

Some hyperbole, sure, but forgivable. What happened next was less so.

Because what happened next was so predictable, given who Jeb is and how Jeb thinks, that even he ought to realize the folly of it all in retrospect.

A LITTLE BACKGROUND is necessary: Jeb did not think of Scripps as a likely Florida prospect on his own. That actually was the dream of British billionaire Joe Lewis, who figured a new campus for Scripps would be just the thing for his 7,000-acre development at Lake Nona in Orlando. Lewis talked to his lawyer, C. David Brown II, who was a big fund-raiser for Jeb. Brown mentioned the idea to him just as he was heading out to California to raise money for his brother in July 2003.

Based on this, Jeb arranged a visit of Scripps's La Jolla campus and, as he is so capable of doing, charmed the pants off Scripps's chairman Richard Lerner, showing off an impressive grasp of the field and flattering the scientists with his energy and interest. Within weeks, Jeb had his economic development staff working up numbers and incentives to turn Scripps's vague idea of expansion into a Florida campus, and to nail it all down quickly.

Pretty soon, though, it became clear that scientists who work at Scripps just weren't as keen on Orlando and the Mouse and all the rest of it as some Floridians are, and Jeb's people scrambled to show Scripps some other locations, too: Tampa, the Naples-Fort Myers area, and Palm Beach County.

This is the part of the story where one of Jeb's principal traits as a leader started leading the project astray: his obsession with secrecy.

The official justification for this—it had come to the point where Palm Beach County's Business Development Board had only known the Scripps visitors' first names as they showed them around—was to prevent some other player from jumping in and luring Scripps away. But what other player? Jeb was dangling more than $300 million, with a smaller but substantial commitment from whatever community was chosen. No other state was even involved.

Once Scripps was onboard with the idea of coming to Florida, letting the local experts like planners and engineers offer their two cents, rather than just accept the word and the judgment of the development community, would have helped find the best possible location for a new campus. Surely it was in the best interests of all Floridians to have an open selection process, right?

But no, Jeb wanted it all hush-hush. Which meant that in Palm Beach County, really the only ones involved in picking Scripps's site were those with strong friendships and powerful ties to the biggest and richest developers. Is it any surprise they picked a site at the edge of the Florida Everglades, a spot the state's huge home builders had been itching to exploit for years? Naturally, all the scientists Scripps would bring in would need houses and grocery stores and gas stations, as would all their research assistants and technicians and so on.

This quite understandably raised the ire of some county commission members, a lot of county residents, and pretty much every environmental group in the state. Mecca Farms, the site chosen, was well beyond the county's "urban services boundary," the line the county had drawn to limit urban sprawl and protect what remained of the county's wetlands by focusing new construction in places where roads, water, and sewer services already existed. Ramming through a 1,920-acre—that's more than three square miles—development out across the street from the J.W. Corbett Wildlife Management Area not only violated the county's own planning rules, but also created a precedent for every other developer wanting the same thing. How could the county tell John Doe and Sons Builders that they could not erect three thousand homes across the street from the Everglades when the county had just done exactly the same thing for Scripps?

Also quite understandably, all these ticked-off people meant that lawsuits were sure to follow. Some of the environmental groups in Florida have deep enough pockets to finance years of litigation, and the headlong rush the county and the various regulatory agencies had taken to give Jeb what he wanted *immediately,* if not sooner, meant that the lawyers would find plenty of nits to pick, if not some serious deficiencies.

Once that was done, Jeb's other fatal flaw as a leader kicked in: his never-admit-you're-wrong stubbornness.

GIVEN THE ire Jeb had shown for anyone who dared challenge his judgment, given particularly the utter contempt Jeb had shown for the judiciary—think of his voucher program, which he rammed through a pliant legislature and then dragged through the courts for the duration of his two terms—it was a foregone conclusion, that Jeb was going to cross his arms and dig in his heels over Mecca Farms. Sometimes right, sometimes wrong, never in doubt.

Not, it is important to note, that he particularly cared about the site— although, admittedly, it no doubt gave him a measure of satisfaction that although the Scripps honchos had chosen to expand into a county filled with people who had voted resoundingly against him and his brother, and served by a newspaper (my own *Palm Beach Post*) he despised, at least the county would have to violate its growth management guidelines and help the hated home builders as part of the bargain.

No, Jeb probably would have been satisfied even if the Palm Beach County Business Development Board had chosen a logical site, and not one that necessarily advanced the goal of putting up new houses and strip malls in every last acre of the county. All things being equal, naturally, Jeb prefers to help his home builder allies. But in this case, had the county determined that a swath in Jupiter—close to the Interstate, close to surface streets and water lines that already existed—or even poor-and-hurting-for-redevelopment Riviera Beach were the best choices, Jeb would have been happy.

But a year later, when the county started second-guessing the Mecca Farms site as the environmental challenges looked ever more serious, Jeb stood firm. Even when lawyers pointed out that an appellate court had forced a developer literally to tear down an illegally permitted development in neighboring Martin County, Jeb wasn't fazed. He was ready to double dog dare a judge to stop him.

In October 2005, Jeb met his match—a federal judge who happened to live in Palm Beach County who held county officials' feet to the fire, demanding to know why they had sought an Army Corps of Engineers permit for the Scripps project totaling only 535 acres, when in fact they were planning to develop the entire 1,920 acres. To Judge Donald Middlebrooks, the reason was pretty obvious: a permit for the total amount would have required a full environmental impact statement, a process that would have taken upwards of two years. The 535-acre permit could be pushed through quickly.

Middlebrooks wasn't amused, and he wasn't fooled, and he wasn't intimidated by the Bush brand. On November 10, he ruled that Scripps's construction on its already begun, 44-acre campus could continue—but that the county could not continue with the roads that would lead to these buildings or the water or power lines that would let it function, until such time that they had an honest permit for the entire 1,920 acres from the Army Corps.

The ruling was, to the legions of old and new Jeb detractors in Florida by that point, a thing of pure poetry. The *Palm Beach Post*'s humor columnist had a field day, imagining years into the future when *President* Jeb would make a surprise appearance at the opening of the Scripps campus, his shirt soaked through because of the three-mile hike from the nearest road, where he would see scientists rubbing two sticks together to get a pot of coffee going.

And so, finally, years after he should have, Jeb backed down and acceded to common sense. Three months later, the county commission put Scripps where it probably should have gone in the first place—in an already built-out section of the county, on a branch campus of Florida Atlantic University.

A CONTEMPT FOR the legislature, a contempt for the judiciary—perhaps those can be explained as the natural predilections of a strong-willed executive trying to accomplish a lot in a limited amount of time. The frustrations are certainly understandable.

But what Floridians could have seen in Jeb, had they chose to, was the ultimate contempt, one that had no such justification in the separation of powers structure, and that was the contempt for Floridians, as expressed in their attempts at direct democracy.

Now, there can be a healthy debate on the wisdom of "government by citizen initiative," as practiced in Florida and other states in recent years. Certainly a well-organized mob can easily drum up the necessary signatures to put hot-button questions on a state ballot that could win a majority while tearing up a society. You don't need much of an imagination to think up some truly wicked things that could find their way into a state constitution. Provisions hurting blacks, gays, and other minorities come to mind right off the bat.

The Founding Fathers had some good reasons to prefer a republic, which would by design be slower to act and therefore less prone to rashness, as well as be more interested in the rights of minorities than the preferences of the majority.

That said, there is a genuine public benefit to having the citizens of Florida decide they're mad as hell and they aren't going to take it anymore, and put a question on the ballot to modify the state's constitution and *force* the legislature and the governor to take action on a given issue. Time and time again, a good idea will be put forth in the legislature but then squashed like a bug by the moneyed interests who can afford lots of lobbyists.

Florida's smoking ban is a perfect example.

For years, groups like the Heart Association and the Cancer Society had been working to limit smoking in public places. Long after no-smoking sections were required in restaurants in many other states, Florida restaurants were under no such mandate. No-smoking areas were voluntary, even though most adults—and all children—in Florida did not smoke. Eventually, eateries larger than a certain threshold were required to set aside 35 percent of their seats for nonsmokers—a huge victory for the do-gooders over the combined lobbying forces of the tobacco and restaurant lobbies.

By the late 1990s, the antismoking forces were pushing to reverse the obvious mismatch: the majority of restaurant seats set aside for smokers when the majority of diners were nonsmokers. On this, the smoking lobbyists were adamant. It was not going to happen. Even when compromises were attempted—such as giving the option of having tougher nonsmoking laws in counties or cities that wanted them—they were shot down, sometimes using the sneaky legislative maneuvers that good, expensive lobbyists always have up their sleeve. The cockiness in their laughter, in the bars after yet another antismoking bill had been successfully killed, was something to behold.

It gave what happened in 2002 a deserved sense of righteousness, when the antismoking groups woke up and realized that although they did not have the Florida legislature in their pockets, they did have the whole-hearted support of Florida's largely nonsmoking electorate, most of whom were tired of having to breathe other people's cigarette smoke every time they went out to dinner. They quickly raised the $6 million they needed to gather the 488,722 signatures necessary to put the question on the ballot as well as buy the necessary advertising and phone banks and other things you need to win a statewide election in Florida.

By July 1, 2003, it was illegal to smoke in public places in Florida, with only a small number of exceptions that were spelled out in the ballot initiative. All the negotiating over percentages of smoking versus nonsmoking, separate ventilation systems—all that was gone. There was *no* smoking in restaurants. Period. There was also no more smoking in bowling alleys, auto-parts stores, barbershops, all of those "traditional" places that used to be hangouts for people who wanted to light up. The one big exception was bars, but only if they were not part of a restaurant and did not serve food other than prepackaged snacks.

All of this was beyond what the heart and lung and cancer people had been hoping to get when they were still *playing by the rules* and trying to work their way through the legislature. The lesson here for legislators should have been simple: as powerful as their need was to suck up to the lobbyists who pay for their campaigns, they needed to curb it, when those lobbyists were pushing interests diametrically opposed to what their constituents wanted. So what lesson did they learn instead? That citizen-generated constitutional amendments were evil, and that the process had to be stopped. And in this belief, they and Jeb were completely simpatico.

OF COURSE, those who railed against the citizen-initiative process in Florida rarely railed against the indoor smoking ban, which, with its 71 percent approval, was a dangerous thing to oppose. Instead, they lampooned the "pregnant pig amendment," an initiative pushed by animal rights activists and environmentalists who wanted to keep giant pig farms out of Florida, which they accomplished by banning the use of small gestation crates.

Jeb, frankly, could not have cared less about the pregnant pigs. He really didn't care too much about the smoking ban, either. He was no longer a smoker, and he wasn't beholden to big tobacco any more than he was to any other big donor. He didn't even get particularly exercised about a series of amendments passed by trial lawyers and doctors in their fight over medical malpractice lawsuits. On the other hand, three particular citizen initiatives absolutely enraged him: one in 2000 that mandated a high-speed rail system among the major Florida population centers; another in 2002 that created a statewide higher education governing board; and, the one Jeb hated the worst, a 2002 amendment that required the state to limit the number of children in public school classrooms by 2010.

No, Jeb did not have a moral aversion to trains, fast or slow. And while he may have believed that a statewide board for public universities was cumbersome and inefficient, that by itself was not the key. And Jeb, in calmer moments, has agreed that smaller classes are better than larger ones, both for children and for teachers. No, what these three constitutional amendments had in common was that voters had passed them over Jeb's strenuous and repeated objections. In the case of the class-size amendment, Jeb's warnings to voters were downright dire—the amendment would block out the sun, it would require massive tax increases or massive cuts in social programs for the old and the sick.

All three also had in common the feature of a single champion who, despite Jeb having been governor and a Bush to boot and their not having been either, had nonetheless bested him. In the case of the high-speed rail amendment, it was a longtime proponent of fast trains who happened to be a millionaire and who was not afraid to take on Jeb. In the case of the state universities, Jeb tangled with Bob Graham, at the time a United States senator and a former governor, who believed he had done his utmost to take politics out of the state universities' Board of Regents, only to watch Jeb abolish it. And in the case of the class-size amendment, it was a shrewd state senator, the son of one of the first blacks elected to Congress from Florida since Reconstruction.

For Jeb, nearly everything is political as well as personal. And, so, naturally, once these amendments passed, he had to do his best to ignore them or even undermine them. His handling of the class-size amendment is such an instructive window on his personality and style of leadership that it will be examined in great detail in a subsequent chapter.

For here, it will suffice to point out that the class-size amendment shared with these other two one last commonality: it was pushed in large part in exasperation with Jeb's autocratic style. Since taking office, Jeb had made private school vouchers the real focus of his education policy. Despite historic budget surpluses thanks to a red-hot economy, Jeb had given *public* schools enough to cover increasing enrollments and inflation and not a whole lot more. Yet as he entered his reelection year in 2002, he was touting a $3 billion increase for public schools in his first term—and glossing over the fact that the money, the bulk of it thanks to local property taxes, not state funds, had done barely more than let schools tread water. State Senator Kendrick Meek's constitutional amendment was an angry response to that: so you're such a big fan of public schools? Let's see how you deal with *this.*

It was even more of an obvious backlash with the other two. In 2000, Lakeland rancher and cattleman C.C. "Doc" Dockery went to the voters to force Jeb to reconsider a decision he had made within weeks of taking office in 1999: undoing the longstanding state policy to bring high-speed rail to Florida. True, after more than a decade, the project seemed mired in endless engineering studies and delays with an actual train still nowhere in sight. Still, few could argue that it was not a good idea. The big cities of Florida are choked with traffic, and a fast, efficient rail line linking the commercial and tourist centers would be a good thing. As a resident of ever-more-congested Miami since 1981, Jeb should have understood this— even if, as a Texan and Houstonian, he was brought up to believe that mass transit is a United Nations conspiracy. All this became even more plainly obvious in the autumn of 2005, when two Gulf hurricanes brought an early preview of three-dollar-a-gallon gasoline: an inevitability, given China's escalating demand for fuel.

But set aside for a moment the relative merits of keeping or canceling the bullet train. Jeb, as governor, was certainly entitled to his position on the issue. More important here is Jeb's failure to understand that there was a much smarter, much more reasonable way to build a consensus around his view that high-speed rail should be terminated, and the money spent elsewhere, than the method that he chose, which was to decree this by fiat.

That rashness, that utter lack of interest in the viewpoints of others, was really what pushed Dockery. Had Jeb made his case to the legislature that first year—a Republican House and a Republican Senate, that were pretty much determined to help him succeed, regardless of the issue—he prob- ably would have gotten what he wanted, the old-fashioned way: with a bill that he would have signed into law, ending Florida's long dalliance with fast trains. Instead, Jeb's imperiousness ticked off a guy who could do something about it. Dockery spent $3 million of his own money to pay for the signature gatherers and the ad campaign to put the matter before the voters. To Jeb's stunned amazement, it passed, even though he had lob- bied against it.

Almost immediately, Jeb began a campaign to get rid of it, arguing that voters really didn't know what they were doing, and had they understood the rail line's cost, they would have defeated it. That line of argument ig- nored that the margin of the amendment's passage, 293,000 votes, was more than *five hundred* times larger than his brother's margin of victory that year in the presidential race in Florida. Did voters also not understand what they were doing there?

Jeb did the bare minimum to implement the will of the voters in 2001—creating inexpensive study commissions and the like—with the idea of quickly getting a repeal back on the ballot. Unfortunately for Jeb, Dockery's wife happened to be a state House member, and one of his best friends was chair of a key committee in the state Senate. The legislature was unwilling to smite two of its own even to please Jeb, and was unwill- ing to put the matter on the 2002 ballot. Jeb had to wait until 2004, when fellow Republican Cabinet member Tom Gallagher led up a statewide political committee to gather signatures. The committee raised $2.2 million, much of it from Jeb's cronies in the development and road-building communities, who naturally stood to lose if the state were to subsidize trains instead of cars. By then, Jeb and his allies had also pushed through a constitutional amendment allowing the government—that is to say: Jeb and the Republicans leaders of the legislature—to put "fiscal impact" statements on all ballot initiatives. The government put a cost of $25 billion for *not* repealing the bullet train, and voters responded accordingly.

After he had finally gotten his way on the matter, Jeb had this to say: "The people have spoken. It's time to move on."

THE MOST amazing thing was that when he said it, he not only kept a straight face, but actually had a strong head of righteous indignation going too.

The people have spoken. True, they do that in Florida and elsewhere on average every other year. But in his two terms, Jeb made it plain that he was interested in what they were saying when and only when they happened to agree with him. Otherwise, they had to be put off, misled, worn down, threatened, or otherwise undermined.

It sounds terribly harsh, put like that, but Jeb's record speaks for itself. Jeb essentially put the bullet train on a barely lit back burner until he could finally drive a stake through its heart. He attempted the same strategy with the class-size amendment, as we will see later. He couldn't quite manage that with the Graham amendment, as the state universities initiative came to be known—partly because it passed with a larger majority than supported Jeb's reelection that year, and partly because even Jeb understood that he couldn't seek to repeal *all* the amendments voters had passed.

Jeb settled on ignoring the newly created Board of Governors as best he could, pushing legislation that gave it as few responsibilities as possible and then loading it up with cronies. Its chair, for example, was the woman who led the political committee Jeb created to organize its defeat. Ironically, Jeb eventually seemed to appreciate Graham's point a year later, when the legislature insisted on a chiropractic college at Florida State University. This was done to honor a leading state senator—a chiropractor, naturally—but was quickly making the school a laughingstock around the nation. What was next, a college of aromatherapy? At this point, Jeb suddenly found purpose for his until-then-dormant Board of Governors, which quickly determined that there was no demonstrable need for Florida to create the world's first publicly supported college of a pseudoscience.

Even more ironically, the Board of Governors the following year would be called upon to put the brakes on new medical colleges at two more state universities. Medical schools are enormously expensive—which is the reason that the original Board of Regents had opposed building a new one at Florida State, the alma mater of former House speaker and Jeb pal John Thrasher. Thrasher outlined his plan to get even—by eliminating the Regents and replacing them with local boards at each of the universities—on a paper napkin over dinner with Jeb one night. Jeb, eager to pay back his friend for two years of turning his legislative chamber over for Jeb's complete disposal, in that instance went along. The Regents were eliminated, and Thrasher got his medical school.

IT WOULD be nice to think that Jeb learned something from this, perhaps even the idea that he personally was not the fount of all brilliant ideas the state has ever had. That, once in a while, good ideas might originate with other state leaders in the legislature or the Supreme Court, or local leaders in the counties and cities, or leaders that came before them in previous years and decades or even—heaven forbid—from the citizens themselves in the form of a ballot initiative.

It would be nice to think this, except for the fact that there is absolutely no evidence to suggest it is true. Sure, Jeb frequently has people stand up beside him at press conferences and he praises them for things they have done, and explains how he has learned from them. But they are props, accessories to help sell the message of what a great job he has done and how smart he is.

In two full terms, only on a single policy did Jeb come forward to admit that originally he had been wrong and that he had come to change his mind, and that was regarding a "sales tax holiday" on back-to-school clothing—a tax cut that literally returned pennies to the great unwashed. Jeb had thought the idea stupid because it did nothing to help the rich "investor class," his preferred tax-cut beneficiary, but eventually came to embrace the annual, weeklong event for its political value. We will examine Jeb's tax cut policies—it is silly to call them merely "tax" policies—in greater detail later, as we will his education policies, his privatization policies, and his quasi affirmative action policy which, ironically enough, gave Kendrick Meek the stature he later used to push the class-size amendment.

In those areas specifically, as well as other policies more generally, Jeb moved with a critics-be-damned attitude that was at once both breathtaking and scary. For that is the Florida he constructed for himself during his eight years: one with a leader as close to being king as can be imagined in a constitutional republic. The people he most empathizes with are corporate executives, and Jeb thought of himself as Florida's CEO. He would get things done that were important to him, with the attitude that those things were likewise important to all Floridians by dint of their having made him their governor. You either helped him succeed, or you got out of his way, or he and his allies would make you suffer the consequences.

For those who disagreed with his views and his policies, perhaps the only saving grace was that he was only governor. At the end of two terms, the natural inefficiency of 160 legislators, even largely Jeb-friendly legislators, limited Jeb's accomplishments. And while Jeb was also able to make the courts considerably more Jeb-friendly at the lower levels, the judiciary nevertheless remained independent enough to check his more adventuresome excursions past the boundaries set by the state constitution. Jeb couldn't call out the state police on people he didn't like, he couldn't start a war, and he couldn't—try as he might—create laws by fiat.

Of course, a president has a lot more latitude in these areas than a mere governor. And, depending on where you sit, the idea of a President Jeb with his personality and prejudices at the levers of national power will either seem incredibly comforting or downright terrifying.

It is an idea that Americans will almost certainly have to wrestle with in the not-too-distant future.

Chapter Six

PRIVATIZE THIS

"Government is an obsolete dinosaur. I don't consider that being from the far left or far right, or far anything."
— JEB BUSH, IN HIS FIRST RUN
FOR GOVERNOR, 1993

"Quietly, without debate, we are transforming our society to a collectivist policy."
— JEB BUSH, 1994

"Market theology can be almost childlike in its ignorance of subjects like the Koran, suicide bombers, and Carpathian ethnography."
— KEVIN PHILLIPS, 2004

It was, as is not uncommon, a chilly January morning in Tallahassee as Jeb stepped to the podium in 2003—the state capital is not in South Florida and gets its share of winter cold snaps.

George H.W. and Barbara were with him and Columba and the kids on the steps of the Old Capitol looking down the hill of Apalachee Parkway, but apart from that it was not a particularly memorable occasion. Jeb had won his 2002 reelection easily, the nation was on the brink of a war with Iraq, and no one expected any major policy shifts.

Besides, Jeb has never been good with formal speeches. As good as he is off-the-cuff, without notes, his prepared deliveries are a dud. The sincerity and facility with the facts that come across in extemporaneous remarks are replaced with a stilted smugness when he reads off a teleprompter. Even the speech was weak—possibly the weakest of all the major addresses that the normally gifted Paul Bradshaw had written for him. It rambled along for fourteen minutes, never finding any real high points or even memorable lines.

Except for one: "There would be no greater tribute to our maturity as a society than if we can make these buildings around us empty of workers—silent monuments to the time when government played a larger role than it deserved or could adequately fill."

In the context of the speech, it was clear what Jeb meant. He was repeating a refrain that both he and George W. have used through the years, that it was impossible for government to make all parents love their children, make all people love their neighbors, and so government had to serve as an imperfect substitute in the case of neglected children and disciplinarian in the case of the criminal justice system.

But words like that spoken by the state's chief executive, in a town where state government is the number one employer, and following four years of proposals to whittle down government by reducing its workforce—well, it's understandable why the emptied-of-workers state buildings remark struck such a sour note.

As governor, Jeb outsourced the meals for state prison inmates to Philadelphia-based Aramark. Five hundred state jobs disappeared in the transaction. He brought in a division of Ticketmaster to handle campsite reservations at state parks, shedding dozens more jobs. He gave Cincinnati-based telecommunications giant Convergys the largest of his outsourcing efforts, a $262 million, seven-year deal to handle the state's payroll and personnel services, eliminating roughly 900 state positions.

Jeb tried to consolidate all state computer and software purchasing into a single office under his control, and then tried to outsource most of that work. He privatized a slice of the state's public school system through a series of school voucher programs. He privatized the state's foster-care delivery system. He outsourced the handling of death penalty appeals to private lawyers. He even tried to get a private, South Florida university to take much of the State Library collection off our hands—and was willing to *pay them* $10 million to do it.

Each and every one of these deals, and more, drew heaps of criticism, much of it from Republicans, for recklessly and hastily undoing state services, sometimes without any cost savings at all. In the case of the State Technology Office, a 2002 audit by the office of fellow Republican comptroller Robert Milligan found numerous instances of "gross mismanagement," conflicts of interest and dismal bookkeeping in the way the office doled out tens of millions of dollars in contracts. Two years later, the agency was forced to rebid two contracts totaling $176 million to consulting giants Accenture and BearingPoint—both, coincidentally enough, major donors to the Republican Party—after it came out that the office's director, Kim Bahrami, had awarded the contracts, quit her job, and within months had turned up working for BearingPoint.

Aramark was accused of supplying meager quantities of food of dubious quality. Convergys became an epithet among state employees. And the school voucher programs were so dysfunctional that they deserve an entire chapter.

Through it all, Jeb led with his chin.

By the middle of his second term, his office calculated that they had saved the state $552 million—a figure opponents called vastly overstated—and cut 9,500 jobs. "To be timid because there have been mistakes and go under a rock and worry about what people write, I'm not going to worry about that," Jeb said.

TRUE ENOUGH, Jeb did not worry what anyone else thought about his privatization plans, not even the "Efficiency Czar" he hired at $95,000 a year in 2001 to provide expert advice. Ruth Sykes spent twenty years in the Air Force as a management and efficiency analyst. She did not last five months in Jeb's office. Not after she started questioning the logic of some of the projects.

"I didn't have access to the governor. I tried," she said after her quiet departure, describing her inability to crack Jeb's "inner circle" of true believers. "I thought that was one of the reasons I was brought in there. . . . But after a while, you start to think, well, if you're not in support of what they want to do, you should be going."

And if after Sykes's departure it was still uncertain why all this was happening, that became crystal clear three years later, when the Department of Children and Families was evaluating two proposals to modernize a welfare program's administration. One was from an outside vendor, and the other from in-house employees. Each showed savings of $69.2 million a year, but DCF administrators added the words "at least," with no apparent justification, to the outsourced model. The only measurable "disadvantage" to keeping the work in-house was that it kept a larger number of state workers than did the outsourcing idea.

So what was DCF's rationale for not keeping the work in-house? Said DCF Secretary Lucy Hadi: "We're sensitive to who we work for."

Probably the most damning of the voluminous criticism in this area came from Milligan, a retired three-star Marine general who handled logistics during Desert Storm. "The people that were doing the analysis were biased in the analysis. They wanted an answer and they made sure they got the answer. It wasn't because Bush demanded the answer, but they wanted to satisfy the boss," Milligan told the St. Petersburg Times two years after he had left office because of term limits. He cited the advice he offered on the Convergys personnel contract—which drew the most angry complaints because it resulted in erroneous paychecks and long telephone hold times for Republican state legislators and their spouses. Jeb's people rammed the proposal through the legislature, believing that the outsourced system could be up and running in nine months. "I told them you needed three to four years to get that system right," Milligan said. "They didn't want to hear it."

You can't get something for nothing.

It is a general principle that most people understand, and it even has scientific roots in the laws of conservation and thermodynamics. In the area of personal morality, Jeb has often expressed his view that gambling, for instance, is evil because it promotes the "something for nothing" culture.

And so it may seem perplexing, on the surface, Jeb's continual claim that he *could* get something for nothing merely by shifting the locus of the activity in question from the public sector to the private.

Jeb defended his efforts to reduce the state workforce as a means of saving taxpayer money and focusing the state's efforts on its core functions— although that claim was belied by his enthusiasm for privatizing such things as the state's foster care system, which most Floridians would likely agree is a core state function.

Like in many areas, the true key to understanding Jeb's worldview comes not from the things he said publicly as governor or during his 1998 run for governor, but from the things he said during his unsuccessful 1994 run—things like: "Government is an obsolete dinosaur." One particularly illustrative example comes from his campaign promise that year to build more prisons, but to do it at a substantially lower cost than proposals by both Democratic governor Lawton Chiles as well as his Republican rivals, one of whom had been proposing a penny increase in the sales tax to pay for all the new cells and the guards to watch over them.

Jeb based this estimate on the assumption that building private prisons would save 15 percent and operating them would save 20 percent against what the state would spend. Not 2 or 3 percent, not 5, not even 10. A full 15 and 20 percent.

Why did he think this was possible? Well, there was no empirical evidence, other than his deep-seated faith that government is inherently wasteful and that private businesses are inherently both competent and efficient.

Part of this no doubt is the result of never having been part of a large private sector organization prior to becoming governor. He spent all of five years with Texas Commerce Bank, and a year and a half of that was starting up a tiny branch office in Venezuela. After his dad's unsuccessful presidential and successful vice presidential runs in 1980, Jeb spent the next seven years working in small businesses, always either as owner or partner. *His* private sector businesses could move fast, be responsive to clients, and turn on a dime because he personally was doing much of the work or riding herd on a small group of individuals who answered directly to him. Maybe because he routinely worked twelve, fourteen, even sixteen hours each day, going full bore, he assumed everybody in the private sector does.

Had Jeb's private-sector experience been with General Motors or Sears or Kmart or any number of other businesses that have proven over time how *in*efficient and sluggish the private sector can be, perhaps he would have formed a different opinion.

Jeb's government-is-wasteful worldview was no doubt also colored by his own brief experience in a small part of government that truly *was* wasteful, the Department of Commerce. The agency was created to maintain and generate business for Florida. How this should be done—and what, if anything, would constitute success in a state with such a phenomenal growth rate—was never quite clear. Former governor Bob Graham had such little use for the agency that he put as its head his lieutenant governor, Wayne Mixson, whose only other chore in the Graham administration had been to nail down the conservative Democratic Panhandle vote. Governor Lawton Chiles did away with the department and replaced it with Enterprise Florida, which has had similarly dubious results, but at least, because of its "public private" nature, has forced business to contribute a greater share to its existence.

In between those two Democrats was Bob Martinez, who gave the honor of leading the agency to Jeb Bush, who in 1987 was the thirty-four-year-old chair of the Dade County Republican Party. Jeb put out press releases about how many tourists the state was receiving, led "trade missions" to other countries, and otherwise did those chamber-of-commerce things that all states do because they feel they must to compete with other states.

If Jeb construed that absolutely none of this served a vital role for Floridians, he would have been correct. Unfortunately, Jeb seemed to have taken his analysis on the efficacy and even necessity of his meaningless little corner of state government and extrapolated it onto the whole.

Viewed in this light, his belief that a private company could save 15 and 20 percent building and staffing a prison gains context, but still remains somewhat inexplicable. Did Jeb really believe that the Department of Corrections staff was so inept that it gave out 15 percent more on construction contracts than it needed to? Did he think that the prison system, which in 1994 was already overstretched and paying some of the lowest wages in state government, was bloated by a full one-fifth?

"Bush is either appallingly ignorant or he is a supreme cynic who is playing the public not merely for fools, but for morons," said *St. Petersburg Times* columnist Martin Dyckman at the time.

This is perhaps the most amazing thing about Jeb: while he is, at times, a cynic, and he really cannot be called ignorant because of his honest efforts to gather facts, he pushes ahead with his most fervent goals anyway, regardless of those facts.

It is a true faith-based government—not faith in any Supreme Being, but in an eighteenth-century Scottish economist and his "invisible hand."

WHEN JEB and like-minded devotees of Adam Smith get going, facts generally are cast aside. The facts from history, for example.

The free-marketeer, antiregulation, *get the government out of the way* types either do not know or do not care what has come before. They complain about environmental regulations, about how burdensome they are to businesses. They complain about unions. They complain about OSHA's picky safety rules. They go on, arms waving, often to cheers and whoops at business roundtables and similar groups, about what a wonderful world it would be if only all these silly rules and regulations would just go away.

Well, the world has already seen how wonderfully an unfettered approach to capitalism works. If anyone needs a refresher course, just read some Charles Dickens. London, England, home of industrial capitalism, the first beneficiary of Mr. Smith's "Invisible Hand," was just a dandy place to live, if you happened to be a factory owner.

If you happened to be a factory worker, well . . . not so much.

Eighteenth-century England was exactly the unregulated dreamland that Jeb and his friends talk about, sort of a Disney World for capitalists. People would lose limbs in the new machines that were making the factory owners rich. Once maimed, these underproductive slackers would get fired, pushed out into the street, and replacement workers would be brought in—of which there was quite a surplus, thanks to the forced migration of the rural poor to the cities. To further help the low-end labor market, there were poorhouses. And because there was none of this pesky, universal public schooling, the ten-and-under set made for a perfect pool of agile, smaller workers more readily able to climb down into the guts of the machines.

Factory owners didn't have to worry about scrubbing their smokestacks or cleaning up their effluent or any of that silly hooey. Why should they have to, when they had the London skies and the River Thames?

The air over London got so foul that the masters of England's universe unintentionally proved one of the central tenets of evolution. Before all the pollution, the dominant color of the peppered moth, *Biston betularia,* was white. After the industrial revolution had been underway for a while, gray became the dominant shade—white became too easily spotted by hungry birds—thereby showing that natural selection really works. And it has taken England the better part of a century to clean the Thames to a point where it is no longer a complete embarrassment.

All these woes had one thing in common: they were factors for which no short-term, natural disincentive existed in the market. If you're not required to pay workers' compensation premiums and face no sanctions from an OSHA-type body, for example, it makes no sense to worry about keeping your workers safe, unless they require specialized training that would cost you time and money. If you can hire a twelve-year-old for a few shillings less than a grown man, why wouldn't you? And as for the pollution, if someone wants to complain about the oily sludge you're putting into the river, you can rightly argue that it's not *their* river, now is it?

Unregulated capitalism has the same rules as unrestricted warfare or a Bush family political campaign, which is to say: none. It's a race to the bottom. Whatever the other guy is willing to do, if you don't do the same and then some, you lose.

It's not as if governments love regulating things. Regulating something that is currently unregulated involves work, and no bureaucratic entity is voluntarily going to add to its workload. We have regulations because human greed is so powerful that people will do just about anything for a buck, including maiming children and poisoning water.

Now, granted, regulations frequently get out of hand. Agencies with overlapping jurisdictions don't communicate with each other. Mid-level bureaucrats love to guard their fiefdoms. Rules and regulations and forms get layered onto each other until a periodic, commonsense analysis of matching desired objectives and necessary paperwork is a good idea.

There is a big difference between wanting to streamline regulations to make them work better and wanting simply to eliminate them. In Florida, Jeb has always been on the far side of this divide.

IN THE AREA of growth management, for example, Jeb's first instinct, and the thrust of his legislative initiatives when he came into office, was essentially to do away with it.

This was the Florida Growth Management Act of 1985, which at the time was a national landmark for trying to manage the construction of new homes and shops and roads and all the *stuff* that goes with it by forcing both local and state governments to lay out rational plans. This part of the county for housing, this part for commercial, and this out here to remain rural, or as wilderness, to serve as "water recharge" for the area ground water. The law was cutting edge, back when it passed, but over the years had faced ever more problems, primarily because local governments—which in Florida are generally the most easily influenced (read: "purchased") by the concrete coalition—have perennially wanted to scrap their original plans in favor of more "job creating, tax-base broadening" development.

Jeb correctly assessed that the law was not working as intended. His solution? "Devolve" the power down to local governments—the same entities that have for two decades sought out ways to get around building restrictions. Would that have helped the quality of life in Florida? *More* strip malls and cookie-cutter homes on roads and schools already packed to overflowing?

Yet that in most cases has been Jeb's answer to solving complicated problems—reducing government's involvement in the solution. That, in fact, goes to an important catechism in Capitalist Theology: all would be well if government just got out of the way. Education and health care "reform," therefore, are predicated on the idea that if you simply end the government "monopoly" of public schools and of the public health systems, education and medical care for poor and middle class and rich alike will improve dramatically.

This is proof positive of how reliant on faith, and how willfully ignorant of actual facts, this ideology really is. History alone should provide some important clues.

Why did public schools even get started? Was it because government bureaucrats badly wanted to interfere in the free market and put out of business all those fine, private institutions providing high-quality, low-cost schooling to all those poor and rural children? Or was it that all those poor and rural children were *not getting* an education because it was something their families could not afford?

Compare primary education, for example, with the manufacture of shoes. Why was it that governments never got into the shoe-making business? (Although, as a side note, recall that footwear manufacture was something that Jeb got involved in briefly, in his "Get Rich Quick" years.) Was it because government bureaucrats somehow forgot to meddle in it? Or might it have been that enough cobblers were out there making a decent enough profit to shod all those people who desired shoes?

And right there is the key to why Jeb's voucher plans failed. For as much as Jeb talks about and reveres the profit motive in the functioning of all things great and small, he ignores its absence in schools and public hospitals.

Because here is a simple fact: you don't get rich teaching children or making poor, sick people better. Education and public health are purely money-losing propositions. If you handed over public schools and public clinics to one of the big Wall Street firms and said, here, maximize earnings from these, they would quickly shut them down and sell off the buildings.

I'm not sure why this is such a difficult thing to grasp. We as a society educate children and care for the poor because we've decided over the past few centuries that it's the right thing to do, not because it's profitable. Sure, the education component produces a fundamental good—a better-educated populace is likely to engage in more economically beneficial activities. But that is a long-term benefit, something that free markets are notoriously bad at evaluating correctly. As to providing health care for the poor—well, to be crass, there isn't even a long-term benefit there at all. (Other than the wickedly devious idea that the poor ought not be allowed to die off too much, lest we drive up labor costs for lawn guys and burger flippers.)

This is not to suggest that companies cannot grow rich by handling outsourced government contracts in these areas. There are plenty of for-profit educators and health-care providers who are happy to take public money for public services and convert a healthy fraction of it into private profits. Bringing in these folks misses the point. These companies in general were not there before government paid for these services and they won't be there if government stopped paying for them.

In fact, here's a pretty handy guide to understanding whether something can work in a profit-driven, market environment: Do the individuals involved in the actual delivery of the services mainly do it for the money? Or do they do it out of a sense of calling?

Most good teachers you've met are smart, dedicated, and love children. They think teaching is doing God's work. They probably could be earning a lot more in some other field, if money had been their primary motive. Same thing with child-welfare workers, police officers, nurses, and the clergy (who, I guess, really *are* doing God's work).

All of these enterprises, with the possible exception of nurses in specialties like plastic surgery, are money-losing ventures. You don't see Goldman Sachs and Smith Barney fighting over who will underwrite a new convent.

THERE IS NO private market for free health care for the poor. There is no private market for high-quality, low-cost schooling. There never has been. There never will be.

And yet Americans have come to expect good public schools and good public health care, even as they suggest through the stated ideologies of the leaders they put forward, that they believe in capitalism and the free market and reject socialism.

That, right there, is the crux of the problem. Our collective knowledge of and interest in economics is so low that we have created any number of institutions that merge the absolute worst features of both government ownership and private ownership with few benefits of either.

Americans say they do not want a national health care system like Canada's because it is socialistic. Oh, really? And what is it that we have today? We have socialist health care for the elderly and we have socialist health care for the poor. In fact, the very concept of insurance—spreading risk across a broad swath to minimize individual costs in the event of calamity—is fundamentally a socialist notion. If we were actually the rugged individualists we think we are, we would pay for the medical care we needed or wanted, without the security blanket of health insurance, and accept the consequences, with the devil taking the hindmost.

The same argument could be made regarding public schools, and public fire departments and libraries and on and on and on. As a society, we have come to expect a goodly number of services from government—services that we see as basic rights, not privileges. Every single one of these things could be handled by individuals on their own, or by private entities through memberships and user fees.

Despite all this, we do not see the "socialism" in these things, and in fact give strong victory margins to politicians who make a big deal out of proclaiming how antisocialist and pro-capitalist they are. In Florida, the most absurd result of this dynamic was the creation and continued support of a state-run property insurance scheme that not only redistributed the risk of losses, but did so in a way that actually helped the well-off at the expense of everybody else.

After Hurricane Andrew wrecked southern Dade County in 1992, Florida elected officials responded to the disinclination of private insurers to write new homeowners policies in areas seen as particularly vulnerable to storms. To growth-mad Florida, this was a potential nightmare: without property insurance, banks would not lend money for mortgages. Without mortgages, the entire real estate business, both commercial and residential, would go to hell. So the legislature's response? Create a state-run insurance company that would handle *only the riskiest policies* that private insurers would not touch. To make sure of this, the company, which in its later iteration became known as Citizens Property Insurance, could not price premiums any lower than the commercially available rate.

That consumer groups did not go absolutely berserk over this was incredible, given that deficits caused by catastrophic, Andrew-type storms would be covered by "assessments" levied on *every* policy in the state, whether it was written by Citizens or a private insurer. Imagine that. The state of Florida had created an entity specifically to maintain the profitability of private insurance companies, at the expense of every resident. The only fair way to accomplish such a scheme would have been to create a single insurance pool, so as to spread the *benefit* of mild hurricane seasons, as well as the downside of bad storm years, across all Florida.

Of course, such a thing would have seemed too much like socialism—even though insurance *is* socialism—and so it was never even discussed. The richest irony of all this is that the main beneficiaries of Citizens are residents of storm-vulnerable areas along the coast. The biggest dollar-value beneficiaries are the residents right *on* the coast, the multi-million-dollar homes and mansions of the state's most exclusive beach cities.

JEB NEVER really encountered that much resistance to his never-ending goal of shrinking government. The union representing many state workers complained, but as Florida is a "right to work" state, the group never got much empathy from the general public.

Jeb probably could have accomplished all of these various outsourcing goals with nary a second glance, had his appointees not screwed them up so badly and attracted numerous audits and investigations. The State Technology Office, as mentioned above, was a complete disaster—so much so that even Jeb eventually conceded as much and abolished the thing, moving its functions into his Department of Management Services. The Convergys contract defied common sense from the start: why would as large an operation as the State of Florida, with some 120,000 employees, want to farm out its human resources work? The whole point of outsourcing is to pay others to do work that you cannot cost-effectively manage yourself. This is why most large corporations do most of their own bookkeeping, their own lawyering, and, yes, their own payroll and benefits. The economies of scale involved in large companies minimize the benefit of outsourcing, not to mention the loss of accountability and control when an outside entity is so integrally involved in such a vital function.

Despite this, Jeb pushed ahead. His people originally promised a savings of $173 million during the course of the $262 million, seven-year contract. Then they revised that down to a $93 million savings. Then things started going badly, as Milligan predicted they would, and the contract ballooned to nine years and $350 million, while the savings shrank to $25 million.

The elimination of one of the three state-paid Capital Collateral Representative offices, which represented death row inmates, was done not particularly to eliminate jobs, but to punish those who held them for performing them too well. It was the opinion of Jeb and his people that as state employees, the lawyers for condemned inmates should be willing members of the death-penalty apparatus. It infuriated them that many of the lawyers in the offices—big surprise here—actually opposed the death penalty on moral grounds, and worked as hard as they could to slow down executions and get their clients' sentences changed to life imprisonment. Which is to say: did their jobs. And so Jeb, with a willing Republican legislature, replaced the northern district office with a registry of private lawyers, many of them with little or no experience in death cases. It got so bad that Florida Supreme Court justice Raoul Cantero—a longtime ally of Jeb before he appointed him to the court—accused the private attorneys of "the worst lawyering I've seen." He said their incompetence was actually slowing down the progress of death cases—which was the exact reason that death penalty advocates Governor Bob Graham and Attorney General Jim Smith pushed for the creation of the state CCR office in the first place, two decades earlier.

A *Palm Beach Post* review of Jeb's privatization of foster care found caseworkers and foster families who saw it as privatization merely for privatization's sake. Said one caseworker: "They were given a pretty well-functioning system and blew it to bits." One foster parent, talking about penny-pinching over basic services, called the old, state-run system an aging but serviceable Chevy with a few dents: "What they did was they traded in the Chevy and got us a Yugo."

Others became more agitated about the penny-pinching, particularly when they realized that Jeb's DCF was letting *for-profit* companies in on the foster-care game. One, Family Preservation Services, actually made $1.3 million in profits on $19.2 revenues for foster-care contracts in southern and central Florida. That upset even Republicans, including state senator Evelyn Lynn: "If you can make a profit on anything we are doing, then that means we are doing something wrong."

DESPITE THESE and other setbacks, Jeb even late into his second term remained so enamored of the private sector that he pushed to extend it to Florida's massive Medicaid program—representing potentially $12 billion worth of new outsourcing. Instead of having the state handle reimbursements to doctors and hospitals, Jeb instead wanted to give private insurers and health maintenance organizations fixed amounts for each patient, and then let those companies decide who could see which doctor for what procedures.

Had this been three decades earlier, when HMOs were still new and being touted as the way to control costs and improve medical care, Jeb's promises that his plan would do the same for Florida's 2.2 million poor people—one of every seven residents—might have held some credibility.

Yet by 2005 and 2006, with many if not most Americans dissatisfied with the hassles required to get even basic care from their HMOs, Jeb's claims were downright laughable. How could HMOs possibly deliver better care to patients when they would supposedly get 9 percent less per patient than what the state had been paying previously, as Jeb's Agency for Health Care Administration was proposing? The only way to manage that, as well as to earn the profits that their shareholders expect, was to deny medical services or create discouraging obstacles to patients who wanted them—which is exactly what HMOs do in the private sector.

It should be remembered that this grand experiment with HMOs was already tried with Medicare, the federal plan for the elderly. And it quickly became evident that the private market could not come anywhere near matching Medicare's 3 percent overhead. Not when 10 to 25 percent of their revenue is tied up paying big salaries to administrators and creating the bureaucracy necessary to say no to services, and then back up that denial with the required layers of appeals. How was all this less expensive than simply reimbursing doctors and hospitals under the traditional fee-for-service arrangement? It was not, at least with Medicare. Not even close.

No matter, Jeb pushed ahead anyway, with claims that, unchecked, Medicaid would swallow the vast majority of the entire state budget within a decade. To its credit, the Florida Senate and its leader, Republican Tom Lee, did not roll over for Jeb, and after a year of haggling gave him a two-year "pilot" program in two parts of the state to see if the proposal actually worked. Any statewide expansion would occur after Jeb had left office—thereby providing a more reasonable chance that facts, not Jeb's personal ideology, would drive the decision.

THERE WERE, through the Jeb years, two notable deviations from capitalist doctrine. One made itself known during Florida's Year of the Hur-

ricane, 2004, when Jeb showed that even he understood full well the public's limited understanding of, and patience with, market theology.

It was during that unprecedented autumn, when four powerful storms
slammed the state within a span of six weeks, that Florida government, *Jeb's*
government, first immersed itself into the gasoline distribution market. One
hand reached out for help, his people calling distributors, requesting that
shipments to certain areas be given priority—even as the other closed into
a fist, threatening gas station owners who price gouged with prosecution.

It seemed a bit odd even then, to have such a devoted fan of the free
market suddenly talking like a member of the Central Committee of the
Worker State. (In fact, a news conference question that alluded to the similarities to a planned economy drew a testy rebuke.) Even the normally
Republican-friendly Fox News asked Florida officials what the distinction
was between "price gouging" on the one hand and everyday "what the
market will bear" pricing on the other.

But, in the end, Floridians from one end of the state to the other were
going through a daily hell, and it seemed like a humane thing to shield
them from this one worry in their time of woe. And so, even those who
might ordinarily have attributed Jeb's motives to the impending election
and the close race his brother was facing tended to give him the benefit
of the doubt, given the circumstances.

Skip ahead one year. This time, it wasn't four hurricanes hitting Florida,
but one massive killer storm hitting Louisiana and Mississippi. Granted, Katrina did first cross South Florida on her way to New Orleans, but the damage was slight. No seaports were severely damaged. No roads were wrecked.
In other words, the storm had done nothing to slow down the transport
or distribution of motor fuel.

It didn't matter. Katrina *did* do a number on the Gulf coast of Louisiana,
shutting down gasoline refineries and pipelines. And that was enough for
Jeb, who vowed that service stations and distributors who price gouged
would be prosecuted.

This was his explanation, when asked how it could be defined as price
gouging if the hurricane in question had not struck anywhere near the
service station with the higher-priced gas:

> I don't know what the law is, but I would consider it price gouging
> even if it's in Alaska. It's price gouging if you are raising your price,
> under our laws, if you raise your price, irrespective of cost, beyond a
> certain threshold. The same commodity, if you buy it at X and you sell

it at Y for a profit, that's great. But when you take advantage of the situation and raise prices even more, I think that's price gouging, irrespective of whether it's in a hurricane-impacted area or in an area that hasn't been hit by the storm. . . . In an emergency situation, all bets are off.

How did he know when the price hikes had gone beyond that "certain threshold"?

I don't understand every little nook and cranny of the gas and oil business, the gasoline business, but if you change your prices three times in a day, or two times in a day, and it's the same gas that you had in your tank, there is no justification for that. So if people are taking advantage of the anticipated higher prices—generally, I think, people accept . . . that [if] you wipe out a significant part of your production, that you're going to have increases in price; that's just Economics 101. In anticipation of that, to raise prices for fuel that you have already purchased at a lower price, that is what our laws are trying to get with. And the commissioner [of Agriculture and Consumer Services], and the attorney general, and this office will work together to make sure that that's not tolerated.

Then he gave out the toll-free number for people to rat out those doing this bad raising of prices, not just in gasoline, but on any commodity that "people desperately need."

Just to make sure I was hearing this right, I asked what a reasonable profit would be on a gallon of gasoline. His answer: "Two or three cents."

Got it?

Point A: Buying something at one price and selling it a price more than a percent or two higher is price gouging. Point B: There's no nexus necessary between an actual disaster event in Florida and the ability of the Florida governor to invoke his disaster-related powers banning price gouging. It's an emergency if Jeb says it is.

BEAR IN MIND here that this isn't a service traditionally provided by government—like the schools—that Jeb believes should instead be done by the private sector. This is an activity that has *always* been done completely by the private sector, which now Jeb believes needs strong government manipulation.

In fact, if ever there was a rationale to letting the market runs its course and set a price, it is in this instance, where there is a limited quantity of a desirable and economically necessary commodity. Let's follow the logic of both scenarios to their conclusion: first, if the gasoline price were allowed to rise freely according to supply and demand, it would no doubt rise to a point where people would buy enough *only* for necessary driving to work and school. Weekend joy rides, short errands, and so forth would likely be curtailed or eliminated, and the reduction in demand would have the effect of preserving quantity, albeit at a higher price. But under Jeb's cajoling and threats, prices would be kept artificially low—thereby failing to discourage the unnecessary driving, and leading to shortages even for those wanting it for necessary driving.

It really was a thing of beauty, this trip down the rabbit hole and emergence somewhere during Mao's Great Leap Forward or Fidel's Glorious Sugar Harvest. The more Jeb tried to explain himself, the more breathtaking it was, hearing from his lips the distinction between appropriate and inappropriate profits. Two or three cents on a gallon of gas.

Should that ratio be applied to others in the buying and selling game? Say, for instance, real estate deals? Say, to be more precise, *Jeb's* real estate deals from the 1980s? How about, for example, we applied this to his Museum Tower deal that saw him earn a $345,000 profit on a $1,000 investment in a span of six years. By Jeb's calculus, a two percent *per anum* profit would have yielded an appropriate selling price of $1,126.16 after six years. Meaning Jeb "price gouged" to the tune of $344,873.84.

Now, this is not to ridicule consumer protection laws generally or even price gouging specifically. Government probably does have a role to protect its citizens who, because of exigent circumstances, are vulnerable to those whose greed outweighs their scruples.

The important distinction here is "exigent circumstances." What was the emergency facing Florida that justified Jeb's intrusion into his beloved free market? What if, instead of a neighboring state, Katrina had hit Venezuela's main oil-shipment terminal? What if there had been no hurricane at all, and demand simply outstripped supply, as it sooner or later (probably sooner) will?

The important lesson here is that for Jeb, the "emergency" was the political one he and George W. could have faced in Florida, if motorists had suddenly faced four-dollar gasoline. Worship of the free market, as it turns out, only goes so far.

It goes exactly as far, in fact, as the political health and well-being of the Bush family. And in those rare instances when there is conflict between the two, as Jeb might say: "All bets are off."

In the end, though, Jeb's adventures with gasoline are useful mainly as an academic case study. Even most die-hard conservatives backed his stance, particularly when the price at the pump leaped past three dollars per gallon. Jeb's second departure from the strictures of laissez-faire markets was somewhat more subtle and, to the typical Floridian, considerably less populist in its effect.

IF YOU DRIVE with any frequency from Florida's Cocoa Beach toward Orlando along the Beeline Expressway, chances are that you will come across one or two or several Mack dump trucks. Great, big giant dump trucks. And inside these dump trucks are small stones—the makings of concrete, the lifeblood of the Sunshine State.

These stones are unloaded at Port Canaveral and then piled into these trucks for transport to wherever new construction is needed in Central Florida, which is to say: everywhere. When we say "piled" into these trucks, we mean literally—so that the tops of the mounds extend well above the rim of the truck bed. Stretched over the top of the truck bed is a fabric covering, ostensibly to keep said stones from popping up and out of the truck bed and into your windshield. However, the efficacy of this safety feature is somewhat diminished by the foot-tall gap between the fabric and the rear of the truck bed.

This means—you guessed it—that whenever one of these trucks bounces over a bump or even a seam in the pavement, a quantity of these stones bounces out of the truck bed to become projectiles for drivers behind them to avoid.

Not to worry, though: once you get fed up dodging this grapeshot and decide to pass said truck, you see the two-inch block letters printed on the rear advising drivers to remain 100 feet back and further advising that objects falling out of the truck are not the responsibility of the trucking company.

It would be funny, if it weren't so deadly. The sign, naturally, isn't legible unless you're within twenty feet. And really, when you get right down it, the physics of the raining rock are such that you're *better off* driving into one from twenty or fifty or one hundred feet—when the stone is still traveling close to the speed of your car—than you would be hitting one from three hundred feet back, when it might be traveling 20 mph compared to your car windshield's 70 mph.

It's a thing of beauty, that sign. Not responsible for falling rocks. Then whose responsibility, pray tell, might they be?

Well, here's the real funny, or deadly, part: in Florida, thanks to Jeb and his allies, the fault might well be yours, by law, and not the trucking company's.

Think about that. Here this company as a general practice overloads its trucks in order to maximize its profits. Then it runs these missile launchers not on its own privately maintained streets, but on State Road 528, a public four-lane expressway.

So what if one of these rocks were to come crashing through your windshield, making you lose control, flip your car, and end up paralyzed from the neck down for the rest of your life with a mortgage to pay, children to put through college, and brand-new nursing costs?

Under bills pushed into law by Jeb under the banner of "tort reform," chances are much greater that you will be out of luck, beyond what your medical insurance, Social Security, and, ultimately, Medicaid would pay.

Now, granted, Jeb is not the only Republican in the country, or even Florida, to push for laws and rules to make it harder to sue businesses. The Florida legislature in 1998, before Jeb was elected, passed a tort reform bill, only to see then-governor Lawton Chiles veto it.

The statistics of the policy debate, whether the number of lawsuits is increasing faster or more slowly than the population, and whether the average, inflation-adjusted jury award is growing or shrinking, are beyond the scope of this book. More to the point here is that for all the lip service Jeb gives to the concepts of accountability and personal responsibility, that pretty much goes out the window when the persons involved are corporate executives and their profit-making businesses. In those cases, Jeb's vision for the interplay between the individual and the community completely flip-flops. In those cases, the greater good for Florida or America or the world is served by letting these entities get away with some measure of negligence and having society as a whole pay for their messes. Better that victims of deadly accidents caused by Ford Explorers or Bridgestone tires be taken care of by socialistic safety nets than the companies and their shareholders suffer financially. Maybe that's a harsh analysis, but that's the one offered by one of the top business lobbyists who pushed for tort reform, Jon Shebel.

Let's accept that at least some of Jeb's enthusiasm for stopping law-suits—even after the 1999 victory, he was back in 2001 trying to limit lawsuits against nursing homes, in 2003 trying to limit lawsuits against doctors and hospitals, and in 2005 and 2006 trying to push even stronger protections for businesses generally—is his view of the trial bar as his po-litical enemy. In what he thought was a private conversation with his sup-porters prior to his 2002 reelection, Jeb said: "We need to whack the trial lawyers."

It's unseemly at best "to whack" any large group, regardless of the po-litical proclivities of its members, but surely Jeb understood the collateral damage of his stance on victims of negligence. He understood it, but pro-ceeded full tilt anyway. For a man who, as a candidate in 1994, was ready to impose strict time limits on welfare benefits and was telling single moms to find husbands, and who, as governor, cannot get through a speech with-out mentioning the need for "accountability," his position was spectacu-larly hypocritical.

IN THE END, Jeb's blind faith in private enterprise and his single-minded goal of slashing state jobs, regardless of the costs and benefits involved, earned him an embarrassing black eye in an area where he should have shone: basic competence.

His harshest critics believe that Jeb's efforts to privatize were simply a "pay to play" reimbursement scheme, in which he steered contracts to top GOP political donors. And while this rationale does surface, sometimes overtly, sometimes subconsciously, in other politicians, I believe such an ac-cusation about Jeb is misplaced. Those critics who make it underestimate the enormity of his ego. Jeb personally does not go out of his way to re-ward political donors with contracts or anything else, because he truly be-lieves he is doing us all a favor by serving as our leader. In that context, he is pleased that rich people and their corporations donate to him and his party, but he sees it more as his rightful due, as the natural order of things, than as behavior that needs to be acknowledged and rewarded. So in a strange way, his core belief that he was born to rule serves to limit venal tendencies. Unfortunately for Floridians, not all, perhaps not even most, of his political appointees got that memo.

Because even in the best-case world, where Jeb could clone dozens of himself and administer his outsourcing jihad without fear or favor, there would still be the difficult problem of proving that a particular contract made sense financially. When low-rent corruption mars the process, an observer doesn't even get to that stage before coming to the reasonable conclusion that the whole scheme was fundamentally screwed up.

A perfect example: two of Jeb's top Department of Children and Families administrators were forced to resign after they were caught accepting gifts from companies that held contracts with the agency. Ben Harris took a $10,000 trip to Australia paid for by InterSystems, a computer company, and a $163 massage from a computer media company during a conference in Palm Desert, California. Glen Palmiere got the same Australia trip but also got a free hotel room along with his massage. And a week after a trip to Las Vegas that included a round of golf with InterSystems representatives, Palmiere wrote to DCF employees to "make sure that all the potential roadblocks that once existed in getting a contract signed with InterSystems do not exist."

An episode like this one, by itself, perhaps could be called isolated. But on top of the Convergys fiasco, the State Technology Office mess, and various and sundry other problems, it was the successes of Jeb's privatization initiative, not the failures, that were the isolated incidents.

In 2005, the former director of the by-then defunct Correctional Privatization Commission was indicted by a federal grand jury for stealing nearly $225,000 in state money. The group had been entrusted with overseeing the state's five privately run prisons, but a state audit found "numerous instances where vendors' interests were considered over state interests." Because of this, and because of the commission's willingness to cover various "questionable and excessive costs," the Department of Corrections' inspector general concluded that there was no way to determine whether the private prisons had been any cheaper to operate than the traditional public ones.

That, writ large, would have been equally true of Jeb's privatization initiative as a whole.

FINALLY, Jeb's efforts to shrink government by outsourcing its duties carried real social costs that deserved some attention but were ignored in the privatization calculus. Put simply: When people who used to get higher salaries, medical benefits, and retirement from the state of Florida stop getting these things, Florida as a whole suffers.

And that, typically, is what happens when private corporations take over services that formally had been handled by state workers. In fact, it *has* to happen. For-profit companies that ran juvenile delinquency centers, for example, paid their workers $17,906 a year, according to a 2005 state legislative analysis done following a *Palm Beach Post* investigation. State workers in identical jobs had median salaries of $22,762.

That is how private enterprise works. Business owners and shareholders are in it to make a profit. In other words, the total amount of money that the state gives to the company to provide that particular service has built into it a profit of 5 or 7 or 10 or whatever percent. That total amount, in theory, should be less than what the government had been spending to perform that same task. The total of those two values is how much less Florida workers get as a result of that particular outsourcing, either from fewer employees or from smaller compensation packages or both. And while some of that new profit went to Florida business owners, much of it flowed to out-of-state corporations and shareholders.

So what happens when people lose their medical benefits? Often they simply show up at public emergency rooms, or end up on the Medicaid rolls. It's the same story when people lose retirement benefits. Ultimately, one way or another, we all pay for those services that we, as a society, have decided that not even the poor should have to do without in the world's richest nation.

Now, most conservatives, many moderates, and even some liberals will argue that it is not government's job to provide work for its citizens. Most people, regardless of their political affiliations, would probably agree that government-sponsored make work is not a good idea.

That, however, is not what we're talking about here. These are existing state programs that provide generally valued services. It's the method of delivery, not the need for the service, that is in question.

And in that question, a fair analysis should take into account that diminishment of wages and benefits to Floridians, versus the increased costs to local, state, and federal governments to provide those people what they have lost. Is it worth it? This transmogrification of money for Florida residents into profits for largely out-of-state corporations?

This, by the way, was an analysis that caught the attention of at least one Republican state House member, Carlos Lacasa—a man so conservative that he listed as a hobby in his Clerk's Manual entry: "capitalism." Perhaps it was that interest, though, that let Lacasa see the big picture of wealth and capital. Discussing the problems with privatized prisons way back in 2001, in Jeb's first term, Lacasa said: "We've transferred wealth from state agencies to the private sector. We're not in the business of transferring wealth. We're in the business of providing services."

During Jeb's tenure, Lacasa's point of view was so scarce as to be nonexistent. Some Democrats were raising those issues, as well as some liberal public policy groups. But within Jeb's administration itself? The questions never came up.

Chapter Seven

KENDRICK MEEK

"Probably nothing."
—JEB BUSH, 1994, WHEN ASKED BY AN
AUDIENCE MEMBER IN A CAMPAIGN DEBATE WHAT
HE WOULD DO FOR THE BLACK COMMUNITY

"Democrats have taken the black vote for granted and Republicans have never tried, but that dynamic has changed."
—JEB BUSH, 1998

"Kick their asses out."
—JEB BUSH, 2000, TELLING AIDES WHAT HAD
TO BE DONE TO END A SIT-IN BY TWO
BLACK LEGISLATORS. JEB LATER CLAIMED
HE WAS REFERRING NOT TO THE
LEGISLATORS, BUT TO THE REPORTERS
WHO WERE HOLED UP WITH THEM.

On November 3, 1998, the governor's race election results generated a tremor that threatened lasting damage to the Democratic Party, not just in Florida, but nationally. It was not that John Ellis Bush had won, becoming only the third Republican governor since Reconstruction—that had been a foregone conclusion even among most Democrats for more than a year.

No, the seismic event was evidenced in the exit polling that found that Jeb had taken a full 14 percent of the black vote that election. On its face, that may not seem like a big deal, but to close observers of American politics, it was extraordinary: not just a Republican, but a *conservative* Republican who four years earlier had offered blacks at best casual indifference had attracted fully one out of every seven black voters, perhaps double what the typical Republican candidate was used to seeing. Even more incredible: it had happened not in some liberal bastion like Massachusetts or Minnesota, but in Florida, a proud member of the Solid South going back five decades.

The implications were enormous. If Republicans could break the Democratic Party's lock on black support, it could completely change the dynamics of elections all over the country. If Democrats who had been used to winning 90 percent of a constituency that makes up as much as 15 percent of the electorate instead began winning only 80 percent, or 70 percent, they would be in trouble in statehouses and congressional districts just about everywhere.

That was in the heady days of 1999. Skip ahead now barely a year, to the opening day of the 2000 legislative session in Tallahassee and the occasion of the largest political demonstration in decades to converge on the capital city. The vast majority of the faces in the crowd were black, and all of them were mad—many holding hand-lettered signs reading "Jeb Crow" and "Bushit."

So what happened? How in a span of just fifteen months could Jeb go from the model of the new, Republican leader who could cross a decades-old racial line, to one being compared to a Klansman?

Well, part of it is, of course, Jeb. He is who he is, and he was bound to do something sooner or later to irritate black people and then, when he was criticized, react peevishly to make matters worse. He has done that to pretty much every constituency in Florida, with the possible exception of evangelical Christians and super-rich investors. The offended parties generally sulk quietly for a while but, knowing Jeb's thin skin and penchant for getting even, do not publicly criticize him, and eventually return to the fold.

What happened differently in this case was the rise of a black leader as extraordinary as Jeb himself, who over Jeb's two terms served as his most effective antagonist and who, without Jeb, would have remained in relative obscurity. Like an unbalanced force in particle physics or an eastern religion, Jeb's own strength of personality helped generate his opposite number—a man who nearly dragged brother George W. down to defeat in the 2000 election and two years later hung a budgetary albatross around Jeb's neck that tormented him through his entire second term.

HE MAY go down in the annals of early twenty-first-century Florida history as the single most important catalyst for improvement in the Sunshine State's dismal public education system. He could be remembered as the man who single-handedly dragged state government, kicking and screaming, to let Florida public schools vault past the likes of Mississippi and Alabama into the middle of the national pack.

To Jeb's unending resentment, he will not be that man. Even worse, it will be his nemesis—the man who inflicted more political damage on Jeb than both his election opponents combined.

Meet former Miami state senator, and now congressman, Kendrick Meek—the anti-Jeb.

For it was Kendrick Meek who strolled into Jeb's suite in January of 2000, and then staged a sixties-style sit-in when Jeb refused to meet with him to discuss Jeb's unilateral ending of affirmative action programs in Florida. A 10,000-person protest march followed on the legislature's opening day that year, and then a massive voter registration drive that summer— a drive that nearly cost Jeb's brother the presidential election in November when black turnout increased 280,000 over what it would have been had it tracked the 1996 pattern. Without Meek, George W. would have won Florida easily, just as most Democratic and Republican politicos had been predicting early on in 2000.

Two years later, Meek accomplished the feat that could make him Florida's foremost champion of education when he pushed for and won a citizen's initiative that enshrined in the Florida constitution a requirement to limit class sizes in public schools. Meek said he was driven to act by the thirty-five children in his own third grader's class—not by the obvious political implications. Whatever the motive, by 2003 Florida's constitution dictated that the legislature and governor would have to reduce class sizes by two children per year until, by autumn of 2010, kindergartens through third grade could have no more than eighteen children, fourth through eighth grades no more than twenty-two, and ninth through twelfth no more than twenty-five.

2000: Jeb explains to black legislators and other Democrats his decision
to dismantle affirmative-action programs and replace them with his One
Florida initiative. The two men seated immediately to his left, Tony Hill and
Kendrick Meek, had staged an overnight, sixties-style sit-in in his office to
protest his decision. Meek, now a Miami congressman, quickly became Jeb's
political nemesis during his two terms as governor.

The year Meek's class-size amendment passed was also the year Jeb ran for reelection. Jeb, in fact, ran harder against the amendment than he did against his Democratic opponent, Bill McBride, particularly by mid-October, when it was clear that Jeb was far ahead.

On November 5, 2002, Jeb had beat McBride. But in a curious turn, Kendrick Meek beat Jeb—thereby simultaneously forcing Florida to spend more on its schools, and making Jeb's top priority of additional, large permanent tax cuts difficult if not impossible.

It's an interesting contrast, Kendrick and Jeb. They are both physically big men. Kendrick played football in college; Jeb played tennis. Kendrick has a big smile; Jeb, rarely so. On first blush, Kendrick can seem bumbling, an inarticulate but well-meaning goofball prone to malapropisms and mispronunciations. Up against Jeb's polish, it doesn't seem a fair fight.

Here, as elsewhere, appearances can be deceiving. For Kendrick Meek, like Jeb, is a legacy politician.

When he was a lad, his mother, Carrie Meek, was in the Florida House and then the Florida Senate, and Kendrick served as a legislative page and tagged along as mom became known for her fiery oratory—her insistence that bills she disliked be killed "black-flag dead!"

In 1992, Carrie Meek made Florida history, becoming one of the first three black members of Congress since Reconstruction following the drawing of black and Hispanic seats in a court-ordered redistricting. Kendrick's success tracked his mother's. He graduated from Florida A&M, where he played linebacker, and entered the Florida Highway Patrol, winning a political promotion through the ranks to make captain and win the relatively cushy assignment of driving around the lieutenant governor.

In 1994, Kendrick left the police business and ran for and won a seat in the House. In 1998, he risked that seat to take on incumbent state senator Bill Turner, beating him soundly in the Democratic primary for the seat his mother had once held.

And it was as a state senator that he got fellow black caucus member Tony Hill to walk down to the governor's office that day and see what trouble they could cause. At that point, a full two months after Jeb had unrolled his "One Florida" plan to eliminate the overt use of race in state contracts and university admissions, most black leaders had expressed statements of regret and disappointment. It took Meek to do something a little more forceful.

In 2001, Carrie Meek announced her retirement, so it was as he was starting the campaign to inherit her seat—a campaign, by the way, that he would have had a tough time losing, given his name and her popularity—that he also started his campaign to put school class sizes on the November ballot.

That spring, he had attempted to run the proposal through the legislature—a so-called "joint resolution" that would permit the ballot question without needing to collect some 500,000 signatures. Naturally, the idea didn't have a prayer with Republicans controlling both chambers. It is a measure of his tenacity that he pushed incredible odds to collect the signatures, fought Jeb's attempts in court to keep the question off the ballot, and then overcame Jeb's enormous and publicly funded campaign to defeat the question at the ballot box.

Ultimately, the class-size amendment proved to be an unending tribulation for Jeb through his entire second term. He hated it, not only because of the money he would be forced to spend on education and not on his beloved tax cuts, but because it was Kendrick. In 2000, when Jeb had learned that Meek was in his lieutenant governor's office, and was threatening to stay there until he could get a meeting, Jeb went down to poke his head in and tell him that he had better get some blankets, because he could be there a while. That remark almost cost his brother the White House. Two years later, Meek had outmaneuvered him again.

JEB IS NOT a racist. He does not believe that white people are better, smarter or more capable than black people, brown people, or any other people. As good an authority as Carrie Meek put it best. "There's not a racist bone in that boy's body," she said even as other black leaders pilloried him for wanting to end affirmative action in Florida. "You're not from a family of bigots. You couldn't be. It's not in your genes."

Still and all, Jeb is a Bush, and the Bushes have a long, uneven history with racial matters—the Willie Horton television ad of 1988 is probably the nadir—that, understandably, makes many black voters suspicious of anyone from the family.

It didn't start out that way.

In fact, great-grandfather Samuel Bush was downright egalitarian about it. At the turn of the century in Columbus, Ohio, the son of an Episcopal minister insisted on sending his children, including Prescott, to public schools not in spite of the large populations of black children and German children in attendance, but because of it.

Prescott, as a United States senator from Connecticut and chairman of the platform committee for the 1956 Republican convention, pushed for stronger civil rights language than supported even by northern Democrats. He wanted federal employment guidelines that banned discrimination, he opposed the poll tax, and he urged his party to praise the Brown v. Board of Education Supreme Court decision. He even supported eliminating the filibuster rule in the Senate—what's now become known as the "nuclear option"—not to load the high court with archconservatives, but to end Southern Democrats' decades-long blockade of civil rights legislation.

But then something strange happened in the next generation.

Barbara Bush, the product of a comfortable suburban upbringing in Rye, New York, allowed as how she had no firsthand knowledge of racial discrimination until 1957, when she and her black servants tried to drive from Texas to Connecticut with the children. She found that most hotels and restaurants in the South did not want black people in their establishments. She recounts staying in Howard Johnson's Motor Lodges, the one chain that had ended its discriminatory practices, and bringing food back up to the room so everyone could eat together. Even when she got to Greenwich, she found that the ferry operators didn't want the black servants, Otha Taylor or Julia Jackson, aboard the boat. She had to invoke Prescott Bush's name for them to make an exception.

Yet seven years later, there was George H.W. Bush, running for the Senate from Texas, telling the voters how he opposed President Johnson's efforts to end discrimination. "The new civil rights act was passed to protect fourteen percent of the people," he said. "I'm also worried about the other eighty-six percent." He made sure it was known that he was opposed to laws that would force private businesses like hotels and restaurants to accept black customers. He called Martin Luther King Jr. a "militant" whose efforts were being financed by union money. He even opposed the elimination of the poll tax, offering the appalling explanation that he did not want the polls to be "swamped with a liberal vote bloc."

After losing that election, George H.W. acknowledged to his Episcopal minister that he "took some of the far right positions to get elected. I hope I never do it again. I regret it." Yet four years later, the Bushes' political party adopted the "Southern Strategy," the more-or-less openly racist appeal to win over Southern whites who were angry at Democrats for helping blacks, and the family's racial record got even more dodgy.

George H.W. by then was seeking reelection as the congressman for the newly carved-out Republican part of Houston, and Johnson was pushing for even more civil rights legislation, this time a fair-housing bill. In later years, George H.W. would cite his support for this bill as a watershed moment, coming after a visit to Vietnam where he saw black servicemen fighting and dying for the country. How could he in good conscience then oppose their right to find a home when they came back? Naturally, what he failed to mention is that he had earlier voted to kill the bill on a procedural vote. Yes, George H.W. had voted against fair housing before he had voted for it.

That same election, number one son George W.—who nearly four decades later would spend much of 2003 and 2004 lauding the new ability of women in Afghanistan and Iraq to vote—in his very first, nonfamilial political campaign helped a guy get to the United States Senate by accusing his opponent of helping black people to vote.

The year was 1968, and the place, ironically enough, was Florida. The Republican was Ed Gurney, a Brevard County congressman, and the opponent was LeRoy Collins, whose progressive attitudes about race a decade earlier helped avert in Florida the riots and unrest suffered by its neighbors. Gurney's campaign turned this against Collins by distributing photos of Collins walking with civil rights leaders Martin Luther King Jr. and Andrew Young. The photo was not exactly in context—Collins was actually trying to negotiate with the two on behalf of the Johnson administration to avoid a strike, not participating in the march—but it didn't matter. Collins, a hero in Florida today, and someone Jeb calls a model, ended his political career. Gurney was indicted for bribery and influence peddling and resigned in 1974.

Two decades later, after two terms of serving faithfully under a president who used an apocryphal story of a Cadillac-driving welfare mother to help cement his rapport with the still–Solid South, George H.W.'s use of Willie Horton to appeal to that same base came as little surprise—it would have been more surprising, in fact, if a campaign run by South Carolinian and attentive student of southern politics Lee Atwater did *not* use such a tactic.

A dozen years after that, the next generation's standard bearer, George W., cheerfully visited that bastion of tolerance, Bob Jones University, and declared that he shared his audience's values. After moving into the White

House, he became the first president since Herbert Hoover to refuse to speak to the NAACP.

Jeb himself, in his 1994 iteration, was little better. When a black questioner asked what he would do for the black community if he were elected governor, Jeb answered: "Probably nothing." Then, to put an exclamation point on it, he pushed hard on his theme of "welfare reform"—which, on its face, was already a not-so-subtle appeal to bigoted white votes—by telling welfare mothers that they should "get their lives together and find a husband."

GIVEN ALL these impediments, Jeb's showing among black voters in 1998 was not just creditable, but phenomenal.

Part of it was due to his active efforts to meet actual black people, in the intervening years, including his founding of a "charter" school in the blighted Liberty City section of his adopted hometown, Miami. He picked up on the idea that many black parents favored private school vouchers so they could send their children to religious schools, and built on that common ground, as well.

But equally important to Jeb's doubling his support from black voters was the Democratic Party's internal fractures over the ousting of their incoming leader in the state House, Willie Logan, who would have been the first black party leader since Reconstruction.

Now, to be fair to the Democrats, Logan was about as slippery as they come, usually working the system for his personal aggrandizement rather than his party's benefit. The job of the incoming chamber leader is to raise money and recruit good candidates for the coming election, and Logan was doing neither. Frankly, he needed ousting.

Naturally, the House Democrats handled it with all the political skills that had become evident in their rapid decline through the 1990s. Instead of making the focus Logan's competency, they allowed Logan to make it his race, and it went predictably downhill from there.

The Republican Party openly pandered to the man, to the point of having the state chairman don waiter's attire and serve his meal to him at a public function. Sure, there were glitches—such as when Logan was forced to return tens of thousands of dollars in Republican money because he had created the wrong type of political committee to accept large donations. Or when Logan, at that moment the blackest man in Florida, blithely joined the party chairman in the Bahamas on his sailing yacht . . . which happened to be named for a family slave from pre–Civil War times.

Jeb, of course, was suddenly not only Logan's best friend, but a handful of other black elected officials', too. The new alliance did what it was supposed to do—distract the Democrats from their overall strategy by having to woo people who should have been part of their solid base—and Jeb won the election handily. As he delivered his victory speech from Miami, directly behind him in the camera shot were Logan and Rudy Bradley, another black House member from St. Petersburg.

WHICH BRINGS us back to how his great rapprochement went to hell.

His governorship started out well enough. To Jeb's credit, he made real efforts to put together an administration that resembled the state that it was leading. For a Republican, particularly, this is a difficult thing. After all, the people beating a path to his door were the friends and acquaintances and distant and not-so-distant relatives of rich Republican donors—very few of whom were anything other than Caucasian. Jeb on more than one occasion went back to his transition team—and, later, his judicial nominating commissions—and asked them to go back out and find good female, Hispanic, and black candidates. By the end of the first year, Jeb had two agency heads who were black and made a respectable effort to bring diversity to the various boards and commissions that he must appoint.

And then along came Ward Connerly, the black affirmative action opponent from California, who wanted to end preferential hiring, contracting, and university admissions in Florida. It was, as he readily admitted, an entirely political move. Jeb's older brother was the likely Republican presidential nominee, and Connerly wanted to put the debate over racial preferences front and center. Jeb's 1998 "compassionate conservative" slogan mirrored his brother's in 2000—both boys had lifted it from their dad, for whom it was invented by a Christian consultant in 1986—and he understood that there was absolutely no upside to teaming with Connerly. White voters with racial resentments were solidly behind George W., regardless of compassionate conservatism—a phrase that former Tennessee governor and current U.S. Senator Lamar Alexander labeled "weasel words." Supporting Connerly's efforts would not add to their support from the closet racists, but *would* tick off both moderates and potential black voters.

Connerly did get a meeting with Jeb in early 1999, but not his support. Jeb said afterward that he did not think that Florida's affirmative action programs had problems. Jeb also put out the word that Connerly was not to find a friendly audience with the Republican legislature, which explained why the man could get neither the Senate president nor the House speaker to meet with him. While official Florida wanted nothing to do with him, though, Connerly found a sympathetic ear with the Florida Associated General Contractors, who saw some money to be made if they could stop government from setting aside portions of construction projects for women- and minority-owned businesses.

When it became clear that the group was helping Connerly raise money with the aim of gathering enough signatures to put the question on the November 2000 ballot, Jeb realized that he had to act. And thus was born the One Florida initiative, Jeb's attempt to outmaneuver one of the few black guys who actually spoke about race like a Republican—in fact, actually spoke about it the same way Jeb had spoken about it just six years earlier.

THERE ARE many ironies to all of this, the most obvious one that it was out of fear of nontraditional black man Connerly that Jeb wound up empowering Kendrick Meek, who then was able to use the traditional, *Republicans-hate-blacks* arguments as a cudgel to pound both Jeb and George W.

A more fundamental one, though, was that One Florida was actually designed to maintain the status quo—to admit just as many black and Hispanic students to Florida universities and award just as many contracts to black and Hispanic businesses as was possible under affirmative action, except to do this without specifically using race. The college admissions, for example, would be done using a "Talented 20" scheme, in which students in the top fifth of any high school class would be guaranteed entrance to a public university, regardless of their actual grade point averages or SAT scores. The net result was to be the same. Students in predominantly minority high schools who scored at the top of their class would have a huge leg up over white students in suburban schools.

This was a program that, had Jeb used some savvy in rolling it out, blacks and Hispanics could easily have embraced—and Ward Connerly and his white allies should have hated.

Jeb's problem, as was typical, was his paternalistic, I-talk-you-listen style. Jeb was proposing to repeal hard-won affirmative action programs that blacks and Hispanics had spent decades fighting for. He reached out for their support only when it came time to roll out the proposal and he needed some black and brown faces to stand beside him at the press conference.

Once black leaders and Democrats started realizing the political possibilities with the issue, things really started to get ugly. Within a few weeks, all his outreach efforts to the black community of the past several years—all the visits to black churches and community centers, all the efforts of his predominantly black charter school—were quickly erased.

Finally, in January 2000, as legislators gathered in Tallahassee for a week of committee meetings, Kendrick Meek took the occasion to take his concerns directly to Jeb. Jeb refused to meet with him, and Meek immediately realized what a coup he had scored. Within minutes his staff was on the phone, informing reporters of the "sit-in" underway in Jeb's suite. Some dozen journalists were allowed in, ostensibly to talk to Meek and his sidekick, state Representative Tony Hill, and a half-dozen reporters decided they would stay, to see how it turned out.

BY THAT EVENING, Jeb got so flustered that he told aides that eventually they would have to "kick their asses out"—unaware that a TV cameraman was rolling tape as he uttered the words. Eventually, Jeb gave in and agreed to a public meeting with Meek. It also was televised, so all of Florida was able to watch him pout as Meek expounded on the need for dialogue and communication.

The conventional wisdom afterward opined that Jeb had exacerbated things by, well, being Jeb. People imagined how the late Lawton Chiles would have handled such an episode, and decided that rather then try to starve Meek and Hill out of his office, as Jeb tried to do, Chiles would have ordered pizza for them or, even better, brought in some wild game he had shot and cooked it up for them right there.

Some of that was nostalgia for the Old He-Coon and some of it was on point. It is important, though, not to sell Kendrick Meek short. He knew what he was doing when he wandered down to the Capitol's plaza level to "see if he could talk to Jeb." By then, a full year into his first term, all of Jeb's weaknesses—his stubbornness, his quickness to anger, his need to win *everything*—were well known. Meek may not have been able to predict Jeb's exact reaction to his demand, but he could have guessed with reasonable certainty that it would not be a smart one.

That Jeb reacted as badly as he did was Meek's good luck. The round of public hearings around the state Jeb was forced to accept served as additional opportunities to beat up on both Jeb and, by extension, George W.

Jeb, naturally, refused to back away from One Florida, and Meek parlayed that into a massive demonstration in Tallahassee, drawing the Rev. Jesse Jackson and the other usual players in these sorts of things. But Meek's even more impressive accomplishment was to put together voter registration and turnout drives that *actually worked*. Black voters in 1996 had accounted for 10 percent of the electorate. In 2000 they made up 15 percent, which worked out to 280,000 additional votes, nearly all of them for Al Gore. So while it's true that some 2,600 votes were inadvertently cast for Pat Buchanan rather than Gore in Palm Beach County because of the "butterfly ballot," and another 25,000 mostly Gore votes were tossed out in Duval County because of the "caterpillar ballot," these events became pivotal toward George W.'s accidental election only because of Kendrick Meek, without whom, Al Gore would not have even been in the game.

As an epilogue to One Florida, it should be noted that Jeb's grand alliance with black leaders in Florida essentially imploded in the months and years following Meek's sit-in, until there was virtually nothing left by the time Jeb left office.

Much of the problem arises from a dynamic discussed earlier: when the first and most important criterion for being hired by Jeb's administration is an unquestioning personal loyalty to Jeb or the Bush family, that limits the pool of qualified applicants. Trying then to find a minority candidate in that small universe is even more difficult.

Both of the two original black agency heads in 1999 left under ethical clouds. The *South Florida Sun-Sentinel* in 2001 found that Ruben King-Shaw, Jeb's Agency for Health Care Administration secretary, had dined dozens of times and taken trips with industry lobbyists, whose clients later received favorable consideration from the agency. King-Shaw accused the paper of racism and trying to disrupt his planned move to Washington to work in George W.'s Health Care Financing Administration. And Lottery secretary David Griffin resigned in late 2002, shortly ahead of an audit that found that he and other top agency officials had improperly accepted meals and gifts from agency vendors.

Rudy Bradley, one of the two black Democrats standing behind Jeb the night of his 1998 victory speech, switched parties and ran for a state Senate seat as a Republican. He lost. So Jeb in 2001 made him a $123,000-

a-year member of the Public Service Commission, the body that regulates utilities in the state. Bradley, a former social worker and school administrator, had no obvious qualifications for a job that required familiarity with a highly technical body of laws and rules. Three years later, Bradley read as his position on a phone rate hike, verbatim, a document written by one of the phone companies seeking the rate increase. Jeb did not reappoint him when his term expired in 2006.

Willie Logan, Jeb's great pal and the other black leader on that stage election night, came to an even more ignominious political end. After term limits forced him from the House, he ran as an independent—with GOP encouragement—for the United States Senate in 2000, for a seat that was won by Democrat Bill Nelson. Within a year, he was under investigation by the state Ethics Commission for misusing state money from the time he was a state legislator. He ultimately agreed in 2002 to pay a fine and receive a public reprimand. That same year, a jury acquitted him for resisting arrest—but never heard about the underlying incident, in which Logan ran from officers who found him masturbating in a men's restroom near a nude beach. A judge had earlier tossed out the indecent exposure charge because he said officers should not have been looking into his stall. The publicity, though, damaged his career, and in 2004 he lost a race for the Miami-Dade County Commission.

Other black leaders who supported Jeb said they made a mistake. Christopher Smith, a Fort Lauderdale lawyer running for the state House in 1998 who had supported Jeb over Buddy MacKay, had switched back by the 2002 reelection campaign. "In '98, we had an unknown who showed a lot of promise. Now that he's been in office we've seen what he's done and not done for the community," said Smith, who in 2004 became House Democratic leader, the same post Logan was prevented from winning. Smith explained why Jeb's support among black voters fell back into the single digits in that 2002 election. "Those who gave him the benefit of the doubt weren't willing to do it again."

The Rev. Joseph Wright, president of the Tallahassee Inter-denominational Ministerial Alliance, went even further. By late 2001 he was back before his congregants to tell them: "I truly apologize to the community for making a bad decision three years ago. I can no longer support the governor's policies. He is a good man and my friend. I love him. And he's a personable young man," Wright said. "Looking back, these programs have really hurt our community. A lot of you had jobs and job security, but you no longer have them today . . . so I'm very disappointed with the Republican agenda and how they handle things."

DESPITE ALL of this, and as bad as it all sounds, it must be remembered that Jeb is not a bigot, in the sense that it suggests that he believes that black people are, by dint of their skin color, inferior in some away.

Of all the Bushes, Jeb certainly understands the ugliness of racial hatred firsthand. He was eager to leave Houston because of the anti-Mexican discrimination that Columba had to cope with there as a young bride. And even in Miami, where Hispanics by the early 1980s were well on their way to becoming the majority ethnic group, his oldest boy had to deal with epithets on the baseball field.

Jeb also had to suffer through the ugly hullabaloo that followed his dad's pointing out Jeb's children to President Reagan as "the little brown ones" at an airport campaign rally. True, that embarrassment must be balanced against the blatant effort that George H.W. made in that election to use daughter-in-law Columba and his grandchildren to counter the fluent Spanish of both Michael Dukakis and Lloyd Bentsen. Columba cut a television ad for the campaign, vouching for George H.W. as a champion for "Hispanics like me." George H.W. then finished the commercial: "As president, I'll have a lot of reasons to help Hispanics everywhere, because I'll not only be answering to my grandchildren, I'll be answering to history."

Jeb also adopted that strategy in his own run for governor in 1994. He told the Hispanic Chamber of Commerce of Central Florida at an Orlando campaign appearance: "I am the husband of a Hispanic, I am the father of three beautiful children who have Hispanic blood running through their veins, my business partner and 75 percent of the former team members of my business are Hispanic."

In Miami, Jeb didn't need Columba's ethnicity to connect with the Hispanic majority. His ability to speak the language and, perhaps even more important, his long and deep support of Miami's virulently anti-communist foreign policy essentially made Jeb an honorary Cuban.

In all these ways, Jeb is about as far from the stereotypical white male Anglo as is possible for a Republican to be. Which, naturally, begs the question: why does Jeb have such a terrible track record on issues important to blacks? And the answer is: for the same reason he has such a terrible record on issues important to poor people. And that is that Jeb Bush has not a clue, not one little inkling, of what poor people go through in this life. He doesn't have any idea what it could be like not to know where your next meal is coming from. The idea that one day he could be old and not have enough money to care for himself has never crossed his mind. And why should it?

By the time he was born, George H.W. Bush was on the verge of striking it rich through Zapata's oil wells. When Jeb was two years old, his family had moved into a 3,000-square-foot house in Midland, abutting a park, and with a pool and cabana. Just to keep things in perspective, the average house in 1950 America was 963 square feet. In late 2005, it was 2,400 square feet.

Jeb came to Florida using one credit card to pay the bill for another, but was raking in more than $1 million within a decade. Surely, if he could pick himself up by his bootstraps, so could welfare moms and other poor people, right?

And because it so happens that in early-twenty-first-century America, a disproportionate number of black people are also poor, so it is that Jeb, unless he undergoes some miraculous epiphany or befalls some incredible *Job*-like series of misfortunes that reduces him to abject poverty, is simply unlikely at this point in his life to change his views on these matters.

Which means that the correct answer of what Jeb would do for black people in the way of dramatic changes to end their disproportionate representation among America's poorest, should he ever take up residence in the White House, is more than likely the same one he gave to that questioner back in 1994: "Probably nothing."

FOR WHAT it's worth, it is not only the poor Jeb cannot empathize with. It is also gays and lesbians.

Not that he actively discriminates against them. As someone whose family has been immersed in the culture of national politics, and who has aspirations for national office himself, Jeb no doubt has had many dealings with gays and lesbians, who are ubiquitous in the Washington, D.C., scene, on both sides of the political aisle.

Rather, he has made it clear that he does not feel any need to specifically protect gays from discrimination. "I don't believe we need to create another category of victims," he told a lesbian couple who heckled him at a 1993 campaign event. Also in that campaign, his staff asked that caterers at a fund-raiser he held at the Tampa Bay Performing Arts Center remove the red ribbons that they regularly wore in remembrance of AIDS victims. Apparently these ribbons were a political statement. The wrong political statement.

And in the now infamous "private" conversation he had with a delegation of Panhandle legislators that was recorded by a reporter who was allowed in with the group, Jeb joked about two sisters who had been picked up in the disappearance of a five-year-old foster child in their custody. "As [Graham] was being arrested, she told her coworkers, 'Tell my wife I've been arrested.' The wife is the grandmother, and the aunt is the husband." Jeb made little quotation marks around the word "grandmother" with his fingers. "Bet you don't get that in Pensacola."

The incident would have been merely juvenile had it not been for the fact that little Rilya Wilson had been missing for more than a year before Jeb's Department of Children and Families took notice, which made the remark appalling.

Jeb later explained that he meant no disrespect by his remark. He was merely conveying a conversation that had been relayed to him by state police. The incident evidently did not harm Jeb too badly. He won reelection a mere month later by 13 percentage points—655,000 votes.

All of which is a long way of pointing out that while Jeb would, in a presidential run and a presidency, hire gay and lesbian staff, the Log Cabin Republicans will probably find a more sympathetic ear somewhere else.

GAY RIGHTS, though, is not a battle that the Republican Party is grappling with in the early part of the twenty-first century. Far closer to the top of the agenda, as evidenced by Republican National Committee Chairman Ken Mehlman's much publicized efforts in 2005, was to bring more black voters into the Republican fold—which brings to a boil that simmering tension between the GOP as the party of the man who freed the slaves versus the GOP as the group that cheerfully and cynically adopted the "Southern Strategy" to pick up the white people angry with the Democrats for helping blacks.

And with the voting rights battles largely behind us, and black people able to sue when they encounter discrimination in the workplace, the most visible remaining flashpoint for all this is, of course, the Confederate flag.

As inane as it sounds, indeed, as inane as it *is,* this is the Southern White Man's litmus test of Where You Stand. In simple, inflammatory code, that says it all. Where you stand on The Flag makes it perfectly plain: do you stand with us? Or do you stand with the niggers?

There it is, crude and nasty. For all the nonsense about the flag standing for Southern heritage, about pride in one's ancestors and so forth, is simply that: pure nonsense. The Confederate flag (technically, the battle flag—it was never the official flag of the seceding states) was and is a hurtful symbol of the fundamental inequity of these United States, a wrong that, until it was righted by Abraham Lincoln and the abolitionists, made our professed love of freedom and God-given inaliable rights an exercise in hypocrisy.

Yes, it may also be a symbol of Southern heritage—but can that heritage realistically be celebrated without implicitly honoring the institution upon which its entire economic structure was based? How would we as a nation react if, say, Bavaria decided that Nazism was an important part of *its* heritage, and people started driving around with the swastikas on their bumpers? If Jewish people objected, would we agree that they had a legitimate beef?

And yet, such is the need to kiss the Southern White Man's ass that something as evil as a symbol of the armed struggle to retain the ability to own and sell another human being on the basis of his skin color is regarded as a question of "states rights."

Remember that? That was the explanation George W. gave in February 2000, as he fought to rebound from his drubbing in New Hampshire in that stronghold of the Southern White Man, South Carolina.

True, this is the same George W. who, as a teenager at Andover in the mid-1960s, made his statement with a battle flag on his dorm-room wall.

It's not really clear what statement he was trying to make. Was it that he was a Southerner, and if all the Yankees up there didn't like it, they could go pound sand? Maybe it wasn't a statement. Maybe it was just a teenager being stupid, as teenagers are wont to do.

Then again, when we put this act in the context of the times, it makes you wonder what exactly was going through young George W.'s head. At the same time he thought that flag would make a nifty dorm-room decoration, both black and white activists were getting murdered in the South for trying to help blacks do the terribly subversive thing of registering to vote.

In that regard, anyway, Jeb has it all over his elder brother. He may have done mean and insensitive things as a youth, but probably nothing *that* mean or insensitive.

To the contrary, a year after George W. as a presidential candidate in South Carolina was offering up mealymouthed explanations of states rights, Jeb unceremoniously banished the "Stainless Banner"—a small Confederate battle flag on an otherwise white field—from the grounds of the Florida Capitol. Previously it had flown in front of the western entrance to the building, along with all the other flags that Florida had flown under in the five centuries since Europeans arrived.

There was no announcement, no nothing. The official reasoning, released after the fact, was that the flagpoles had all been taken down anyway for some renovation work on that side of the building, and, when it was over, it was decided that the Confederate flag would not go back up. Simple as that. Passive voice construction—it was decided—and that was the end of it.

No one really noticed, in fact, until the local paper got a complaint from the head of the Sons of the Confederacy, the self-described nonracist group that is merely interested in preserving Southern heritage. To his credit, Jeb did not back down. He didn't even waste much breath defending his decision. The action spoke for itself.

Jeb's disrespect for the Confederate flag did not become an issue in his reelection. For one thing, there was no real Republican primary, when the Southern White Man's vote becomes much amplified. And then, in November, there was Jeb against Bill McBride, who, although he had fought in Vietnam, nonetheless seemed to tolerate blacks and gays and all the rest of them entirely too easily.

What was the Southern White Man to do? Either vote for Jeb or not vote at all. Most, it seems from the results, decided to vote for Jeb.

It will be interesting to see how Jeb handles the issue on a national stage. The Confederate flag, in the end, is not a pivotal matter in Florida, which is not really a "Southern" state demographically anymore. But that totem remains important in Georgia and South Carolina, two important GOP primary states. It may happen that by 2008 or 2012, the flag is not a top issue anyplace in the South, and Jeb will, as Bushes have traditionally done, do very well there.

But if the banner is again a touchstone for the Southern White Man vote, Jeb will be faced with choosing between the compulsion to denounce something he knows is a reminder of an evil era, as he quietly did in Florida, and his compulsion to win.

It will be an interesting choice.

Chapter Eight

VOUCHER MADNESS

"A high school diploma, do you know what that means in this state? What it means is you show up and breathe oxygen regularly and exhale CO_2."

—JEB BUSH, 1994

"I believe smaller schools, smaller classrooms, are better, and I think the school shows that."

—JEB BUSH, 1997, ABOUT HIS
LIBERTY CITY CHARTER SCHOOL

"I have a couple of devious plans if this thing passes."

—JEB BUSH, 2002, IN AN UNGUARDED REMARK
ABOUT THE PROPOSED CLASS SIZE
AMENDMENT, WHICH VOTERS APPROVED
OVER HIS STRONG OBJECTIONS

In Jeb Bush's educational system, you could get a publicly funded, private school voucher to send your child to a Baptist school that would teach her that Jews, Hindus, and other infidels were going to hell—even though the state constitution said that no public money was supposed to go to religious institutions.

In Jeb's educational system, children at public schools had to take the rigorous, much-feared and overly important FCAT—the Florida Comprehensive Assessment Test—that would determine whether children would advance to the next grade and whether the entire school would be rewarded or punished. Children who accepted one of Jeb's "Opportunity Scholarship" vouchers to escape a failing public school could attend a start-up, for-profit private school with no qualified teachers, no academic curriculum, no accreditation. Though they still had to take the FCAT, neither they nor their private school were ever held to account for their scores. In fact, no one outside Jeb's education department—with the exception of a single friendly "researcher" at a pro-voucher think tank—was ever allowed to know the scores. Children getting other brands of vouchers were not required to take any standardized test, ever.

In Jeb's educational system, disabled children at public schools were entitled to receive an individualized learning plan, including, if need be, teachers with specialized training. Parents unhappy with their child's education were entitled to a judicial hearing. Disabled children who took a so-called "McKay Scholarship" and went to a private school were not guaranteed to get any specialized instruction. Three-quarters of McKay voucher schools, in fact, had no special education teachers. Voucher-taking schools, in fact, were under no obligation to have teachers with any sort of training or experience whatsoever.

Voucher-taking schools, to put it bluntly, were under virtually no obligations at all. They did not have to run criminal background checks on their employees. They did not have to use academically recognized curricula. They could use the proceeds of the voucher money to proselytize children, to pay shareholder dividends, or to buy the school owner a beach cottage in Aruba. Florida taxpayers had no right to know.

Florida, under Jeb Bush, became Voucher Land—with more children attending private schools using public money than any other state.

This is not to say that Jeb did not talk about the public schools. He did. Public schools and their students, we were constantly told by Jeb and his people, were performing better than ever before. But in the end, the 2.7 million children in those schools barely marched in place, compared to other states. Their scores went up slightly on the state's proprietary FCAT, but largely stayed even or fell compared to the rest of the country. This should not have come as a surprise. Florida had always been stingy when it came to public education, and Jeb did his best to keep it that way.

As poorly as Florida's schoolchildren were served by Jeb's policies,

2006: Jeb attends a rally staged by a wealthy political supporter and school voucher proponent a month after the Florida Supreme Court struck down Jeb's prized Opportunity Scholarships vouchers. Lawyers had warned Jeb when he pushed the legislation through in 1999 that the program was likely illegal under the state's constitution, but Jeb didn't care.

PHOTO: STATE OF FLORIDA

though, they may have been better off than the voucher children in 1,200 or so private schools. Most of the serious, academically oriented secular schools never participated in Jeb's voucher programs. And, by the middle of Jeb's second term, the Florida Catholic Conference was getting increasingly weary of taking abuse from Jeb and his staff for supporting even minimal accountability legislation, which led the single largest group of academically oriented religious schools to back away from the programs, as well. That left the hard-core evangelical schools that saw voucher children as religious recruits, the mediocre private schools that had trouble filling their classes in the open market, and, sadly, a good number of profit-oriented "entrepreneurial" schools, set up specifically to accept state vouchers.

Near the end of Jeb's second term—just before the Florida Supreme Court struck down one voucher program and laid the groundwork to end the other two—the three voucher programs hit a total enrollment of 30,374 children . . . and that is just about all we can know about them. For all of Jeb's vaunted "A-plus education plan" and its insistence on holding schools and their teachers and their administrators *accountable*, and for *measuring* the success or lack of it, because you cannot improve what you cannot measure, and for all the noble aims of brother George W.'s No Child Left Behind and tracking *individual student progress*—despite all of those things, no one on God's green earth had one clue how well those 30,374 children did academically, and whether schools did a good, great, fair, poor, or downright criminally awful job educating those kids using taxpayer money.

It was, truly, voucher madness.

WHERE TO BEGIN, with the self-proclaimed Education Governor's education policies?

· The sad part is, Jeb came into power in 1999 with the rarest of opportunities to make a real difference in this area. He had won a convincing mandate over his Democratic opponent, and had significant majorities in both chambers of the legislature led by allies who honestly wanted to make him succeed. The last Republican governor, Bob Martinez, was a decent guy but a disaster as the state's chief executive, almost from the day he took office.

True, Republican legislators, who had only taken full control in 1996, were not particularly interested in improving public education, given their long history of sitting in the back benches and generally opposing Democratic attempts to spend more on schools. But just as it took Nixon to go to China, it could have been Jeb—the Republican All-Star son of America's First Family—to persuade his own party to take the bold step of making public education a *Republican* issue and pushing Florida out of the cellar in national rankings and into the top tier.

Not since Democrat Bob Graham gambled a sizable chunk of his political capital on vastly increased school spending and higher standards for teachers and students in the early 1980s had a governor made public education a serious priority. In the intervening decade and a half, Florida public schools had gradually sank back down to their usual spot. It was high time for another powerful advocate in the Governor's Mansion, and Jeb had all the stars lined up to be that savior. All his education talk during his 1998 campaign could have even provided him the political cover for announcing shortly after his election that a thorough review of the public school financing formula had convinced him that the only way to move Florida forward in this area would require an enormous financial commitment that would have to take priority over all else.

And so what did Floridians get?

Pretty much the same per-student spending on schools as before Jeb took office, but combined with a time-consuming and draconian testing scheme that screamed "improve or else!"—with the threat that failing schools would have to pass out private-school vouchers to their students. The ensuing but predictable emphasis on test-taking practice to drill for the FCATs each February angered parents who watched the curriculum narrow, while the school grades and voucher threats demoralized the teachers. That was probably not the main intent of the vouchers—the main intent of the voucher program was, of course, to have lots of publicly financed private schools—but if they gave heartache to teachers, so much the better. Jeb hated the teachers union, which supported his Democratic opponent in each of his elections.

Jeb loved to talk about how much more his administration was spending on public schools—it was a favorite theme during his 2002 reelection campaign: $3 billion more in four years. But that's what it largely was: talk. After taking into account inflation plus the year-after-year increases in public school enrollment because of Florida's growth, Jeb's real increases for schools during that first term were almost nonexistent: all of fifty dollars per child, or 0.9 percent.

Such a performance might have been forgivable, had these been tough budget years for the state. There is the real scandal. Jeb was lucky enough to be governor in a span when the state revenues, all except the period after September 11, 2001, were constantly marching upward. Unfortunately for public-school children, Jeb's main priority was a massive tax cut for the wealthiest 5 percent of the state's residents. That consumed a big chunk of the state's real "disposable" income, leaving Medicaid, children's protective services, road construction, the environment, and public schools to fight over the rest. The only reason schools didn't actually lose ground in Jeb's years was the absurd increase in Florida property values, which brought in a corresponding increase in property taxes for schools.

But perhaps the most telling aspect of Jeb's attitudes toward public schools was his position on the citizen-approved "Class Size Amendment" that was added to the state constitution on the same ballot that gave Jeb a second term. The amendment required, within eight years, that public school classes not exceed eighteen in kindergarten through third grade, twenty-two in grades four through eight, and twenty-five in grades nine through twelve. It was a plea from a fed-up public for at least one, real, tangible improvement in their children's education—the same feature, coincidentally, that just about every quality private school also brags about, small classes with more individualized attention.

Quite naturally, Jeb hated it.

He hated it with an undying passion, and fought harder against its passage than he did the Democratic nominee who sought to unseat him that year, Tampa lawyer Bill McBride. At virtually every campaign stop that summer and autumn, Jeb talked about himself, he talked about McBride, and then he talked about what a disaster the class-size amendment would be for the state were it to pass, how it would cost some $27 billion to implement, forcing massive budget cuts in other programs as well as tax increases.

It's important to keep in mind here *why* Jeb hated it. After all, he himself attended two extremely expensive private academies that boast of their tiny classes. He sent his own children to private schools that similarly use small classes as a selling point. Even Jeb conceded, while claiming there was little scientific proof that smaller classes lead to higher student achievement, that all other things being equal, both parents and teachers understandably prefer smaller classes to larger ones. And it was not even the fact that his most effective political foe, Democrat Kendrick Meek, was the amendment's architect and leader, or that the hated teachers unions served as Meek's foot soldiers.

No, the reason that Jeb hated the class-size amendment so much was that "tax increase" bit. Jeb had come into office vowing to cut taxes generally, and the "insidious" intangibles tax that almost exclusively struck his wealthy backers particularly, and he was damned if he was going to raise taxes for something like public schools. And yet, Meek's strategy to bypass the legislature and put the class-size language directly in the state constitution seemed as if it would force Jeb to do exactly that. Having to do something so directly against his "head-banging conservative" political philosophy was bad enough, but blemishing his record with a big tax hike? How would that play in New Hampshire's Republican primary someday? Or even worse, South Carolina's?

And so unfolded the twisted education legacy of Florida's 43rd governor: parents could opt to send their children to low-quality, highly religious private schools with no testing or financial accountability with Jeb's blessing. But parents who wanted small class sizes like they have in good private schools at their neighborhood *public* schools, Jeb thwarted them every way he could, even after they passed a constitutional amendment to that effect over his strenuous objections.

SO THERE'S no misunderstanding, Jeb Bush is not the reason Florida has a lousy public education system. No, it was that way already when he got his hands on it.

By just about any standard—graduation rate, college entrance exam scores, teacher salaries, school size, reading scores, per-student expenditures—Florida is in the bottom half of the fifty states and the District of Columbia, and usually in the bottom fifth. It's apparently a deep-seated tradition in the state, that the schools be terrible, because it has been the case for generations. Yes, there are many excellent teachers and some excellent schools. But, in general, we have lived by a slogan that former State Universities chancellor Charlie Reed coined about the public colleges but which was equally on-point about the K–12 system: "We're cheap, and we're proud."

Florida's schools are, as a whole, just plain bad. For years, education advocates have joked that our motto ought to be: "Thank God for Mississippi." And even that, in recent years, may have been an insult to the nation's poorest state.

And that right there gets at the saddest part of this, which is that Florida is not a destitute state. True, we're not New Hampshire, Connecticut, or New York, but we're not Mississippi, Louisiana, or West Virginia, either.

In the U.S. Census's 2004 income report, Florida's per capita income was ranked number twenty-three of the fifty states, at $31,455, sandwiched between Michigan and North Dakota.

Unfortunately for the 2.7 million schoolchildren consigned to the public schools, income and wealth are not spread equally across the population. Rather, they are disproportionately in the hands of the elderly, which has given rise in our fair state to the ugly concept of the greedy geezer. The retiree, often of moderate to better-than-moderate means, who enjoys golf and tennis and the rest of the active lifestyle, but gets mad as hell when somebody suggests a tax increase to improve the schools. Their view is that they already paid their taxes in Ohio or New York or Michigan to put their own kids through school, so why should they have to pay again?

There are only a few politicians left in Florida who have the backbone to tell these folks: because both childless households and empty nesters back home in Ohio, New York, and Michigan helped put *your* kids through school, that's why. No, instead, what the vast majority of the recent generation of Florida politicians has told them is: oh, you're absolutely right. You shouldn't have to pay.

Maybe they assume that parents who really want a quality public education would never be so foolish as to set up residence in Florida. Maybe they think these sticklers for children learning to read Shakespeare and do algebra by high school would vote with their feet and relocate in Massachusetts or Iowa or Minnesota. Maybe they're right.

This view has cut, by the way, across party lines. Democrats ran the entire legislature until 1994 and had control of the Governor's Mansion until 1999, with brief exceptions between 1967 and 1971, when eccentric Republican Claude Kirk was in office, and 1987 through 1991, when Bob Martinez was in. Former governor Lawton Chiles, a long-beloved Democratic legend who spoke passionately about education, did little to force the legislature to spend more for schools beyond a special session he called in 1997 to find money for school construction. Bob Martinez did little for education in his single term, despite his background as a schoolteacher, but did send schools more money thanks to the newly instituted Florida Lottery.

Only Democrat Bob Graham among modern governors successfully pushed for significant increases for the public schools. A major goal of his was to push teacher salaries into the upper quartile of the fifty states. He didn't quite achieve that level, but got as close as Florida has ever been. He did this by using the only real weapon a governor has: the threat of repeated special sessions, right through the summer, if necessary.

Tallahassee has many charms, being as it is essentially a small Georgia town that happens to be Florida's capital, including its weather in both autumn and spring. Summer, though, is another matter entirely—all the stifling heat of the Florida peninsula with none of the cooling sea breezes. Legislators do not like having to be away from home more than the required sixty days a year. They particularly don't like having to be in Tallahassee in June, July, or August, when the afternoon thundershowers typically leave a windless steam bath, rather than offer any relief.

So there was Graham's genius, in 1983. He vetoed the entire education section of the budget, just weeks before the start of the school year, and told legislators he would keep calling them back unless they came up with an additional $100 million for public schools. They moaned, but they eventually gave him what he wanted.

The point is that a governor, although in Florida as in some other states constitutionally weak, can set the agenda and dictate the schedule, if he's willing to spend political capital and tick legislators off.

Jeb, of all people, had no problem with either, as he has shown. He had called special sessions to eliminate legal appeals for condemned killers, to subsidize a new campus for a biomedical research institute, and to implement slot-machine gambling in Fort Lauderdale. He even called those much-despised, midsummer special sessions when his medical doctor allies wanted laws protecting them from malpractice lawsuits.

During his two terms, he never called a special session to increase spending for public schools. The thought that he should never occurred to him. And why would it have? Just about every budget that legislators passed—Republican legislators, mind—allocated more money for schools than Jeb had asked for.

Spending more money for schools was never the point.

WHICH ALL comes around to suggest that there is great reason to empathize with those who want to escape the public schools in Florida.

Parents who want the best education for their children have good cause to question the idea of entrusting them to a system of public schools that, as a whole, produces the kind of national rankings alluded to above. Who can blame them? Children have a single chance at a good start. Parents who value education do not want to risk that—particularly the parents handpicked by Jeb's people to put a human face on the benefits of school vouchers. Typically they are black single moms, sometimes not terribly long ago on welfare, who want a good education for their babies so they do not have to grow up repeating their moms' mistakes.

You have to hand it to Jeb and his machine, in terms of PR value. They know how to phrase an issue to their best advantage.

And, before we go further, we ought put those single moms wanting a superior education for their children in the context of parents of most children, not just in Florida, but the whole country. There is something to be said, here, that much of the responsibility of our generally dismal state of education is the generally lackadaisical interest parents have in their children's schooling.

This sounds harsh, but think about it. Go to any mall in America on any weekday after school, and you will see middle school and high school children not doing homework, not saving for college, not doing any of those things that would indicate even a passing interest in learning. If parents believed that education was so important, would they let their kids loiter in the malls all afternoon and watch television late into the nights instead of, say, making them take tougher courses and forcing them to do the extra schoolwork that entails?

And so, there is easy and understandable empathy for the idea that if low-income parents desperately want to escape a bad public school and get their children into a good school, then why should we not help them escape the morass of mediocrity and indifferent parents that is our public school system?

The countervailing view to this is that the single greatest determining factor of a child's academic achievement is the parents' degree of involvement. Therefore, a parent who cares will make sure that his or her child will excel in school, be it public or private.

There is much truth to this. It's a cliché, but an accurate one: the squeaky wheel gets the grease, and it is easier for a public school bureaucracy to honor a parent's request that a child get more attention or help or advanced instruction than to keep listening to that parent's complaints.

According to Jeb, all he tried to do with his voucher programs was give poor parents who wanted a quality education the same opportunity that middle-class and wealthy parents already had. The argument was a powerful one, especially when it came to muting the objections of liberals and Democrats, who for generations have staked out the high ground on the issue of compassion for the poor and equality of opportunity for all.

Jeb, naturally, speaks from firsthand experience about escaping the public schools. He himself attended "government" schools, as so many in his right-wing base prefer to call them, only briefly as a young boy, from kindergarten in Midland to first, second, and part of third grade at Grady Elementary in Houston, where his father had moved the family in 1959 so as to be closer to the offshore oil business. When Jeb was eight, his mother enrolled him and brothers Neil and Marvin at the Kinkaid School, one of the most elite in town.

Then, as his grandfather had done with his father, George H.W. Bush, when Jeb reached that ripe old age of fourteen, shipped him off to Phillips Academy in Andover, Massachusetts, commonly known as Andover.

Jeb, as a parent some fifteen years later, continued the family tradition and sent his own children to private schools—The Gulliver Schools in Miami and, for Jeb Jr., his youngest, the Bolles School in Jacksonville. Both are elite, expensive schools—they haven't the national cachet of Andover, but are well known and respected in their communities as top academic institutions.

(Another note in the interest of full disclosure: I personally enrolled my own children in a private school. I did this when, upon visiting our neighborhood elementary school when my older son was ready to enter kindergarten, I found a class of some twenty-six five-year-olds. I was informed that the class size was likely to be the same the coming autumn. I was further informed that there was no guarantee of a teacher's aide. I smiled, walked out, and drove to the private, accredited, academically oriented school where some of my friends' children were enrolled, which had maximum class sizes of twenty, plus a teacher's aide in every kindergarten. I mention this because, although I believe it is irrelevant to the subject of this book, Jeb evidently believes it extremely relevant when it comes to refuting my work. He and his press office and his pro-voucher allies have taken pains to mention where my children go to school to other reporters.)

The idea that poor people's children should have the same opportunities as rich people's children is, however, an odd argument to hear from someone as opposed to egalitarian principles as Jeb. This is, recall, someone who firmly believes that rich people ought to be able to pass on their riches, intact, to their offspring, on down through the generations. This is a governor who wanted to limit the quality and quantity of state Medicaid programs because of their cost. This is the man who, as a candidate for governor in 1994, had supported strict limits on welfare programs, including, at one point, a threat that parents who remained on welfare would have their children taken as wards of the state.

For such a fan of capitalism, this was indeed a strange argument to hear from Jeb. Most liberals, and most socialists, for that matter, would certainly agree: it would be great for all children to have first-class educations. But there are many things that rich parents can obtain for their children that poor parents cannot. Foreign travel, for instance. A new, safe Volvo to ride in, rather than a beat-up Chevy Cavalier with a second-hand car seat. Healthy, nutritious meals at home, three of them a day, would also be a good start.

Follow the rabbit down that hole, and you come out wearing a Mao jacket and carrying a little red book.

Surely Jeb cannot mean this, can he? The cynical answer, but likely the correct answer, is that no, he does not. For if he were serious that children poorly served by the public school system get a chance for a better education in the private schools, he would have done two things: he would have made certain that the public schools had the money they needed to compete with quality private schools, and he would have required that children escaping bad public schools enroll in academically superior private schools. Jeb did neither, and instead argued that the mere threat of competition would force both the public schools and the private voucher schools to improve.

IT IS a curious thing, this article of faith that competition will improve public schools—that you can apply the supply and demand principles of Burger King versus McDonald's to the primary and secondary education systems.

And it seems to go back to Jeb's bedrock faith in capitalism, for it does not appear to be based in any actual facts about the actual, real world. In the real world, tuitions at academically superior private schools rise every year—rise, in fact, faster than the consumer price index. This is because these private schools already compete with public schools in attracting quality, experienced teachers. They often don't have to pay as much as the public schools because they offer other important benefits, like smaller classes and parents who are, as a whole, more interested in their children's educations. But they must keep up with salary increases in the public schools to prevent the wage gap from growing.

Compare this with McDonald's and Burger King. Adjusted for inflation, fast-food hamburgers are the same price or even cheaper today than they were five years ago, or ten years ago. McDonald's "Value Meals" have cost about four dollars pretty much forever, it seems.

In reality, what Florida's overemphasis on testing has done is create a system that Jeb, as a conservative, should abhor—the homogenization of curriculum and instruction to ensure a mediocre conformity. Gone is any incentive to tailor instruction to children with particular talents. Gone, ironically, is any incentive for a gifted program.

If a child enters the third grade reading at the fifth-grade level, that ought to be a child who presents a challenge for the teacher to get him or her reading at the sixth or seventh grade level by the end of the year. But in Jeb's system of minimum standards, that is instead a child who does not present a problem for the teacher at all, save for finding him or her a place to sit quietly and read while the teacher works like hell to get the children who are reading at first- or second-grade level up to par, so that that teacher and that school are not punished by the FCAT results come springtime.

So, in a sense, Jeb has indeed brought competition to the public schools—a competition to be mediocre. Because that is what is rewarded, or more accurately, goes unpunished. Not excellence—children performing to the best of their ability—but mediocrity—*all* children performing just enough to get by.

In a way, it *is* like McDonald's and Burger King. We don't except much when we go there beyond hot, or at least lukewarm, calories that are salty enough to choke down while we drive. We're not paying much, and we know we're not going to get much in return.

Just like our schools in Florida.

GETTING BACK to public schools competing with private ones: let's contrast how Jeb's ideal for education delivery, the educationally oriented private schools, handled testing compared to Florida's public schools.

(It's necessary to distinguish "educationally oriented" schools because a great many private schools are not educationally orientated, but rather have as their first mission the inculcation of their particular religious viewpoint. Old-line dominations like the Catholic or Episcopalian or Lutheran schools are less prone to this than the schools of the more fervently evangelical denominations, like the Southern Baptists, the Pentecostals, or the Assemblies of God.)

At almost all quality private schools, children are given a standardized test each year, typically in the late spring, typically over a number of days. Parents are informed of the upcoming test, and are asked to make sure their children attend unless they are extremely ill, and to make sure they have had a good night's sleep and a good breakfast.

And that's it.

No cramming for the test for weeks on end, no pep rallies about doing well on the test, no special classes on test-taking—none of the absurd gyrations that Florida's public schools go through each year in the weeks and months preceding the FCAT.

In other words, the test—typically the Stanford 10 or, at Catholic schools, the Iowa Test of Basic Skills—is administered to show teachers and parents the areas in which the child is doing well in addition to the areas in which the child needs help. The low-key administration of the test is part of that concept. There should not be any attempt "to cram" for an assessment test, because that defeats the purpose. Nor should teachers try to "teach to the test"—for the same reason.

It is important to note here that the FCAT, on its own, is not a bad test. It was developed in the 1990s, prior to Jeb's election, by committees of teachers under the guidance of the state Department of Education. At the time, it was designed to identify children who needed help in certain areas and to identify schools that for whatever reason—typically high poverty rates—also needed additional help.

It can fairly be argued whether poorly performing students and schools got the help they needed under Jeb's predecessor, Lawton Chiles. It can be argued that school districts had employed a separate-and-unequal scheme that funneled better teachers, newer books, and more money to white, suburban schools to the detriment of majority black, inner-city schools.

All of that is fair criticism, and generally accurate. But what Jeb did was take this diagnostic test and, in the first year of his tenure, turn it into a high-stakes week of torture. Eventually, children who did not pass the third-grade FCAT were held back, as were children who did not pass the ninth-grade FCAT. Schools were graded based on the results of their student scores, and schools that got F's two years out of any four had to give out private school vouchers. Toward the end of his second term, Jeb even tried to use children's FCAT scores to hand out bonuses to teachers.

All this, obviously, was only for public schools. For private schools? Well, if the parents of the voucher kids were happy, then Jeb was happy. End of discussion.

• • •

In other words, Jeb instituted a dual-track approach, with two completely different financial and academic standards.

For taxpayers, it meant that our money that went to the public schools had to be accounted for down to the last penny and last paper clip. State money flows to the sixty-seven countywide school districts, which, through locally elected school boards, are responsible for the day-to-day operations of the schools. However, every dime, whether it comes from the state or is raised locally through property taxes, is considered public money, the spending of which is considered a public matter. Anyone from any part of the state (or even outside the state, for that matter) could walk into a school district office and ask to see the ledgers detailing everything from the superintendent's salary to how they purchase toilet paper. It's our money, and the manner in which it is spent is completely our business.

The state government, by the way, wholly supports this transparency, and in fact adds to it with a wide-ranging system of oversight and audits. Local school officials complain that all these checks and balances are time-consuming and unnecessary, but few in Tallahassee believe that state money should simply be signed over to the counties and then forgotten. To the contrary: oversight and "controls" increased, with the support of both Jeb's administration and the Republican legislature, during his eight years in office.

On the other hand—the state money that went to about 1,200 voucher-taking schools? Well, this might aptly be considered one of Jeb's biggest *faith-based* initiatives. Because taxpayers essentially were told to have faith that their money was actually being spent educating children, let alone that it was being spent wisely.

A Floridian who strolled onto the campus of a private school and asked to see the budget—even a school where the majority of the operating budget came from state vouchers – would have been told it was none of his business. If he persisted, the school would have called the police.

Similarly, state officials had no idea how our tax money was being spent at these schools. One of the three programs, the corporate tax credit vouchers, essentially outsourced all administrative functions to the wealthy GOP donor whose $100,000 check led to the program's creation. And in the other two, the extent of the state's oversight was to see that a list of participating students matched up with the number of checks going to each school. That was it. The state didn't know how much was going for school-books versus televisions for the teachers lounge, for the school chaplain versus a nurse, and, most important, for teacher salaries versus the owner's profits (yes, for-profit schools were eligible to participate in Florida's voucher programs). The state didn't know any of these things and, under Jeb, it didn't want to know. The schools were not required to submit audits, and the state was not allowed to audit them.

Jeb and his conservative allies justified this lack of accountability with the claim that the state money was actually only going to the parents, not to the schools, so that it was none of the state's business how the schools were spending it.

The mendacity here was simply breathtaking. Would Republicans who have been talking up the idea of better accountability and slashing waste have taken a similar attitude toward food stamps or Medicaid? Just cut the check and forget about it? Because, after all, the money was for the recipient, and if he wanted to use it for cigarettes and booze or an unnecessary MRI, why was that any of the state's concern?

INCREDIBLY, Jeb's educational system took a similar laissez-faire attitude when it came to academic standards at the voucher schools, too.

The state's 2.7 million public school students were forced to undergo a weeklong, high-stakes standardized test each winter. On those results were based the school's annual letter grade, which in turn determined whether the schools received a hundred dollars per student in reward money, to be spent at the discretion of teachers, administrators, and parents (some went for such things as pizza parties), or, if the school "failed" for two years out of any four, whether it had to offer vouchers to all its students.

Let's repeat that the Florida Comprehensive Assessment Test is not a bad test. If used for its original purpose, it can help parents and can also help county and state education officials flag problem areas. Let's also state right up front that the standards for school success were not terribly high. By Jeb's seventh year in office, 45 percent of the schools received As and 21 percent received Bs. Which meant that two out of three schools were above average. In Florida. On its very face the idea had a Lake Woebegone absurdity—but let that go for a moment.

What's more important here is the vast gulf between the academic tracking of the public schools and total lack of academic oversight for the voucher-taking private schools.

The public schools have to teach to the Sunshine State Standards, which spell out in precise detail what needs to be known by the various grade levels. The standards state, for example, that by the fifth grade, a student should "understand significant achievements in the humanities to the time of the Renaissance (e.g., Roman architecture and Greek art)." And that by the eighth grade, a student should "know that there is an energy difference between an electron near the nucleus and one further away." The FCAT, in addition to testing for reading comprehension and mathematical skills, also looks to see whether students are meeting these benchmarks.

So given this intense interest to make sure that public school students were actually learning, there would have been an equal interest to ensure that children getting public money to attend private schools were also learning, right?

Wrong. Jeb's interest in seeing how the voucher children were doing was approximately zero. Zilch. *Nada.*

Even six years after his voucher programs began, a taxpayer had absolutely no way of knowing how well, if at all, students using private school vouchers were doing academically. The latter two programs created, the McKay voucher for disabled children and the corporate tax voucher for poorer children, had no testing requirement at all. The original plan, the Opportunity Scholarship voucher, engendered the most debate of the three in the legislature and thereby the most—comparatively speaking, of course—oversight. Children getting that voucher had to take the FCAT every year.

But Jeb's education department kept the results of that testing secret from the public, arguing that federal privacy laws prevented them from disclosing, even in the aggregate, how voucher children at any given school had done on the state test. The only person given access to these scores was Jay Greene, a researcher at the pro-voucher Manhattan Institute.

This issue arose as an aside during the Florida Supreme Court oral arguments in the voucher case in 2005, when Justice Fred Lewis asked how the children taking the vouchers were doing on their tests. Jeb's lawyers floundered for a few moments, and then announced that Jay Greene said they were doing just great. Justice Lewis was not impressed.

Testing was merely one missing element in Jeb's lack of concern. While the public schools must track uniform standards in their curricula, the voucher-taking schools could use whatever curriculum they wanted. The laws for public schools said they had to use certified teachers who had undergone intensive criminal background checks. The voucher laws said that private schools had to use teachers who had a bachelor's degree, or three years of experience, or "have special skills, knowledge, or expertise that qualifies them to provide instruction in subjects taught." Since these "special skills, knowledge, or expertise" were not defined anywhere, the schools could interpret that any way they wanted. They could use homeless guys as teachers—in fact, one voucher school in Miami's Liberty City area did exactly that, inviting men from the homeless shelter across the street to help out in class. Voucher schools also did not have to bother with criminal background checks for anyone other than the owner and principal.

Public schools had to provide teachers with special training for students with disabilities. Voucher schools could receive, under the McKay program, the large dollar amounts that came with each disabled child, but were under no obligation to provide any services. Astonishingly, 77 percent of the schools taking the McKay voucher for disabled children had no teachers trained to teach disabled children, according to a *Palm Beach Post* analysis I did in 2003.

As long as the parents who kept their children at these schools were satisfied, the state was satisfied.

Who cared what they were learning? What difference did it make if the teachers had any experience? Or were certified to teach? Or if the curriculum was any good? Jeb and his allies in the legislature declared that once the parent had chosen a private school instead of a public school, that act, in and of itself, was a metric of success.

This double standard led to an obvious but absurd conclusion: if you were a parent who chose to put your child in a public school, you were not deemed capable of determining whether the school was doing a good job and therefore needed Jeb's education department as a constant nanny.

But the instant you took a voucher and moved your child from a public school and into a private one, you were fully and instantly endowed with all the insight and intelligence you could possibly need to make an informed choice about your child's school.

In other words: public school parents were morons. Voucher-school parents were geniuses.

A REVEALING example of this double standard came in late 2005. The issue was "intelligent design," which was under trial in a Pennsylvania federal court, but which was being taught as scientific fact in many, perhaps most, of the voucher-taking schools in Florida.

In contrast, Florida's Sunshine State Standards in the area of science—written, by the way, in 1996 under the leadership of education commissioner Frank Brogan, a Republican who later served as Jeb's lieutenant governor during his first term—included specific knowledge about how genetic mutations occur and how natural selection allows these variations to dominate or die out. These ideas, of course, are the fundamental concepts underlying the theory of evolution. (It is necessary to stipulate this because Jeb claimed, mystifyingly, that the Sunshine State Standards did not include Darwinism or evolution.)

This is not a trivial thing. The theory of evolution, after one hundred and fifty years of experiments and refinement, is now considered the basis of modern biology. Students who want to study science in college, or even want to get into a competitive college, pretty much need to know and understand evolutionary biology.

So how about Florida's private, voucher-taking schools? What sort of science were they teaching? Well, as it turned out, a good many of them were teaching "science" as understood by Bob Jones University and Pensacola Christian College.

A seventh-grade Bob Jones science book, *Life Science for Christian Schools,* includes the subchapter: "How Biological Evolution Supposedly Took Place." The book explains: "The Bible tells us that God directly created all things (John 1:3). The Bible contradicts the theory of evolution. In doing so, the Bible does not contradict true science, since evolution is not science."

The Pensacola Christian College books—sold under the brand "A Beka," after the husband and wife team who founded the college—also teach that evolution is false and that the universe and everything in it were created as per the story in Genesis. It prints an eighth-grade book titled *Matter and Motion in God's Universe* that ends, according to the publisher's catalog, "with a chapter on science versus the false philosophy of evolution." A Beka's sixth-grade science book, *Observing God's World,* teaches "the universe as the direct creation of God and refutes the man-made idea of evolution."

One fourth of all voucher-taking schools in Florida were secular, and a similar percentage were religious schools, like Catholic schools, that nonetheless tracked many of the Sunshine State Standards, including the theory of evolution. But the results of a 2003 *Palm Beach Post* survey of voucher schools found that 43 percent of the religious schools that responded reported using either A Beka or Bob Jones or both. Applied to the statewide total, it means about 375 voucher-taking religious schools, educating about 8,700 students, used one or both of those curricula.

No one questions whether parents have the right to indoctrinate their children thusly. But a fair question was: did these parents have the right to get taxpayer money to help them do so? According to Jeb, the answer was resoundingly yes.

What was really astounding about his defense of this maligning of science using state money was that it was done *at exactly the same time* as Jeb's half-billion dollar attempt to bring Scripps Research Institute to Florida. The irony was nothing short of magnificent. All Scripps scientists do is prove, day in and day out, the validity of evolutionary biology through their experiments that reveal more about the genomes of both humans and the diseases that attack us.

What are the chances that a child who learns all she knows about biology through the A Beka or the Bob Jones texts will have a shot at doing some of that research in years hence? And how did that advance Jeb's claim that voucher schools provide parents a better academic foundation for their children?

So I asked exactly that question one day: should children attending voucher schools get the type of science background that would enable them to work someday at Scripps?

There was a long, long pause as Jeb sorted through the possible responses, until finally: "That is so loaded. That's like—you've already written the article, why do you want me in it? It's not fair."

I pressed: is that a no?

"No, that's nothing. That's no comment. The governor refused to comment. That's what it is in the article: the governor refused to comment."

Conservative Christians, in fact, and the need to placate them, no matter how outlandish their demands, was a core element to Jeb's entire voucher scheme. Nothing demonstrates this better than Jeb's choice for his top education aide for most of his two terms. In fact, I would go further—that it is impossible to understand Jeb's education policies in Florida without first understanding that one woman, Patricia Levesque.

Levesque was truly an oddity in the Jeb Bush inner circle. Many were longtime acolytes, going back to the 1994 run and further. Some had worked in his father's campaigns or in his White House. All were personally devoted to all things Jeb, and that was their ultimate qualification.

Patricia Levesque was different, an outsider with precursor loyalties to someone in Tallahassee other than Jeb, the sort of person he generally did not permit inside the star chamber. Even more unusual, she was extremely smart—in terms of pure intellectual horsepower, she was probably smarter than Jeb. True, Jeb wanted bright people around him, but he wanted this quality because it enabled these people to more efficiently fulfill his wishes. Jeb enjoys being the smartest guy in the room, and it became clear over the years that he didn't really want people smarter than him working for him. The fact that she was, and remained in such a high-profile spot for so long, was completely out of character. Finally, and most important, she had her own agenda—making her possibly the only staffer who achieved that level of power and access in Jeb's world with that distinction. She had an agenda, and she was pushing it full-bore before she joined his team, and she continued pushing it full-bore after she was given his imprimatur. Again, this would not have been tolerated with anyone else. But Patricia Levesque, as we will see, got away with it and for a very good reason.

She had come to Tallahassee to work for Daniel Webster in 1996, when he became the first Republican to become state House speaker since Reconstruction. She was an education policy adviser and, by his second and final year, she pushed a kindergarten voucher plan as a way to twist the Senate president's top goal of early childhood education around to suit her own ideology. Democrat Lawton Chiles was still governor then, and the moderate Republican Senate had little interest in sending public money to religious schools, either, and her plan went nowhere.

A year later, when Jeb had replaced Lawton and Jeb pal John Thrasher replaced Webster as House speaker, Levesque pushed her way to the top education staff post in the House, from where she warded off changes to Jeb's cherished, school-testing-and-vouchers "A-plus" plan as it moved through the legislature. Her assistance was not forgotten. Nor was her enthusiasm in finagling through the legislature and then expanding two other voucher plans in 2000 and 2001. So that in 2002, when the education slot came open in Jeb's Office of Policy and Budget, Levesque was a shoo-in. And once she had regular access to Jeb, it took her only a year to rise to deputy chief of staff, still overseeing education issues.

It was from that perch that she single-handedly laid waste to any and all attempts to bring common sense oversight to either vouchers or the testing scheme that generated vouchers for Jeb's prized "Opportunity Scholarship" program. This meant quashing proposals from in-house reformers like Robert Metty who dared suggest that Jeb's Department of Education had an obligation to keep track of participating students and schools. When Metty put his claim of an attempted cover-up in writing, he was transferred to a do-nothing job under a supervisor who was technically below him on the food chain. When Metty then began speaking out to the press, he was fired.

Levesque approached her mission of keeping public money flowing to religious schools with a ruthlessness that cowed opponents. You were either with the program, or you were a fifth columnist siding with the liberal media and other enemies of school choice. She vilified the Florida Catholic Conference, which had been Jeb's original ally in vouchers—whose schools, in fact, had taken a majority of the first batch of voucher children. But the Catholic Conference came to see that the string of publicized abuses in the programs proved the need for stronger financial and academic oversight. Which is to say, the Catholic Conference had gone to the dark side, and Levesque quickly banished them. And when a colleague and I got close to exposing a scammer who had set himself up as a voucher administrator, Levesque schemed to cook up a plausible reason to boot him from the program while covering up the real reason they were doing so.

These last steps should have been career-enders, particularly for an outsider like Levesque who did not have a long history with Jeb. Openly attempting to lie to the public and—incredibly—leaving an e-mail trail to document it? Ostracizing a major religious group because of a policy disagreement? After all, Jeb was a Catholic. Didn't that count for something?

Not in this instance, because Levesque, you see, was a fundamentalist Christian. Not just any fundamentalist, mind, but an honest-to-God, Bob Jones University graduate. Yes, Bob Jones, where it is taught that Catholics and other impure Christians are going to hell, just like Muslims, Jews, Hindus, and all the other heathens.

She was the sort of person who, as a staff member for the House, publicly dressed down a Jewish state senator who dared question a provision Levesque had tried to sneak into a rewrite of the school code that encouraged prayer at public schools. She was the sort to proselytize coworkers, and explain to them how their choice of a church home was the most important decision they could make.

With this in mind, the arc of Jeb's voucher fixation, and his tolerance for someone as intolerant at Patricia Levesque begins to make sense.

For it was clear from the get-go that Jeb's voucher scheme as drafted would not stand. Florida's constitution was unambiguous in its prohibition of public money going to sectarian institutions. This was a no-brainer, and the Florida Supreme Court spelled it out early in Jeb's final year in office. So why put so much energy, so much capital, so much in outside legal fees, for something that was doomed from the start?

Ultimately, the only explanation that made any sense was the political benefit of satisfying the 23 percent of the state's electorate who thought the way Patricia Levesque thought. These voters already knew that judges were godless-secular-humanist liberals. When they struck down a godly program like school vouchers, this gave Jeb yet another rhetorical club with which to clobber them—and yet another chit with the Christian Right.

POSSIBLY THE worst thing about Jeb's vouchers was the attention they stole from the state's public schools, which, under the state constitution, should have been the focus of both Jeb and the legislature all along.

Instead, the public schools became Jeb's whipping boy. True, he visited a great many of them, and frequently had his photograph taken within them reading to small, black children. Those relatively few teachers and principals who bought into his do-better-or-else regimen of school reform were given the honor of appearing with him at ceremonies and news conferences to herald the latest great achievement of schools under his guidance.

It came close to self-parody, by the end. Each year, just as the old Soviet Union would congratulate itself for once again smashing all production records, so Jeb and his Department of Education would announce how school grades had astonishingly improved for the third or fourth or fifth consecutive year. By his second term, the vast majority of all schools in the state were getting As and Bs. Florida public schools had become like the children of Lake Woebegone.

How was this possible?

Of course, it was not. The children and the schools did get better at taking standardized tests—at considerable expense in terms of time and curriculum—and the relatively small improvements were enough to move schools up in the letter grades. Let's for the sake of discussion accept the argument that having to drill for the reading test forced poorer readers to improve to some degree. The fact of it remained: looking at national rankings, the picture was nowhere as rosy. Florida remained mired near the bottom in terms of both inputs, like spending, and outputs, like scores and graduation rates. It was for this reason that a group led by former Democratic attorney general Bob Butterworth and former Republican comptroller Bob Milligan recommended that the state do a better job of comparing its scores and its progress against other states, particularly against other states in the region.

Milligan, a former Marine general and one of the few Republican officeholders in Florida who did not feel any compulsion to kowtow to Jeb, put it plainly and simply one day in the seventh year of Jeb's vaunted "A-plus" plan: "We're measuring ourselves against ourselves," he told legislators as he presented the highlights of the report. He added that the comparisons of Florida to other states should set off "a political hand grenade," given the state's rankings. "Right now, we're not doing so red hot."

Really, by year seven, this should not have come as a surprise. In the area of giving raises to his inner circle and his political appointees, Jeb subscribed to the Fortune 500 philosophy that quality talent costs and deserves quality compensation. Not so when it came to education. There, as in most areas of state government, Jeb held the conservative Republican view that *just throwing money at the problem wasn't the answer.* Which is why attracting better teachers by increasing teacher pay was not remotely a priority. Schools would improve, Jeb's reasoning went, because the threat of vouchers would force them to.

Into this mix wandered Kendrick Meek, the ambitious former state trooper son of Carrie Meek, one of the first three black members of Congress from Florida since Reconstruction. Meek, recall, had clawed his way into the state Senate from the House, beating an incumbent thanks to his name and his willingness to campaign hard. In 2000, he goaded Jeb into a foolish reaction to his sit-in over Jeb's efforts to reorganize affirmative action in Florida, thereby sparking the largest demonstration march the capital had seen in decades. He followed up with a massive voter registration drive and turnout effort, nearly costing George W. the election that fall.

Two years later, as Jeb positioned himself for reelection, Meek was at it again, this time pushing a citizen's initiative that, while it did not prevent a second term, redefined what Jeb would be able to accomplish in that second term. The class-size reduction amendment, in fact, quickly became the center point to the entire campaign. Jeb maligned it at every turn, speaking out more forcefully against it than his Democratic opponent that year, Bill McBride.

We've already examined Meek's political skills and timing. Even ascribing to Meek the most impure motives imaginable—that his class-size crusade had nothing to do with the thirty-child kindergarten his daughter was assigned to in Miami, but that it was designed purely and solely to hurt Jeb—the important thing here was that it resonated with ordinary Floridians. Jeb and his allies tried to dismiss the backers of the amendment as the usual liberal special interests, and, it is true, Meek was eventually able to get substantial financial backing from the teachers unions and the liberal People for the American Way. But that doesn't explain why rank-and-file teachers—not union rabble-rousers, but the ordinary, at-work-by-six-thirty-each-morning sort whom Jeb professed to respect and admire so much—were volunteering in supermarket parking lots collecting signatures. It doesn't explain why T-ball moms were downloading petitions off the Internet and passing them around at practice.

TOO MANY PARENTS, in too much of Florida, had for too many years been forced to put up with the type of public schools that are the inevitable consequence of a political philosophy that holds low taxes as its highest virtue. We can debate how it got to be that way, and what share of the blame these selfsame parents bore in that, because it is a fair question. Still, by the spring and summer of 2002, it had become abundantly clear that things were not going to get much better in the schools under Jeb, unless your idea of better was more standardized testing and more vouchers. And since the odds of Jeb winning a second term were looking pretty good, the odds of seeing more state money for more teachers and more schools anytime soon were looking pretty grim.

And then . . . out of the blue, along came this amazing idea, this radical promise that public schools, by force of the state constitution, would have to provide the type of small classes that only rich people who sent their children to quality private schools had heretofore been able to enjoy.

Small wonder that it captured the imagination of not only most public school parents, but even most likely voters, according to polls. Obviously, such a thing would cost a lot more money than Florida had been accustomed to spending on something as pedestrian as public schools. How much more was not specified in the petitions that people were signing. What was specified was that the state, not the local school districts, would have to supply the cash.

Small wonder that it captured the imagination of Jeb and his antitax allies in the Republican legislature and in the business community—much like a terrifying nightmare that zeroes in on the thing we fear the most and makes it so real that we wake up in cold sweats. For Jeb, that nightmare was having to raise taxes—not the smaller "user fees" and built-in tax hikes that he could explain away, but a big, serious tax increase to build lots of new schools and hire lots of new teachers to work in them. The sort of big, serious tax hike that would not play at all well in a Republican primary someday in Iowa or South Carolina.

NOT THAT Jeb personally had an aversion to small classes. Not hardly.

As a child, he attended the Kinkaid school in Houston and then Andover. As a parent he sent his children to the Gulliver Schools in Miami and the Bolles School in Jacksonville. Jeb, when asked, explains that he chose schools for his sons and daughter because of their reputation for academic excellence.

Okay. And what do the schools themselves say about it? They attempt to prove their academic excellence . . . in part by bragging how small their classes are. Gulliver Schools aimed for between sixteen and twenty children in each class. Bolles said it had a policy of no more than twenty. Andover's Web site showed its commitment to a quality education with a class-size limit of fourteen. Kinkaid brags to prospective teachers about its standards of excellence, one of which is small class sizes.

Of all the policies Jeb pursued during his tenure in office, this was easily the most hypocritical. Jeb honestly believed that lowering taxes on the rich is the best way to ensure economic prosperity. We might argue that his belief was not based on actual facts, that this was quasi-religious dogma, but his belief appeared to be genuine. Same even with vouchers. We might suggest that his faith in their efficacy was just that, faith, because no empirical evidence showed that they improved the performance of students who received them. Still, there was no denying: Jeb truly believed that private school vouchers were a good and fair and just policy.

On the issue of class size, there was only hypocrisy, pure and simple— and not only because of Jeb's own schooling and his school choices for his own children. Recall that one of his main justifications for supporting school vouchers was to give poor parents the same opportunities for a quality private school education enjoyed by the rich. Okay. So why didn't that logic apply to public school parents who wanted private school class sizes? In fact, it was not merely public school parents who wanted smaller class sizes. When the *Palm Beach Post* surveyed voucher-taking private schools in 2003, what was one of the top reasons that parents gave for choosing them? Yup, small class sizes—along with their desire for religion instruc-tion for their children. Parents attending the massive pro-voucher rallies or-ganized in part by Levesque confirmed this, frequently citing smaller classes as a reason they liked private schools. (Another reason they would often give: to escape the public schools' never-ending emphasis on the FCAT, the standardized test that Jeb made all-important for students, teachers, and schools.)

The truth of it is that even if every child in Florida were given a voucher today, there are not enough private schools, let alone *good* private schools, to enroll even a tiny fraction of the children in the public schools. And those who believe that the free market would over time solve this proba-bly need to go back to economics class. *Good* private schools cost good money: as much or more than what the public schools are given. Jeb, of all people, should know this from all the tuition checks he has written.

So never mind that all that the people who signed those petitions wanted was a feature that voucher-taking parents considered impor-tant. Never mind that reducing class sizes had been a bipartisan legislative priority—admittedly a minor one—since the mid-1990s. It was never a *Jeb* priority, at least not for the public schools, and he was not about to let it become one.

AN IMPORTANT point that frequently gets lost on this issue is that Kendrick Meek, before he went the route of standing outside Publix su-permarkets holding a clipboard, tried to get his fellow legislators to do something "within the process," as its defenders call it, to lower class sizes. Meek had urged lawmakers to expand the legislative efforts to reduce class size, which for several years had been $100 million a year—a literal drop in the bucket, in a multibillion-dollar public schools budget—until Jeb abolished the effort as part of his A-plus plan.

In 2001, Meek and some fellow Democrats sponsored a constitutional amendment within the legislature—they needed three-fifths vote in both chambers, and then voter approval in the next general election—to impose caps of sixteen, twenty, and twenty-five students per class, depending on the grade level. The House, then run like the old Soviet Politburo by Jeb ally Tom Feeney, killed the proposal in committee, citing a $12.2 billion cost estimate by a team of state economists. Remember that number, be-cause it is significant in what was to follow.

Meek shrugged off the defeat and said that if Jeb and his friends in the legislature wouldn't do something about class sizes, then the people would. He started a political committee to raise money and went about collecting signatures to put the question on the ballot in 2002, except that instead of sixteen children per class in the lower grades and twenty in the middle grades, the citizen initiative called for a cap of eighteen in grades kindergarten through three and twenty-two in grades four through eight. The cap of twenty-five for high school classes was left alone. The caps also were to apply only for core courses—not music, art, or physical education, for example—and the state, not the local school districts, would be responsible for finding the money.

At first, Jeb's people laughed off Meek's threat. Despite the abuse the citizens initiative process in Florida gets, it is not an easy thing to get one-tenth of the number of registered voters from the last general election to sign a petition, get the Florida Supreme Court to approve the technical language of your proposal, get all your signatures verified, and then raise money to pay for an ad campaign to fight whatever interest groups line up against you. By October 2001, they weren't laughing anymore, as Meek had successfully gathered the 50,000 signatures he needed to get the question before the Florida Supreme Court. By April 2002, they didn't think it was funny at all, as the court ruled that the question satisfied the stringent demands of their review process and could be on the ballot come November.

Jeb went into full battle mode. The initiative, still lacking the necessary signatures to make the ballot, was enjoying support in various polls of near seventy percent. Jeb, though, was convinced that if people believed the amendment would bankrupt the state, they would vote against it, and that was what Jeb set out to show—using the machinery of state government at his disposal.

He rammed through a willing legislature a law requiring citizen initiatives—but *only* citizen initiatives; ballot questions put on by the legislature were exempt—to receive a formal cost estimate. This would be done by economists appointed by Jeb and by his allies in the Republican-led legislature. If it sounds like a stacked deck, it was. That was the idea: the Revenue Estimating Conference would come up with an enormous price tag on the idea, and that number would be printed on all the ballots that voters would see as they went to cast their votes. Meek and his supporters cried foul and went to the courts as Jeb's people forged ahead.

. . .

THE MOST amazing part of this whole process was that the economists came up with an estimate of *only* $27 billion. Actually, Jeb's people had pushed for an even bigger number, more like $50 billion, but were eventually talked down from the ledge with the argument that, should the amendment pass, it would be hard to explain at that point why the state should spend any less than $50 billion. Actually, that same argument wound up applying with the $27 billion figure—but we get ahead of ourselves.

First off, the $27 billion was arrived at using a method never before used by the Revenue Estimating Conference, which over the years had earned a reputation for nonpolitical economic analysis. Typically, the economists would consider one-time costs, usually start-up expenses or construction of new buildings, and then recurring costs, or the annualized expense once the new program was fully up and running. Recall the 2001 House of Representatives' estimate of $12.2 billion? That was for a class-size reduction proposal that had even smaller classes at the lower and middle grades, and therefore should have been *larger* than the estimate for Meek's ballot initiative. That's because the 2001 estimate was done honestly—using the same methodology that economists had used for years. In 2002, under the gun from Jeb's office to cook up a really big number that would terrify voters, the economists came up with a new algorithm that would give Jeb something closer to what he was looking for.

Instead of counting total capital costs plus the final, end-of-implementation annual operating cost—the $12 billion figure from 2001, for example, was about $9 billion to build classrooms, plus $3 billion a year extra to pay all the new teachers—this new estimate used a *cumulative* total for the operating costs. So instead of $9 billion to build schools and $3 million a year to operate them, the state's economists determined that Meek's amendment would cost $9 billion to build the schools and *$18 billion* more to operate them over the eight-year ramp-up period.

It made absolutely no sense, and such estimates had never been done that way before, for anything. Why produce an estimate totaling the cost over eight years? Why not ten or two or thirty? There was no logical or defensible reason. The purpose of the Revenue Estimating Conference had been to match up costs of new projects to the state's revenue streams: how much one-time, capital money would something cost? How much would it take each year to operate? Now, under Jeb, that had been corrupted to produce a sufficiently scary number. No less than the senior member of the Revenue Estimating Conference, Ed Montanaro, said as much when the committee released its price tag. (Montanaro had worked at the Capitol for some three decades; he was gone within a year.)

The complaints of a single, obviously *liberal* economist, naturally, could not stop Jeb's $27 billion juggernaut. Nor could the *liberal* newspapers that reported on this interesting new analytic method. By the end of the summer, though, the Florida Supreme Court did put a significant damper on Jeb's mission by declaring unconstitutional his plan to give voters cost estimates. Justices ruled that the citizen-initiative process was created in the constitution, and only a change to the constitution could impose such new requirements.

Jeb, predictably, was livid, as he was pretty much any time the judiciary interfered with his plans. He called the decision "incomprehensible" and lashed out at the justices. "The court appears to be condoning a situation that would leave Florida voters in the dark concerning initiatives that will have a significant impact on our state's economy for decades to come."

Well, not exactly. What the court was saying was that the governor and the legislature could not, without the approval of the voters, diminish a right that the voters had given themselves in the Constitution of 1968.

Jeb, also predictably, did not accept the court's ruling as final defeat. That would come only after a grueling autumn campaign that saw him hammer at the class-size amendment as a budgetary Armageddon. At campaign stop after campaign stop, he warned that passing the amendment would mean cutting nursing home care for old people or laying off child abuse investigators. That the amendment would "block out the sun," was another favorite, as was the threat of a massive, broad-based tax increase. The Lieutenant governor, Frank Brogan, pointed out how the $27 billion estimate represented fully half of the state budget at the time—which was about as relevant as comparing it to the gross domestic product of Peru, insofar as the $27 billion would be spent over eight years, not one.

With his relentless pounding, Jeb was able to drive support for the amendment from its lofty 70 percent approval ratings down . . . down. . . . If the campaign had lasted another week, he might have been able to beat it. But he could not. It passed with 52.4 percent of the vote.

So even as voters resoundingly gave him a second term, they saddled him with an educational mandate that he had warned would mean the end of the world as we knew it. It was as if they were saying: Jeb, we think you've got the right stuff to be our governor. We just think you need some clearer direction.

. . .

A GOVERNOR with perhaps a wee bit smaller ego might have noticed the discrepancy in the vote tallies, that the class-size amendment had won some counties that he also had won. That voters had apparently taken his warnings of program cuts and tax increases to heart, but had then voted in favor of better, more expensive public education anyway.

Another governor whose brother had carried a state by a mere five hundred thirty-seven votes might have seen a hypocrisy issue in challenging a ballot initiative that passed by 232,530 votes.

Jeb Bush was neither of these governors. The election results had not been officially certified before Jeb and his people were already scheming how best to push a repeal. Actually, he had already telegraphed this strategy during the campaign, when, unbeknownst to him, a reporter had recorded his candid promise to Panhandle officials that he had a "couple of devious plans" to undo the amendment if it somehow were to pass. Although he later apologized for his use of the word "devious," he did not apologize at all for his vow to fight a voter-approved constitutional amendment.

On March 4, 2003, exactly one hundred twenty days after voters had both reelected him and passed the class-size initiative, Jeb stood at the dais in the Florida House chambers and explained that voters simply did not understand. "So I believe we must go back to the voters and have them make a decision with all the information in hand," he said in his State of the State speech, as his office pushed for a special election that September.

But Republican dominance in the Florida legislature was not so lopsided as to give Jeb's party the three-quarters majority he needed in both chambers to get a special election. In fact, even a number of conservative Republicans were uneasy about telling the electorate so soon that they knew what they were doing when they reelected Jeb and maintained GOP control of the legislature, but that they got stupid a little further down the ballot. A special election was a must, by the way, and not a 2004 general election ballot question because the last thing Jeb wanted was to rile up Meek and the Democrats again as his brother sought reelection.

His next major repeal push came after George W. was safely ensconced for a second term, in the spring legislative session of 2005. This time, Jeb's plan really was devious, at least compared to his previous *"You idiots! Take it back!"* approach.

For the first time since Jeb became governor, he made a serious push for higher teacher salaries. The minimum salary in Florida would be $35,000, lifting the average starting salary by about $3,500, and guaranteeing every teacher at least a $2,000 raise. As Jeb explained it, there was nothing more important than highly qualified school teachers, and the only way to get this quality was with higher pay. Of course there was a catch: voters had to repeal the class-size amendment as part of the package.

In terms of sheer mendacity, this one probably wins hands down.

For one thing, there was absolutely no reason to tie the higher salaries, an admittedly important goal, to eliminating the class-size mandate. Since Jeb took office, he and his legislative allies had slashed the recurring tax base by $1.6 billion a year. Had they instead applied that money to teacher pay, they could have made the starting teacher salary in Florida $40,500 and the average salary $49,100, putting Florida in the top quartile in the nation on both counts, according to a *Palm Beach Post* analysis. Even in that single year, 2005, Jeb could have paid for the bulk of his $488 million teacher salary proposal by forgoing the $430 million in new tax cuts he was seeking.

Not even Jeb could come up with a passable explanation of why it had taken seven years into his term to press for higher teacher pay. Asked directly, Jeb paused to think about it, and then said: "That's a good question."

The answer, of course, is simple: the proposal had less to do with helping teachers than it did with dividing the teachers union and generally punishing South Florida, where the voters who most enthusiastically supported the amendment resided. Starting teacher salaries in South Florida counties were already right around $35,000, meaning teachers there would have received the least benefit. And because those counties have the worst classroom crowding, parents there would have lost out on the benefits of the amendment just as it was starting to have a real effect. Under the law legislators passed in 2003, class sizes had been measured by countywide averages through the 2005–06 school year, but were to use school averages starting in 06–07. The difference in cost between the two methods was staggering, as were the reductions in class sizes at fast-growing suburban schools.

Even Jeb's inordinate hold over Cuban-American Republicans from Miami-Dade County was not enough to overcome the obvious detriment to South Florida contained within Jeb's proposal. In fact, the first state senator to get up and speak against Jeb's plan when it came to the floor was Alex Villalobos, the Senate majority leader. He announced that a repeal would hurt his constituents, while Jeb's teacher salary proposal would provide teachers in his district with minimal help. When he voted no, the two other Miami Cubans in the Senate, both Republicans, voted no as well. In the end, Jeb's repeal went down 19–21 in a state Senate that had twenty-six Republicans. He needed twenty-four votes to pass a ballot question, but he couldn't even get a majority.

Ironically, one or two modifications to his plan probably would have mollified Republican critics from South Florida. A starting teacher salary indexed to the local cost of living, for example. But doing so would have made the proposal less punitive to South Florida, and Jeb was not willing to budge. It was he, in fact, who insisted on a recorded floor vote on his proposal, even though he should have known beforehand that he was going to lose. There was some measure of embarrassment in a recorded tally, sure, but the vote sheet was worth it. Now he had an updated list of whom to punish.

IF THAT were the worst thing Jeb did regarding the class-size amendment, trying to persuade legislators and voters to undo it, that would have been one thing. That might have been somewhat rude, but tolerable, so long as he was at the same time complying with its obligations.

Were that the case, he could argue that he was merely trying to do right by Floridians, doing his best to warn them off of something he just knew was a terrible public policy, yet at the same time understanding his responsibilities and carrying them out.

With Jeb, Floridians got a governor who not only harangued them for four straight years for ignoring him and putting the class-size caps in the constitution, but who then also flouted their will on the matter. Sure, Jeb claimed forcefully and often that he was complying with the constitutional mandate by setting aside hundreds of millions of dollars for "class-size reduction" in each year's budget.

The politest way of describing his approach was that it was a complete sham—lip service, and barely a dime more.

In fact, Jeb's bullheaded insistence in the summer of 2002 on proving just how costly the amendment would be if it passed wound up providing his critics in every subsequent year the proof of just how shamelessly he was ignoring the amendment.

The state economists, while disingenuously totaling eight years of operating costs to come up with the staggering $27 billion figure, actually went to great pains to detail each individual year's costs. And those individual estimates were actually done fairly and accurately. They assumed, logically, that construction money would have to be poured in heavily in the early years, in order to get schools built in time to meet the more difficult class-size reduction targets in the later years.

At the time, Jeb defended the validity of the Revenue Estimating Conference's numbers, pointing out how carefully they had been put together. He had only been trying to get an honest assessment of the proposal's cost, he had insisted, and not ginning up a big number so as to generate sticker shock. Recall also that Jeb's people had originally tried to get an even bigger number, more like $50 billion.

So what sort of money did Jeb and his GOP allies in the legislature wind up spending for smaller classes?

Well, in the first year, the economists had estimated the state would have to spend $628 million more to hire new teachers and staff than it otherwise would have, and spend $2.4 billion to jump-start school construction.

Instead, Jeb spent just $2.7 million more for staffing than public education's historical budget trend in recent years would have provided, and only $600 million for school construction.

In the second year, the economists said the state would need to spend $1.3 billion more for teachers and other staff—the original $628 million plus a new $651 million—plus another $2.3 billion for construction.

Instead, Jeb spent a total $5.8 million more for teachers than the schools likely would have gotten anyway, and $100 million for construction.

The third year was even more miserly. The economists had predicted the state would need to spend $1.9 billion more for teachers and staff than without the amendment, and set aside an additional $2 billion for construction.

Jeb spent $10.1 million more for teachers and absolutely nothing more for construction. Nothing, as in zero. *Nada*.

Cumulatively, the first three years following the passage of the class-size amendment should have cost the state $10.6 billion more than it would have spent without the amendment, according to the Revenue Estimating Conference methodology that ultimately gets to $27 billion by the eighth year.

Jeb, whose office pushed for an estimate *twice* the size that economists ultimately produced, instead spent over those first three years a total of $729 million more—or less than 7 percent of the estimated total.

Notwithstanding this, Jeb claimed at news conferences, in press releases, in public speeches, and in e-mail correspondence that he was spending on the order of $500 million more per year, more than $1.5 billion by the third year, to implement the amendment and reduce class sizes. What he failed to mention was that those figures did not represent *additional* money to the schools beyond the historical growth rates, as the state economists in 2002 had contemplated. Rather, he was simply taking that base amount and carving a category out and calling it class-size money. In other words, Jeb's idea of paying for class-size reduction was to make school districts pay for it out of the money they were getting all along.

In retrospect, it was not just a sham. It was, to borrow from Woody Allen, a travesty of a mockery of a sham.

AND SO, after two full terms of Jeb "Education Governor" Bush, Florida public schools were in a place not terribly different from where they were the day he took office.

Despite all his talk about testing and "raising the bar" and closing the achievement gap, et cetera, et cetera, that is the sad truth of Jeb's education legacy—a lot of sound and fury, signifying not much of anything. Even more damning: the progress that *was* made was done so despite Jeb's best efforts, not because of them.

This thread goes back to the idea of an enormous missed opportunity. If Jeb had used his clout with the legislature, his mandate for change upon his 1998 election, and honestly made public education his focus and his top funding priority, just imagine what he could have accomplished.

The billion that went out the door the first year in tax cuts, the half billion the second year—what if that had gone to making school class sizes smaller? Making schools smaller (like he himself had suggested in 1997)? Paying teachers even a little closer to what they were worth? What if, in other words, Jeb had done even a little bit to make the public schools more able to deliver the kind of education that his beloved elite private academies can?

But no. To do so would have cost money, and that was not part of the game plan. Even when voters, despite his repeated entreaties, *told* him they wanted more money spent on schools, and they specifically wanted smaller classes, like the kind they had at the schools where he sent his own children, Jeb found a way to spend the bare minimum possible, all the while scheming to undo the mandate.

Instead, we got testing out the yin and yang and we got vouchers.

The vouchers, in the end, were largely a distraction, ultimately struck down by the Florida Supreme Court. They never got to more than a tiny fraction of Florida schoolchildren, and as they were designed to be unaccountable, it was impossible to know whether the schools that received them could offer any sort of lesson for the state's public schools.

It is important here to restate the challenges that public schools face generally, but particularly in Florida. Our public school system is charged with giving children an elementary and secondary education that will let them compete with children from all over the world, including many places where the culture values schooling far more than we do here. The schools must provide this education to the children of parents who care about these things—but even more important, the schools must provide this education to the children of parents who do not. They must provide this education to children with both mild and severe handicaps. They must provide this education to children without the faintest knowledge of English. In Florida, this last subgroup makes up a significant chunk of the population.

They must perform these tasks despite the antipathy of what is now the governing party in Florida, leaders of whom will chant, like a mantra, that merely throwing more money at schools is not the answer. There is some truth to that, yes. Schools need to be run smartly, perhaps even with a passion, in order to succeed. But really: when a serious lack of money is a big part of the problem, then, in that case, yes, throwing money at the schools *is* a big part of the answer.

Jeb, while ready to devote the state budget to areas he favored—like corporate incentives and massive tax cuts for the state's wealthiest sliver—clung to his idea that all the public schools needed was a kick in the pants to make them improve, and he and Patricia Levesque guarded this goal to the end.

In fact, the most telling clue of this policy comes from how they dealt with not a political opponent, not a midlevel manager like Robert Metty, and certainly not a journalist, but with a high-ranking member of their ruling clique who dared propose the idea that their high-stakes testing regimen was missing the point.

Jim Warford came to Jeb's education department early in his second term. Unlike Levesque, Warford was a product of and a believer in public schools, having grown up poor with a difficult home life, and with public school teachers his only hope of escape. He went on to be a teacher, an administrator, and eventually the elected schools superintendent of Marion County in conservative, north-central Florida. He was a big believer in Jeb-style "accountability," which is why he signed on as public schools chancellor in the reorganized Department of Education when it came under Jeb's direct control.

It didn't take him long to see that all the testing, while measuring progress of schools, was perhaps misdirecting the state's resources. For one thing, the higher scores that Jeb continually touted were from the lower grades. Those were the children who, in Florida and nationally, were already doing relatively well, compared to other countries. The extreme emphasis on FCAT testing in the elementary schools did indeed ramp up those scores—but did nothing to improve scores in middle and high schools, where the state, and the nation, fall rapidly behind schools around the globe. In other words, Jeb's educational focus had been completely misplaced. He had reaped the low-hanging fruit, but the real problems remained.

Warford was not completely naïve, and he kept these views to himself. His downfall was in trying to push what he believed would be an improvement to the testing regimen. He believed that the FCAT test as structured was unfairly not crediting the efforts in big, urban "failing" middle and high schools, where upwards of 90 percent of students were coming in reading not just below grade level, but three and four and five grades below their appropriate level. All of these students would get the lowest possible score on the FACT—even if their teachers had succeeded during the year advancing their reading by two or three grade levels. Was that fair, he wondered, when teachers in the rich suburbs merely had to maintain their students' already high reading ability to earn good FCAT scores?

Warford suggested incorporating a different type of test, one designed to show precisely a student's reading level, in the annual testing schedule. The test only took about twenty minutes to administer as a stand-alone measure, as opposed to the several days required for the FCAT, but there wasn't even any need for a separate test. The FCAT itself was already indexed for its intrinsic reading level, and a grade-level score could easily have been generated and included on the score sheet that went to parents as well as into the state's massive database.

What would doing this show? For one, it would show a year-to-year assessment of a child's reading level, in plain, easily understood English. If, in fact, teachers at poor, black inner-city schools were getting two and three years' worth of reading improvements out of their children, then wasn't that worthy of mention and accolades, even if the kids were still below "grade level" as defined by the state?

Warford thought it was. His bosses vehemently disagreed. Why? Because it was exactly these black, inner-city schools that, by getting an F grade two out of any four years, were generating the vouchers for Jeb's beloved "Opportunity Scholarship" program. If the reason for this failing grade was mitigated by the exceptionally low level of entering students as well as their marked improvement while there, that would call into question the fairness of that F grade as well as the ensuing vouchers. As long as Jeb was governor, there would be no calling into question *anything* about vouchers. Period.

So when Warford's heresy in this area was compounded by his insistence on pushing for other mushy things like better training for teachers and principals, it was only a matter of time until he was shown the door. Warford saw this coming and suggested to Jeb's education commissioner, John Winn, that he would finish some projects and leave after about six months. That was on a Friday. On Monday morning, Warford was brought to Winn's office, where general counsel and Levesque crony Daniel Woodring showed Warford both the resignation letter he was to sign, and if he chose not to, the termination order that would formalize his firing.

In Jeb's education shop as elsewhere—you were either with Jeb, or you were against him. And God help you if you were against him.

Chapter Nine

WHO WANTS TO KNOW?

"No comment, asshole."
—GEORGE W. BUSH, "LOYALTY ENFORCER,"
GEORGE H.W. BUSH PRESIDENTIAL
CAMPAIGN, TO REPORTERS, 1988

*"This is just a friendly reminder to check if there are reporters at
events. I was more forthright than I would have been had I known.
Thanks, team."*
—JEB BUSH, IN A NOTE TO HIS AIDES, 1999

*"I would say that for anybody that leaks information to the press . . .
rather than provides information to prosecutors—there's a problem
there."*
—JEB BUSH, 2005, EXPLAINING WHY WATERGATE'S
"DEEP THROAT," MARK FELT, WAS NOT A HERO

At a Christmas party at the Naval Observatory residence in 1986,
the vice president of the United States and a number of his holiday-punch-
cheered guests sported big yellow buttons on their lapels that asked: "Who
is Max Gomez?"

The question had recently been the buzz of Washington, D.C., as the long-simmering Iran-Contra affair reached full boil with the revelation that our country had secretly sold weapons to anti-American radicals in Iran, then used the proceeds to fund a by-then illegal war against the Nicaraguan government. The scandal would fritter away what was left of Ronald Reagan's effectiveness in his second term, but on that particular night, to Vice President George H.W. Bush, it was all a big joke.

Because Max Gomez was really a cover name for Felix Rodriguez, a Bay of Pigs veteran, friend of George H.W. and CIA operative up to his neck in the arms-for-hostages-for-money-for-*contra*-rebels operation. And George H.W., in his attempts to misstate his lack of knowledge of the affair, had mistakenly referred to Max Gomez as *Felix* Gomez, thereby letting sharp-eared reporters make the connection.

So while Congress, the media, and the public might have been outraged that the executive branch had run amok, conducting a secret foreign policy in direct contravention of the elected legislature, George H.W. and his pals actually thought it was kind of funny. Funny enough to print up buttons. Funny enough to welcome the linchpin of the operation, Marine lieutenant colonel Oliver North, when he showed up.

The buttons and the camaraderie with North, of course, were mere tokens—much like Che Guevara's wristwatch that Gomez/Rodriguez kept as a reminder of the time he had interrogated the Cuban revolutionary prior to his execution by Bolivian soldiers. What should really have made Americans mad was the way George H.W. stonewalled Iran-Contra prosecutor Lawrence Walsh, refusing to turn over diaries detailing his knowledge of the events until after he had been defeated for reelection in 1992—and then pardoning everyone involved, effectively ending Walsh's investigation.

The most amazing part of it all is that George H.W., through none of this, ever doubted that he was in the right. Richard Ben Cramer, in his detailed study of the election of 1988, in fact described George H.W.'s unsuccessful push to keep the whole thing under wraps as the only forceful dissent he had displayed in his entire eight years in the Reagan White House. George H.W. himself wrote in his diary the day he learned that secretary of state George Schultz had handed over seven hundred pages of notes of his meetings with Reagan: "I found this almost inconceivable. Not only that he kept the notes, but that he'd turned them all over to Congress. . . . I would never do it. I would never surrender such documents and I wouldn't keep such detailed notes."

Would never surrender such documents.

Sound familiar? Because if America generally did not get enough of that mind-set with George W. in the White House, we in Florida certainly got used to it here under the Jeb regime.

Here, as in many places: like father, like son.

IN A HEALTHY republic filled with knowledgeable citizens actively participating in the responsibilities of self-government, this one Bush family trait would get them run out of town on a rail the very first time it showed itself.

To put it succinctly: government secrecy is anti–American. Period. End of story.

Sure, an argument can be made for battle plans and such in a time of genuine war, but those should be rare and limited exceptions. It's our government. It's our money. All those documents being generated at the behest of this powerful interest or that inside player? They are being written on *our* dime, using computers and printers and paper that *we* paid for. People fortunate enough to get elected work for *us,* not the other way around.

Yes, Bush family politicians say some of these same things during political campaigns. But it's clear that they don't really mean them. In fact, their view of it is generally quite the opposite. Their ideal government operates on a "need to know" basis. Unfortunately, in the vast majority of cases on the vast majority of issues, you the average citizen simply do not need to know what the Bush in charge is up to.

From George H.W.'s almost pathological need for secrecy to George W.'s insistence on keeping under wraps details on everything from the nation's energy policy to the response to the September 11 terrorist attacks to Jeb's undermining of Florida's open government laws—it's all of a piece. We know better than you. We are your leaders. Trust us. We'll take care of it. No need to bother your little heads.

To understand why Jeb's incarnation of this secret-squirrel paternalism was particularly offensive, it is necessary to appreciate the primacy of the state's Sunshine Laws, as they are known. They have been a Florida tradition for nearly a century, having been on the books since 1909. In 1992, voters actually enshrined them in the state constitution. Today, if lawmakers want to take a public record that is currently available for inspection and make it exempt from the law, they must do so with two-thirds vote of both legislative chambers—a high threshold that, for open records advocates, makes it easier to defeat such attempts.

Even before that constitutional amendment was passed, both trial court and appellate court judges have taken the open records law and the public meetings law seriously. Local officials, in fact, have gone to jail for refusing to turn over documents to people who asked for them or, more commonly, having even the briefest discussion with elected colleagues outside the confines of a formal meeting. The law is quite clear about this. A city council member cannot discuss an issue that is under consideration by the council with other members except in the format of a public meeting for which adequate notice has been given so that the public can attend. Meaning: no phone calls, no "chance" encounters over lunch to build alliances, no horse-trading on the golf course. If this sounds drastic, it is—and it's the way Floridians like it. In fact, when it became clear that legislators had avoided putting themselves under the rules that the Sunshine Law imposed on the state executive branch and on all local governments, citizens in their 1992 constitutional amendment approved provisions making it unlawful for three or more state legislators to hold an unnoticed meeting to discuss a vote on any bill. Further, the governor could not meet with the legislative presiding officers unless that meeting, too, had been duly "noticed."

So what did Jeb do on his very first full day in office?

Naturally, host a secret meeting with the House speaker and the Senate president.

By that point, he had been a resident of Florida for eighteen years. He had been familiar with county and city governments in Miami, through his position as chairman of the Dade County Republican Party. He knew, from his experience as a developer, how these entities such as zoning commissions were supposed to function properly. He had been the state secretary of commerce under Governor Bob Martinez.

It was not decades of experience, no, but it was enough for him to have a general familiarity with the open meetings law. And yet, when he was confronted about it that day by news media, there was neither contrition nor shame. Instead, it was annoyance edging on anger, that reporters—*reporters!*—had the gall to question his ability to meet with his Republican legislative allies. It was the first opportunity Capitol press corps journalists had to see the new governor in ticked-off mode, complete with crossed arms and flaring nostrils. It would not be the last.

Jeb that day promised he would abide by the constitution and open future meetings to the press and public. He did not, however, promise to abide by the spirit of the law. A year and a half later, during the summer of 2000, Jeb invited the new incoming speaker and president to the Governor's Mansion for a private lunch. The menu was fish, cooked in a Chinese sauce. The ingredients were purchased with taxpayer money. The meal was prepared by a chef on the public payroll. The topics under discussion had to do with state government, which, last time I checked, was of reasonable concern and interest to the taxpayers of Florida.

Jeb, incoming Senate president John McKay and incoming House Speaker (and former Jeb running mate) Tom Feeney all defended their decision to lay out the framework of their two years together behind the Mansion's iron gates. Feeney, who loves to talk about the Founding Fathers and the Federalist Papers, explained how it was so difficult to get anything done in public, how it stifled the flow of ideas. Well, take that to its logical conclusion, and it begs the question of why we would want any public meetings at all—or, for that matter, even a representative government. An enlightened despot would really get things done far more efficiently.

In the end, unfortunately, there are any number of ways for a determined governor to get around the open meetings law. Phone calls to one legislative presiding officer at a time, for example. Or a meeting of top aides, whose role as staff makes them immune from Sunshine Law requirements. And, it's true, Jeb quickly turned to these less press-confrontational methods from that point forward.

It's also true that previous governors had used similar gimmicks to avoid scrutiny. What distinguished Jeb Bush's administration from its predecessors was a comprehensive strategy to undermine the second and, frankly, more important of Florida's open government laws: the state's public records statute.

Jeb's office tightened control of public records requests, centralizing decisions on what to release and to whom to release it and how to release it. They set up new barriers and invented new, time-consuming processes.

This should have been a complete outrage to Floridians. Again, Jeb worked for them and any documents created in the process of this work belonged to them. So what was the public response? A vast, lethargic yawn.

Jeb correctly read how unconcerned average Floridians were about his moves to consolidate control over the flow of state government information and took aggressive advantage of it.

2000: Jeb, with much fanfare, releases his first "e-budget" on compact discs. Jeb promised his administration would be the most open of any in Florida, but in the end became the most secretive in modern history, routinely stonewalling and creating barriers to the release of public information. As Jeb released his proposed budget for the coming year, two black lawmakers continued a sit-in in his office to protest his dismantling of affirmative-action programs.

PHOTO: STATE OF FLORIDA

Given his personality, given his family, this really should not have surprised anyone.

S OMETIMES WHEN politicians get elected to office and they have lousy relations with the news media, it can be blamed on their unfamiliarity with how journalism works. They don't understand core concepts like, for example, a daily deadline. An evening news segment will air that night regardless of the quality or truthfulness of the elected official's "side" of the story. A newspaper reporter will file an article that evening for publication the next day, whether or not the politician's people get back with her answers to questions. This is basic, nuts-and-bolts stuff, but it still occasionally happens that elected leaders and the press corps who cover them get sideways over it.

This was never a problem with Jeb. To the contrary, it was not that Jeb and his people did not understand the news media well enough, it was that he understood the media too well.

He understood the "inside access" that too many of us crave. He understood the dynamics of statewide and regional competition among newspapers. He appreciated that most journalists, particularly younger ones, are cowed by power and are therefore more than willing to give a governor the benefit of the doubt. He knew that reporters, generally speaking, do not understand math—literally, with many unable to calculate simple percentages. He understood the he-said-she-said conventions of modern journalism, and how those rules could be turned to his advantage.

Most important of all, he figured out how to turn the independence and initiative of his most effective journalistic critics against them, successfully persuading the media herd that these people, and therefore their work, was biased.

In short, he understood all of our weaknesses, and he and his people exploited them masterfully.

To be fair, Jeb was not the first governor to play the media. Previous ones also were smart enough to understand that, to journalists, information was the singular coin of our realm. The more rare or the more sought-after the information, the more its worth. Democrat Lawton Chiles, as he prepared to roll out his proposed state budget each January, would parcel out bits and pieces of it to the Capitol press corps, on the basis of region or the reporter's particular interests. The *Orlando Sentinel,* for instance, might be given the "scoop" on Central Florida tollway construction. The *Miami*

Herald might get the inside track to the Everglades restoration proposal. The point to this was to get better "play" for an otherwise dry, bureaucratic article: "Governor proposes budget."

Yes, the selected leaks tended to benefit favored reporters. And yes, Chiles's press people frequently called up reporters to complain about a story they didn't like and even called to try to steer them away from "unfavorable" tacks on certain articles as they were being written.

But in all that previous governors did, their efforts and their effectiveness were embarrassing failures, compared to what Jeb brought to bear after he took office.

I<small>T</small> <small>PROBABLY</small> should have been obvious even during the 1998 campaign the regard Jeb held for a free and independent press, such as the sort that Thomas Jefferson two centuries earlier had opined was more important than government itself. During that campaign, the *Tampa Tribune* wrote a tough series of articles about Jeb's business background and associates and so on. In Jeb's eyes, the stories were inaccurate. In Jeb's eyes, the *Tribune* had to be punished. And so his campaign cut them off. Their reporters were not invited to travel with his campaign. Their phone calls were not answered. Their offices were not even sent schedules or press releases.

It was the damnedest thing. Here was Jeb, running for governor of Florida, the *entire* state of Florida, which would include the two hundred thousand or so residents of greater Tampa who subscribed to the *Tribune,* and Jeb crossed them out with his index finger and pretended they no longer existed. It was childish, it was petty—and to the everlasting shame of the rest of the Florida media, we let him get away with it.

What we should have done was to rally around the *Trib* reporters, writing articles about Jeb's actions and telling his staff that it was out of line and we weren't going to go along with it. Regardless of what we personally thought about the *Tribune's* coverage, we should have zealously guarded their right to print it. That's what freedom of the press is all about.

Of course, we didn't. Some of us thought Jeb was going too far but thought the *Tribune's* stories were unfair and we did not want to seem to be defending them. Some of us thought the stories were basically dead on, but did not want to say anything for fear of suffering the same fate as our *Tribune* colleagues. And some of us, sadly, saw Jeb's not talking to one newspaper as an opportunity for increased access for ourselves.

Once the election was over, Jeb appeared to understand that as a public official, he had certain responsibilities that he did not have as a candidate. The *Tribune* was off the disappeared list, and Jeb's transition office began dealing with the media and the public in a generally normal manner.

For about a week.

Which was about how long it took for us to realize that Jeb's people were not going to release documents they were collecting and producing as part of the transition. Again: here was a guy, occupying publicly owned office space, using publicly owned telephones, fax machines, and computers, with publicly paid employees, doing the work of the public—yet arguing that we did not have a right to see that work product.

On this, others agreed with me and my *Palm Beach Post* editors that we could not let the governor-elect get away with this one or we would see a guy used to the unaccountability of the private sector set up his government office on that model. A group of us newspapers, including the *Post* and the *Tampa Tribune,* got our lawyers to draft a lawsuit under the state's open records law. We were prepared to file it—indeed, we would have filed it on Jeb's inauguration day, had his staff not come to our editors with a compromise: they would not admit that a transition team was, in fact, a public body subject to the open records law, but they would give us full access to all the documents we were seeking.

I and a few others were wary of Jeb's offer. We believed that a governor's transition team was by its nature and its funding in Florida unequivocally a public agency. Accepting Jeb's deal meant, in essence, accepting that Jeb was *choosing* to give us these records out of the goodness of his heart, not because the law compelled such access. Unfortunately, we were outvoted. Newspapers are businesses, and editors are responsible for meeting a budget. They looked at it this way: we were getting a look at the documents we wanted, and so what if Jeb did not concede the central point? At the moment of his inaugural, Jeb was unarguably a public official, and there would never again be a Jeb Bush transition team in Florida. We took the deal.

It was a huge mistake.

JACK SISSON was a seventy-seven-year-old retiree who wanted to know what the state's guidelines were for patient care. He did what any resident has a right to do and filed a public records request of Jeb's Agency for Health Care Administration.

Sure, AHCA officials told him, but only after a judge finally forced them to concede they had the documents in question. We'll be happy to provide them—for a mere $61,815.

Now let's take it as a given that Jeb and his people had little interest in helping Jack Sisson. Fifteen years earlier, he had suffered a brain trauma when he was hit by a red-light runner. With that experience with doctors and hospitals, and with years of background in state government, Sisson believed, quite passionately, that if only the state enforced those patient care guidelines already in existence, it could dramatically reduce medical malpractice in Florida. He wanted the documents in hand so he could testify about this before the state legislature when it discussed Jeb's proposals to crack down on medical malpractice lawsuits.

Let's further accept that Jeb's people may have believed that Jack Sisson was a royal pain in the behind, and helping him would only obfuscate a serious crisis. Let's give Jeb the benefit of the doubt here and assume he wasn't merely trying to prevent Mr. Sisson from expressing a position that Jeb opposed.

It doesn't matter.

Florida law says that Jack Sisson had a complete and absolute right to those records, even if his intent was to fold them up into paper airplanes and toss them off his roof. Because giving ordinary citizens access to information about their government and its functioning is the fundamental purpose of the public records law. And here is a perfect illustration of the effect on one such ordinary citizen by Jeb's new policies to impede access to public documents.

True, Jeb didn't create these new policies specifically to shut out guys like Jack Sisson, although there is no evidence that he felt any consternation about having done so. No, the evolution of a policy over several years that would stiff regular Joes like Sisson was a direct result of the press corps' unwillingness to take him to court back on his inauguration day.

Because what Jeb and his people learned from that episode was that, when it came down to it, the state's newspapers were too cheap to take a public records lawsuit against him to court, where it would cost tens of thousands of dollars, even hundreds of thousands of dollars, rather than merely taking lofty positions on their editorial pages. Jeb had already proven that the voters of Florida were more loyal to him than they were to the editorial page writers. He didn't care about bad press, certainly not on an issue that most Floridians did not consider particularly important.

And so, what Jeb did was, gradually, make his compliance with the law ever more grudging—never to the point of egging on a lawsuit, but nevertheless over the weeks and months altering the generally accepted standard for meeting the law's letter and spirit.

In Florida, the law states that custodians of public records must make these records available in no more time than it literally takes to make the records available. It had become accepted practice that for cities and counties, that meant if you asked for a copy of a contract or a letter or a memo in the morning, you should have it in your hands by lunchtime. More voluminous requests might take a day, or two days.

Even at the start of his administration, which he promised would be the most ethical and open in history, Jeb's office was never that forthcoming. At first the excuse was that they were still settling in, that we in the media had to be patient, and permit them to get a system in place, and then everything would be fine.

But the more that Jeb's "system" got into place, the longer it took for Jeb's press office to turn over documents.

One piece of this in particular shows the utter contempt Jeb had for the whole idea of accountability and transparency. When he took over, a good number of low-level clerical workers from the Chiles administration remained in the governor's office, including one in the press office. In Chiles's shop, she'd been a clerk, answering the phones and taking messages. She possessed neither the experience nor the organizational skills for much more than that. Under Jeb, she was placed in charge of all public records requests.

It was, if you were trying to sabotage the processing of public records requests, utterly brilliant. Jeb's people used her incompetence to suppress the flow of information, while, at the same time, being able to point to how broad-minded they were: giving real responsibility to a black, single mom. Meanwhile, they chortled to themselves how the liberal press corps would never be able to criticize either them or her for precisely that reason. You guys are always defending affirmative action? Here's some affirmative action for you.

And here was the beauty part: they didn't even have to nudge her to stonewall us or anything so unseemly. All she had to do was to be herself.

One new hire to the press office, not immediately realizing the strategy, sounded out reporters on background, asking if the public records clerk was doing a good job and then sounding concerned when we replied that no, she was not. Naturally, this concern did not translate into any action. The newbie learned soon enough that *not* filling records requests quickly and efficiently was exactly the point.

The clerk did eventually leave the press office. She was promoted to "Director of Communications" at the Florida Lottery, at more than double her original salary.

THERE WAS, naturally, a good reason for delaying the release of these records, at least from Jeb's point of view. These documents, most particularly the e-mail correspondence among his own staff, were as a rule generating the most damaging press coverage the administration was getting.

The longer you could delay the release of this harmful material, the less its likely impact and the more likely that the reporters in question would have lost interest and moved on to more fertile ground by the time they finally received it.

With the more dogged journalists, this didn't always work. One *St. Petersburg Times* reporter, after a lengthy delay, got a trove of e-mails regarding Jeb's attempt to stack the trial-level and appellate courts with judges who were "ideologically compatible" by creating a shadow nominating system behind the formal one that gave the governor only so much power. But, warned deputy general counsel Frank Jimenez in an e-mail about the scheme: "We need to be careful, because we don't want (to) create a 'kingmaker' perception."

After a while, it became clear to Jeb's people that a mere delay was not by itself enough to stop the most damaging articles. Florida law allows governments to levy a photocopying charge for each page released to the media. Jeb's press office quickly realized that this was a pretty handy way to run up a bill. Particularly in the case of e-mails, which by their nature carry with them a long train of previous correspondence and responses, you could easily drive a records request up into several thousands of pages, translating into several hundreds of dollars. And if the e-mails had long documents attached, especially spreadsheets, so much the better. That made the cost that much higher, while large spreadsheets often become so confusing as to be meaningless, when they are printed out without headers on each page.

This trick worked for them for a while, until some of us started requesting e-mails and their attached documents in their native, electronic format—something the public records law specifically allowed us to do.

It is impossible to overstate the advantages this provided. First, it reduced the duplicating costs from hundreds of dollars down to less than a single dollar, the price of a blank compact disc. Even more important, though, was the ability to organize and search the material using a computer. Instead of getting boxes and boxes of printed out e-mails, many of them out of sequence and separated from their attachments, we started getting a CD loaded with an electronic folder containing all of Jeb's e-mails for a particular week or month, or to and from a particular group of people. We were able to sort by date, by recipient, by subject. We were able to search e-mails using a word or a name. Even more useful: we had instant access to attached electronic files, which meant we could learn when they were created and on whose computer. This last bit was potentially devastating. It could show, for example, which lobbyist had actually written a given regulation or piece of legislation, and how it changed as it passed from one Jeb aide to another.

The *Palm Beach Post* ran precisely this sort of article, in fact. Jeb's proposed "compliance form" to fix all the screw-ups in his voucher programs was actually written by the private schools and home-schooling lobbyist and e-mailed to Jeb's education aide, Patricia Levesque, at 6:26 p.m. on August 11, 2003. She had titled it "Suggested DOE Database for Private Schools Participating in Scholarship Programs." Exactly thirty-one minutes later, Levesque had forwarded the proposal, minus the word "suggested" in the title, to the Department of Education, with the instructions: "Will you please have someone take this document and put the DOE logo on top?" and "Will you please take a look from a formatting perspective and make any edits to make it look more official?"

That same batch of e-mails and attached documents also provided the proof that, as a *Post* colleague and I closed in on a correspondence school operator who appeared to be scamming the voucher program to the tune of a quarter million dollars, Levesque worked to get ahead of the impending bad press by kicking the problem "Scholarship Funding Organization" as well as a second suspected scammer out of the program, but doing so in a way that did not reveal the problems to the public.

"The governor may want to say that we have too many SFOs now and in order to ensure accountability at the state level he will recommend only having 'x' SFOs—whatever the number of the SFOs currently minus the two we have concerns about." But then, seeing possible flies in the ointment, she added in italics: *If the press asks how we would eliminate some of the current ones, the answer can be first-come, first-served—if that gives us the ones we want (Alex, please check) or he could answer whichever ones the commissioner recommends as being the most accountable to participate in the program.*

She was basically scheming up an elaborate lie, and leaving a rich paper trail—or electron trail, rather—in the process.

In other words: by getting e-mail in this format, we had hit the mother lode.

Now, I fully understand that Jeb and his people could not have been happy reading these articles in the newspaper. Seeing your names in print in that light could not have been fun.

However, I will respectfully suggest that the proper way to avoid seeing those kinds of articles about oneself is to avoid letting a lobbyist with a self-interest in proposed regulations from writing that particular regulation. If one doesn't want articles questioning one's honesty, then one ought not be dishonest.

Jeb and his staff, though, chose a different method than altering their behavior. Instead, they altered the price they would henceforth charge for releasing public documents, even a CD of e-mails worth less than a dollar. From then on, Jeb's press office decided that the charges for a similar CD with, say, five hundred e-mail messages on it would total roughly $1,500. One dollar for the CD, and $1,499 for processing the request. Jeb's education department took an even more creative approach. Not only would they charge for the time of the high-ranking public official—read: expensive—who had to sort through his documents, but they would then bill for the hours that a department lawyer—read: even more expensive—would need to read through them all looking for and "redacting" things that might be exempt from release under the records laws. Oh, and the lawyer liked having said documents in a big stack, not on a computer screen, so we would also have to pay fifteen cents per page for printing them all out. The department estimated it would cost us $7,000 to get nine months' worth of e-mails from three top officials.

Just to test my theory that they were inventing new and unreasonable charges, the *Post* requested one week's worth of e-mail from those same three gentlemen. They charged us $351, and this is what we got: twenty-nine e-mails from the department's No. 2 man, with no redactions; seventeen documents from the department's finance chief, with no redactions; 246 e-mails from the department commissioner, with three redactions—two in notes from the same parent discussing educational philosophy and mentioning, in passing, that his child had been suspended for stealing, and one when the lawyer whited-out the cell phone number of the education commissioner. There does not appear to have been any legal basis for either redaction, which, under state law, can be done only in specific circumstances: the home number or address of a police officer, for example.

IT IS IMPORTANT to realize how effectively an invoice for $1,500 or $2,000 can close down an avenue for obtaining public documents. Only the major daily newspapers in Florida can afford such a tab on a regular basis, and even none of them really wants to. Smaller dailies and weekly newspapers simply cannot afford this kind of price.

It is also important to appreciate how big of a scam charging that much money for a public records request like this really is. In a modern e-mail program, it takes exactly ten seconds to filter a folder using a keyword. So with six keywords, one minute. Two minutes if you don't know how to type. One more minute to narrow that set to a selected period of time. Allow another five minutes to burn a CD, and the public official in question has invested all of eight minutes to comply with the public records law. In other words, obeying that law has never been as fast, as easy or as inexpensive as today, in the era of computers and optical discs. Instead, Jeb Bush made production of these public records more expensive than ever.

This was nothing short of outrageous, and most likely illegal, given the strict guidelines set out in the public records statute.

But Jeb fully understood that, by and large, his disregard for that particular law would not directly affect the vast majority of Floridians, who typically go their entire lives without filing even a single public records request with a government agency. He correctly assessed that only the news media would whine about this policy, and that we would get no public sympathy whatsoever.

The news media rank right up there with politicians and trial lawyers, when it comes to popularity and respect among the citizenry. Some of this is because of the relentless demonization of the *mainstream media* by the extreme right wing of the political spectrum, including Rush Limbaugh and Fox News. Some of it is because of our failure in the "MSM" to stand up to these bullies. Some of it is self-inflicted—our eagerness to pursue "news" about celebrities instead of news that really matters, and our occasional carelessness with the facts about important news. And yet, as disliked as the media are, we are the only independent check on government. We are the only group that routinely and regularly reports on what those in charge of public money are doing with that money.

When Jeb choked off access to this data stream, the effect was to make his public pronouncements and "official" statements account for a proportionally larger share of the information available in the public domain about his administration and its performance—which was, of course, the whole idea.

For the record, not all of Florida's statewide officials, even Jeb's fellow Republicans, had such contempt for the public records law. Treasurer Tom Gallagher routinely turned over large data sets for the cost of a blank CD or, sometimes, the actual cost of someone from a data processing office to run a query and produce a spreadsheet—twenty or thirty dollars. And Charlie Crist, as an elected education commissioner who was running for attorney general, turned over a pile of travel expenses and calendars to the *Post* in a timely manner. The resulting article showed that Crist had arranged his fund-raising schedule to coincide with his public schedule— and sometimes vice versa—to allow him to travel to his fund-raisers on the public dime. He understood when he turned the documents over that that was what the article would show. He complied with the law anyway, and without delay.

Contrast this to Jeb's attitude. To him, the public records statute was never a real law, just one of those annoying obstacles that are sometimes thrown in the way of real leaders like himself. It didn't take him long at all to figure out a way to get around it.

Even if it meant charging Mr. Sisson $61,815.

UNDERMINING LAWS designed to keep government accountable to its citizens took some measure of devious cleverness but was primarily a matter of sheer chutzpah. Just doing what you're intent on doing and daring somebody to challenge you.

That, though, is in reality just a small piece of "message" control for the simple reason that most journalists have neither the time nor the inclination to pore over hundreds of e-mails. Usually getting Jeb's side of the story top billing was more a function of the parallel task of manipulating the press corps. And in that area, Jeb shone.

He started out, naturally, with an enormous natural advantage. He is Jeb Bush. Even in 1994, during his first run for governor, he was the articulate, dynamic, *tall* son of a president. The star treatment he got from the general public was mirrored by the political press corps in Florida. The story line, too, was compelling: the rising son of a defeated president, taking revenge upon a fading Democratic war horse in his twilight years. Reporters seemed stunned when it didn't turn out that way.

Four years later, it was a foregone conclusion that Jeb was going to become Florida's next governor, and many journalists started early with the trading-favorable-coverage-for-better-access game. It was the sort of barter that Jeb clearly understood, and his people, many of them veterans of his father's White House and his presidential runs, played it not just like pros, but with a ruthless enthusiasm.

Most elected officials have favorite journalists—those they believe are most likely to put them in a positive light or, at the least, give their side of a negative story prominent play—and Jeb made sure his top two pets were also the established leaders of the Tallahassee press corps: the bureau chiefs of the state's two biggest papers, the *Miami Herald,* and the *St. Petersburg Times.* Whenever a major announcement was forthcoming, chances were good that one of these two reporters would get an early tip or an exclusive interview. And, in return, they offered a largely sympathetic portrait to their readers—in the case of the *St. Petersburg Times* reporter, an almost exclusively sympathetic portrait. When Jeb staged a press conference to bat down a rumor that he was having an affair with a department head, it was these two who lobbed him the softballs that let him lament the poisonous political atmosphere in Tallahassee. This was a question no journalist appropriately detached from Jeb would have asked. We at the *Post,* who by then were at the top of Jeb's enemies list, did not even want to write the story. We had no reason to believe the rumor was true, and even if it was, it wasn't any of the public's business unless it was affecting his job performance, which not even the rumormongers were suggesting was the case. But such are the tradeoffs for "access," and the reporters who make these bargains must live with their consequences.

Jeb, though, made an even more valuable partnership than with the top reporters at the state's biggest papers when his office cultivated the new correspondent with the Associated Press in 2001. The wire service has a critical role in a state capital, far more so than in Washington, D.C., which has an enormous press corps that daily scrutinizes each other's work. Without the AP "picking up" and retransmitting a given newspaper's investigative report in Florida, chances are slim that it will be seen in other newspapers. It was to Jeb's great advantage, then, to discourage the AP from picking up articles critical of him or his administration and thereby "containing" the damage to a small portion of the state. That way, readers of the *Florida Times-Union* in Jacksonville would not see a tough story by the *Miami Herald*. Readers of the *St. Petersburg Times* would be oblivious to an investigative piece in the *Palm Beach Post*.

Jeb's press office was usually on the phone to the AP by early morning the day a damaging article had run in one of the state's daily newspapers, asking that it not be picked up. They would sometimes call other newspapers, too, in the event reporters were considering following up on the story by themselves, without waiting for the AP. Sometimes they would offer one-on-one interview time with Jeb in return. Far, far too often, their offers of these little trades paid off. Too often, reporters let their competitive instincts outweigh the public service to their readers. Jeb's people understood that dynamic and pressed it to their use whenever possible.

And, being Jeb's people, they were fully prepared to use the stick, when the carrot wasn't working. A big giant stick, studded with spikes and rusty nails.

The most obvious, of course, was denying access to reporters they didn't like. This meant that if you wrote an article that made Jeb mad, you could pretty much rule out traveling with him on the state plane to an event anytime soon. Or getting five minutes of "exclusive" time with him. Or even getting your phone calls answered on basic queries to the press office.

True, these tricks had been used in the past by other governors. But Jeb took this strategy to new levels by trying to actively hurt the careers of reporters whose work he didn't like.

Jeb and his staffers aggressively went after a *Tampa Tribune* reporter who was aggressively writing stories about one of his department heads—the same one whom Jeb would later hold a press conference to announce that he was not having an affair with. When the reporter ultimately left the paper, Jeb personally acknowledged in a meeting with the *Tribune's* editorial board that he was glad the paper had taken care of their "little problem" in Tallahassee.

Jeb went after me personally because of my series of articles about the problems in his voucher programs. His press staff denied that was the reason, telling other reporters that I had been abusive to one of them but refusing to say exactly how. As an aside, this was a beautiful character assassination technique—the naughty word in question was "goddamned," which they knew would not outrage too many reporters. By refusing to be specific, they let my colleagues imagine the worst.

They banned me and all *Post* reporters from the softball, year-end interviews with Jeb, when he gets to explain what a phenomenal year he had. Knowing how important "scoops" are in our business, they leaked to the *Palm Beach Post*'s archrival, the *South Florida Sun-Sentinel*, the fact that Jeb was bringing Scripps Research Institute to Palm Beach County, and then made it clear to our beat reporter on that issue that they had done so to punish me. They intentionally gave away the details of a major investigation a colleague and I had been working on for weeks to the *Miami Herald*. The *Herald*, certainly, was not immune to this treatment in their own investigative stories. As they closed in on a dynamite story about failures in the child-protective services agency, Jeb's people gave the details to the Associated Press, which naturally presented the information with the obligatory pro-Jeb spin.

I do not mean to sound whiny about Jeb's treatment of the press corps. Unlike with public records and public meetings, there is nothing in either the state constitution or in state law saying that public officials have to be cordial or even civil to journalists. I and, I believe, most journalists would not want any such provision. But I do think it is important to point out that Jeb's press office bore little resemblance to earlier governors' press shops, which saw their role as basically to field press queries and organize the distribution of information, with some spin control thrown in. Jeb's people were all message control, all the time, and used hardball tactics to keep people in line.

It was in press relations as in all other things: you are either with us, or you are against us, and if you are against us, we will make you pay.

JEB'S RELATIONSHIP with the media, however, offers a valuable insight into an important aspect of his personality: how he deals with people he doesn't like.

This is not to suggest that Jeb dislikes only reporters. Far from it. Jeb dislikes trial lawyers, legislators, judges, teachers—anyone or any group, in fact, that has opposed him or his policies. But journalists were the only group that he had to deal with on a continuing basis. The others he could ignore, or lash out against in op-ed pieces or with punitive legislation. But reporters, even had he cut back on his press conference schedule, could still hound him daily. Unlike the president of the United States, who using the excuse of security can insulate himself in a bubble pretty much 24/7, a Florida governor usually has several public appearances a day, with only one or two state security officers to keep people at bay.

Now, to be fair, Jeb does not dislike all journalists, or all trial lawyers, all legislators, and so on. In truth, it is probably more accurate to say that he does not respect their professions, and is therefore predisposed to dislike them as individuals. There are exceptions. Reporters, judges and legislators who profess their admiration for Jeb can break through the wall, if they work at it. (Florida's teachers of the year, for example, were generally fawned upon by Jeb's administration. Coincidentally enough, many of them seemed far more supportive of Jeb's education policies than teachers generally, who as a whole thought Jeb was a horrible governor and his education policies were destroying public schools.)

Jeb worked a news conference, particularly when queries started coming that didn't concern the "message of the day," like a playground bully, glibly brushing off questions and questioners he didn't care for, sparring with those who persisted and then, when he really got steamed, embarrassing them into silence.

To understand this, you have to remember the physical dimensions of the man. Jeb is huge. On those occasions when he is attempting to seem approachable and humble, he stoops slightly (also when he appears beside his brother, the president . . . presumably so he doesn't seem to overshadow him).

When he's in bullying mode, the stooping bit goes out the window. He stands upright, arms crossed, heels dug in. He'll answer a question with a snippy retort, or a devastating counter question designed to reveal the questioner's ignorance. His eyes flash, his nostrils flare, and those of us of median height or less are treated to the sight of his twitching nose hairs.

You see now why most journalists—as well as most legislators, most judges, etc.—do not care to pick a fight with the man. Contrary to popular opinion of journalists as rude, aggressive, and argumentative (well, okay, some of us *are* like this), most reporters are like most regular people: mild-mannered, shy in the face of authority and conflict averse. And this explains how Jeb generally has avoided really critical treatment in the press. I mean, really: who wants to get humiliated by a tall, mean guy with a giant head and twitching nose hairs?

Jeb has taken enough reporters down enough times that anyone thinking of asking a question that challenges his orthodoxy or could remotely be considered "off topic" usually thinks twice.

For Jeb, dealing with the Liberal Media, like pretty much everything else, is a contact sport.

. . .

An illustration of this is the evolution of Jeb's press office over his first term, from a traditional governmental media affairs shop to a virtual extension of Jeb's permanent campaign.

Usually, elected officials only need look within their ranks of loyal acolytes to find people to get their versions of reality out to the public. Especially in state government, one would think this would not be so difficult. After all, the budget is what it is. Test scores, crime rates, tax revenues, and so forth are all measurable quantities that are relatively easy to relay to the public.

Jeb, in his first few years, did rely on young true believers to get out the good word. His first press secretary, Cory Tilley, was an amiable guy who would put forth the Jeb party line but would do so understanding that journalists had their own jobs to do, and reflecting Jeb's point of view was only a small part of it.

Tilley had some experience in this, having worked in that capacity for the governor of Maine—admittedly not as turbulent a place as Florida, but state government nonetheless. He had interned for Jeb confidante Sally Bradshaw in George H.W.'s White House political office, and fell in with the Jeb crowd in 1993, serving as his press spokesman during the 1994 campaign, and then with the campaign-in-waiting of Jeb's Foundation for Florida's Future until the second run officially began in 1997.

Tilley was promoted to deputy chief of staff within a year, and was replaced by another true believer, Justin Sayfie, another young, amiable guy who appeared to make an honest effort to balance Jeb's need for spin with the public's right to know.

Tilley left relatively soon to open a public relations business, and Sayfie, who had young children, decided like many others with families that Jeb's workaholic nature was not for him. He was replaced by Katie Baur, another young Republican true believer who started as an intern in George H.W. Bush's White House and migrated to Florida in 1998 to work for Jeb ally John Thrasher, who that November became speaker of the state House.

Baur, by the time she moved over to run Jeb's press office, similarly had some idea of what dealing with reporters meant in a government capacity. To her credit, she tried to honor Florida's open government tradition, which naturally put her somewhat at cross purposes with Jeb's predilection to withhold and delay the release of public records whenever possible. Baur also had a tough time keeping a straight face when trying to sell the more implausible public positions Jeb would sometimes take. She had known the Capitol press corps before working for the governor, and many of us considered her our friend.

And so when she, too, was burned out by Jeb's workaholic nature and with a surprisingly tough reelection challenge imminent in 2002, Jeb took the opportunity to make a qualitative change in the press office leadership.

Tilley and Sayfie and Baur, it seemed, were simply too honest, and simply too willing to act as advocates for the news media as representatives of the public's right to know about their government.

In other words: they behaved in the way that press officers have traditionally worked in Florida, prior to the Jeb era.

ENTER INTO this Jill Bratina.

It is difficult to understate the significance of her arrival. Unlike her predecessors, Bratina had not worked for Jeb before. She had not worked for any of the Bush family. She had not, in fact, worked for any governmental entity. Rather, she came from the "private sector," as the news release announcing her arrival had put it.

Now, the vast majority of public relations jobs in the private sector involve answering questions about a given company from reporters and putting out press releases trying to get positive coverage for said company. *Acme Widgets boosted sales 70 percent over last year, thanks to an aggressive marketing campaign to enter the Asian widget market. Mr. Elmer Crumpet, vice president of sales for Acme Widgets, recently won the National Widget Association associate of the year award, and is available for interviews.* That sort of thing.

Bratina's private sector background was a little different. Prior to coming to work for Jeb, she had worked for Bridgestone-Firestone. Yes, that Bridgestone-Firestone. The woman quoted in papers around the country, and on the TV news about how Firestone tires were perfectly safe, and it was the Ford Explorer that was so badly designed that it kept rolling over in accidents—never mind that the National Highway Traffic Safety Administration blamed the tires for 271 deaths and more than a thousand injuries? That was Bratina.

Here's a good one from May 21, 2001, when she told the *Houston Chronicle:* "Our tires are not defective. . . . We believe the August recall was more than adequate to protect the public, and more importantly, when you look at the data, you'll see the differences when these tires are on Ford Explorers and other vehicles, and we need to understand why." Three weeks later, she told Newhouse News Service that the tires were performing "at a world-class level."

Prior to Firestone, Bratina, working for a public relations firm, had spun her magic for such clients as American Home Products/Wyeth-Ayerst, the marketers of the diet drug fen-phen, and Dow Chemical, which had some issues with silicone breast implants.

Not to put too fine a point on it, but Bratina was basically a professional liar—a hired gun who specialized in helping companies who had severe customer relations problems improve their public image. It is more than a little interesting that Jeb felt his press shop needed this type of industry pro. Bratina, who had won *PR Week's* coveted "Top 30 Under 30" award for her work with troubled corporations, did not disappoint. She brought "message discipline" to the press office—which is to say, robotically repeating the same meaningless phrase ("rising student achievement," for example) over and over until reporters got tired of asking—presumably because the previous spokespeople had been too willing to engage in back-and-forth with reporters.

Bratina successfully instilled her brand of take-no-prisoners press management within the office as a whole, so that, even after she left in 2004, her protégé, Alia Faraj, continued running the office in that style. As discussed, news organizations willing to give Jeb favorable treatment were given access and "scoops" against their competitors. Others, including the *Palm Beach Post,* who would not play ball, were shut out. Perhaps most notably in this regard, Bratina and Faraj were the ones to co-opt the Associated Press Tallahassee office, which was handed major scoops, including those that had been investigative stories being pursued by member newspapers. The AP in that time period failed to "pick-up" and retransmit to its members a substantial number of articles critical of Jeb and his agencies by the Tallahassee press corps—a major coup by Jeb's press office because it meant that negative stories would run only in a particular newspaper in a particular part of the state, rather than in newspapers around the state and around the country.

When the *Post* broke a story about how Jeb's education staff had chosen to promote the book *The Lion, the Witch and the Wardrobe* just as the film version was about to hit the theaters, and how the film had been been produced by a major Republican donor and evangelical Christian, and how Jeb's office had never in his six previous years so promoted a new movie, well, the AP decided that simply was not very interesting and that its other Florida members were better off without it.

But what Bratina succeeded in most was enforcing a rigid expectation among reporters that Jeb's position and statements on a topic were, by the very fact that he had come to them, to be treated as proven facts. Which is a complicated way of saying that if we expected to get our phone calls answered, we needed to treat as true the press office's statements, even if they were lies.

WHICH GETS to that troublesome word: lie. It's a touchy one, for newspapers. Maybe because it's so harsh.

Liar.

For such a short word, it wields incredible power. A word with more invective per syllable is hard to conjure. You use it, and then it's out there forever, and, typically, the one who resorts to it winds up as muddied as the intended target.

Liar.

And yet—it's quick and to the point. And, sadly, sometimes not to use it, for the sake of civility, is the greater disservice.

It's important, first, to distinguish what is meant by liar.

Yes, technically, just about everyone lies, just about every day. The rules of etiquette revolve around a whole host of small lies. *I am fine, thanks. You don't look a day older than the last time we met. We must do this again soon.* We teach our children to lie. *Tell Grandma her casserole was delicious. Tell your aunt you can't wait to see her.*

To be clear, these conventions are not a bad thing. Maybe the world would be a more precise, more honest place if everyone said exactly what was on his or her mind. But it would also be a meaner place.

Of course, we're not talking about taking umbrage at our politicians for engaging in normal social relations using standard social conventions. We're not even getting too upset about leaders who use the face-saving lie that most of us do—an untruth told out of embarrassment or guilt. *Sure, I read the report just last night. I mailed the check two days ago.*

We're not even too upset about lies about sex. The public's reaction to Bill Clinton, both to Gennifer Flowers in 1992 and Monica Lewinsky in

1998, proved that. We understand lust and lack of personal discipline, probably because most of us have either succumbed or have been tempted, at one time or another.

No, what we're talking about is a purposeful deception, either premeditated or continuing, to advance a policy or agenda or even a resume that would not otherwise be widely palatable. And by this measure, Jeb is, alas, not only a liar but an accomplished one.

MAYBE THIS is a family thing.

For all the talk Americans have gotten over the last twenty-five years from the Bush family about the importance of bedrock values like integrity and honesty, the nation has gotten an astonishing volume of subterfuge and, at times, whole-cloth fabrications.

Maybe it's something the "bred-to-rule" class talks about in their boarding schools and country club dining halls, the need to reveal less than the whole truth—sometimes a great deal less than the whole truth—when interacting with the rabble. Whatever the origins, we've now had two generations of a family where dishonesty has played a significant role in their lives.

Jeb's father, for example. Possibly the single, universal attribute that George Herbert Walker Bush enjoys is that he is a nice guy.

Even political foes remarked before, during and after he was president that he was a decent fellow, and tried to win the friendship and trust of most he met. So it comes as something of a shock to review his early public career, his 1988 campaign and his presidency and see the evidence that George H.W. Bush, nice guy extraordinaire, was a frequent, almost recreational liar.

Yes, that sounds harsh. There, in black and white, it even looks harsh.

Still, there is in his record over the years clear evidence showing how George H.W. would employ both slight mistruths and flat-out deceptions to get what he wanted.

Most blatant was probably the already mentioned, open refusal to turn over evidence in the Iran-Contra affair that contradicted his claim that he was "out of the loop," but there were many others. In 1974, writing in his diary, he described how his job running the RNC meant "bending, stretching a little here or there" when it came to telling the truth. In 1975, angered that a public stink over secretary of state Henry Kissinger's family flying free on government planes was now forcing him to pay $1,600 for a ride Barbara had received, he wrote out the check to the United States Air Force and then told Kissinger's aide: "Now you tell them I paid in advance." When, obviously, he had not. In 1988, he told a writer profiling him that two decades earlier he was the only member of the Texas delegation to vote for the Open Housing bill. In fact, he was one of nine Texas congressmen who voted that way.

George H.W. biographers Michael Duffy and Dan Goodgame, two *Time* magazine writers who put together a retrospective of his White House years, described him as having a "well-practiced and ruthless use of deception."

The predisposition for untruths irritated even those who generally liked him. Brit Hume, then with ABC and now with Fox, got so fed up with George H.W.'s petty misstatements on whether he was planning a new arms-control deal that he put together a montage of Bush saying one thing about a particular policy one day, and then doing exactly the opposite just days later.

Most telling was Bush's reaction to the coverage. Visibly angry, he came into the back of Air Force One and basically pouted, playing silly word games with the reporters. "I can't go into the details of that," George H.W. said, when asked whether he'd had a good night's sleep. "Because some will think it's too much sleep and some will think it's too little."

He was mad that they had gotten mad. Evidently, a president should be allowed to say whatever he wants. On one day the sky is blue; the next it is orange, and who is the press to question it?

If that was the extent of the untruths—the desire for maximum publicity or surprise—that would have been one thing. But that was not the extent of it.

In the run-up to the first Gulf War, for instance, George H.W. lowballed the number of troops he would deploy in order to win support both at home and in Saudi Arabia—which was nervous about hosting a huge, infidel force in the Muslim holy land. And then, when Americans did not appear to be terribly keen about going to war merely to defend Kuwait, George H.W. began raising the specter of a nuclear-armed Saddam—the identical ploy first son George W. used a dozen years later.

In fact, the whole "truth management" strategy has been adopted and perhaps even expanded by this next generation. Whole books have been devoted to the various dishonesties of George W.'s statements and policies, both in Texas and in the White House.

In Florida, Jeb was disturbingly comfortable about describing his proposals and policies a certain way, even though facts he was aware of suggested a completely different reality.

IN 1998, for example, Jeb was touting the same school voucher plan he had pushed with little success in 1994. Only this time, as part of the overall strategy to change the campaign tone without touching the underlying content, Jeb emphasized all the testing all schoolchildren would undergo every year, with only repeatedly failing schools having to offer private school vouchers to their students.

This remained as controversial in 1998 as it had been in 1994 because of the wording in Florida's constitution that prohibited sending state money to religious institutions—wording that had been in the constitution since Reconstruction and which was specifically renewed in the 1968 revision when parochial schools started clamoring for state help.

Jeb unveiled his proposal at a middle school in Tallahassee, flanked by running mate Frank Brogan and lots of adorable children (many of them black, as per the new strategy of the national voucher movement, as formally adopted in 2000 by Children First America, a group of primarily superrich white guys who want vouchers for all). Jeb was asked about the language in Florida's constitution, and how religious schools could participate given that wording. He offered up his usual smug grin (as opposed to his brother's well-known smirk) and said, in that case, church-and-state sticklers had "nothing to worry about."

As it turned out, Floridians who believed that the state ought not be giving tax money to religious schools should have worried quite a bit. Because Jeb's big education law he rammed through during his first legislative session specifically allowed religious schools to receive state money—in direct contravention of the state constitution.

Yes, Jeb knew what he wanted as he stood in that classroom. He also knew that many voters—including many Republicans—would be uneasy with his plan. And so he lied.

It was not his first dishonesty in his public life. That one actually came shortly before Jeb first ran for governor, at a political picnic in Orlando a week before the 1992 election, rumors were already flying and a reporter asked whether he planned to run for governor in 1994. Jeb raised a plastic cup of beer he was drinking and said: "Do you think I'd be doing this if I was running?" Within three months, Jeb confirmed that he was, in fact, running in 1994.

That political campaign and the ones to come saw a number of stretched, distorted, and even some completely made-up facts. Unfortunately, this practice was not confined to the rough-and-tumble of the campaign, but enthusiastically embraced in the governor's office, as well.

From the deceptive claims made in his education budgets—taking credit as new spending, for example, a decrease in cost for the teachers' retirement plan—to the mischaracterization of the beneficiaries of his tax cuts to the repeated, inaccurate claims that his education department was overseeing his pet voucher programs, Jeb as governor made truth a relative concept.

He even acknowledged as much in a note to his top aides following an education speech he delivered in Naples early in his first term: "This is just a friendly reminder to check if there are reporters at events. I was more forthright than I would have been had I known. Thanks, team."

In other words, the truth was something to be told only when the general public wasn't around to listen.

THE TROUBLE with catching lies and writing about lies, of course, is proving intent. Maybe the guy really does believe the nonsense he's saying. And so, as journalists who can only print what we can prove, as opposed to what any person employing his common sense would be able to determine, we are continually frustrated by politicians who weave their public statements with just enough of a fuzzy area to maintain, if it comes to it, well meaning ignorance, rather than conniving mendacity.

Which was why the black-and-white proof of Jeb's top education aide not just lying, but caught in the middle of cooking up a great, big, juicy whopper in an effort to cover up how the lousy oversight in Jeb's school voucher plans had allowed a scammer to steal $268,125 from one of them was such a phenomenal coup.

We learned of this several months later, after Jeb's office finally turned over e-mails sent and received by the aide, Patricia Levesque. We prepared the story, with the top editors still squeamish about using the word "lie" in the paper. We agreed we could go as far as "fabricate" in the lead paragraph, because the first definition in the dictionary was "make or manufacture."

(So what did the copy desk do, when it came time to laying out the front page? "Fabricate" is an awful long word. . . . You guessed it: "E-mails: Bush aide mulled voucher lies.")

Fabrications, stories, lies—it was a tough article, backed up with hard proof. So what was the reaction? Yawn. No other newspapers followed up. Neither did the Associated Press, which by then had a close working relationship with Jeb's press shop.

Oh, and Patricia Levesque? Not to worry. Jeb promoted her, to deputy chief of staff—where, two years later, she and press secretary Alia Faraj again tried to cover up Levesque's efforts to prepare legislation in anticipation of an adverse ruling in the voucher case. Their subterfuge in that instance amounted to a flouting of the public records law, but by then, even that was old hat. Nobody cared. It was almost the eighth and final year of the regime, and they had already done so much worse.

HOW A SYSTEMATIC use of dishonesty would reflect on Jeb should he ever seek to inhabit the White House, however, may be a different story.

In most things, being perceived as smarter is better. Not so in lying.

When it comes to telling untruths, it is far, far better to be thought a little slow on the uptake or, even better, ignorant. Two cases in point: Ronald Reagan and Jeb's brother, George W.

Reagan probably got the most benefit of most doubts, pretty much from the 1980 campaign onward. He seemed like such a genuinely nice guy, like how everyone wishes their grandfather could be, that people were willing to forgive him the minor things—like being accurate with facts.

He was so prone to saying the most outlandish things—welfare moms driving Cadillacs, trees causing pollution, et cetera—that it was never completely clear whether he was edging into the blurry fog of senility, or merely pretending to. Once people had watched him drift off into one of his "memories" of a war zone he'd never actually been anywhere near, it was pretty much a given that you ought not take him at face value. So when his defense to the revelations that his aides had concocted a scheme to sell arms to Iran and then illegally funnel the profits to the contras in Nicaragua was that he simply had no idea how this could have happened . . . you almost had to shrug. Maybe he didn't know anything about it.

George W. Bush has such a practiced ignorance that people are unwilling to believe the worst about him. People, even those outside his "base," are more likely to believe that he simply doesn't know any better than think he is being dishonest. The invasion of Iraq is a perfect example: despite all the articles and all the books suggesting otherwise, more Americans were more comfortable with the explanation that he really thought Saddam Hussein had dangerous weapons than were willing to accept that he was looking for an excuse to invade from the start. The "outing" of CIA operative Valerie Plame is another—somehow George W. was able to sell the idea that whatever nastiness happened in his White House, he personally had nothing to do with it.

When it comes to telling untruths, though, being a smarty-pants is a killer. Just ask Bill Clinton. He knew so much that whenever something he said didn't ring true, it was immediately assumed that he was willfully lying.

Jeb has the same problem, only without Clinton's disarming ability to empathize. Rather, Jeb's smugness comes to the fore when he pushes factual boundaries—the famous smirk and outthrust chin: That's my story and I'm sticking to it. Go ahead . . . prove I'm wrong.

Fortunately for Jeb, and unfortunately for America, proving he's wrong will probably be left to the news media who, if past is prologue, probably will not be up to the job.

BECAUSE AN important corollary to message control and media management is the broader cultural efforts by Jeb and his cohorts in the conservative wing of the Republican Party to delegitimize the news media in this country. In the end, this effort represents a much greater threat to the centuries-long tradition of an independent press, and therefore deserves some discussion.

First, let's take the issue of the "liberal" media. Proof of this is usually offered up in the form of polling data that shows that a larger percentage of journalists register as Democrats than Republicans, or that journalists are more likely to have "liberal" attitudes in the areas of education, social welfare, criminal justice and foreign policy than "conservative" views.

I'm never sure what this is supposed to prove. That there's a giant conspiracy to keep conservatives out of newspapers and broadcast news? Would this be the same conspiracy that keeps conservatives underrepresented in such fields as social work, teaching, and nursing? Or could it be that college-age conservatives don't generally queue up to enter fields where years of experience and loads of talent are rewarded with little pay and no respect?

My personal favorite is the new trend to try to prove a liberal bias in the nation's universities by showing that professors disproportionately vote Democratic. I'm not sure this is a wise avenue for conservatives—proving that the nation's top intellectuals, the country's best and brightest, consider themselves liberal. It's interesting that no one seems to be as interested that there is a marked paucity of liberal Democrats among top corporate board-rooms, elite country clubs, and fraternity houses at Southern colleges.

But no matter. Of *course* most journalists are going to be liberal. Many if not most reporters become reporters because they believe in social justice and helping the downtrodden. Because they think that only an informed citizenry can govern themselves wisely. All that idealistic stuff. (Well, except for sports reporters. Sports reporters get into it for the free food.) Does this sound like the kind of thing that would attract the typical Young Republican?

The test at hand is here not whether those reporting the news are liberal or conservative. The test ought to be whether those reporting the news have the smarts and the toughness to cut through the spin, whoever happens to be dishing it out, and find and publish the facts, the truth—or as close to it as possible.

Those who decry cultural relativism, typically socially conservative Republicans, ought to like this vision, this idea that there is absolute truth out there. But no, this type of conservative seems to prefer uncritical stenography. Anything beyond that is proof of liberalism. Factual accuracy is not a criterion—"balance" is everything. In this view, if an article contains a criticism of a Republican or his policies, then he and his defenders should get equal time, word for word. Taken to its logical conclusion, I suppose, a prosecutor whose eyewitness and scientific evidence paints a murderer's undeniable guilt over the course of five hundred words in a newspaper article ought to be balanced by five hundred words worth of "I didn't do it" and "I was framed."

Now, this is not to suggest that American reporters are fantastic and thorough and their product should be believed and trusted. No, American journalism has serious shortcomings—but it's not because reporters are biased. It's because reporters can't do math.

It might sound bizarre, but think it through: the most important service reporters provide is to chronicle the operations of our government, from the local sewer board to the White House. Much of that, indeed most of that, is keeping track of the public's money. And yet . . . most reporters have to think twice, three times, and then go ask for "expert" help when doing something as simple as figuring percentages.

That, right there, is why so many stories about government are largely works of stenography: this is what officials say they are doing. Or, only slightly better: this is what officials say they are doing, but this is what those who oppose those officials say is really happening.

If there is no attempt to independently determine "the truth," or get as close to it as is possible, then journalism is falling down on the job.

Obviously, Jeb and many of his ilk disagree with this view wholeheartedly. Reporters, in their view, should report. Literally. As in write down what they say, word for word, using the charts and graphics and other visual aids that have been so helpfully created, and then put that on the air or in the newspaper or on the Internet. That's it. End of job description.

If you ask critical questions, then you're no longer a reporter but an editorial writer. If you crunch their "official" numbers and come up with a contrary finding, then you are *liberal* and/or *biased*. In Jeb's particular view, you'd be *liberal* and *biased* anyway, just because, but this reckless independent streak—well, that's just further proof.

(Of course, do this in a political campaign of a Democratic candidate—just write down what he or she says and print it—and you're basically just a Clinton-worshipping toady. Jeb's people chide: "Dammit, man! Open your eyes! Think, for once!" Nope. There's no winning this one.)

THERE IS, sad to say, another problem with journalism that deserves mention, and that is the peculiar separation too many political reporters have with the actual planet Earth.

How and why this happens is not exactly clear, particularly since most political reporters start out having covered some form of government, be it local, state, or federal. But once freed from the daily grind of writing about budgets, laws and such, many of these folks appear to leave all knowledge or interest about these matters behind, choosing instead to immerse themselves in the horse race.

Stories about a candidate's record, his or her actual performance in office or in the private sector, are done only grudgingly, early on in the "election cycle" when few actual humans are paying any attention. And once that chore is put behind them, the political writers are free to pursue their favorite topic: who is going to win?

Instead of analyses of historical facts, we get "insider" stories featuring high-priced political "strategists" who explain how their guys will lay down a base of positive, feel-good, biographical ads before moving over to rip the other guy's throat out. Instead of competing to see who can deliver the most comprehensive biography of the candidate, this breed of political writer competes to see who can most accurately predict the outcome of the election.

And there, I believe, is where horse race journalism does not merely fail to deliver much value to the reader, but is actually detrimental. Because to get these inside stories, with insider quotes and insider polling data, political writers must be on friendly terms with their sources—in effect turning them into a brand of sports reporter. (One time I inadvertently got allowed onto a conference call with a bunch of sports reporters interviewing the general manager of the Florida Marlins, who at the time were in the middle of attempt number three to get a second, $60 million handout from the state of Florida to build a new baseball stadium. Yes, this would have been about nine years into their first, thirty-year, $60 million handout. The sports writers' questions were almost without fail of the following variety: *Gee, Mr. Good and Wise General Manager, why do state legislators in Tallahassee seem unable to see the need for a baseball-only park for the Marlins when all the other teams are getting one?*)

You can't get pithy quotes and tracking poll and focus group data from Jeb and his people if you write stories that tick off Jeb and his people.

Jeb himself remarked on the sort of scribblers who thrive on this brand of coverage to the family's authorized biographers, Peter and Rochelle Schweizer: "Most of these people are not the most brilliant people in the world."

So it was doubly hilarious when Jeb—after successful selling the notion to most political reporters in Florida in 1994 that the standard that ought to be applied to the $4 million bailout he got from the feds for a failed savings and loan was whether any laws had been broken, rather than whether getting such a bailout was sleazy, particularly for a conservative, antigovernment, antiwelfare candidate—then turned around to praise the fine reporting of these selfsame, "not-the-most-brilliant" political reporters.

"I have been investigated by the best and the brightest in this state and in the country," Jeb said in a debate with Democrat Lawton Chiles. "And if they had found something that was wrong in my business dealings, then you would've heard about it already."

FINALLY, this is as good a point as any to mention a problem of the American news media in the early twenty-first century, and that is, of course, Fox "News."

Imagine for a moment that Michael Moore decided that he wasn't reaching enough people with his movies and instead wanted to create a "news" network so all his fans could avoid the conservative slant of the mainstream media. He could call it the "Truth and Accuracy" network.

How do you suppose that would go over? Would anyone believe, even for a second, that people with traditional, conservative viewpoints would get a fair shake?

And yet, despite the outlandishness of a Michael Moore News Channel, at least Moore has been in the business of digging up and presenting actual facts. Sure, his documentaries have a point of view. Most documentaries do. But documentaries by their very nature document some aspect of human existence, using provable facts.

Contrast this to the founder and chief of the Fox "News" Channel—who was actually a Republican political consultant for decades before he got into the "Fair and Balanced" business. Not just any political consultant, mind, *but a guy who helped dream up the Willie Horton campaign!*

This, frankly, is mind-boggling. Roger Ailes, the media genius who made Michael Dukakis, the son of immigrants, look like an elitist dweeb while making George H.W. Bush, the son of a United States senator with an oceanfront mansion in Maine, look like an accessible commoner, has gotten away with a joke of epic proportions. A TV channel that shamelessly uses jingoism and McCarthyist tactics to intimidate those who might question George W. has made itself known for fairness and balance, when it employs neither.

Fox escapee David Shuster described a network that encouraged him to go after Bill Clinton, but wasn't so interested in toughness when it was George W. "With the change of administration in Washington, I wanted to do the same kind of reporting, holding the (Bush) administration accountable, and that was not something that Fox was interested in doing," said Shuster, who jumped over to MSNBC, to a college audience in 2005. "But the bigger issue was that there wasn't a tradition or track record of honoring journalistic integrity. I found some reporters at Fox would cut corners or steal information from other sources or in some cases, just make things up. Management would either look the other way or just wouldn't care to take a closer look. I had serious issues with that."

It would all be funny, like the scene in *Catch-22* where the soldiers are forced to sing the national anthem, recite the pledge of allegiance, and sign countless loyalty oaths just to get fed in the mess hall, if the consequences weren't so corrosive. Fox's powerful ratings have cowed other networks into aping the flag-waving foolishness, at the expense of the aggressive reporting that ought to be the hallmark of a free society.

It used to be, in America, that we were unlike most Latin American countries and many European countries in that we had a truly independent press. In these other places, there is a tradition of a "socialist newspaper" and a "Christian Democrat newspaper" and so on. Readers know that they are getting an inaccurate take on the news in favor of the paper's leaning.

We were different. Here, the press was beholden to no person and to no ideology. Now, that's changing. Fox openly backs conservative Republicans—like its founder. Can something akin to the Michael Moore News Network be terribly far behind? And once we have our tribes getting their news from sources that pander to their prejudices, does anyone honestly believe we'll be better off?

IN THE END, just as his brother effectively neutered the national press for one full term and part of a second, so Jeb was largely able to freeze out the Florida media during his eight years. The strategies were somewhat different—Jeb, unlike George W., could not realistically question a reporter's patriotism for writing a negative article—but the effect was the same.

George W.'s people were not at all shy about playing the with-us-or-against-us card—in 2005, White House press secretary Scott McClellan questioned columnist Helen Thomas's commitment to the "war on terror"—as well as using their power to make more and more of what they did secret. With a cumbersome federal bureaucracy and an expensive court trip to use the Freedom of Information Act, they were able to get away with it.

In Tallahassee, Jeb divided and conquered the press corps, intimidating some, giving special access to others, to get out his message—all the while making it more and more time consuming and ever more expensive to pry loose public records.

And by the end of his second term, nobody, apart from maybe a few dozen journalists and maybe an equal number of editorial writers, cared. Not even a little bit. Which is another way of saying that when Jeb finished his second term having markedly diminished Floridians' right to know about their own government, much of the blame must be borne by Floridians themselves.

It's a harsh indictment, but there it is. Maybe journalists must share in the blame, for not effectively explaining why when Jeb was stonewalling us, he was actually stonewalling the general public. I say "maybe" because I'm not remotely persuaded this is true, even though it has become quite fashionable to blame the media for their lack of relevance. Usually this is attributed to scandals in recent years involving fabricated stories and forged documents and so forth, but I think this misses a more basic point. The difference between the media today and the media fifty years ago, I think, is that the media today have much more precise means of determining what Americans want to read in their newspapers or see on television. It's not only political candidates who use focus groups and polling.

Are Americans more ignorant of their government because the news media do a worse job of covering it? Or do the media do a worse job covering politics and government because Americans don't care about those things as much? As politically correct as it might be to blame both equally or society as a whole, as someone who has watched the business from the inside for two decades, I think I must blame the news consumer. In a competitive market such as journalism, the customer is always right, and in this area the customer has shown that he values information about movie, television and sports celebrities and their entertainment events more highly than information about his school board and his governor. If you doubt this, come look at the respective travel budgets at your home-town newspaper for its state capital bureau and its sports department. Compare the typical salaries at a metro newspaper for the county commission reporter versus the gossip columnist. If readers demanded more in-depth coverage of the state legislature than they did the pro basketball team, trust me, editors and publishers would respond. If viewers demanded more coverage of their Congress than the latest missing white woman, believe me: the cable news networks would turn on a dime.

With the Florida open government laws as clear as they are, there was a simple way for the news media to obtain the public records that anyone in the public is entitled to receive in a timely manner: take Jeb to court. It would have been a clear-cut case. The language was not ambiguous. Years of case law were on our side. So why didn't it happen? Lawsuits are costly and time consuming—and our readers really didn't care if they got the information or not. The public records in question were not about Britney Spears. They weren't about the Miami Dolphins.

And so, the end result is that people like Jeb, who have mastered the modern art of "message," can advance their careers with a minimum of scrutiny and analysis. Voters by and large know about Jeb only what Jeb wants them to know, countered to an extent when the opposing party puts out its own paid message during election times. Since Jeb thus far has been far more competent at getting out his message as well as flat out louder than his Democratic opponents, to date it has been no contest.

Should Jeb ever find himself in the White House, Americans can expect a government-in-the-dark-closet policy that makes his brother's administration look open and forthcoming in comparison.

Will anyone other than the usual whiners like us in the news media care? Unfortunately, if history is a guide—no, probably not.

Chapter Ten

LET THEM EAT TAX CUTS

"I don't believe you can 'reinvent' government unless you can constrain the beast, first and foremost."

—JEB BUSH, 1993

"Our budget proposes a $277 million reduction in the insidious 'intangibles tax,' which punishes our seniors and small businesses for saving and investing."

—JEB BUSH, 2001, ABOUT A TAX THAT
ALMOST EXCLUSIVELY HIT THE WEALTHIEST
4.5 PERCENT OF FLORIDIANS

"I was a federal prosecutor: insidious is what you call a serial murderer. A tax is not insidious."

—INCOMING FLORIDA HOUSE
DEMOCRATIC LEADER DAN GELBER, 2006

Fact one: of all the Florida governors since 1970, Jeb Bush presided over the lowest job-creation rate.

Fact two: of all the Florida governors since 1970, Jeb Bush created significantly fewer actual jobs than one of the three previous two-term governors, and barely more than another, despite having the largest economy of all of them.

On their own, these facts mean little. The Florida economy is a tiny fraction of the national economy, and even a president, who has the ability to influence the nation's monetary policy and federal tax policy, still has but limited control over the big picture. What's more, Florida was on the receiving end of a massive migration pattern during the 1970s and 1980s that generally saw Americans leave the northeast and the Rust Belt states and move south and west to the Sun Belt. The 1990s saw a lessening of that trend—as common sense and sheer physical limits suggested it had to.

But on a political level, these facts are enormously important, because they belie Jeb's perennial claims that job growth had been unprecedented under his watch, and said job growth was specifically attributable to his tax cuts.

Because as Jeb's own labor department's statistics show, job growth during his two terms did not equal that of his predecessors' numbers. Given that, the tax cuts lose their justification as a tool of economic growth and must stand alone on their own merits.

And by that analysis, the combined tax cuts of Jeb's two terms reveal why it is that Florida's wealthy overwhelmingly backed Jeb during his reelection:

Jeb made them even richer. A lot richer.

Constitutionally barred from imposing an income tax, Florida prior to Jeb's arrival in 1999 really had only one levy that exclusively hit the wealthy. Over his two terms in office, Jeb made that go away, almost completely by his seventh year, and forever. The other main tax cut that Jeb liked to talk about? An annual "sales tax holiday" on back-to-school clothes and supplies. That cut typically lasted only nine days, and it had to be reauthorized by legislators each year, so that in some summers, there was no tax cut for the little guy. Only in his final year as governor did it occur to Jeb to try to make that tax break a permanent one.

With a few exceptions, the "intangibles" tax on stocks and bonds in 1999 hit the richest 4.5 percent of Floridians. Their average annual savings: $1,523 per household. The average annual savings for the typical Palm Beach County millionaire: $7,980.

The sales tax holidays were available to anyone buying clothes, notebooks, backpacks, and so forth that cost less than, depending on the year,

$50 or $100. The average savings: $16 per household in those years the "holiday" was held.

The rich got filet mignon. Everybody else got little scraps of tofu.

PART OF the problem for Jeb's opponents was that the singular focus of his tax-cutting *jihad,* the intangibles tax, was so difficult to understand. What, for example, *is* an intangible, and why was the state taxing it?

To put it bluntly, the tax was passed in an attempt to soak the rich— particularly the Yankee rich who were moving to Florida to build winter getaways during the early part of the twentieth century. In a state where the income tax was then and is to this day constitutionally off the table, the intangibles tax was created to bring some measure of progressive taxation.

By the mid-1980s, the tax was applied on stocks, bonds, and other financial instruments—*intangible* things, as opposed to cars, jewelry, or land— at the rate of $1 per $1,000 of value. There was an exemption on the first $20,000 worth of securities for a single person and $40,000 for a married couple. On top of that, there was a minimum pay feature of five dollars, meaning you owed nothing at all until you had $25,000 in assets as an individual or $45,000 as a married couple. There were also other broad exemptions: cash held in checking, savings, and money market accounts was exempt, as were any and all assets held in retirement accounts like IRAs or 401(k)s.

With that last provision especially, you were left pretty much with people who had maxed out on their retirement plan contributions but had managed to put away some savings on top of that—or, more likely, those who had inherited a nest egg from a parent or other relative.

In the early 1990s, as Florida was hammered by recession, first Republican governor Bob Martinez and then Democratic successor Lawton Chiles approved increases in the tax. A second tier was created, so that holders of portfolios larger than $100,000 for single filers and $200,000 for couples paid at first fifty cents more, and later a full dollar more per $1,000 in assets.

Later in the 1990s, the tax was reduced somewhat. First the minimum pay threshold was raised from five dollars to sixty dollars, and then the exemption amounts were increased to $40,000 for individuals and $60,000 for couples.

Bottom line: by the time Jeb took office in 1999, not a whole lot of people were affected by this. In a state of some 15.6 million people, only 717,000 (approximately 239,000 single filers and 478,000 married couples) were filing the tax. It is possible that some who owed the tax were not paying it—we'll address this topic a little later.

But even for those who *were* paying it, most were still paying less, even a lot less, than what they would have been paying had they been living in other states that have an income tax.

As IN many areas, Florida in the region of taxes was a mess long before Jeb got his hands on it.

It is today one of the seven states that do not levy an income tax and is therefore largely dependent on its sales tax, which since 1987—under an increase by Jeb's former boss, Governor Martinez—has been 6 percent on most goods. Things such as most groceries, prescription drugs, and long-term rent are exempt, but the tax remains fairly regressive. Poor and lower-middle-class people spend a larger proportion of their incomes on necessities such as gasoline, clothing, and cars, and all of those things are subject to the sales tax.

A couple of Jeb's predecessors tried to change that balance, but in the end were not terribly successful. An income tax, which is employed by most states as the fairest way of financing state services, is actually prohibited in Florida's state constitution, and most politicians, Democrats included, will not admit to even contemplating a change.

Still, in 1970, Pensacola Democrat Reubin Askew ran for governor on the platform of introducing a corporate income tax in Florida. Business groups naturally opposed this idea and fought hard against it and him, claiming that prices for consumer goods would rise dramatically, should the state start taxing corporate profits. Askew countered this by holding up two identical shirts, one purchased from a Sears in Georgia and the other from a Sears in Florida. They were priced the same, even though Georgia already had a corporate income tax.

Askew won (true, this was more because he was a Democrat in what was then an overwhelmingly Democratic state that by 1970 was getting over its odd attraction to eccentric GOP incumbent Claude Kirk) and promptly pushed through a 5 percent tax on corporate profits.

It was, at the time, a big deal. When it was fully implemented, the corporate income tax became a huge revenue stream for the state, which at the time had a sales tax rate of 4 percent. In 1972, the corporate income tax brought in $148 million, 8.1 percent of general revenues for that year. By 1979, that proportion had grown to 10 percent.

But in the coming years, that proportion started to shrink. By the early 1980s, Governor Bob Graham, who succeeded Askew in 1979, thought he knew why. In a special session he called to increase education spending by $100 million, Graham pushed through the so-called "unitary tax," which made it harder for multistate and multinational corporations from "hiding" profit in low-tax jurisdictions while reporting low profits or even losses in higher-tax areas. Instead, businesses would have to pay corporate income tax based on their total profit and the proportion of their business that was sited in Florida.

The big national corporations were blindsided by Graham's quick action, but soon responded with an all-out lobbying blitz. The implications were enormous. What if other large states copied Florida?

In short order, leaders in both the House and Senate were clamoring for a repeal, even if it meant increasing the corporate income tax rate by a quarter point to 5.25 percent, to make up for the money the unitary tax was bringing in. Graham went along with this, since it was clear they had the votes to override him. What has never been clear was how businesses that are based in and limited their activities to Florida got so badly hoodwinked into supporting the unitary tax repeal, but they did—even though it meant a significant tax increase for them and the elimination of a provision that did not harm them. (Well, that's actually a dumb question. They got hoodwinked into supporting it the same way they get hoodwinked into supporting any number of bad ideas—they believe their lobbyists, and their lobbyists get more money from the big boys than from the mom-and-pop outfits.)

The next and last major attempt to flatten Florida's tax pyramid started in the final year of Graham's tenure, when the legislature agreed to "sunset," or phase out, every single sales tax exemption—most of them on the various service industries—the following spring and only reenact those with a compelling state interest.

The basic idea was that it made no sense to charge sales tax on a pair of grooming scissors but not charge it on a haircut at a barbershop. That you should charge sales tax on a restaurant meal but not on a meal catered at your house. In other words, businesses that offered services should be treated no differently than businesses that sold goods, when it came to the sales tax.

Graham's successor, Republican Martinez, supported the services tax concept, particularly if it meant a rollback of the state sales tax rate, which by then was 5 percent. (Martinez's commerce secretary, it should be noted again, a Mr. John Ellis Bush, also publicly supported the idea: "If this is a way to broaden taxation and at the same time lower the rate, I think a lot of people would really go for it.")

After that spring's legislative session, though, legislators passed, and Martinez approved, an expansion of the sales tax to include most services but did not reduce the rate in the process. Proponents argued that Florida had a number of things it needed but could not afford without the extra billion dollars the new tax would bring in.

Whether that failure to lower the rate proved to be the tax's downfall is debatable but doubtful. In any event, all the big-money service providers—among them: accountants, architects, engineers, and, yes, the print and broadcast media—collectively piled on and demanded a repeal. Within months, Martinez called the special session to give it to them, but kept the just-passed larger budget in balance by increasing the sales tax rate to 6 percent.

IT'S IMPORTANT to bear in mind what a services tax would have done to the state tax structure.

The poor and the working poor spend much of their paychecks on the basics of life—groceries, the rent, a cheap car, the gas to make it run, clothes for work, clothes for children—but relatively little on services.

Most of the big-money service providers—accountants, lawyers, engineers, consultants, and so on—are hired by other businesses or relatively well-off individuals. Similarly, the manicurist, the fancy hairdresser, the pool guy, the lawn guy are all expenses that folks living from paycheck to paycheck normally don't worry about.

Related to this, many of the service providers and their lobbyists claimed that all consumers would, in the end, pay the higher taxes because businesses would simply pass down the costs to the retail-level customer. It was, of course, not really true. (Anytime a business lobbyist claims that a tax will simply be passed down to the consumer, you should question its veracity. Why, if a business can simply pass a tax along, would the business owner bother lobbying so hard against it?) Costs can be readily passed down in areas where there is little elasticity of demand, where people need to buy things almost regardless of their costs—gasoline, say, or staples like bread and milk, or medicines. But in other areas, particularly luxuries, demand will certainly go down as cost goes up.

In other words, the overall tax burden would have shifted somewhat to hit the more well-off.

WHICH GETS us back to the biggest tax cut of Jeb's time in office, the intangibles tax, which by the end had diminished the state treasury by $1 billion a year. An analysis of that policy should start with two fundamental questions. The first: given Florida's poor rankings in various quality-of-life measures—the health and welfare of its children, the care of its elderly, the quality of its schools and colleges, etc.—were large tax cuts appropriate public policy? And second, once you have decided that tax cuts were appropriate, was the intangibles tax the most appropriate one to cut?

On the first question, Jeb is part of the wing of the Republican Party that believes as a fundamental truth that taxes are too high. Period.

If Jeb were a resident of New York or Massachusetts or Sweden, he could easily make the argument that compared to other large states or other Western nations, taxes were too high and therefore ought to come down. But Florida?

Survey after survey shows the Sunshine State near the bottom when it comes to overall per capita state taxes and about in the middle when it comes to local taxes. That Jeb could start with the premise that Floridians are overtaxed is a telling statement.

Further, the inability or unwillingness to quantify what the ideal taxation level is or where Florida stood compared to that benchmark leads to a peculiar end. Through two terms of Jeb's rule, he and his allies pushed the idea that when the economy was good and tax collections increasing, that was a perfect time to cut taxes. But then, when times turned bad and tax collections decreased, the argument then became—you guessed it—that a recession is no time to raise taxes and, in fact, can be cured only by cutting taxes.

If taxes should be cut in good times and they should also be cut in bad times, what is the desired end here? That taxes should be zero?

No, with Jeb, the desire for lower taxes was more an article of faith than a conclusion based on a study of economic data. Here, like school vouchers and the push to privatize state government, the policy was not beholden in any significant way to facts.

The second question, of whether the intangibles tax was the one that most deserved cutting, takes us into a similar fact-free zone—a favored stamping ground, in fact, of the other political Bushes.

IF YOU cut taxes on the rich, everyone benefits.

There, in a nutshell, is the Bush Family Economic Theory, boiled down to nine words.

It's important to distinguish here that the emphasis is not to cut taxes for everybody. That, of course, is not a terrible thing, so long as taxes are cut proportionately more for the wealthy—or, in Bush parlance, the *investor class*, the *risk takers*, the *job creators*.

In the 1980s, after George H.W. renounced his attack on Ronald Reagan's broad tax-cutting plan as "voodoo economics" and joined in his administration, there was a mishmash of this general theme. Reagan wanted and won across-the-board reductions in all income tax rates. These were partly undone in subsequent years, especially for the working poor and the middle class, who saw massive payroll tax increases to bail out Social Security and Medicare. That remains one of the least remembered pieces of the Reagan legacy, lost in the broad-brush portrait of Reagan as a tax cutter: middle and lower-class people actually were paying higher federal taxes after Reagan left office than before he came in. But these were largely Reagan's priorities and compromises—the vice president had little to do with economic policy.

What George H.W. really cared about, and what became apparent when he himself moved into the Oval Office in 1989, was the tax on capital gains, or the amount stocks and bonds or other assets appreciate over the period that an investor owns them. Throughout his term, that was the priority—a tax cut that would have sent 60 percent of the benefit to the richest 1 percent of the population earning more than $200,000 a year. During the now-infamous budget-cutting, tax-raising deal of 1990, George H.W. was able to leave capital gains rates where they were while other taxes went up. And then, when the recession hit, George H.W.'s ready answer was to push Congress into cutting capital gains taxes.

Others pushed him to cut payroll taxes on a one-time basis, a move that would have helped middle- and lower-class workers the most because Social Security and Medicare taxes make up a proportionately larger share of their tax burden than it does for wealthier taxpayers.

George H.W. even resisted extending unemployment benefits, pushing instead to reduce the tax rate on investments, ostensibly so that the rich would be more apt to sink money into expanding businesses or starting new ones.

When George W. took office, he picked up where his father had left off. The 2001 tax cuts were skewed toward the wealthy. The 2003 tax cuts—with the reductions in the dividend tax rates as well as the capital gains rates—were mainly for the wealthy.

In Florida, meanwhile, Jeb was already valiantly fighting the good fight on behalf of the Sunshine State's wealthy.

NOW, simply coming out and saying that you're helping the rich doesn't play well, outside of exclusive golf courses and yacht clubs, so Jeb and his people came up with a host of other reasons to eliminate the state's one tax on the rich. These covered the waterfront, from the tax's inefficiency to its alleged "unfairness" to its supposed ill effects on the Florida economy.

The first two had to be admired for chutzpah, if nothing else.

Jeb knew it would be tough to create any public empathy for the actual "victims" of this tax, and so he and his people invented a new description for them: "seniors and savers." They produced statistics to show that a disproportionate number of people who paid this tax were elderly. And indeed, many, maybe even most of them probably were "savers," insofar as they hadn't spend their entire fortunes on yachts and furs.

But this is one of those uses of statistics to pretty much tell a lie, or at best, tell only a small fraction of the truth. Yes, it was true that people sixty-five and older disproportionately paid this tax. That's because, particularly in Florida, the elderly are disproportionately wealthier than the rest of us. There's nothing wrong with this. We should expect people who have spent their lives working to have amassed a nest egg. But to suggest that the design of the tax discriminates against old people was simply dishonest.

Jeb tried a slightly different tack on the "discriminatory" aspect of this tax in his later years. In his proposed 2004–05 budget, Jeb explained that the intangibles tax was unfair because it affected only a few hundred thousand people out of a state population of, by then, some seventeen million. It never quite got around to explaining that the one common factor these 233,000 people all had was that they were *rich*. The average single filer, by that point, with most of the payers already taken off the rolls, had a portfolio worth $1.1 million. Those are assets, remember, held outside of retirement accounts and not including plain old checking and savings accounts, which have always been exempt. The average married couple had assets totaling $2.1 million.

Jeb had no problems with these sleights of hand. In fact, he reveled in them, particularly the catchword *insidious,* which he tried to use whenever he was talking about the tax. "The insidious intangibles tax," he never tired of saying. At one point, his aide and antitax soul mate Brian Yablonski yucked it up in a 2000 e-mail exchange over how they'd tricked the *Tampa Tribune* into using the phrase in an article.

"People may not know what (the) heck the word means, but just the sound of it conjures up images of a guy in a black cape rolling his pencil-thin mustache between his fingers with the word 'villain' underneath the screen," wrote Yablonski.

"Exactly! An alliteration. It is poetic!" responded Jeb.

Funny stuff. The joke, unfortunately, was on the actual "seniors and savers" who thought, incorrectly, that their retirement accounts were being taxed by the state and that Jeb was helping end this outrage. Those accounts, naturally, had never been taxed to start with, but if the confusion created additional people supporting the elimination of that "insidious" tax, then, well, that was just serendipitous for Jeb, wasn't it?

Of course, there were a small but significant number of actual seniors who were not that wealthy but who were paying this tax. These would be people who had, say, inherited a dead spouse's pension plan that was converted to stock and had never been part of a qualified retirement account. Widows such as these might have a total nest egg of $50,000 or $80,000, the modest earnings from which supplemented their Social Security checks. Jeb and his legislative allies could easily have written some specific exemptions to take care of people like that.

But what did Jeb do instead? He let the poor widows keep paying their annual taxes, while he lowered the tax rate for the wealthiest filers. That's right. Instead of initially cutting the tax for those with portfolios smaller than that $100,000 threshold for individuals and $200,000 for couples and who therefore paid only $1 on $1,000 in assets, Jeb went after that second dollar per $1,000 in assets that was applied to the largest portfolios. In his first year in office, that second dollar was reduced to fifty cents. In his second year, the additional rate on the larger portfolios was eliminated entirely.

In other words: the supposedly poor seniors who were forced to eat cat food and cut their pills in half because of the intangibles tax (yes, some Republicans actually claimed on the campaign trail in those years there were such people) actually got absolutely no relief whatsoever—until the third year of Jeb's tenure, when Senate Republicans read articles in the *Palm Beach Post* explaining the issue. At that point, legislators, rather than further lowering the tax rate, which is what Jeb wanted, instead increased the exemptions to $250,000 for singles and $500,000 for couples—which finally took care of the widows living off of their modest nest eggs.

THE SECOND reason Jeb and friends gave for eliminating this awful tax was that the seriously rich knew how to evade it. Again, this was true—although how true, nobody really knew, because there were no accurate records documenting it. Nonetheless, the way the intangibles tax was structured, you paid annually based on the value of your portfolio that was held at a Florida address on January 1 of each year. So, if you had the energy to do this, you could have transferred your assets to an out-of-state trustee for a day or two and then transferred them all back. (You wouldn't have wanted to just keep your holdings out of state, because then you would have had to pay income taxes on the annual proceeds.)

However, all of this cost money, to pay the accountants and lawyers who actually did the transfers. When Jeb took office, with the tax rates in effect then, a portfolio had to be worth about $2 million before the tax you avoided paying was greater than the accounting fees. By the time that second tier rate was eliminated in 2000, that threshold had increased to $4 million.

But take a step back and look at the big picture: Jeb was arguing that the tax should be eliminated because people had figured out a way to avoid it. Imagine for a moment that the loophole had been in the sales tax or tolls on state highways. You suppose the response would have been the same? A shrug of the shoulders and a regretful decision to do away with the levy? Of course not. Jeb and the legislature would simply have closed the loophole. Doing so in the case of the intangibles tax would have taken one of Jeb's staffers about fifteen minutes to draft the necessary language—to require quarterly or monthly "snapshots," for example, rather than annual ones.

Jeb, though, had no interest in making the tax more efficient and more enforceable. Quite the opposite, in fact.

BUT WHETHER the *really* rich or just the somewhat rich paid this tax, and whether it was excessive or a pittance compared to other states—all of that was meaningless next to Jeb's secret weapon against the intangibles tax: the claim that getting rid of it was working. That without it, the Florida economy would be unshackled and produce all manner of high-paying jobs.

The proof, he would claim year after year, was in the periodic employment numbers, which continually showed Florida at or near the top of all states in terms of new jobs. Budget chief Donna Arduin at one point actually tried to reduce this to a direct correlation, and Jeb himself directly tied the two in speeches to legislators, civic groups, and on the stump. Because of his tax cuts, primarily the intangibles tax cuts, Florida was leading the nation in job growth.

In these claims, Jeb had a powerful ally: the lack of much institutional memory in the Tallahassee Capitol press corps. Because had anyone bothered to look, they would have seen that previous governors, including Democrats Lawton Chiles and Bob Graham and Republican Bob Martinez had made identical claims. Their economic policies—which in the case of all three, had included tax increases—had resulted in more jobs for Florida.

Finally, in Jeb's seventh year in office, I couldn't help myself and asked the obvious question: insofar as past governors have also taken credit for job growth, how do you *know* that Florida's job growth is the result of your tax cuts?

Jeb looked at me like I was from a distant galaxy before replying. "It is counterintuitive to me . . . that if you raise taxes and you make the burdens on the business, the job-creating entities, the entrepreneurs, and the small businesses of our state, that if you increase costs for them, that you increase the chance for job creation." He did concede, though: "I haven't paused to do any research on this."

None of this should have been a surprise. In 1993, he predicted on CBS's *Early Show* that Bill Clinton's tax increase would bring economic disaster for Florida and the nation—no doubt leaving him thoroughly confused when, instead, both Florida and the nation had an eight-year run of strong growth.

But that morning when I asked him about his own tax policy, Jeb couldn't leave his answer be. Of those previous governors, he said: "I'm not sure that they had the kind of growth we've had."

Maybe Jeb really believed this. If so, the hubris is staggering but, given Jeb, not completely surprising that he thought, without the least bit of evidence, that he had outperformed previous governors in the area of job growth.

And, in fact, research into Jeb's own labor statistics—the same ones that quarterly trumpeted the latest employment figures—showed that compared to the previous four governors going back to 1970 (which was how far back Jeb's Agency for Workforce Development kept comparable data), Jeb had been a total and utter slouch, in the area of new jobs.

All four of the previous governors had higher job-creation rates—ranging from a little higher, to markedly higher. That measure is the most fair because Jeb took office when the state's economy was much larger than when his predecessors took office. An even more telling statistic was that Jeb was the only governor whose job-creation rate was less than the population increase rate. All the governors going back to Askew in the early 1970s saw jobs growing at a faster rate than the general population.

Compared to the nation as a whole, Jeb's record exceeded only that of Lawton Chiles. All the other governors had job-growth rates that were better than the national average by a larger margin than Jeb's. And even under the crudest of scales, the number of total jobs created—a measure that should favor Jeb, because of his larger economy—Jeb still was not the best. Bob Graham created 125,000 more jobs through his first seven years than Jeb did, even with an economy that was fully a third smaller.

Bear in mind here that all of the previous governors had significant tax increases in their terms. Two of them, Martinez and Chiles, had raised the exact same intangibles tax that Bush claimed was a job-killer. Reubin Askew had been even worse, instituting a corporate income tax where none had existed previously, surely as deadly a disincentive to business as can be imagined. So who had the highest job-creation rate? Askew.

Which, using Jeb's logic, brings us to this unexpected conclusion: maybe Jeb had it all wrong. Maybe the way to encourage job growth is not to cut taxes, but to increase them!

THE WHOLE discussion, of course, is more than a little silly.

Florida has had rapid job growth over the past four decades because Florida has been growing like a tumor over those four decades, with little regard for existing roads and schools or future quality of life.

Eventually, though, things come back into balance. More and more newcomers realized that Florida wasn't all that it was cracked up to be, that jammed roads, lousy schools, and low wages don't make up for lots of sunshine and low taxes. More and more, the in-migration was being reduced by out-migration, both of relative newcomers and longtime residents who had had enough. Many of these people are heading back up the Interstate and stopping, interestingly, in North Carolina, which *has* made a significant commitment to public education. It was bound to happen, and it wasn't really Jeb's fault—although his policies did little to improve these central concerns.

As net population growth has slowed, so has job growth. Simple enough.

Jeb's folly was to draw direct connections between tax cuts and job growth, although, to his credit, he stopped doing so after the *Post*'s article on this issue, thereafter making only general claims about Florida's low taxes and favorable "business climate" being responsible for job growth.

Nevertheless, Jeb's insistence—with no facts whatsoever to support him—that cutting taxes for the state's wealthiest would create jobs and help the state as a whole is perhaps *the* central tenet to his family theology. It is, of course, part of the whole "supply side" theory used during the Reagan era that claimed that massive tax cuts could pay for themselves by increased economic growth, so that total collections would actually increase. Massive budget deficits by the end of Reagan's tenure showed that the theory didn't quite pan out in the real world, but let's assume for the sake of discussion that there is validity to Arthur Laffer's curve.

The idea is that if you lower the top marginal rate for the so-called investor class, these folks would be more likely to risk their money on new factories and businesses in the hopes of getting higher returns. These new factories and businesses would hire more people, who would then spend these wages buying more stuff, thereby keeping the cycle going and making everyone happy. Yes, the rich would get even richer, but everyone would benefit.

This was Jeb's advertised reason for eliminating the intangibles tax—that doing so would encourage additional investment that would create more jobs in Florida.

But nowhere in his policy was any mechanism to connect the reduction of the tax to Florida investment. The tax was eliminated, period, with no strings of any kind. People were not required to invest the money in job-creating enterprises in Florida. They could spend it on summer homes in the Swiss Alps or a bigger yacht in the Bahamas. Even those who decided to invest in new or expanded businesses had no incentive to invest in *Florida* businesses. If a tax-cut beneficiary put all her savings into a broad-based mutual fund, for example, the vast majority of those businesses were located outside of Florida. Floridians could expect, at best, pennies of job creation for each dollar of tax that was cut.

It is important to note that Jeb could easily have created such a link between the intangibles tax cut and Florida jobs, if that's what he'd really wanted.

Creating an intangibles tax credit for people who invested in Florida businesses would have been the simplest way. Or a tax credit against investments, whether in Florida or not, that could prove they had created new jobs in Florida. Local, state, and federal governments create these "targeted" credits all the time, to encourage investment in areas that policy makers believe are being missed by the free market.

More to the point, though, if Jeb had really wanted to see tax money go back into the economy and generate more jobs, then the consensus approach most economists advise is to cut taxes on the poorest, not the richest.

The rich, when they get a tax cut, have a lot of choices. They can make the Bermuda vacation three weeks long instead of two. They can add that second hot tub at the condo in Aspen. They can diversify their portfolio by adding a Latin American stock fund. They can just let the money sit in a mutual fund and grow. Only one of those, the fourth, helps the Florida economy even a tiny bit.

But those at the bottom end of the economic food chain tend to spend every dollar they can get their hands on as quickly as possible, typically right in their local communities. Maybe new shoes for the family. Maybe a new muffler to replace the one held in place by baling wire. If they choose to vacation, it will almost certainly be local—a day trip to Disney World, for example.

So how much did Jeb help out Florida's nonrich, so they could help Florida's economy?

WHILE THE wealthy were being delivered from the only tax Florida had that specifically hit them, the rest of us mainly got pennies. Literally.

For between a week and nine days in most years, Floridians were given the opportunity to purchase clothes, shoes, school supplies and, in one year, books. The event took place in the final days of July and early days of August—timed to coincide with the start of Florida's school year. (In Jeb's seventh year, a Democratic-inspired hurricane supplies tax "holiday" was passed, but this ostensibly aimed at storm preparedness, not tax relief.)

In terms of hype, this one had it all over the intangibles tax. Jeb would typically hit a Staples or a Target or a Macy's and pile his shopping cart full as TV cameras rolled. In 2005, he outdid himself. He went to Bealls Department Store in a Tampa suburb on a Saturday, the Target in Tallahassee the following Wednesday, and a Macy's in Orlando two days later. It was great stuff. Jeb in a store, just like a normal person, buying notebooks and pens and socks. Newspapers and local television ate it up, explaining in breathless detail which exact dates shoppers could hit the mall and save.

Some quick math here: in a county with a penny sales tax on top of the state's 6 percent, a pack of Spider-Man underwear costing $4.99 would save you thirty-four cents. A refill of notebook paper costing eighty-nine cents would save you six cents. After all was said and done, say you bought $200 worth of clothes and $50 in school supplies for your children. You would have saved seventeen dollars and fifty cents. For the year, that's what Jeb Bush's tax cuts would have given you. That example, by the way, was slightly larger than the $16 savings that the average household enjoyed.

In contrast, the average person who paid the intangibles tax got a $196 break the first year, and an $1,523 extra in their pocket—year, after year—by the time Jeb left office.

Not once did Jeb hold a media event at a brokerage house or a country club to celebrate all the extra money the members would be able to enjoy. An oversight, no doubt. Or an unfortunate scheduling conflict.

Almost as significant as the relative size of the two tax breaks, though, was their permanence.

The sales tax "holidays" were, until Jeb's final year in office, all contemplated and passed as one-time events, with the legislation specifying the exact dates in that coming summer. In those years where no law was passed, there was no "holiday."

Now the ostensible reason provided for this was that legislators could not know, year to year, what the budget situation was going to be like, and so they did not want to tie the hands of future legislators. That lawmakers and Jeb could manage this explanation with a straight face is a marvel of nature. The cost of these holidays was generally in the $35 million range—a tiny fraction of the recurring, year-after-year costs of the intangibles tax cuts.

Of course, the real reason Jeb and the legislature did not make the sales tax holidays a permanent fixture in state law was that they rather liked the ability to brag on their generosity to the great unwashed each year, particularly during election years. This pass-it-every-year strategy, however, does bring up an interesting point: Jeb could have saved the state a lot of unnecessary heartache by making the intangibles tax cuts "annual" holidays, too.

Doing this would have required some extra work of the Department of Revenue, but certainly no more than it had to do to implement the sales tax holiday. The department could have sent out notices to its intangibles tax payers that, for the coming year, no tax would be due, on account of the state's robust finances and Jeb's desire to give a little something back in a time of plenty.

And then, in times of budgetary crises, like after September 11, 2001, when tourism to the state fell off dramatically, the state could have not held its intangibles tax holiday the following year and immediately had an extra half billion to a billion dollars on hand.

But that option was never even on the table. Democrats took the blunter approach, hammering Jeb for cutting a tax on the rich at all. Jeb would typically respond by arguing that if he had not pushed a tax cut, that lawmakers would simply have spent the money, probably on recurring expenses like schoolteachers or Medicaid services.

"Let me ask you, do you think if there weren't tax cuts that there would be $1 billion available to spend next fiscal year?" he wrote me in a 2001 e-mail. "Given your long-standing commitment to pointing out the spending habits of the legislature, it is hard for me to believe you think that the money would have been reserved. Can you clear this up for me?"

That is true, as far as it goes. But it does not go very far. First, it argues that Jeb was fiscally prudent by taking money away from legislators before they could spend it unwisely. For Jeb to make that case, he should have held that money in reserve, for use on a rainy day. He did not. He "spent" it— on a tax cut, which was every bit as recurring as the recurring expenses Jeb wanted to avoid.

Further, Jeb's argument presumes that there were only two choices: a permanent tax cut, like he wanted, or more teachers or social workers at higher salaries, like Democrats wanted.

But there were other options, as well. Had he truly wanted to preserve a ready reserve in the budget for lean years, Jeb could easily have told legislators that he was earmarking, say, $500 million from the intangibles tax for that purpose and would only agree to spend it on "nonrecurring" projects. That way, the following year, that $500 million would once again be fully available if it were needed in an economic downturn, and Floridians would have gotten a half billion dollars of badly needed schools, water treatment plants, environmental preservation, or other "capital" projects. The state has a long backlog of such needs, and this would have been a smart way to eat into that list.

And, of course, if it were deemed absolutely necessary that the rich get relief, Jeb could have offered, as discussed above, their intangibles tax cut, but only in years with hefty surpluses by structuring them as "holidays," the same way the nonrich were getting their much smaller tax cut.

In reality, none of this was even considered. These other things—building new schools, buying environmentally sensitive land and so forth— were a priority, but they were not the top priority. Tax cuts were. The type and size of these were set first, and the rest of the budget was built from there.

THERE IS, in this antitax *jihad,* a method to the madness.

The goal is a smaller government, doing fewer things—even though that is completely the opposite of what constituents, even constituents who call themselves conservative Republicans, say they want. If taxes are cut and cut and cut, eventually, during a recession, voters will be given an ultimatum: what do you want, higher taxes? Or larger class sizes or worse nursing home ratios or less children's health insurance?

The bet is that voters will go for the lower taxes and worse services, particularly since, at the state level, the only real service that most middle-class people get is public education. Medicaid and child protective services and subsidized health insurance—most of that stuff is used by the poor and the marginalized. The sort of people who do not vote.

This is essentially the "starve the beast" theory of cutting government, the strategy that many conservative Republicans adopted after the straight-ahead, let's-just-start-cutting-these-middle-class-entitlements approach of Newt Gingrich and his Class of '94 army didn't work so well at the federal level.

But whether Jeb's approach will work in the long run in Florida is not clear. The vast majority of the state budget is education and Medicaid. Jeb tried to hold the line on education spending by offering and approving annual budgets that barely exceeded inflation and student growth, but instead was handed the class-size amendment in the same election he was reelected. Voters basically told him his vision of public schools wasn't good enough. With Medicaid, Jeb faced a different problem but with similar results. Much of the massive program is dictated by the federal government in services that must be offered. And even with those that are discretionary at the state level, the nation and Florida have come quite a ways since the days before Lyndon Johnson's Great Society. George H.W. Bush poked fun at Medicare during his unsuccessful Senate run in 1964, saying that "medical care of the aged" made about as much sense as providing air-conditioning for animals being transported in ships—"medical air for the caged." (I didn't say it was a *good* joke.)

George H.W. came to regret those remarks, and in later years moved into the American mainstream in terms of his public support for Medicare, Medicaid, and Social Security. It is interesting to note that in 1994, Jeb was still closer to where his father had been three decades earlier, calling government programs like these "creeping collectivism" and a "silent march toward socialism."

But four decades after George H.W.'s lame joke, both politicians and voters, including many Republicans, get queasy when explaining how it's necessary to cut back on pediatric visits for poor children while others are getting a tax cut. Basic health care has moved in the past two generations from something for the rich and middle class to a fundamental right of all Americans. Never mind that we were oh-so-slow getting there, compared to other Western industrialized countries.

That we got there at all drives conservatives like Jeb bonkers.

PERHAPS WHAT'S needed to appreciate Jeb's handling of tax matters is a primer on the tax structure that the economic conservative wing of the Republican Party, that group that believes this nation is headed toward socialism, would favor in an ideal world.

First, right off the bat, let's go ahead and concede that if socialism is used so broadly as to include quality health care and education for all citizens—rather than the more precise economic definition in which the state owns most of the factories and farms, the "means of production"—then yes, absolutely: Jeb and his allies are right. America is well on her way.

In the economic conservatives' perfect world, government's role would be limited to national defense, roads, police, courts, prisons . . . and that's pretty much it. It's not clear how such issues as pollution and environmental preservation would be handled, but we'll let that go for now. The money to pay for these limited goals would come from a small tax levied equally on all citizens.

Government would not be in the business of providing health care or education. These would be handled by individuals, paying for the schooling of their choice and the medical care of their choice. Because catastrophic medical care is so expensive, those who wanted to pool their risk and buy insurance for such care could do so. Yes, shared risk is an inherently collectivist concept—but hey, heart attacks hit conservatives, too.

Under this worldview, the levies needed to finance socialistic goals like Social Security and Medicare, then, are by definition immoral, confiscatory taxes. And adding both insult and injury to it all is a federal tax code designed to hit the wealthy proportionately more than the poor.

And it is this fundamental opposition to the "progressive" income tax—which in theory sounds an awful lot like Karl Marx's "from each according to his ability" (yes, it also sounds an awful lot like what the New Testament said about Jesus in Acts—"distribution was made unto every man according as he had need"—but let us be charitable and assume that conservatives are offended by Marx, and not Christ)—that drives the periodic calls for a flat tax, or a national sales tax, or a value-added tax. The publicized reasons for this are generally to weaken or eliminate the much-reviled Internal Revenue Service, or to simplify the tax code, or to save time, or a combination of all of these. Rarely do proponents advertise the real effect of these other tax schemes, which would be to shift the burden down the economic ladder—a shift that started after Ronald Reagan took office in 1981.

In these broader schemes, Jeb's tax policy in Florida fits right in.

WE LIKE MYTHS, we Americans, particularly about ourselves.

We like to believe we have the best health-care system in the world, even though, measuring outcomes of most users, we clearly do not. We like to believe our scientific research is without parallel, even though, without a steady stream of foreign students, we could not begin to compete against nations with superior educational systems in the Far East and Europe.

We like to think our Founding Fathers demanded independence from mother England because of our love of political and religious freedom, when in fact our "revolution" was really more of a tax revolt.

Our tax structure generally, in fact, has come to reside more in the land of myth and legend than reality. Ronald Reagan is probably the best example of this. Most Americans seem to believe that he was a tax-cutter of heroic magnitude. Particularly since his death in 2004, that view has attained the level of sacred dogma. If you challenge it, your patriotism is suspect.

In fact, while Ronald Reagan did push for and win big, across-the-board tax cuts in 1981, just a year later Reagan signed into law the biggest peace-time tax increase in the nation's history. The TEFRA of 1982—for Tax Equity and Fiscal Responsibility Act—was, as a percentage of gross domestic product, even larger that Bill Clinton's tax increase in 1993. And Reagan the year after TEFRA signed a massive Social Security tax increase, the result of a commission tasked to figure out a way to keep solvent America's retirement plan of last resort. Additional tax increases followed, so that by the end of his two terms, most Americans were paying more in Social Security taxes than in income taxes, and most Americans were paying more in federal taxes in 1988 than they were in 1980. And, oh yeah, the annual budget deficit and the total national debt were both setting records each year.

Reagan, though, honestly seemed to believe that if taxes were to be cut, then all Americans should share in the windfall. And on that point, he and the Bushes parted ways.

When George H.W. became president, he raised taxes to balance the budget, true, but even as he did this, he fought for lower tax rates on capital gains, favoring his beloved "investor" class that does so much for the country by taking all those terrible risks to make more money. Where the father did not succeed, son George W. did, managing to lower taxes on both capital gains and dividends to rates significantly lower than those applied to "earned" income.

It is a distinction sometimes lost in the popular media, but it is of tremendous importance for the Bushes, who over the generations have accepted the premise that money made from the ownership and sale of stocks and bonds is somehow more moral than money made from wages. It is nothing short of bizarre, when you think about it: If you work in a widget factory, your total federal taxes—income taxes plus Social Security and Medicare—are between 25 and 30 percent. But if your livelihood is based on owning stock in that same widget factory, then your federal tax rate should be no higher than 15 percent. Meaning that making money off the sweat of someone else's brow should be less taxing than making money off the sweat of your own.

SOMEDAY, someone, or more likely a large group of someones, will have to pay for the financial disaster left by George W.

There is no free lunch, not when the children of the holders of U.S.

Government securities in various foreign countries can do math so much better than our own children can. The question is at what point reality will finally set in and we will stop running up the national credit card and compounding our woes.

Jeb Bush, in Florida, held the reins of a low-tax, low-service state, but still insisted on lowering the taxes further for his favorite constituency, even though it meant running up the state debt in the process. Taxes were reduced a cumulative $14 billion, while state indebtedness went up $6 billion. Running the national government would mean controlling a beast nearly two orders of magnitude larger, but one that, thanks to his brother, has also gotten used to even lower taxes but even greater spending.

It is impossible to predict what sort of national consensus might emerge in the coming years about taxes and the budget. Maybe a group of deficit "hawks" will take control of Congress, and insist on balancing the books even if it means raising taxes. Maybe a deficit hawk will win the White House in 2008, and veto tax and budget bills over and over until a package comes across that starts reversing the long-term prognosis.

All of that is speculation. Here is something that is not: if undoing the tax cuts of George W. is what is necessary to fix the nation's finances, Americans cannot expect a president John Ellis Bush to be even remotely interested in doing this. This is one area where the Heritage Foundation blinders that Jeb wears to enable him to think "outside the box" are, in fact, surgically attached to his skull. It is impossible for him to see evidence that raising taxes could increase revenues and thereby reduce the deficit when he already *knows*—just as he *knows* the sun will rise tomorrow in the east— that the *exact opposite* is true.

This is part of Jeb's faith-based governance, and nothing, not even facts, will persuade him otherwise.

Chapter Eleven

IN GOD'S NAME

"Thank the Lord for George and Jeb Bush"
—HAND-LETTERED BILLBOARD ALONG
INTERSTATE 95, JUST SOUTH OF THE MIMS
EXIT IN BREVARD COUNTY, FLORIDA, 2004

"While religious conservatives may not be a majority in the country, we are by far the biggest single minority voting block. With our grassroots organization in our churches, and with our dedication and discipline, we are the difference that will provide the margin of victory."
—REV. JERRY FALWELL, 1992

"But it does me no injury for my neighbor to say there are twenty gods or no God. It neither picks my pocket nor breaks my leg."
—THOMAS JEFFERSON, 1782

Jeb believes in wealth. Wealth is good. Wealth is the creator of jobs, of industry, of progress. Wealth creates the economic conditions that enable reelection. And as such, wealth must be nurtured.

Jeb believes in low capital-gains taxes. For man nurtures wealth through low taxes on capital gains. And capital is wealth and wealth capital.

Jeb believes in profit and the free market. (Except, as noted earlier, in the instance of motor fuels during hurricane seasons. In that particular instance, Jeb is a socialist.) The profit motive and competition improve all things, especially the public schools.

Jeb believes in himself, indeed in the whole Bush family, as a leading light in America.

These are the things Jeb believes.

These are things in which he has faith. More accurately, these are the things, given his record, in which we can prove he has faith. Because these are the difficult or impossible to prove things that Jeb, at his core, knows to be true, without needing proof. And that is the essence of faith.

WHAT ABOUT the other kind of faith? The kind that involves, in the Christian religion, an acceptance of the Father, the Son, and the Holy Spirit?

Ah, that gets into touchy territory—one that gets into the uncomfortable region of a man's personal faith, and whether he has been true to it in the course of his life. In a perfect world, this would be between Jeb and his god or gods. What he chooses to believe, or what his spirit or his conscience leads him to believe, is really none of my business, or yours.

But we do not live in a perfect world—in fact, in the sphere of the relationship between church and state, ours is an imperfect corner of the world, and one that seems to be getting more imperfect by the day. And if those who would impose their particular notion of a Supreme Being upon the rest of us appear to be holding a stronger hand these days, it is at least partially because both Jeb and his brother the president have proudly and loudly pushed us in that direction. Both the political Bushes of this generation have made it quite plain that if you are not as as pious as they are, well, then you are a bad person.

Through his two terms, Jeb injected religion into state government at seemingly every opportunity. He started right off the bat by insisting that religious schools be allowed to take state taxpayer money in the form of tuition vouchers, even though the Florida constitution clearly prohibited the practice. He signed into a law a divisive "Choose Life" Florida license plate that helps antiabortion groups raise money. He used state money to set up so-called "faith-based" prisons. He insisted on provisions in a prekindergarten program that allow religious schools getting state money to discriminate in admissions decisions on the basis of a four-year-old's religion. He used the legal and financial might of the state to fight Michael Schiavo in a family dispute regarding the wishes of his brain-damaged wife. He pushed through money to let his office fund antiabortion billboards along the state's highways.

And through it all, he wore his sanctimony on his sleeve, a self-righteous *jihadist,* fighting any and all infidels who dared question his goals or even his methods. When some in the press wrote articles examining his decision to stick by his choice to lead the child welfare agency even after the man's biblically-based, pro-spanking views came to light, Jeb wrote to a supporter in an e-mail: "I am no longer amazed at the anti-Christian feelings in the press."

IN BARTOW, Florida, was a woman who considered herself an "overseer prophetess" in the Deliverance Worldwide Crusade Ministry. A major part of her church apparently was to get money from the state school voucher programs.

In Clearwater, Florida, is a major outpost for the Church of Scientology, founded by science-fiction writer L. Ron Hubbard. According to former members, church doctrine evidently holds that humans are actually reborn alien spirits called Thetans, banished to this planet seventy-five million years ago by the evil galactic tyrant Xenu. To help you better understand all this, the church offers training and the use of an "e-meter"—in exchange for "auditing" fees that run into the tens of thousands of dollars.

In Salt Lake City, Utah, is based the Church of Jesus Christ and the Latter Day Saints. Their religion was founded by a con man from western New York who said he found some golden tablets in a hillside. Their "Book of Abraham" teaches that God lives near the star Kolob. They believe the Garden of Eden was located in Missouri.

Now here is one crucial point: there is absolutely zero objective, observable proof that the Garden of Eden was not in Missouri. Or that we are not actually Thetans. Or that Betty Jives Mitchell of Bartow, Florida, is not an overseer prophetess.

Just as there is no proof that Jesus Christ was not the son of God or that Lord Krishna was not the reincarnation of Vishnu, the preserver of the universe.

Which brings us to another crucial point: those who want to believe in the divine goodness of Overseer Prophetess Mitchell are just as entitled to their religion as devotees of Scientology are to theirs and Mormons are to theirs and Hindus are to theirs and Southern Baptists are to theirs.

And one final point: those who choose to believe in a religion other than evangelical Christianity have just as much right to be ticked off when they are told they will go to hell for not accepting Jesus Christ as their personal savior as evangelical Christians have when a Hindu tells them they will come back in their next lives as tapeworms.

All this is a long way of getting to the point that most thoughtful people understand that religion is one of those areas where folks are hypersensitive to taking offense precisely because there is no objective standard of truth. Faith in any particular religion—except for perhaps a religion like Buddhism or a pantheism that does not recognize discrete, personal gods—is a willing suspension of disbelief. Intellectually we know there's something wrong with the idea that a piece of wafer actually becomes the body of Christ, but we accept it because that is what we are supposed to do. Yet, at the same time, we get defensive when someone questions that—because we cannot defend it, other than as a matter of faith.

Which is why basing a public policy argument "on Scripture" really serves no purpose with those of other faiths than to insult them.

Jeb is plenty smart enough to understand this. And yet, time after time, he cozied up to religious bigots in the evangelical Christian community who saw every government program as an opportunity to proselytize.

Sometimes these were open and blatant—private, religious schools, particularly unaccredited religious schools, getting tax money to help advance their religious missions. The "crisis counseling" groups, getting tax money to lead women away from abortion and toward Jesus.

Other times, though, the spreading of the word was done more with a wink and a nod. A Department of Education program to encourage fathers to get involved in their children's lives, for example, linked to a Christian group's Web site that told dads they needed to read the Bible, if they were looking for a guide to good family life. And at the Department of Children and Families, fundamentalist Christian Jerry Regier began an "Adopt-a-worker" program that encouraged employees to partner with churches to pray for social workers they "adopted."

Jeb himself would often talk about faith in God, and how it was always good, and how only antireligious zealots could possibly suggest that the state ought to stay out of matters of faith. At a 2005 school voucher rally at a church that took up residence in a decrepit Jacksonville shopping mall, he proclaimed: "I used to be in the real-estate business, and I love the fact that a vacant shopping center has now got the Holy Spirit now running throughout it. Nothing wrong with that."

At times, the commentary seemed gratuitous, like in 2004 when a Tallahassee principal had attributed her middle school's high grade in the annual rankings to God. "By the way, all power does go to the Lord, on everything, always, and I'm glad you brought that up," Jeb told her.

And yet . . . here was Jeb, so often living his do-as-I-say-not-as-I-do life, spending little time with his own family, not in the least bit reluctant to employ both profanity and obscenity to bully others—including, in at least one instance, representatives of his own Catholic Church—and ignoring vast swaths of politically inconvenient tenets of his professed Catholic faith, such as opposition to the death penalty and the Iraq war. Here is the brutal, unvarnished truth of it: while Jeb frequently disagrees with Catholic doctrine, he rarely disagrees with the orthodoxy of evangelical Christianity, a faith whose followers make up a crucial 23 percent bloc in the Florida electorate and have reliably given their support to him. Heading into the 1994 Republican primary, for example, Jeb was pulling 42 percent of the evangelical vote. His next closest rival was only getting 20 percent.

There are many areas where critics opposed Jeb on his policies but could not question his sincerity. Religion, alas, is not one of them. In terms of sheer moxie, Jeb's use, or misuse, of God as a political tool during his Florida reign was surpassed only by his calling himself the "Education Governor."

IT IS PROBABLY useful here to digress and explain exactly what is meant by evangelical Christians, because they make up—despite their public policy victories under George W.—still a relative minority of the national electorate.

Evangelical Christians typically are also fundamentalists, in that they believe that the Bible (that is, the King James Version) is the revealed word of God. Everything in it is irrefutably true—like, for example, that God created the world in six days. True fundamentalists do not want to hear that the word "days" might mean an age, when speaking of the Lord. Six days means six days. Fundamentalists believe that there is only one way to heaven, and that being good to one's fellow man and performing "good works" has nothing to do with it. Rather, it is by accepting that Jesus is God's son and that he redeemed us by dying on the cross and that he was resurrected three days later. Evangelicals take this a step further and believe they have an obligation to convert and thereby "save" as many people as possible before Christ's second coming as foretold in the Bible.

Perhaps the easiest way to understand the worldview of this group is to pick up a copy of one of the *Left Behind* series of novels. If you have not read one you should, because the series explains a lot.

The premise of the books is the arrival of biblical end times in contemporary America. Obviously, there are plot features that might insult readers other than fundamentalist Christians—only those who have accepted Jesus into their hearts, for instance, are sucked up into heaven in the Rapture. But there are many other details that go a long way toward explaining the popularity of George W. and similar-minded Republicans among this reddest of red-state constituencies. One example: the antichrist quickly ascends to become the head of the United Nations, which then takes over much of the world, including the United States.

To nonbelievers, this might sound just plain goofy, but to many evangelicals, the U.N. and its emergence is a sign foretold in the Book of Revelations. The good guys are Christians who were not taken up during the Rapture but are redeeming themselves by working to bring about Christ's triumphant return and thousand-year reign on earth. They are aided by the occasional Jew who has accepted that Jesus is in fact the Messiah.

These are ideas that nonfundamentalists just don't get but which are basic dogma to evangelicals. The United States is a Christian country that has lost its way. We are in a holy war against Islam. The United Nations represents not merely an un-American ideal of international cooperation, but a satanic conspiracy to bring about One World Government.

To blue-state liberals and social moderates and all the rest of you who cannot understand how George W. could have bungled Iraq and let Osama bin Laden slip away and still have gotten reelected on his ability to defend America, you are failing to understand how fundamentalist Christians viewed him. When George W. flipped the United Nations the bird and decided to go into Iraq alone (or, technically, with his coalition of the willing that included Britain as well as major powers like Azerbaijan and Mongolia), conservative Christians cheered him on. So what if Iraq hadn't technically been involved with September 11? The place is full of Muslims, who have given us nothing but trouble since the fall of the Shah. Just as important, weakening Saddam Hussein and Iraq strengthens Israel, which, even though it is full of Jews, nonetheless has a crucial role in biblical end times prophecy. Which is why some of Israel's strongest defenders in America today—particularly Israel's expansionary settlement policy—are fundamentalist Christians.

Last and, to nonfundamentalist Christians probably most important, evangelical Christianity as it exists today does not believe that religion should stay out of politics. To the contrary, it is vitally important that only those who agree with its religious goals get elected to office.

THAT THE two political Bushes of this generation have both allied themselves with a movement that seeks to inject Christian fundamentalism into the body politic is somewhat ironic, given their lineage.

George Herbert Walker was raised a Catholic but as an adult did not really concern himself with spiritual things. Samuel Bush was the son of an Episcopalian minister—the Episcopal Church being the American affiliate of the Church of England, which, recall, was founded by King Henry VIII because the Pope would not grant him a divorce from Catherine of Aragon, the first of his six wives.

Perhaps because of those roots, the church has acquired the reputation through the years of being somewhat bloodless—a cold, formal religion that does not make unreasonable demands of its parishioners. (After all, when the founder is a guy who had two of those six wives beheaded, it sort of limits the level of sanctimony.)

Prescott Bush was an Episcopalian who ran for office back in the days when politicians, at least those in Connecticut, did not have to wear their godliness on their sleeves. Dorothy, Bert Walker's daughter, was in charge of family piety, reading religious homilies at breakfast and drilling into the children the important things in life: try your hardest. Don't boast. Go to church.

Their second son, George H.W., also considered himself an Episcopalian, which is to say, he went to church and, when he became a politician in 1962, started mentioning his faith in God as a matter of course. But he wasn't a fanatic about it. George H.W. Bush the congressman from Houston, in fact, was known as a pro-choice candidate, one of whose major policy initiatives was dealing with overpopulation. He was the main House sponsor of Public Law 91-572, the Population Control and Research Act.

Indeed, religion did not become even a medium-sized deal with him until he started running for president in 1978, and he noticed how the Republican Party had radically shifted beneath him to the right. Many people forget this. That the Republican Party, while actively pandering to Southern racists in 1968, was still the party of Nelson Rockefeller, too. Even Richard Nixon, a foreign policy hawk regarding Vietnam, was hardly a right-winger by today's standards. Recall détente with the Soviet Union? That was Nixon. So was opening relations with Mao's China. So were wage and price controls. Repeat that one a couple of times, to remember: Wage and price controls. The government telling employees and businesses, both, how much they could earn and how much they could charge for goods. Daniel Patrick Moynihan, let us not forget, worked for Nixon, in his domestic policy shop, looking for ways to end poverty.

By the 1980 election cycle, though, Ronald Reagan was the front-runner after giving Gerald Ford a serious scare in 1976. Reagan appealed to both economic conservatives with his talk of tax cuts as well as social conservatives (despite being on his second wife and having a dysfunctional family) with his talk about ending welfare and putting God back in schools and overturning Roe v. Wade.

George H.W. wanted to be president more than he wanted to be pro-choice, and he quietly jumped on the antiabortion bandwagon. He also started talking more about God, but he was never comfortable doing it. This was pretty obvious, whenever he tried to articulate his views beyond the easy cliché in a speech.

As he geared up for his second run in 1988, this time as the sitting vice president, Bush was asked about his personal relationship with Jesus by Assemblies of God minister, and pal of George W., Doug Wead (who in 2005 admitted having taped conversations with him when George W. was president) in a made-for-the-Christian-Right book called *Man of Integrity*. This is how George H.W. answered: "If by 'born again' one is asking, 'Do you accept Jesus Christ as your savior,' then I could answer a clear-cut yes. No hesitancy. No awkwardness."

Sound pretty convincing? Amazingly, it sounded like a resounding affirmation, compared to his explanation of what was going through his mind after he was shot down in the Pacific during a World War II bombing run: "Mom and Dad, about our country, about God . . . and about the separation of church and state."

George H.W. won the Christian Right support in 1988 but, in another factor contributing to his defeat, lost the group's confidence in 1992.

. . .

As in many things, the current Bush political generation learned from the mistakes of the last. Neither George W. nor Jeb has ever done anything to antagonize that crucial, reliable bloc of Republican primary voters.

George W., in fact, actually joined their ranks in the 1980s, in time to become the liaison between his father's 1988 presidential campaign and conservative Christians who were not quite sure whether a Massachusetts-born, raised-in-Connecticut Episcopalian could really accept the mantle of Ronald Reagan. Exactly when George W.'s conversion took place is a matter of some debate.

The official story is that George W., as he approached midlife, started thinking about his directionless youth and where it had taken him and whether it was a good place, and that one day, when family friend Billy Graham was visiting Kennebunkport, the good reverend asked George W. if he was right with God, and George W. replied that he was not sure, but that he would like to be. And so came the famous walk on the beach with the world-famous evangelist who "planted a mustard seed" in George W.'s soul.

True, that doesn't explain the account given by Arthur Blessitt, an itinerant evangelist who got himself in the *Guinness Book of World Records* for having hauled around a 12-foot cross with him as he proselytized. In 1984, his travels took him through Midland, Texas, where he was supposed to have a revival meeting. Before that event, he learned there was someone who wanted to talk with him, but did not want to go to the revival. And so Blessitt met George W. and fellow oilman Jim Sale at a coffee shop in the Best Western motel, where they talked for a while and where, that morning, George W. came to Jesus.

Well, if you were George W., you would promote the Billy Graham version over the guy-with-the-twelve-foot-cross-on-a-wheel version, too.

In any event, George W. was "born again" to the satisfaction of those who monitor such things, and has been faithfully in the fold ever since. In fact, he and his mother once got into a theological argument over who could get into heaven. George W. said only those who had accepted Jesus as their personal savior could, while she suggested that that was somewhat of a narrow reading. Barbara decided to settle the matter by getting the White House operator to get Billy Graham on the phone. He agreed with George W.

Cousin John Ellis gets amused when Democrats and journalists accuse the president of pandering to religious conservatives. "I'm always amazed when I read that George Bush is moving this way or that way for the religious right. George W. Bush is the religious right."

As governor of Texas, George W. unapologetically worked to please evangelical Christians who wanted state money to deliver social services and, along the way, proselytize. He tried (but failed) to create a school voucher system that would send public money to religious schools. He even declared June 10 as Jesus Day. (It's not clear whether Texan Hindus are still holding out for a "Krishna Day" or Texan Zoroastrians for an "Ahura Mazda Day.")

As president, it was more of the same—promises to let religious groups get more federal money to dole out services, constant references to God in his public utterances, and even, in the case of failed Supreme Court nominee Harriet Miers, a blatant reference to assuage his base by making it clear that he had looked into Miers's heart and seen a good, evangelical Christian.

WITH GEORGE W., in fact, first Texas and then the nation got a full dose of his newfound godliness. And if George H.W. actually thought about the separation of church and state so much that it went through his mind as he bobbed about in the South Pacific praying for rescue while his raft blew back toward Japanese-occupied Chichi Jima, that particularly American principle seems never to have crossed his eldest son's mind at all.

The morning of Jeb's first inauguration in Tallahassee in 1999, George W. and George H.W. and Barbara were all accompanying him at a prayer breakfast before he was sworn in. A reporter asked a generic question about whether religious faith was important for elected leaders. George W. flashed the smirk he has become famous for and retorted that it was impossible to lead if you didn't believe in a higher authority.

It seemed at the time such a sophomoric response. Was he seriously suggesting that agnostics and atheists were incapable of leadership? Because they could not be moral enough? What about the many deists and other out-of-the-mainstream types among this nation's Founding Fathers?

In retrospect, it is clear George W.'s answer that morning wasn't just something he tossed out because he was at a prayer breakfast and it seemed like a good thing to say. This is an idea he has repeated so much, over and over through the years—that overt piety was a good thing—that it came as a bit of a shock when he declared during one of the 2004 presidential debates that it made you no less of an American if you did not believe in God. For three and a half years, he seemed to have been saying the exact opposite.

If that remark had the effect of antagonizing his long-cultivated base in the Christian Right, it did not show up at the polls, at least in the states that mattered. Religious conservatives had overwhelming turnout in both Florida and Ohio, giving him a healthy margin in the former and just enough to win in the latter.

In any event, probably the worst that can be said about George W.'s public religious pronouncements—he sided with biblical creationists, for example, in their attempt to get their renamed "intelligent design" theory equal footing with evolutionary biology in the public schoolrooms—is that he is what he is. He took to his new religion fervently because he does all of those few things that interest him fervently—exercise, for example, or political campaigning.

Now, Jeb and his new religion . . . well, that is something of a different story.

ON SEPTEMBER 11, 2001, Florida's top government officials gathered at the state's hurricane-proof Emergency Operations Center in the chaos that ensued after the terrorist attacks. The giant projection television screens in the center of the room showed the smoldering ruins of lower Manhattan.

Jeb came out into the press conference room for a final briefing for the day and answered the expected questions about what the state would be doing to guard against new attacks and whether state offices would be open or closed the next day, and what about schools and colleges and was there a need for a state security response apart from the national one. And finally someone asked where Jeb was going next.

With the familiar, pinched grin, Jeb told us: "I'm going to Mass."

Something like that, on a day like that, there should have been absolutely no reason for it not to ring true. And yet . . . it was somehow off, just a little bit. The reasons for this were not completely evident at the time, given the circumstances, but later it became more clear why.

Jeb's response to that question seemed staged because it was. He wanted badly to tell us he was going to pray, and was pleased when he got the opportunity. Hence the odd smile. Part of it was no doubt his long-standing view that journalists are not just nonreligious but anti-Christian, and here was an easy opportunity to taunt us: *I'm going to go pray and you're not.*

There was another element to it, though. He knew that whatever he said was likely to be widely reported. He was going to Mass. He was a good Catholic, and in a time of trouble, he was seeking solace in prayer.

Why the need to get this message out? Because unlike his brother, who created a persona openly comfortable with the religion of the Republican Party's base, Jeb had never been a particularly public Christian. Sure, he had always been a vocal supporter of religion—his voucher plan specifically included religious schools, for example—but that wasn't the same thing. It was one thing to support Christianity. It was something else, and far more important, to be a Christian, and in the immediate aftermath of September 11, in the high-contrast, Christianity-versus-Islam worldview that set in, even a deeply suspect denomination like Roman Catholicism could, in the ensuing crusade, be safely marked by conservative Christians in the "with us" column.

THE FACT IS, Jeb's association with his chosen religion has been somewhat of a moving target over time.

Jeb, like his parents, was an Episcopalian through his formative years, to the extent that the label mattered, which was not terribly much. George H.W. and Barbara, for example, attended a Presbyterian church in Midland, where Jeb was born and spent his youngest years, but returned to an Episcopal congregation when they moved to Houston.

The first time anyone in the general public much cared about Jeb's faith, though, was nearly three decades later, in 1989, in newspaper articles about Mexican-born Columba, who was daughter-in-law to the new United States president. Jeb and Columba told journalists that he had converted to her religion back in 1973, just before they got married upon his graduation from the University of Texas. That was the same story that was sold four years later, when he announced he was running for governor of Florida. At that time, in the slew of newspaper and magazine profiles that attempted to reveal everything about Jeb from his golf game (scratch) to his favorite television show (*American Gladiators,* for reasons still unclear), his people let it be known to reporters that Jeb had been a Catholic for two decades.

Okay. So far, things are unremarkable. Most people's religious affiliation comes from their parents or their significant others.

But then, following Jeb's loss in 1994 and reemergence in 1997 as the 800-pound front-runner gorilla for the 1998 contest, there came to pass a new story-line. According to this one, Jeb converted to Catholicism just before Easter in 1995, following all the family troubles that came to a head with the election loss. His daughter was having problems with drugs, Columba was upset about his having spent so much time away from her and the children—Jeb rededicated his life to his family, and part of that was accepting his wife's faith as his own. Weekly classes in the church's "Rite of Christian Initiation of Adults" finally let him take communion with his wife, he told the *St. Petersburg Times*.

"It turned out to be a real blessing to do it. It was very therapeutic to go through the class after the election, through the Easter Sabbath. The people that attended were wonderful people, from the real world, not from the never-never land of politics," Jeb said in the 1998 interview. "The rituals are comforting. The symbols are powerful. . . . It was easy for me to convert because of my wife, but as I got into it I found there was true beauty and comfort in the religion."

It made for an honorable and touching story, his hard work to pull his family back together. But . . . what of his 1973 conversion to his wife's faith? Astonishingly, not a single newspaper that mentioned his religion—and there were plenty—in that slew of stories prior to the 1998 election even noted that discrepancy.

Even this, by itself, for ordinary people, would not be a big deal. People commit themselves to all sorts of things—exercise, healthier food, less alcohol, yard work, God—and then slack off, and then recommit themselves. Maybe this is what happened with Jeb, and if so, it showed only that he was human, and that, perhaps, the 1994 election loss had made him a better person, if in fact it forced him to focus on his family. That certainly was the point of the narrative he and his campaign people put out there.

But then, seven years later, Floridians got yet another iteration, in which family had nothing to do with his decision.

This latest version was offered just before Jeb left Tallahassee in April 2005, on his way to Rome as part of the United States contingent for the seating of the new Pope. Pope John Paul II had died, and George W. sent his Catholic brother as his personal emissary to congratulate his successor, Pope Benedict XVI.

Jeb remarked on the details of the trip, when he was leaving, when he was coming back, what he thought of the church's new leader, and then a reporter asked him the circumstances about his own conversion to the faith. And this is what Jeb said:

"I think I remember going to one, when I was Episcopalian, to one place where the guy, the preacher, whose name will remain nameless, started to talk about political issues, that I thought was completely inappropriate. My dad happened to be there, and I didn't think he needed to get lectured by an Episcopal priest. I said, 'I've had it.' "

Well, that particular sermon occurred at St. Ann's Episcopal Church outside the family compound in Kennebunkport. The priest was Bishop John Allin, the former head of the Episcopal Church in the United States, and he pointed out that the United States was building prisons faster than it was building schools, and that the nation should end its preoccupation with communism and start paying attention to problems at home.

Leave aside for a moment Jeb's great umbrage at a religious figure discussing political issues—has Jeb shared this concern with, say, James Dobson or Jerry Falwell? The important detail is that the offending sermon's date was August 25, 1991, which is neither 1973 nor 1995.

So there you have it. Jeb's becoming a Catholic, like so many other things in the political odyssey of the Bush clan, seemed less to do with the merits of the issue and everything to do with who was loyal to the Bushes and who was not.

NOT THAT it matters. Not even a little bit.

Jeb attended Mass and would carry a rosary when a hurricane was about to smack Florida, but it was hard to discern any sort of doctrinal identification with the Catholic Church. True, the church opposes abortion and Jeb also opposes it, but on public policy matters, it is hard to think of other such agreements. What makes this all the more significant is that, unlike most people who are born into a faith and then find themselves at odds with certain doctrines, Jeb came to his religion as a fully formed adult, knowing exactly where he was, and where the church was.

The Catholic Church, for example, opposes the death penalty for the same reason it opposes abortion: because it considers human life to be sacred. It believes only God has the authority to forfeit a man's life, regardless of how heinous the crime. Jeb has always supported the death penalty. As governor, he seemed less rabid about it than, say, in 1994, when it became the singular issue on which his overreach allowed incumbent Lawton Chiles back into the contest. The church also opposed the wars against Iraq, both his father's and his brother's. Jeb supported both, although admittedly, it would have been difficult for him, even as a loyal Catholic, to publicly oppose his family.

But perhaps the most telling disagreement is not over a hot-button campaign issue, but on the church's major emphasis on alleviating human suffering and poverty, particularly in the Third World. These general policies sprang from the Second Ecumenical Council of the Vatican from 1962 to 1965, which came to be known as Vatican II. In Latin America, this new direction led to Catholic clergy helping lead land-reform movements and otherwise redistribute wealth in countries where a small ruling class owned most of everything.

To put it mildly, Jeb's interest, particularly since he allied himself with the émigré community of South Florida, has never really been on redistributing wealth. To the contrary, when it came to foreign policy, Jeb sided with the moneyed classes trying to put down land-reform movements and other "socialist" rebellions. And at home, Jeb's tax policies were not about redistributing wealth, but about letting the wealthy get even wealthier.

No, Jeb may officially be a Catholic, but in terms of philosophy and public policy, his head and heart are far more in line with evangelical Christianity as it is promoted by the likes of Amway and other nakedly capitalist organizations than with any leftist priests in South America.

I DO NOT MEAN in these pages to ridicule faith or trivialize its importance. The universe around us can be a big, scary place, with people and Mother Nature both doing awful, inexplicable things. Science will take even the most arrogant among us only to a certain level of peace with our world before it forces us to contend with a yawning emptiness.

On a more emotional level—anyone who's ever had a child in an emergency room, or at a pediatrician's office to get some scary test results . . . well, that's a person who can tell you firsthand about faith and its importance, when it looks like it could be all you have left.

At its best, religion is an acknowledgment of mankind's humbling niche in this universe, a well-meaning attempt to find order among laws of nature that seem bound only by the Second Law of Thermodynamics—that all systems must eventually spin out to tepid, random chaos. At its best, religion organizes us to bring aid to the stricken, comfort to the weary, and does so out of openhearted charity. When seen with an ecumenical eye, religion teaches us that we, all members of the family of mankind, have more in common than that which divides us.

All of that is religion at its best. There is also religion at its worst.

Religion at its worst has worked to divide us and keep us apart. It makes us teach our children that our tribe is right and everyone else is wrong. In earlier times, this teaching was accompanied by the corollary that if others did not accept our tribe's god(s), that it was okay to do something drastic about it.

Recall Christianity's great crusades, when it was perfectly acceptable for those in the service of Jesus to chase down infidels on horseback and run them through with pikes. The followers of Muhammad also were perfectly okay in those years to improve their relative numbers using the scimitar: convert or die.

(Some would argue that the terrorist attacks of September 11 show that some Muslims continue to see a religious imperative to kill non-Muslims. Others, I believe correctly, argue that those attacks seemed as much about anti-colonialism and Saudi nationalism as they were about God and the proper way to worship him.)

To this day, Hindu fundamentalists in India believe it's just a dandy idea to burn a mosque to the ground (and to stone any Muslims who happen to be nearby) because, four or five hundred years ago, a Hindu temple had stood there instead.

Obviously, in this discussion of religion in politics, we're not talking about primal yearning and the need for understanding of our universe. We're talking about elected leaders and candidates taking this force and twisting it to mobilize political support.

TAKE, for example, the extreme ethnocentrism of politicians who pander to Christian conservatives about the placement of the Ten Commandments in the public square or—even worse—in the public schools.

Read the Ten Commandments. Which one is the first commandment: the one about murder? Or theft? Or adultery? No. It's about monotheism, and its superiority over polytheism. The next three commandments are similarly about the core beliefs of Judaism and, later, Christianity and Islam—not about the public morality that is so often touted when the Ten Commandments are advocated as universal truths.

There are well over a billion people of Indian descent on this planet, the vast majority of them Hindus—whose religion teaches that there is not one God, but a great number of gods. A goodly number of these folks live in the United States, where they pay taxes and vote. Can anyone think of a good reason why tax money should be spent to proselytize their children in public schools that there is one single, true God?

Maybe it's just ignorance that lets these folks talk about the Judeo-Christian tradition as if it's the only one going. (It's also a bit curious that Islam is typically left out of that line. Really it's the Judeo-Christian-Islamic tradition, that dominates western religion, insofar as Muslims also believe that the one God who asked Abraham to murder his son as a test of devotion, who then sent Jesus to earth, is also the same God who now insists on prayers five times a day and a month of fasting each year.) In that same vein are fundamentalist Christians who insist on teaching creationism as an equally valid alternative to evolution—yes, absolutely. Let's teach about the lotus flower that springs from Lord Vishnu's navel, which becomes Brahma the Creator. And let's also teach about Baiame and the Dreamtime ancestors, as the Australian aborigines believe. And after those three, teachers can spend equal time on the dozens of other equally unprovable versions.

It must be noted that Florida is not Alabama, or South Carolina, or even Tennessee, where fundamentalist Christians appear to have a strong grip on state politics.

No, Florida is much less homogenous than those places. Miami can seem like a Latin American capital, with feisty, at-times-entertaining, at-times-ludicrous politics—but not much in the way of religious fervor. Fort Lauderdale's Broward County may as well be an honorary borough of New York City, and has a strong, politically active Jewish community. Southwest Florida is like Ohio or Indiana—conservative, but not fanatically so. Tampa and Orlando have become large urban centers with increasing minority communities, and once solidly Republican St. Petersburg is becoming increasing liberal.

In Florida, the Bible Belt stretches across the northern tier, from Pensacola eastward, looping around the college town/state capital city of Tallahassee, and then continuing on into Jacksonville and then southward down the middle of the peninsula about as far as Ocala.

Demographically, this area represents a minority of the state—which perhaps explains why Christian conservatives have never held a majority in the state Senate. They have had much higher stature in the House, where they grew tight particularly with speakers Tom Feeney and John-nie Byrd, both of whom were quite content to use fundamentalist support to further their own political careers.

In a National Annenberg Election Survey released in 2004 correlating the percentage of self-described evangelical Christians in a state against that state's voting patterns, Florida ranked squarely in the middle—most definitely a "swing" state, not a "red" one.

Pandering excessively to the Christian Right is a dangerous tactic, one just as liable to alienate everybody else as it is to solidify "the base."

In 2000, former congressman Bill McCollum, with strong scores from the Christian Coalition, was nonetheless beaten by Insurance Commissioner Bill Nelson for an open United States Senate seat. In 2004, for another open Senate seat, Republican Mel Martinez, who ran on an antigay platform in the primary, nearly lost to Democrat Betty Castor, even though he had powerful Hispanic support as well as the full support of the White House.

In this climate, Jeb played an interesting religion card.

During his first term, he took all the positions Christian Conservatives would want—signing into law a "Choose Life" license plate, a parental consent of abortion bill, school voucher bills. His legal office quietly looked for ways to make sure that his judicial nominating commissions came up with nominees with "ideologically compatible" philosophies. But Jeb's tone was mild, particularly compared to that of his brother.

After winning reelection in 2002, though, it was no-holds-barred. His Department of Children and Families sought to bar a minor girl who'd had sex while in the state's protective custody from having an abortion. He pushed through a law strictly regulating abortion clinics, but no other comparable outpatient clinics. He created "faith-based" prisons, where all inmates get religious counseling, courtesy of Florida taxpayers, without any idea or interest whether it would help the recidivism rate. He got money in the budget for his office to finance antiabortion groups who counsel women to carry pregnancies to term.

The usual suspects complained about all of these efforts—the ACLU, pro-choice groups, the newspaper editorial boards. Jeb didn't care. If the Christian Right liked an idea, Jeb liked it.

IN AUTUMN OF 2005, Jeb's statewide reading program sponsored a contest to get Florida's schoolchildren to read a book and, depending on the grade level, write an essay or draw a picture or produce a short video. The winner in each category would get to stay at a Disney resort and watch the premiere of the movie made from the book. The book Jeb's office chose? *The Lion, the Witch and the Wardrobe,* C. S. Lewis's classic parable of Jesus' life and crucifixion.

Let's agree right up front: generally speaking, anything that gets Florida schoolchildren reading more is a good thing. As discussed earlier, college football, theme parks, and beaches are some of the few things Florida does well. Public education is not.

But there were a couple of interesting things about this contest. It was the first such contest, for example, that was timed to coincide with the theatrical release of the film adaptation of the chosen book. The previous year, Warner Brothers had released the movie version of *The Polar Express.* Chris Van Allsburg's modern classic about a magical trip to Santa's North Pole won a Caldicott medal, but that didn't win over Jeb's "Just Read, Florida!" office. Tom Hanks's film got no promotional help from Florida taxpayers. In earlier years, theaters around the Sunshine State and the nation had premiered movies based on the Harry Potter books. Surely, if any single human can be credited with bringing the love of books to young people today, that would be J. K. Rowling. But, no matter. Neither her storytelling ability nor her popularity was enough to attract the attention of Jeb's people. The movies were sent out to fly or flop on their own. Florida held no contest to promote them.

So what made *The Lion, the Witch and the Wardrobe* so different? Well, Jeb's people explained, the film's producer, Walden Media, happened to be a "partner" of the reading program. It had helped promote an earlier contest, with the winner getting a walk-on role in the filming of that particular book, *Hoot,* Carl Hiaasen's children's novel. Walden had also ponied up $10,000 to help sponsor a conference for the state's reading coaches and school principals.

At least, those were the explanations Jeb's people offered. Here's one they somehow neglected to mention: Walden was owned by Denver billionaire Philip Anschutz, a devout Christian who by then had given some half million dollars to the Republican Party and Republican candidates over the past decade and who was on a mission to bring "traditional values" back to Hollywood movies.

So is everybody clear on the ground rules?

If you are a big, evil Hollywood movie company (read: owned and run by secular-humanist liberals) making films from books about wizards and witchcraft or a secular Santa Claus, then Jeb wants nothing to do with you.

If, on the other hand, you are a conservative Christian and a reliable Republican donor who is popularizing the work of perhaps the most famous Christian apologist of the twentieth century, well, then, the state of Florida wants to know how it can help.

THIS IS NOT to denigrate C. S. Lewis or *The Lion, the Witch and the Wardrobe.* It has been a children's classic for half a century, and rightly so.

But should taxpayer resources help give a religious book the state of Florida's imprimatur? It would be one thing if the book were part of a survey of children's literature across the world's religions. But do you suppose Florida will next be encouraging its public school children to read the *Mahabharata,* the stories from ancient India? Florida Hindus ought not hold their breath.

Naturally, the director of Jeb's reading program argued that *The Lion, the Witch and the Wardrobe* can be read purely as a fantasy novel. Then she added that she hoped children would read the book "and decide for themselves."

But to suggest that *The Lion, the Witch and the Wardrobe* can be seen in a purely secular light borders on the absurd. Frankly, unless one is familiar with the story of Jesus' life and death, why Aslan does what he does and how he comes back to life would make no sense at all. That doesn't make it a bad book. That makes it an overtly Christian book. If this were not the case, Walden's Media's own Web site would not have been featuring a discussion board that offered a "17-week Narnia Bible study for children."

And as to the idea that all of Florida's children should read the book and decide for themselves—should they also be encouraged to read Jewish, Muslim, and Buddhist children's stories and decide for themselves with those, too? Children are easy to proselytize. That's why we proselytize them into our own religions before they are old enough to make a rational decision. And yet, here was Jeb, suggesting that all Florida children be inculcated with the idea of death and resurrection in the name of redemption, the singular tenet of Christianity.

Barry Lynn, a minister with the United Church of Christ and head of the Americans United for the Separation of Church and State, called the book "totally inappropriate" as the exclusive selection in a state-sponsored reading contest. He compared it to the state asking children to watch Mel Gibson's *The Passion of the Christ* to enter a contest with the prize a trip to Rome.

"He seems to be tone deaf," Lynn said of Jeb's inability to sense the line between things ecclesiastical and things governmental.

The Reverend Lynn, though, got it wrong.

Jeb's hearing is pitch perfect, but not to Lynn's brand of open, affirming Christianity. Lynn's church opens its doors to gay people, drug addicts, and the mentally and physically abused. It runs soup kitchens and shelters. It doesn't do much in the way of evangelizing. Those types of Christians, the ones who take Jesus' Sermon on the Mount literally, those Christians are Democrats.

Jeb's favorite Christians are Republicans. They vote in primaries, they work phone banks, they pass out voting guides at their churches. When they get rich, they share their blessings generously with like-minded GOP candidates.

Barry Lynn's Christians, the ones who whine about the constitution and keeping church and state separate, well . . . frankly, they are too much like the Christians who got fed to the lions. Those Christians are losers.

Jeb's Christians are the ones who went on the Crusades in ages past, and now fill the ranks of Amway and like-minded, profit-loving organizations. They see nothing wrong at all in turning the resources of their government to spread God's word. Jeb's Christians are winners.

And remember: Jeb likes to win. In fact, his alliance with the Christian Right was, as politicians love to say, a win-win situation. They helped Jeb's brother become president, helped keep him there for a second term, and helped to give Jeb two easy election wins as governor. They helped him win, and he seemed determined to make sure they would win, too.

ONE BIG AREA where they won during Jeb's tenure was education. Jeb's push for school vouchers, of course, dovetailed nicely with the home school movement and startup, evangelical Christian schools.

A large percentage of parents who home school in Florida do so for religious reasons, and the various voucher programs that catered to home schooled children helped make him a hero in their eyes. And evangelical churches that dreamed of starting schools for their children but could not afford to do so under Jeb suddenly found themselves able to get state vouchers ranging from $3,500 through $10,000 or more, for children who had disabilities.

Indeed, it was in the area of school vouchers that showcased another open battle between Catholics and some evangelical Christians.

Starting in 2003, as my newspaper and some others in the state starting printing article after article about how the state was spending more than $100 million in its various voucher programs with no clear idea of which children were receiving them or what they were learning, the state's Catholic schools were the first to ask for strict oversight to prevent bad schools as well as outright scam artists from getting state money. This immediately drew the ire of Jeb's top education aide Patricia Levesque, who believed that any type of restriction on vouchers was giving in to the "liberal media" and other opponents of school choice. It so happened that Levesque is a graduate of Bob Jones University, which has a history of virulent anti-Catholicism and still promotes the idea that only Christians who accept Jesus as their savior, such as themselves, will go to heaven and that everyone else, including Catholics, are going to hell.

So which side did Jeb take? The Bob Jones University side, naturally. From that point forward, Jeb allowed Levesque to essentially shut the Florida Catholic Conference out of any further involvement with the administration's "voucher accountability" proposals. This even though it was the Catholic Conference, in 1999, that helped move Jeb's original voucher bill through a decidedly uneasy Senate. And when the first batch of fifty-eight students got vouchers that fall, it was four Catholic schools in Pensacola that enrolled all but the handful of them who went to a Montessori school.

None of that mattered. Because of their treasonous behavior on the voucher bill, the Catholic Conference was out. Two years later, when the Catholic schools publicly objected to the way a new universal prekindergarten program allowed schools to discriminate on the basis of religion, Jeb personally criticized their education lobbyist while Levesque and others tried to get him fired.

EVEN IN cases where specific personalities were not involved, Jeb's coziness with fundamentalist Christians made for suspect educational policy for everybody else. A perfect example was in the autumn of 2005, with the backdrop of the "intelligent design" trial going on in Pennsylvania and a review of the state's Sunshine State Standards for science looming in the coming year.

Some important background: Jeb's own professed faith, Roman Catholicism, has made its peace with science. Sure, the Vatican burned the monk

Giordano Bruno alive for declaring that the sun was the center of the solar system and put Galileo under house arrest for the last four decades of his life for the same offense. But the church has gotten over that, and has come around to the view that faith and science are complementary, not in conflict. Mainstream Catholic schools in Florida teach the theory of evolution in their biology classes.

Some even more important background: just two years earlier, in 2003, Jeb had successfully courted the renowned Scripps Research Institute to branch out into a second campus in Florida, and had persuaded the legislature to give the company $310 million in state money to do it. Among the ostensible benefits was that Florida would be at the cutting edge of biomedical and pharmaceutical research, with all the prestige that would bring in the academic world.

And what exactly does Scripps do? Molecular biology and genetic manipulation using recombinant DNA. And what are those based on? Charles Darwin's theory of natural selection, modified and developed over a century and a half of scientific experimentation.

Although most of the state legislators who voted to give Scripps the money probably did not realize this—an honestly bizarre moment was watching one of the Scripps scientists explaining gene sequencing to the Florida House of Representatives . . . something which anyone who has ever seen the Florida House in action knows is only slightly less silly than trying to teach quantum mechanics to a tribe of orangutans—Jeb is certainly knowledgeable enough to understand the inherent irony. This is probably why he took such umbrage when I asked him whether children at voucher schools ought to get the science background they would need if they wanted to work someday at Scripps.

He knew there was no way to answer and not royally tick off somebody. "No" would have antagonized taxpayers who believe that children whose education is paid for by the state should be learning science, including evolutionary biology. "Yes" would have raised hell in the evangelical Christian community. Jeb chose not to answer.

That autumn of the trial in Harrisburg also happened to be when Jeb's education department hired creationist Cheri Yecke as chancellor of K–12 education in Florida. Yecke had been forced out of a similar job in Minnesota after trying to sneak "intelligent design"—the new code phrase for creationism—into the public school curriculum there. She denied that had been her intention, and claimed that the whole episode was pure politics—a Democratic legislative chamber saluting a Republican governor. She sought refuge at a conservative think tank, from which she was rescued, naturally, by Jeb.

Whatever the motives behind her hiring, it raised eyebrows among school administrators and science teachers, who suspected the worst. Jeb did little to assuage them when he was finally asked whether "intelligent design" should be taught in public school science classrooms.

Jeb paused, and said: "It's not part of our standards. Nor is creationism. Nor is Darwinism or evolution, either."

Huh? The state's Sunshine State Standards for science, last modified in 1996 (prior to Jeb's ascension), are actually quite clear about evolution. Eighth graders are expected to know that the "fossil record provides evidence that changes in the kinds of plants and animals in the environment have been occurring over time." High school students are expected to understand how genetic mutations occur and how "natural selection ensures that those who are best adapted to their surroundings survive to reproduce"—the two fundamental concepts underlying evolutionary biology.

When I pointed this out to Jeb, he claimed that he had been told by his education commissioner that the standards did not include evolution—not a terribly likely scenario given that his commissioner by that point, a former science teacher, had been part of the education bureaucracy in Florida for a dozen years before Jeb took office.

So then Jeb said: "I like what we have right now. And I don't think there needs to be any changes. I don't think we need to restrict discussion, but it doesn't need to be required, either."

It was an extraordinary revealing exchange. Jeb does not like to be caught flat-footed on any topic, let alone one in which, as the self-professed "education governor," he should have had mastery. And yet, when forced to choose between looking ignorant and admitting that he has allowed godless secular humanism to remain in the public school science curriculum nearly seven years after he'd taken office, Jeb picked ignorance.

Such is his fealty to the Christian Right.

WHICH GETS US, finally, to the low point in Jeb's handling of religious matters, the long, drawn-out death of Terri Schiavo.

It's a hard thing, to call someone vindictive in print. It just starts out sounding petty and goes downhill from there. As a rhetorical device, it is therefore probably counterproductive. Still, sometimes, a spade must be called a spade, and the aftermath of the Terri Schiavo case is one of those times.

First, recall, it was not Jeb who put the Schiavo issue front and center, but Johnnie Byrd, easily the most self-parodying caricature of a megalomaniac Florida has seen in recent political memory. Byrd was the House Speaker who succeeded former Jeb running mate Tom Feeney—and was so bad that he actually made Feeney look sane and reasonable.

In the autumn of 2003, Byrd, using his legislative perch to run for the United States Senate, saw the Schiavo affair as the perfect way to outflank his opponents in the Republican primary, which has in Florida became a flat-out race to the right. This took place during the special session Jeb called to lure the Scripps Research Institute to Florida.

The Senate leader at the time was Jim King, who had written the right-to-die law in the first place a dozen years earlier, which meant he felt no need to jump into the Schiavo case. Court rulings had run their course, and her feeding tube had been removed. Which made it the perfect moment for Byrd to pounce.

One afternoon, his campaign put out a release advising people to watch Fox News that night, because Johnnie Byrd was going to outline how he was going to save Terri Schiavo's life. King was furious. Byrd had just finished telling King how, if there was no consensus to do anything, then he was not going to bring it up. Byrd's press secretary was furious. She had just gotten done telling reporters that nothing was going to happen in the Schiavo case when the campaign e-mail was pointed out to her. And Jeb's people were, curiously, silent. They saw the difficulty of writing a law to affect just one person, and saner heads in the Governor's Office wondered about the wisdom of getting involved at all.

Within forty-eight hours, Byrd had successfully brewed political nitroglycerin. While normal people watched in disbelief, elected Republicans were put in the position of either you passed some of kind of bill to do something, or you were one of Terri's executioners.

King caved, and led his Senate in passing a bill that, essentially, only applied to Terri Schiavo. Bush quickly signed it and ordered the feeding tube reinserted while Michael Schiavo's lawyer started the legal groundwork to have the new law struck down as unconstitutional, which, of course, it was.

Jump ahead now a year and a half. Byrd is gone, so the House, though still conservative, is no longer run by a kook. King, though no longer Senate president, is still a power broker in that chamber. But now, oddly, it is Jeb Bush who has become the prime mover in the Capitol for a Terri Schiavo bill.

This was a hard one to decipher. The easiest, most cynical explanation is that he was simply pandering to the Religious Right. All those folks who put tape over their mouths and tried to sneak water in to Terri, even though she was incapable of swallowing it, these are the people who vote disproportionately in GOP primaries, and who therefore must be appeased at all cost.

In fairness, Jeb was hardly the only conservative Republican who made a spectacle of himself during this episode. Remember newly minted United States senator Mel Martinez, passing out a memo explaining how Republicans could make political hay from the Schiavo family's trauma? Remember Senate majority leader Bill Frist, diagnosing Terri via videotapes distributed by her advocates? And remember the president himself, staying up way past his bedtime, to show how much the conservative Christian vote meant to him by signing a bill putting the question (briefly) into federal court?

True, it was Jeb who helped spur some of this along, calling Mel Martinez the day before Schiavo's feeding tube was removed to tell him it was not looking promising that he would be able to persuade the Florida Senate to go along with yet another Terri Schiavo law.

(Indeed, not only did the Senate not go along, but it also gave Jeb one of two stinging rebukes it delivered him during the 2005 legislative session: a floor vote defeating the governor. A governor who was the brother of the sitting president. To appreciate the significance of this, you must understand how rarely things are defeated on recorded votes in the Florida legislature, particularly the Florida Senate. This is a collegial group where members work out their differences behind closed doors. If something cannot pass the Senate, it generally just never comes up for consideration on the floor. To defeat something, particularly to defeat an initiative of a governor from your own party, is unheard of. It happened with the Schiavo bill, and then it happened again a few weeks later with Jeb's attempt to repeal the class-size amendment. There was more than a little joy in the upper chamber when these votes went down, by the way. After six years of Jeb's my-way-or-the-highway approach to legislation, the Senate was happy to give Jeb directions to the Interstate.)

Conservative Christian pandering is the best explanation of the congressional action. Martinez' infamous memo, the one that emphasized how the issue could be exploited politically and used to shore up support from the "pro-life base," documents this pretty well.

This is not the case with Jeb. His name is gold with conservatives in the party, and even more valuable with religious conservatives. He doesn't need to pander—and yet, as the obvious end drew nearer, his actions got more desperate, to the point that his Department of Children and Families officers, backed up with Florida Department of Law Enforcement agents, were actually rolling toward the hospice to seize Terri Schiavo and put her in protective custody. They backed down when local police told them they had no intention of allowing anyone to take Terri without a court order.

At this point, Jeb was not pandering. By this point, he was way past pandering. He was doing what he does best: he was playing to win.

The most telling detail into Jeb's personality came after Terri Schiavo finally died March 31, thirteen days after her feeding tube was removed. (Michael Schiavo argues that Terri died mentally and in spirit fifteen years earlier, on the morning of February 25, 1990.)

By then, the Washington politicos had blustered a bit about federal judges not heeding the will of Congress and so forth, and then shut up when the poll numbers started coming out showing that the overwhelming majority of Americans—including the majority of self-described Christian conservatives—wanted the government to stay out of the Schiavo family's problems.

Instead, this is what Jeb did: following the long-awaited autopsy report that cleared Michael Schiavo of all the nutty allegations that advocates for his wife were making (that he had broken her bones, etc.) and that also vindicated the many neurologists who had diagnosed that Terri was in a persistent vegetative state, Jeb wrote a letter to the prosecutor for that county. He said he was "troubled" by the discrepancy in the exact time Michael Schiavo called 911 after finding his wife on the floor, and the time that he told CNN's Larry King that he had done those things.

"Between forty and seventy minutes elapsed before the call was made, and I am aware of no explanation for the delay," Jeb wrote to Pinellas County state attorney Bernard McCabe. "In light of this new information, I urge you to take a fresh look at this case without any preconceptions as to the outcome. . . . Mrs. Schiavo's family deserves to know anything that can be done to determine the cause and circumstances of her collapse fifteen years ago."

Let's think this through, for a moment. Jeb was asking, essentially, for a criminal investigation of Michael Schiavo for the death of his wife. Jeb, under the protection his office afforded him, was essentially calling Michael Schiavo a murderer.

No, technically that word never issued from his lips. But the implication is perfectly clear: the governor of the state believes that Michael Schiavo may have been a bad actor in—may have been responsible for—his wife's death.

Can anyone imagine, say, a media organization making such a charge? We'd be sued for libel. Check that—anyone can sue anyone for anything. We'd be *guilty* of libel, saying something like that without the first fact to back it up. But here is the governor of the state, making that same charge, and releasing it to the world. Compare this with the usual obstreperousness of the Bush press office when it came to releasing Jeb's correspondence. This is particularly amusing since McCabe was on vacation at the time, and could not have possibly responded to the letter in a timely fashion.

Even for defenders of Jeb, this was beyond the pale. Here was an autopsy report that in its entirety supported Michael Schiavo and refuted most of what his in-laws' supporters were saying. It found, for example, that the part of her brain that controlled vision was gone—therefore, the claims that she understood what she was seeing when she "smiled" at her family (the part of the videotapes that Dr. Frist found so persuasive) were not correct. Somehow, Jeb took it all and twisted it around to read as an indictment of Michael Schiavo.

Thirteen days later, McCabe did respond, writing Jeb that too much time had passed for a meaningful inquiry, and that, more to the point, a mere variance in recollection of the exact time something had happened years earlier did not justify an investigation. McCabe said the important thing was that Michael Schiavo had consistently said that he called for help immediately after finding Terri unconscious. He also wrote: "(You) urged that this inquiry be conducted without any preconceptions as to the outcome. We have attempted to follow this sound advice unlike some pundits, some 'experts,' some e-mail and Web-based correspondents, and even some institutions of government that have, in my view, reached conclusions regarding the controversy surrounding Mrs. Schiavo based upon such preconceptions and/or misinformation."

In other words: Thanks, Jeb, but no thanks. I want no part of your kangaroo court.

Of all the things Jeb did in his two terms in office, this is probably the most troubling to the most people. Jeb wanted the Schiavo case to turn out a certain way. It did not turn out that way. In his mind, Jeb lost. In his mind, Michael Schiavo had beaten him. Michael Schiavo had to pay.

BY LATE 2005, the Bush family's long-cultivated courtship of the Christian Right was starting to show strains.

Apparently the hundreds of billions of federal tax dollars that George W. was forced to promise to rebuild New Orleans was not the sort of Christian charity that many evangelicals favor. And then, to cap it off, came his appointment of his buddy and personal lawyer, Harriet Miers, to the United States Supreme Court.

The fire-breathing Right had evidently assumed that when the time came to replace a swing vote on the court, it would be with an ideologically proud Christian, whose record would match the many years of "Dred Scott" and "crisis pregnancy centers" hints that George W. had been dropping. Instead, they got a stealth ally at best, and a possible David Souter turncoat at worst. And were they ever ticked.

American Family Association founder Donald Wildmon complained that George W., after asking for and getting evangelical Christian support for years, had started acting like he was "embarrassed to be seen in public with us," and that Christians did not understand why.

Really? He seriously doesn't understand? Well, let's try to puzzle through it for him.

Evangelical Christians feel compelled to spread their religion to all of us who are not "born again." This is annoying at best, and often downright insulting, because most of us wouldn't dream of trying to impose our own Catholicism or Buddhism or Hinduism or Islam or Judaism upon them. And then, when the attempted conversion on the basis of how much peace and happiness it will bring us doesn't work, they resort to the argument that only those who have truly accepted Jesus into their hearts—such as themselves—will see the kingdom of heaven.

And this, Mr. Wildmon, is why national politicians who pander to evangelicals prefer to do so in code, talking about the "culture of life" and "Dred Scott" rather than coming out and walking beside them, hand in hand. The rest of the nation—and this includes the majority of Republicans—are not intolerant about matters of faith, and it troubles us to see our leaders all kissy-face with those who are.

How hard the Donald Wildmons and the James Dobsons of America will push George W. in his final two years in office, and how much he can appease them, will factor heavily in how much Jeb can rely on this crucial bloc if and when he ever takes the plunge himself.

The Christian Right was never completely comfortable with George H.W. in 1988, and supported him grudgingly and only after an intense outreach campaign orchestrated by George W. on his dad's behalf. By 1992, that support had evaporated after George H.W. gave them gestures and talk, but little more.

Evangelicals took a chance supporting the father's eldest son in 2000, but did so with the knowledge that George W. was, literally, one of them. If despite this, it turns out that he winds up not giving them the one thing they really wanted—a high court stacked with sympathetic justices who will outlaw abortion and make America Christian again—then they may well write off the Bushes once and for all.

This, though, is a drastic and unlikely step. After all, George W. has given them a gaggle of friendly federal district judges and appellate judges who will be legitimate choices for the top court in coming years and decades. George W. also started knocking down the wall between church and state to give them access to federal money in the distribution of various social services.

If and when national journalists and religious activists start investigating Jeb's years in Tallahassee, they will see those same good works of George W., except even more so and done with a more aggressive leading with the chin.

Because there's the crucial difference between the two brothers, in this area. Their particular professed faiths as mature adults are not really revealing of their character—a much more telling clue is that each brother joined the religion that happened to be most politically useful in his particular state. In this area, especially, Jeb has been happy to ally himself with the evangelicals, even when it meant—particularly when it meant—making others mad.

Had Jeb been president in late 2005, he would have appointed not merely a Sam Alito, but the most open, most vocal, most conservative judge he could find with the longest, most clear record on abortion, gay rights and every other hot-button issue. He would have picked this person, and he would have double dog dared the Senate to do something about it.

• • •

AND SO, strangely, Jeb the Catholic would likely be able to rally the support of that big block of Republican votes in the evangelical community more reliably even than his brother, the born-again Protestant. Fundamentalist Christians to whom unquestioning faith is such an all-encompassing part of their religion would not even need such faith when it came to scrutinizing Jeb. They would not need to know his heart, as George W. so frequently asked his followers to do. They would just have to look at his record, and they would have to agree that it is good.

True, there is a possibility that they may never have the opportunity to do that. It could well be that by the end of his second term, George W.'s presidency has sunk to such a disastrous low that it is simply impossible for anyone with the last name of Bush to run for state assemblyman, let alone president of the United States, for years to come.

Were that to happen, it would twist around and bring an ironic epilogue to one of the creepier notions held by many Christian conservatives during the 2004 reelection campaign: that God personally wanted George W. Bush to win in order to advance His plans for the world.

As perverse an idea as this might seem in a modern, pluralistic society, it was a very real element of that election campaign. Many George W. supporters saw his invasion of Iraq—"Babylon"—as divinely inspired, if not actually prophesized in the Bible. Bush-Cheney '04 rallies in Florida featured many homemade signs suggesting that God was on George W.'s side. At a Fort Myers rally, the warm-up country western singer announced that he had accepted Jesus Christ as his personal savior and got a standing ovation from the crowd filling a minor league baseball stadium.

This was more than a little scary. After all, nineteen extremely God-fearing men carried out what they thought was the Lord's work on September 11, 2001—and killed some three thousand innocents along the way. Theirs was also the God of Abraham.

Going from the creepy to the absurd: the idea of a personal God taking an active interest in American electoral politics brings with it a number of theological questions, the most obvious of which is why He did not ensure that George W. got more votes than his presumably godless opponent in 2000. Why not give him a clear mandate and make it easier for George W. to get His work done?

But never mind. If, ultimately, a George W. second-term meltdown

2006: Jeb speaks on the Capitol courtyard on National Guard Day during the annual spring legislative session. Two weeks after this photo, Jeb went on an unannounced visit of Florida Guard troops in Kuwait and Iraq along with two other governors. He said afterward that he wanted to be in Iraq on Easter—a statement with deep connotations for Christian conservatives who believe his brother is carrying out biblical prophesy by invading "Babylon."

makes a Jeb presidency impossible, then Bush family opponents can turn this whole argument on its head, thusly: the Lord knew full well that of the Bush brothers, it was Jeb who would be the more effective at implementing the Bush vision for America and the world. God knew that Jeb, with his unrelenting focus and speaking ability and grasp of small facts, and not George W., would actually bend the world more to the Bush family's liking.

And so, He allowed George W. to win in 2000, and then again in 2004—not because He particularly wanted the guy in the White House, but because He knew that George W. would bollix things up so badly that by the end of two terms, there would be no way whatsoever that Jeb could ever follow in his brother's footsteps.

And then, both Bush supporters and opponents would finally have something to agree upon: the Lord does indeed work in mysterious ways.

Chapter Twelve

WITH US OR AGAINST US

"We rescued the emir of Kuwait. Now, if I knock on your door and say I'd like to borrow your son to go to the Middle East so that this dude with several wives, who's got a minister for sex to find him a virgin every Thursday night, can have his throne back, you'd probably hit me in the mouth."

—Ross Perot, 1992

"G. met with Arafat and said he was charming. Amazing. Whoever thought that we'd recognize him—a sworn terrorist? . . . One man's terrorist is another man's hero."

—Barbara Bush diary entry, 1993

"I had no compelling reason to go to Vietnam."

—Jeb Bush, 1994

In June 1989, pediatrician-cum-terrorist Orlando Bosch sat in a federal detention center, where he had been for a year since illegally trying to get back into the United States. Bosch's primary stunt in this country had come two decades earlier, when he had towed a bazooka through downtown Miami and then fired it at a Polish freighter in the Port of

Miami. The round did little damage to the ship, but Bosch was given four years in prison. He violated parole by leaving the country.

It's what he did where he went next, Venezuela, that held the attention of the U.S. Justice Department. Investigators found dozens of instances of sabotage and violence in the United States, Panama, Puerto Rico, and Cuba through the 1960s, but nothing to compare it to the midair bombing of an Air Cubana DC-8 en route back to Havana in October 1976. Seventy-three people died, including a group of athletes returning home from the Pan American Games, and although Bosch was acquitted three times of the charge in Venezuela, U.S. investigators called the evidence "overwhelming."

"We must look at terrorism as a universal evil, even if it is directed toward those with whom we have no political sympathy," said Joe Whitley, acting associate attorney general. "The conclusion is inescapable that it would be prejudicial to the public interest of the United States to provide a safe haven for Bosch."

So that was it, right? The good Dr. Bosch was sent back to Venezuela or Cuba or wherever to face the music for his deeds, right?

Wrong.

Because in Miami, Florida, the Cuban revolution of 1959 continued through the 1970s, the 1980s, and right on through into the early twenty-first century. So sure: maybe Bosch, according to our own government, was implicated in a host of assassinations and murders, not to mention the destruction of an entire airliner off the coast of Barbados. But he was doing it *to oppose Fidel Castro.* Which meant that in Miami, he was so much a hero that the city commission declared March 25, 1983, when he was still in a Venezuelan jail, to be "Orlando Bosch Day."

Which meant that in 1989, John Ellis Bush, honorary Cuban, went to bat for the sixty-two-year-old accused killer, lobbying the government of his father, the president of the United States.

Which meant that by July 1990, Orlando Bosch was a free man.

USUALLY WHEN WE elect a man president, the nation's foreign policy for the coming four years is a big question mark. Because regardless of what a senator or a governor *says* he will do in foreign affairs, his perspective obviously changes dramatically once he is behind the Oval Office desk. This is not meant as a criticism. The president obviously has access to far more relevant information than do even members of congressional oversight committees, let alone the chief executives of state governments.

All that is a way of prefacing the caveat that should Jeb Bush achieve his destiny and take his perceived rightful place in the White House, we really have little idea of how he might conduct American foreign policy for his four or eight years. More so than in any other area—education, welfare, taxes, the environment, all of which have analogs at the state level—Jeb's views on, say, the Third World debt crisis or the appropriateness of the World Court are a blank slate.

Now, that said, it is also true that more so than any other potential candidate for the presidency in recent times, there are clear clues as to how Jeb would handle foreign affairs, should he be given that honor. And in this area, as in all of those others, what you think of these clues likely depends on where you sit.

Jeb supported the covert American effort to supply the right-wing militias making up the Nicaraguan *contras* in the mid-1980s. He has long supported the overthrow of Fidel Castro in Cuba. In 1997, he signed onto the Project for a New American Century, a group that included many of the neoconservative architects of the Iraq invasion, which called for a "Reaganite" foreign policy of military strength and "moral clarity"—although in 1998, the year he was running a second time for Florida governor, he was not a signatory to the group's call to invade Iraq and depose Saddam Hussein.

Jeb is a big proponent of private charities getting public money for the distribution of aid, even if that aid comes then with a dollop of proselytizing. This would presumably be the case with foreign aid, too, with Christian groups freed to spread the Gospel along with federally financed water pumps and building materials.

And Jeb is big on capitalism as perhaps not the only way to economic success, but certainly the best way—meaning guaranteed friction with an increasing assembly of Latin American nations that have, in recent years, rejected the United States-favored candidates and chosen socialist leaders.

But as important, perhaps even more important, than the specifics of what Jeb would do is how he is likely to go about doing it. And it is here than even those who agree with his worldview might find reason for pause. Because foreign affairs is the one area of government where the nation gives the president extraordinary latitude to set policy, pretty much by himself.

On budgets, taxes, education, the environment, on all the domestic issues, there are interest groups who can push back when they believe they are getting the shaft, and institutions like Congress and the judiciary who can step in if the executive gets too far out of line. In our dealings with other nations, particularly those that seem threatening to *our way of life,* we give the president pretty much a free hand.

Given Jeb's history in Florida, his willingness to push every institutional and political advantage to its limit, his phenomenal stubbornness . . . is it such a good idea to give him that level of control over anything, let alone the power to make war?

BY THE END of the presidential term in 2009, the Bush family will have been in the White House, either in the number two job or the presidency, for twenty out of the previous twenty-eight years.

In that time period, the United States' once cozy relationship with dictator and thug Manuel Noriega—whom George H.W., as CIA chief in 1976, actually paid $110,000 as an agency operative—deteriorated to the point where George H.W., as president, felt compelled to invade Panama to capture him.

In that time period, the United States' ally in the Persian Gulf, Saddam Hussein, who had access to an annual $1 billion in American "farm" credits through the 1980s as he waged a nasty, chemical weapons war against Iran, went rogue and invaded Kuwait. Both George H.W. and later George W. felt compelled to take him on.

And in that time period, the esteem the rest of the world holds the United States in has fallen. In the years following George W.'s invasion of Iraq, it has gone into free fall. Not that we were well loved before. In 1975, an American diplomat wrote: "The American people do not have any concept of how others around the world view America. We think we are good, honorable, decent, freedom loving. Others are firmly convinced that though they like the people themselves in our country, that we are embarking on policies that are anathema to them. We have a massive public relations job to do on all of this."

That diplomat, of course, was George H.W. Bush, at the time the U.S. liaison to China under President Ford. By that time, he had already been the country's ambassador to the United Nations under President Nixon, so his belief that the nation's problem with the world was merely a "public relations" issue is simply mystifying. He was correct in his assessment that most Americans had no idea what the rest of the world thought of us then, and he would be correct to make that assessment again today. He would also be correct if he went further and said that many, if not most, Americans do not *care* what the rest of the world thinks of us. But is it really possible that a man like George H.W., whose job it was to understand world opinion, could really have believed that all these other people in the world, the Europeans, the Africans, the Asians—all of them merely misunderstood what the United States' objectives were?

Amazingly, and sadly, the evidence seems to indicate that not only George H.W.'s view of the world and America's place in it these last fifty years, but also that of his comrades in leadership and certainly his two political sons is similarly fantastic.

IN THE summer of 2005, as George W. spent his August, as he is wont to do, in Crawford, Texas, a California mom who lost her son in Iraq a year earlier responded to the president's description of the war as "noble" with this: "If it's such a noble cause, why aren't his daughters over there?"

It's a good question, one that will hang heavily in the air for as long as Iraq continues. For between the Bush family's political brothers of this generation, there are five children, every single one of prime military service age. Not a single one wears or has worn the uniform.

This is of great interest because the nation seems to be in a new trend of more military engagements, not fewer, and one of the Bush family's political strengths has always been great support from the military establishment.

In the case of George H.W., this is entirely logical and deserving. He was among "The Greatest Generation" who turned back Hitler and Mussolini and Tojo. He flew a dive-bomber off a tiny converted cruiser in the South Pacific and nearly died when his plane was shot down during one bombing run.

Yet somehow, support for George H.W. has translated into support from the military and retired military for his political sons. This is extraordinary, given their choices during Vietnam, when both were old enough to do what their father had done—enlist at the earliest opportunity and seek out a combat role—but chose not to.

George H.W. Bush supported the war in Vietnam, and made it clear that he thought poorly of those lads who chose not to fight. In a March 1998 letter to Tom Brokaw, who was writing a book about the World War II generation, George H.W. put it like this: "I have contempt for those who, when called, fail to serve. I hated the Vietnam syndrome—when people who served were vilified and spat upon. Those who ducked and dodged and fled only to let some underprivileged take their places particularly offend my sense of honor."

This contempt, naturally, was reserved for other people's children, not his own. In a 1990 interview, George W. explained why he turned to the Air National Guard in Texas, rather than, say, trying to join the Marines or Army infantry: "I was not prepared to shoot my eardrum out with a shotgun in order to get a deferment. Nor was I willing to go to Canada. I decided to better myself by learning how to fly airplanes."

The actions of the Bush family's Vietnam generation, certainly, do not impugn the decisions made by the Bush family's current, Iraq generation.

There is nothing dishonorable about George W.'s daughters or Jeb's sons and daughter not volunteering to head over to Iraq. At the risk of seeming unpatriotic, one might even infer some level of common sense in their failure to be there. Maybe someone, maybe their naval aviator war hero of a grandfather, taught them the distinction between, on the one hand, a genuine threat to world peace like a Hitler or a Tojo that requires all good men and women to come forward and sacrifice, and, on the other, a war of political convenience or ego or carelessness or fossil fuels in which the better part of valor is to have "other priorities," like Dick Cheney did during Vietnam.

A much more pointed question of the Bushes would be directed at George W. and ask, given his spirited defense of Vietnam as a young lad at Yale, why he didn't make more of an effort to take part in the glorious defense of South Vietnam instead of finagling his way into a squadron of obsolete fighter jets whose task was to guard Houston?

John Kerry and his supporters did ask this question, more or less, in 2004, and it didn't seem to matter to most Americans. Vietnam was done. Everyone of that era made a choice, and it was so long ago and it was time to move on.

But what happens when that question is asked of Jeb?

IN 1968, as brother George W. was finishing up four years of macho Texas talk about Vietnam at Yale, young Jeb was still at Andover, just turning fifteen. Lyndon Johnson was so battered by the war that he did the unthinkable and decided not to run for reelection. Robert Kennedy was murdered that year. So was Martin Luther King Jr.

The flames of 1968 seemingly had no effect on George W., who entered the National Guard, did his basic training, and continued talking about the war as if he personally was going hand-to-hand against black-pajama-clad VC.

Jeb wasn't so sure.

In later years, he called himself a "cynical little turd at a cynical little school." Perhaps. Or maybe that is the answer he likes to give now to explain away a young man more sensitive to his world than his political "base" of red-meat, Southern White Man Republicans care to understand.

The fact of it was, Jeb was deeply troubled by Vietnam and Johnson's handling of it. So troubled, in fact, that in the coming years, not only did he not sign right up to join the infantry but instead went to talk to his father, the congressman, U.S. Senate candidate, and United Nations ambassador. He was seriously considering filing for conscientious objector status, and wanted to run it past his dad.

Doing so would have put a serious crick in George H.W.'s career. Yes, he had given up a safe House seat in 1970 and run for the Senate at the urging of President Nixon, only to lose when liberal target Ralph Yarborough had been taken out in the Democratic primary by Lloyd Bentsen. But Nixon had taken care of him with the U.N. appointment, and George H.W. Bush was already plotting his next moves, including possibly replacing Vice President Spiro Agnew on the 1972 ticket. Having a son duck out of the war, when Nixon was still aggressively pushing it, would not have helped his career opportunities.

To George H.W. Bush's credit, and notwithstanding his later, withering criticism of those who did not fight, he told Jeb that he would support whatever decision he made. Barbara, in a 1984 interview with United Press International, described it this way: "George said, 'Whatever you decide, I will do. I will back you one hundred percent.'"

In late 1971, Jeb, a lanky eighteen-year-old with hair longer than his parents might have liked, decided to back his father's political career. He went into Houston to get his physical.

ALMOST FROM the start, George W. has been insensitive to the point of callowness about the young—and, in the case of many reservists, not-so-young—men and women left dead or maimed by his decision to invade Iraq. He does not go to funerals, he makes only rare visits to soldiers' families, and he most certainly does not meet with the families of dead soldiers who openly oppose the war.

That was not much of a surprise, given his predilection to surround himself only with those who share his views. But in the case of a war that he himself created, his refusal to deal with the human consequences has seemed downright cowardly. One Saturday during that August in 2005, as Cindy Sheehan camped out in protest of his refusal to talk to her about the war, George W. was able to make time for a two-hour bike ride. He was asked afterward how he could claim, as he had been doing, that he was too busy to meet with the lady. He replied that he had to get on with his life.

As ruthless and as mean as Jeb can be, it is hard to imagine him being quite that bad.

Jeb also surrounds himself with people who agree with him, and does not take kindly to dissent or protest. But were he in George W.'s shoes, he likely would have made the time to meet with Cindy Sheehan and take her abuse. He would have felt it his responsibility as the one who sent her son to his death.

While that is more grown-up and more gentlemanly, it probably should not comfort those who worry whether another Bush White House would mean another recreational war or two. That one is difficult to predict. There is the fact of his own disinclination to go fight in the jungles of Southeast Asia. One might hope that he would be unwilling to ask others to kill and die in a situation where he himself did not wish to do so. Perhaps the empathy that is so lacking for people who did not have his advantages will reveal itself in an area where he does have personal experience.

This, though, ought not be counted upon.

Bear in mind that Jeb himself, during his run for governor, denied that he had considered seeking conscientious objector status—that despite his own mother having admitted that he had. Further, there is the rejection of things related to his youth in general and to Andover in particular that Jeb came to in his thirties and forties. It should be remembered that Jeb also took part in the Socialist Club at Andover, not a group he would possibly be associated with today.

Finally, and most important, Jeb after all the hand-wringing ultimately went down for his physical, and his birthday ultimately produced the draft number twenty-six. Had Nixon and Congress not wound down the draft,

Jeb would likely have been called up. So he can argue that although he wrestled with the prospects of fighting in a war, in the end he did the right thing by his country.

In fact, the revising of the story line to an acceptably heroic version has already begun. Running for governor in 1994, Jeb told the *Miami Herald*: "I wanted to get married, work, and have a family. I had no compelling reason to go to Vietnam." A half-dozen years later, he told his family's official biographers: "I was prepared to serve if called."

So unlike Bill Clinton, who was actively deterred from putting American troops on foreign soil because of his own unwillingness to do so as a youth, Jeb's own past likely will not prevent him from shipping soldiers and sailors off to distant corners.

Which leaves the question of whether a Jeb presidency would be as likely as his brother's to pursue a foreign policy that would result in armed confrontations in distant corners. And the answer to that is probably.

THIS IS certainly what we would expect, anyway, based on the Bush family's long track record when it comes to a readiness to push the limits of American empire. As an example, although there is a great contrast made today between George W.'s and George H.W.'s styles in foreign affairs, the end result has largely been the same: a foreign policy that unabashedly puts American "interests" first, even when it means embracing both hypocrisy and cynicism.

George W., for example, drew plenty of criticism for hyping the danger of nuclear, biological, and chemical weapons in the hands of Saddam Hussein as justification for his 2003 invasion. But apparently forgotten is that George H.W. used the same mushroom-cloud imagery to whip up the nation against Saddam the first time around, a dozen years earlier.

It was the autumn of 1990, when the first Bush White House found that polls were showing slipping public support for military action based solely on the desire to "liberate" Kuwait. So, upon George H.W.'s return from a Middle East trip, he started hyping not only Saddam's known (and previously winked-at) chemical weapons capacity, but also the shaky claim that he was close to acquiring a nuclear weapon.

Similarly, the "transformational" Middle East policy created by the neoconservatives can be seen as less about bringing democracy to that part of the world than it is about ensuring a new staging ground for American intervention, come the inevitable day that the authoritarian Saudi regime falls to home-grown militants. In that respect, the invasion and continuing military presence are merely a new tack on the same, old Realpolitik strategy of the Cold War.

The irony of all this is that the Bush family's entrance into the world of international politics was more or less accidental, the result of the entrance of conservative Democrat Lloyd Bentsen into the 1970 Texas Senate race. George H.W. had been counting on a rematch against liberal Ralph Yarborough, who had beaten him in 1964 thanks in part to Texan Lyndon Johnson's strength at the top of the ticket. That advantage was gone six years later, with Richard Nixon in the White House. Unfortunately, Bentsen beat Yarborough in the primary, and then, mouthing pretty much the same views George H.W. was offering, trounced him that November.

And so, in 1971, George H.W. needed a job and Nixon, who had urged him to abandon his safe House seat from Houston to run, felt obliged to find him one.

So it came to be that George H.W. Bush, having just finished another Texas statewide campaign in which ridiculing the United Nations is de rigueur, became the United States Ambassador to the United Nations. Not that he remotely had any of the qualifications that might be considered necessary. At that point, he had been a two-term congressman from Houston, and prior to that, the cofounder of an oil drilling business. His international experience was limited to bombing Japanese-held islands during World War II and then traveling to foreign countries on behalf of Zapata Offshore to win drilling concessions. That and, perhaps, using the phrase "Unleash Chiang" in his everyday lexicon—an urging used by the John Birch–type Right in the 1950s and 1960s to spur the United States to help Chiang retake mainland China.

In foreign affairs, George H.W. could not even claim qualification based on the accomplishments of his family. The extent of his parents' and grandparents' foreign policy involvement was the overseas investments of father Prescott—who, as his son was enlisting to become a Navy pilot at age eighteen, referred to the fight against Germany and Japan as "Mr. Roosevelt's War"—and grandfather George Herbert Walker, some of them quite controversial. Like many American investors, Walker had money in Bolshevik Russia after the 1917 revolution, and both men were involved in a Dutch company owned by an early and major supporter of Adolf Hitler.

None of that seemed qualification enough for an ambassadorship to a body that the United States not only hosted, but in which it was a permanent leader. The choice angered Nixon's secretary of state, William

Rogers, who called him a "lightweight." Both the *New York Times* and the *Washington Star* published editorials criticizing the choice, and even one of George H.W.'s best friends, Lud Ashley, asked him: "George, what the fuck do you know about foreign affairs?" George H.W. responded: "You ask me that in ten days."

What newspapers or even the State Department thought, though, was not important. George H.W.'s father had been a United States senator, and the most exclusive of all clubs looked kindly upon the child of one of their own and confirmed him for the job. Soon it became evident that not even Nixon considered the United Nations role particularly important, as George H.W. learned to his chagrin when the administration let him push a pro-Taiwan policy in the U.N., while it was secretly supporting communist China. George H.W. was probably the only high-ranking American surprised when the body voted to admit Mao's China and expel Chiang's Taiwan.

Important votes in the General Assembly, however, accounted for only a small portion of George H.W.'s time as ambassador. The vast majority of it was spent socializing—receptions, dinners, luncheons, making small talk and chitchat with the world's representatives. And in this area, George H.W. excelled—so much so, that he later made personal relationships the core of his foreign policy. Whether it was fishing with Canadian prime minister Brian Mulroney or speed-boating with French leader Francois Mitterrand, George H.W. seemed to believe that he could make the world like us as a nation if only he could get other world leaders to like *him* personally. This was, of course, pretty much the same tactic he used in every field—diplomacy by friendship, no different than tax policy by friendship or media relations by friendship. It was George H.W.'s entire political philosophy, insofar that he had one: if people liked him, they would support him.

THIS IS NOT to say, though, that George H.W. let his obsession with being liked get in the way of ruthless foreign policy objectives. He did not.

As a candidate for president in 1980, for example, he criticized Jimmy Carter for not doing enough to prop up the Shah of Iran, a brutal dictator whose secret police routinely tortured and murdered political opponents. Later, as vice president and then as president, he fully supported the policy to appease and to arm Saddam Hussein, a sociopath who was by the mid-1980s using chemical weapons against both Iran as well as the Kurdish minority in his own country. As late as the spring of 1990, George H.W.'s administration was happily using Saddam the Murderous Nut in the continuing, cynical geopolitical game that George H.W. knew so well from his brief stint at the CIA. In that one year before the 1976 election, he helped conceal from a prying Senate such things as the agency's involvement in the 1973 coup in Chile that murdered democratically elected socialist Salvador Allende as well as "our" dictator Augusto Pinochet's complicity, along with Jeb pal Orlando Bosch, in the 1975 car-bombing assassination of former Chilean ambassador Orlando Letelier in, of all places, Washington, D.C.

George H.W. also fully supported the secret war that President Reagan authorized against the Sandinista government in Nicaragua, which included the mining of its harbor and the arming of the contras rebels, many of whom had been brutal henchmen in the *Guardia Nacional* of deposed dictator Anastasio Somoza Debayle.

And yet, George H.W. seemed to take extremely seriously the responsibility of sending American soldiers and sailors into a war. He agonized over sending troops into Panama, and then even more so in the days leading up to the start of the Gulf War. No doubt it was the result of his own experience as a young man, just out of Andover and thrown into the thick of the mayhem in the South Pacific. He had not been there long when he saw a seaman killed before his eyes when a plane crashed as it tried to land on the converted cruiser *San Jacinto*. He wrote about seeing the man's severed leg on the deck, and hearing an officer screaming to get things cleaned up to let the planes continue landing. He wrote home to his parents that he hoped his younger brothers would be able to avoid combat: "I hope John and Buck and my own children never have to fight a war. Friends disappearing, lives being extinguished. It's just not right. The glory of being a carrier pilot has certainly worn off."

It's somewhat disconcerting, this vast gulf between the concern for the lives of American soldiers he would send into battle, and the indifference toward the men and women and children of other nations who faced those soldiers or the proxy armies created by Oliver North and others. George H.W. correctly felt awful about the twenty-three American servicemen who died in his Operation Just Cause to take out his operative-gone-rogue Manuel Noriega. But in that splendid little action, as many as *four thousand* Panamanians died. Four *thousand*. And in Nicaragua, exactly what did George H.W. suppose the contras were doing with all those American munitions that we were openly providing prior to the Boland

Amendment and then covertly providing afterward? How many dirt-poor Nicaraguan peasants were murdered during those years for supporting the ruling Sandinistas, not to mention the babies and children who died for want of basic preventive medicine? Did George H.W. ever bother to find out?

HIS LACK of concern about "enemy" human life notwithstanding, at least with the first President Bush there was that genuine concern about American human life. His offspring appear to have lost even that.

Back when George H.W. Bush was trying to figure out a way to sell a war against Iraq to a skeptical public, he invited his sons to a dinner with Air Force chief of staff Merrill McPeak, where, after some encouragement from Barbara, all four boys volunteered their view that their dad should deal with Saddam Hussein harshly. That he should release a list of targets that would be destroyed if Hussein did not comply by a certain deadline.

There is, of course, the chutzpah of four grown men who among them had never seen a shot fired in anger urging their dad, who *had* personally witnessed the horrors of war, to send American troops into combat.

More important, though, is the insight it offers into George W.'s and Jeb's worldview—a *we can and therefore we should* take on foreign affairs. This, upon reflection, should not come as a surprise. Winning is perhaps not everything, but it is the most important thing. So the history that we, the United States, just a few years earlier had encouraged and helped arm Saddam Hussein so that he could kill Iranians was not important. What was important at that moment was that Saddam Hussein was thumbing his nose at the United States, and for that he needed to pay.

Few Americans then and maybe only a few more now would argue that Saddam Hussein was anything other than a murderous tyrant. Saddam made for an easy bogeyman. And, now, we've also had the opportunity to see how George W. deals with this sort of situation. The big question going forward is how far Jeb, when it's his turn, would take this attitude with other leaders—leaders who are less unsavory and less easily vilified.

Brother George made it clear he personally disliked North Korean leader Kim Jong Il. But North Korea is a nuclear power. An invasion there would bring all kinds of potential calamities, not just for our troops but for South Korea and possibly Japan. When Kim or his successor insults the United States on Jeb's watch, how will North Korea be forced to pay?

A far more likely flashpoint is not in any far corner of the planet, but a mere day trip south across the Florida Straits. True, Fidel Castro may have died by the time Jeb can make it to the Oval Office, but what if he hasn't? What, then, is the man who many Miami Cubans consider an "honorary Cuban" to do? Invade? The pressure for him to do something beyond merely continuing the embargo will be intense, given his heated rhetoric over the last quarter century.

And how about Venezuela, where Jeb lived for three years in Caracas and which is now run by Castro ally Hugo Chavez? And how about Evo Morales, the socialist and Chavez ally who in late 2005 became president of Bolivia? Or fellow socialist Michelle Bachelet, who in early 2006 became president of Chile? Never mind that all three were democratically elected—that didn't mean much for Salvador Allende in Chile, either. Because the exile community in Miami doesn't like them, and when the exile community speaks, Jeb listens.

For years, he has listened—and then acted.

JEB'S WORK to free terrorist-in-Venezuela, hero-in-Miami Orlando Bosch is just the most high profile of his work for and with the émigrés in Miami over the years.

Throughout the 1980s and 1990s, the city was the nexus of anticommunist activism in Central America. Salvadorans, Nicaraguans, Cubans all conspired to defeat the socialist foe, and for most of that time, Jeb was their unofficial conduit to the White House. Jeb, who spoke their language fluently. Jeb, who accepted without reservation their need to overthrow leftist governments and hunt down and kill leftist rebels. Jeb, who would show up in a guayabera shirt at rallies, chanting *Libre! Libre!* with everyone else.

In March 1985, when a Guatemalan doctor wanted to help the contras get medical assistance, it was Jeb who wrote his dad a note and marked the envelope "Walker" so it would quickly get to his father as family correspondence. George H.W. wrote back to Dr. Mario Castejon: "Since the projects you propose seem most interesting, I might suggest, if you are willing, that you consider meeting with Lt. Col. Oliver North of the President's National Security Council staff at a time that would be convenient for you. My staff has been in contact with Lt. Col. North concerning your projects and I know that he would be most happy to see you."

Just weeks earlier, in January, Jeb had met with Felix Rodriguez, the former CIA operative and wearer of Che Guevara's wristwatch, who at the time was serving as North's chief supply officer in the arms flow. Despite this, Jeb later claimed, just as his father did, that he had *no idea* anything illegal was going on. "That's crap," Jeb told the *Boston Globe* in response to a question about whether he was his father's Florida point man in the scheme. "I believe the freedom fighters should be supported to the maximum and that their cause is noble and just. But I know the difference between proper and improper behavior because I was brought up well. I would never do anything to jeopardize my dad's career. That would be a dagger in my heart."

By late 1986, with the whole Iran-Contra Affair dominating the headlines and hammering the White House just as George H.W. got ready for his long-awaited run for the presidency, Jeb was splitting hairs as to how much, exactly, he had known about the shipments from Florida to Honduras, and thence onward into Nicaragua. "What I have done is a far cry from being part of a arms supply link to the contras," he said, but acknowledged that he had helped with "nonlethal" assistance.

First, there is really no reason to take Jeb at his word about this any more than there is to accept his father's "I was out of the loop" explanations. Jeb is a smart, details-oriented guy, and his disdain for the legislative branch is legendary. His view would have been that the president had every right to ship guns to whomever he wanted, and to hell with Congress—a view also held by his dad, who in his diary on January 13, 1991, called the congressional "use of force" vote a usurpation of the president's powers. But second, even if we do accept his claim at face value, the claim itself is so weasel-wordy that it smacks of his father's successor in the White House. "Nonlethal" assistance should not be confused with medicines and toys for children. Nonlethal meant food, boots, uniforms, canteens, rucksacks—in other words, all the other equipment that a militia needs apart from guns and rocket launchers. If there is a finite amount of cash available, then even "nonlethal" equipment is, in essence, lethal, because it allows the limited money to purchase more weaponry.

In any event, neither Jeb nor the émigré community in Miami generally ever *regretted* the arming-the-contras scheme—just the fact that it was exposed and, because of a tenacious special prosecutor, that some of them might have risked going to jail, had it not been for the pardons George H.W. gave out as he was leaving the White House. In 1987, for example, Miami—where candidate Bob Dole that year got a rousing cheer when he denounced Castro but only silence when he denounced Pinochet—and its Cuban Americans were proudly pitching in for Oliver North's defense as investigators closed in. Prominent Republican donor Carlos Perez created the "Concerned Citizens for Democracy" to help pay North's legal bills.

WE NEED to be careful here not to impute all or even a majority of the nation's foreign policy woes on the Bush family, for their views and tactics have not really been terribly different from that of other leaders.

And, taking it a step further, if America has been ill-served by our leaders in their dealings with the world, that is the fault of us Americans. We don't know much about other countries or their problems, and we don't seem to care. That could not be plainer. Simply listen to National Public Radio, which probably provides more international news than any other American broadcast network, and compare it to the BBC World Service. People in the rest of the world know a whole lot more about our government than we know about theirs. And, unfortunately, what they know, they do not like.

The unvarnished truth is that there's a lot not to like. We Americans have, and have had for some five decades, a straight-face problem, when it comes to foreign affairs. We talk out of both sides of our mouth. We say one thing but do another. We absolutely do *not* treat the citizens of the rest of the planet the way we would like them to treat us.

We can even lay aside the old saw about our being the spoiled kids of the planet, how we make up less than 5 percent of the world's population, yet consume 25 percent of the planet's goodies. This came to be because, first, our ancestors had the foresight to find a lightly populated continent with abundant natural resources and steal it for themselves from the natives and, second, we were the only major power that did not have its infrastructure damaged by World War II. And even though our response to this type of complaint over the years has been, one, we bought those goodies fair and square; or two, we've earned them; or three, tough noogies, in reality it doesn't matter. The world has caught up with us, and emerging powers China and India will soon rebalance that population-resources ratio.

Anyway, the rest of the world is not mad at us because we revere ostentatious consumption. The rest of the world is mad at us because, under George W., our foreign policy has become even more hypocritical than usual. For decades, we have properly extolled the virtues of liberty and self-determination. And for decades we have sidled up to dictators and murderers who provide us military bases or chant the correct slogans. We propped up dictators in South America, we befriended oil-rich oligarchs in the Middle East, we apologized for the racist, minority-rule government of South Africa, we supported terrorists who harassed Cuba—the list goes on and on.

The world, from the 1950s through the 1980s, was seen by Washington through a Cold War lens. If you weren't with us, you were with the Russkies. For decades, for example, the United States sided with Pakistan, a military dictatorship for most of its history, over India, the world's most populous democracy, because India did not want to get in the middle of the U.S.-Soviet rivalry. Most American foreign policy makers from the 1950s through the 1980s honestly could not imagine a world that did not share their life-and-death, with-us-or-against-us view. Nevertheless—there it was. Hard to believe, perhaps, but there were farms, towns, entire fishing villages, whose residents were able to go days if not weeks at a time without worrying whether it was the United States or the Soviet Union at that moment leading the race for global domination.

Sometimes, this hubris and hypocrisy has come around to bite us in the rear. The Mariel boatlift of 1981, in which Fidel Castro emptied his jails and mental hospitals as part of a massive migration to Florida, was a perfect example. Sure, Vice President George H.W. Bush was correct when he asked if it was reasonable that Castro should pawn off all his dangerous killers and lunatics on an unsuspecting populace. But was it any less reasonable than our government trying to murder him during the 1960s with exploding cigars?

More recently, in 2002, George W. told the United Nations that it was worthless and weak if it did not support an invasion of Iraq. (That we sided with the Butcher of Baghdad in the 1980s, atrocities and all, during his war with Iran didn't help our credibility much—particularly since many of the same individuals so outraged by Saddam's behavior in 2002 more or less turned a blind eye to it two decades earlier.) In 2003, we were forced to grovel before U.N. member nations to help bring peace to a country that they never believed needed to be involved in a war in the first place. Was it a surprise when they told us to go pound sand? The Indian government particularly must have taken no small satisfaction in telling the United States to take the long walk off a short pier. After decades of supporting India's dictatorial, terrorist-friendly neighbor Pakistan, America in the summer of 2003 wanted to borrow a full division of Indian troops to help occupy Iraq. New Delhi almost gleefully told Washington: we'd be happy to consider it—as soon as you get United Nations approval.

At the same time—as the rest of the world knows well—Americans have among the most generous hearts on the planet. Let there be an earthquake in Turkey or Guatemala or Uzbekistan, and American food and medicine and blankets and money flow freely. If a category five hurricane were to devastate Havana, does anyone doubt that we would not respond immediately and compassionately, Castro or no Castro?

Therein lies the confusion for foreigners. How can a people who are so warmhearted and caring have a government that behaves like such a jerk?

The answer is that while Americans are incredibly generous, we are also incredibly ignorant. We are vaguely aware that the rest of the world hates us but cannot understand why and cannot be bothered to find out. Call it a failure of public education, call it the rise of the infotainment culture, call it plain old intellectual laziness. Whatever it is called, it is not new. Alexis de Tocqueville recognized the powerful strain of anti-intellectualism in American culture nearly two centuries ago.

In 1979, when radical students stormed our embassy in Iran and took hostages, how many of us remembered that their anti-Americanism just maybe was fueled by the 1953 CIA coup that removed popular nationalist Mohammed Mossadegh from power and replaced him with the oil-industry friendly shah? As a nation, we don't have a terribly good grasp on our own history, let alone the history of the rest of the world. Most Americans to this day could not place Vietnam or even Iraq on an unlabeled map. We don't know who Mossadegh was or, for that matter, from our own hemisphere, Augusto Sandino or Jose Marti or Salvador Allende.

We don't know these things and, even worse, we don't care. So that when a president tells us that we need to arm "freedom fighters" in Nicaragua, or that we need to invade Panama, or that Saddam has nuclear weapons, or that Saddam conspired with Osama bin Laden to attack us on September 11, or that Osama and his followers hate us because of our freedoms, rather than because of our support of the repressive Saudi Arabian ruling family, we nod vaguely and change the channel.

At some point along the way, didn't we kind of get the government we deserve?

SOMEDAY OUR foreign policy will change—either when we lose so much power in the world that we become irrelevant or when we the people wake up and pay attention. The first likely could not happen for at least several decades, and the second will not happen in the foreseeable future. Which means that, for the present, the question of how Jeb might deal with the rest of the world will likely matter a great deal.

Again, it's almost impossible predicting how potential leaders will react once they are actually behind the desk in the Oval Office. Who would have guessed that John F. Kennedy, for all of his talk of a new, idealistic tomorrow, would get the country embroiled in a faraway war that would last a full decade? Who would have supposed that tough-talking Richard Nixon would have opened the door to China and eased tensions with the Soviet Union?

Then, of course, there is George W. Bush, who as a candidate in 2000 talked about conducting a "humble" foreign policy but who, in the months after taking office, quickly backed out of international treaties and implemented the most unilateral foreign policy in decades.

In at least one way, a Jeb-directed foreign policy would be different from that of his brother, if only because Jeb would take a personal interest in it. George W. is not a details guy. Jeb is. George W. also was open about his lack of interest in countries other than our own, and had done precious little foreign travel before becoming president. It was a provincialism he no doubt got from his mother, who in one of her memoirs offered the observation that an official Japanese ceremony she attended involved "some weird chanting" and in the other shared this take on neighboring Korea: "Have you ever noticed how many Koreans are named Kim? Lots." (She evidently did not research whether Koreans ask each other why so many Bushes are named George.)

Jeb, in contrast, not only majored in Latin American studies but actually lived for the better part of two years in Venezuela without the accoutrements of officialdom. Whether this results in a different overall direction or merely a more competent version of the same old story cannot be known.

Overall, though, it is hard to imagine that the basic thrust of American diplomacy would be terribly different. Jeb would have far more knowledge of this hemisphere, but countries in South and Central America need to understand that this is not necessarily a good thing. It's not enough, for example, to be a democratic nation. You must also then vote for pro-capitalist leaders—a mandate that a growing number of South American nations have been ignoring in the first part of the twenty-first century.

Even when the election that followed the end of the contra war produced a winner whom Jeb had raised money for and whose inauguration he and Barbara had attended, he still wasn't happy with the results. Violeta Chamorro had not gotten rid of all the Sandinistas in the government, he explained three years later in 1993, and she had not reinstated all the private property that Daniel Ortega's government had seized from wealthy landowners.

Jeb could put aside his personal preferences and deal with decidedly un-Republican leaders respectfully and openly. I suppose that is possible. But given his vindictive streak—just ask voucher whistle-blower Robert Metty, for example, or Michael Schiavo—he is just as likely to pick a fight with them, to the detriment of us all.

But the number one foreign policy problem in the coming years is likely to be oil, and our strategy for dealing with its dwindling supply as well as the planet-damaging effects of its continued use. Jeb, as governor, talked more about the environment than George W. did in Texas, but that's because Florida is a much "greener" state than Texas, and even Republicans are forced to talk about the environment, if they want to win. But Jeb is also quite a friend of industry and profits, so it's not likely he would put the country on the Kyoto Accords bandwagon if given the opportunity.

In a Jeb Bush White House, America's hunger for fossil fuels will continue to drive the foreign policy, and it is difficult to see how there would be much difference in our relationship with Saudi Arabia. As long as that embrace of an undemocratic friend continues, our efforts to seed the rest of the Middle East with democracy will continue to be seen as hypocritical. And so long as we're seen as oil-grubbing hypocrites in a region where plenty of young men grow up willing to kill themselves in the course of killing others, we will continue to need tedious airport screening and color-coded terror alerts.

While it would be nice to think that Jeb might be the one who breaks the cycle and leads the country down a new, more evenhanded path in foreign relations, it is also highly unlikely. Jeb, recall, was one of the original signatories to the Project for a New American Century, which advocated a strong military to pursue a "Reaganite" foreign policy. Jeb is also an astute student of politics. He saw how well xenophobia and fearmongering worked for his brother's reelection campaign. There is no reason whatsoever to believe he would abandon a proven tactic. In terms of the oil economy, he made some token efforts to give tax credits to alternative fuel ventures—but that was more than counterbalanced by his cancellation of high-speed rail, a project that would have been far more fuel efficient than the car travel it would have replaced.

Eventually, of course, this has to end. The Saudi royal family will fall, as will Kuwait's, either through elections or revolution, and our special access to the oil spigot will be no more. On top of that control issue will be the price issue: a billion Chinese, a billion Indians—between them, they account for one-third of the entire human race. They work hard, they are ambitious, and they are getting richer and more envious of our "stuff" by the day. What happens when they are wealthy enough to want one car per family? How about one car *and* one SUV per family? Can you say: gasoline at ten dollars per gallon? Can you say: global warming hell?

IT DOES NOT have to be a dismal future, but it will—perhaps sooner than later—require drastic, fundamental changes in many areas. And that will require leadership that truly "thinks outside the box" and can explain unpleasant economic truths.

After watching him in Florida for the better part of two decades, it does not seem likely that Jeb can offer such leadership. He, like his brother, was content to rule with a "50 percent plus one" strategy, of winning an election with whatever it took, and then pushing an agenda that, on its own, could not possibly have won majority support. In poll after poll, Jeb personally outperformed his education and tax cut policies—just as George W. has consistently been better liked than his policies. It is hard to imagine Jeb calling for a new gasoline tax or some other radical measure that could hasten reliable alternative energy schemes.

Apart from the inevitable reshuffling of the economic world order, there will also be the ongoing national security issues.

The nuclear genie has been out of the bottle for a while now, and it will only get easier for a group or even a person without the necessary moral restraint from using such a weapon. What will our reaction be when this happens? People who are afraid for their safety and that of their children will understandably be willing to trade liberty for security.

If we truly believe in individualism and freedom, the challenge will be to resist this. Because, in the end, nihilistic terrorists could destroy a building or two every year, or even a city, but not threaten the fundamental existence of the nation like, for example, Hitler or Stalin did.

It will require a huge change in thinking, to recategorize what would be an act of war, in terms of its destruction and death toll, instead as a mere crime. But what is the alternative? If a renegade Pakistani physicist were to produce a suitcase bomb and detonate it in Union Station, do we have to invade Pakistan? And Afghanistan and Iran for good measure?

A more evenhanded foreign policy, one that actually treats other countries the way we'd like to be treated and does not talk out of both sides of its mouth would go a long way to reducing anti-American resentment. The rest of the world follows the news, too, and can see the hypocrisy of lauding women's suffrage and democracy in Afghanistan and Iraq but not in Saudi Arabia and Kuwait. You don't need to be a cynic to figure out the pattern in that one.

We can't know for sure how Jeb might react to these things. Jeb has never actually been in charge of a foreign policy—not counting the bizarre Florida version that revolves around the Miami-Havana axis—so there is the chance that he will be far more thoughtful and forward-looking than one might expect. His public pronouncements backing his brother over two terms might merely have been sibling loyalty, rather than heartfelt support. Maybe he will chart a new course and bring the nation an optimistic worldview that embraces the future.

Maybe . . . but, sadly and given his track record, probably not.

Chapter Thirteen

TOO MANY BUSHES?

"Do you think I'd be doing this if I was running?"
—JEB BUSH, OCT. 15, 1992,
HOLDING UP A PLASTIC CUP OF BEER
AT AN ORLANDO POLITICAL FUNCTION
AFTER HE WAS ASKED WHETHER HE WAS
RUNNING FOR FLORIDA GOVERNOR

"I have every intention to run."
—JEB BUSH, FEB. 17, 1993,
AFTER HIS MOTHER "LEAKS" TO THE PRESS
THAT JEB WILL RUN FOR GOVERNOR

George W: "Listen, I didn't grow up wanting to be president of the United States."

Jeb: "I did."

George W: "Yeah. You did."
—THE GOVERNORS BUSH, 1998

Blame it all on Gerald Ford.

If the mere thought of a Bush Dynasty makes you twitch, take it out on the Only President to Become President without Running in a National Election. If, on the other hand, you think that the Bushes are the answer to what ails this nation, then you should thank Michigan's Finest.

It's one of those moments of history with such amazing consequence, that night in Detroit back in 1980. For it was there that "Bush" went from being the answer to an incredibly difficult trivia question to a household name around the planet.

Two years earlier George H. W. had decided that his brief stints in Congress, at the United Nations, the Republican National Committee, the U.S. liaison office in Beijing, and at the CIA made him the obvious choice among discriminating Republicans as their candidate to turn Jimmy Carter out of office. He ran a smart campaign at first, concentrating his limited dollars on Iowa and winning important momentum before getting snaked by Ronald Reagan at the infamous Nashua debate.

In the end, the Reagan juggernaut was too big, and George H. W.—ignoring the advice of young Jeb, who wanted to go down guns blazing, like Butch and Sundance—had finally thrown in the towel. He had hoped, naturally, that Reagan would pick him for the number two spot, but by the time of the convention in Detroit, it was clear that it was not going to happen. New York congressman Jack Kemp was the "movement conservative" favorite, but then even Kemp was overshadowed by the rise of the Dream Team—a partnership between Reagan, who would beat Carter, and Ford, who had lost to him four years earlier. It was unusual, sure, but it offered both moderate Republicans and conservative Democrats a ticket that promised proven steadiness and foreign policy experience.

More to the point, Reagan had bought into it—which meant that George H. W. and his family gathered at the Pontchartrain Hotel were in the dumps. Jeb suggested that there was no point in staying. That they should just go home. But George H. W. would have none of it. He was classy enough to know that you just didn't do that. He had a role to play, and he would play it.

And then, Ford went on national television and explained to Walter Cronkite his vision of how it would work. Reagan, see, would handle domestic policy, while Ford would take care of the foreign stuff. After all, Ford reasoned, that's where their respective interests and strengths lay. So Cronkite asked: "It's got to be something like a copresidency?" And Ford said: "That's something Governor Reagan really ought to consider."

In his own hotel room, Reagan went ballistic, jumping off the couch and pointing at the television: "Did you hear what he said about his role?" And that, pretty much, was that, as far as the Dream Team went.

Sure, it seemed a bit much—watching Ford explain all this on national television. But look at it from his point of view. Okay, he had never stood in a national election before becoming president—in fact, had never even stood in a statewide election in Michigan. Notwithstanding this, he had acquitted himself reasonably well in the two years following Richard Nixon's departure. Further, it must have been tough for him, to see this former actor who had wounded him in the 1976 primaries, thereby making it even harder for him to hang on that November, now looking like the winner Ford could not be.

In any event, Reagan had never been keen on the Ford idea in the first place, but had been talked into it by his advisers as the best way of making sure he would beat Carter. Still steamed, he turned to an aide: "Now where the hell's George Bush?"

And thusly was born the Bush Dynasty.

Think of it: without Reagan's late-night phone call inviting him to join his ticket, where would George H.W. have been? He had lost two statewide elections in Texas, served two terms in the House, and survived on four political appointments from Nixon and Ford. Reagan would have won reelection in 1984 whoever his vice president had been. So even if George H.W. had still had the inclination in 1988 to give it another go, it's not likely he would have gone far, running against Reagan's vice president.

And where would that have left the next generation of Bushes? Down here with the rest of us peons, is where.

George H.W. did well in the oil business through persistence, rich relatives, and friends—plus one stroke of very good luck. He did reasonably well in politics in the 1960s and 1970s because his father had been a United States senator. How far would he have gone if his dad hadn't been a senator? Harris County GOP chair? Perhaps. U.S. House? Maybe. But in all likelihood, he never would have run for the Senate himself. And he almost certainly would not have gotten any of the political jobs he held after that second Senate loss.

Jeb and George W. would have had an even tougher time. Having your dad run the CIA might help you get international "consulting" jobs, but it probably would not help as you ran for office. Same with having a dad who had been a mere congressman. There are 435 of those, and only the ones in leadership have any real pull.

Having a dad who was vice president and then president—well, that's in a whole different league. In the sort of league where, when you decide at age forty that it's time for you to be governor of the nation's fourth largest state, you're instantly the front-runner, even though you've never held elective office before.

Sure, George H.W. would have remained a wealthy man if Ronald Reagan hadn't made that call in Detroit that night. He may even have been a lot wealthier, if he'd spent his prime earning years back in the oil business. No doubt George W. and young Jeb would never have had trouble finding work, with daddy's connections.

But governor? President?

No. For that, they need to thank Mr. Ford.

THE OTHER person fans of a continued Bush family dynasty need to thank is Osama bin Laden.

It sounds perverse, stated like that, and it is not to suggest in the least that any Bush ever supported the terrorist or his attacks on Americans. Nevertheless, as a historical fact, it cannot be denied.

Where was George W. in the summer of 2001? Stagnant in the polls and seemingly unable to do anything about it. With California getting taken to the cleaners by Enron's scams, his big energy plan was in trouble. He'd gotten his tax cuts, but it was not clear whether he would get any more. He'd lost control of the Senate by ticking off Vermont Republican Jim Jeffords to the point where he left the party. His great big education bill was going to pass, but only after Massachusetts Democrat Ted Kennedy had insisted on stripping out the Religious Right's pride and joy: vouchers.

At first, he'd won a sense of goodwill, even from the plurality of Americans who'd actually voted for Al Gore. Most were ready to accept the Electoral College quirk that had allowed such a thing, and were ready to overlook the shenanigans in Florida that appeared to have reversed the intent of a majority of voters there, as well.

That grace period, though, quickly evaporated, due not in small part to George W. and chief strategist Karl Rove's insistence on governing as if they had won a popular vote landslide.

Even more ominous, major media from around Florida and around the country were preparing a long, exhaustive series studying the 2000 balloting, and would conclude that Al Gore likely would have won a manual, statewide recount—which the Florida Supreme Court had ordered but the U.S. Supreme Court stopped. The original questions of legitimacy would be revisited, and this time bolstered with real, painstakingly acquired numbers.

And then Osama bin Laden struck, killing 3,000 Americans on actual American soil. This had not happened since Japan's attack on Pearl Harbor in 1941, and had not happened on the United States mainland since the War of 1812.

Overnight, George W. was a hero—the right man in the right job at the right time. Many Christian fundamentalists believed it was God's will, that the attack was a signal of "end times," and that it was similarly part of God's plan that a good, born-again Christian like George W. should be in the White House at that moment. Hard-core Republicans felt vindicated by the results of 2000—after all, who in their right minds would have wanted Al Gore at the helm at a time like this? Democrats, including Gore, rallied around George W. and supported his leadership because he was the president and the nation had been attacked.

Even the news media, a group that the radical right likes to call treasonous and anti-American, pulled its punches with the Florida recount stories. Most papers either buried the stories or spiked them entirely. Editors acted in what they thought was the national interest—when the country had been hit and thousands were dead, it was deemed unpatriotic to run articles questioning the president's legitimacy.

The tone of subsequent articles also was different, as traits in George W. that previously had been characterized as weaknesses overnight became strengths. His unwillingness or inability to see nuance in issues was labeled as decisiveness. He wasn't stubborn anymore. He was *resolute.*

George W. had been instantly and thoroughly rehabilitated from inarticulate buffoon to fearless leader. And Jeb's political future, which had been looking dimmer by the day, was once again viable.

IT'S HARD to predict what might have been, once we start venturing down the path of alternative realities. Perhaps the economy would have recovered quickly, if Osama had never attacked us. Maybe George W. would have settled for a less confrontational style, if the 2002 midterm elections had, as expected, consolidated the control that Jeffords had given Senate Democrats. In short, maybe George W. would have turned it around, and made himself a strong candidate in time for 2004.

Perhaps—but all we can know is that this scenario wasn't looking likely in the summer of 2001. And a George W. loss in 2004 almost certainly would have ended any presidential aspirations Jeb might still have held. What were the chances that even hard-core Bush family supporters in the Republican Party would have gambled on yet another Bush, after the first two had been thrown out of office after a single term? Jeb himself appeared to sense this. He was, in fact, considering not even standing for reelection.

Instead, Jeb's star in the GOP firmament today is as bright as ever.

Now, granted, it might have been brighter still, had George W. taken the mandate that he was given after September 11 and not squandered it invading Iraq. Imagine if he'd committed the number of troops he sent to overthrow Saddam Hussein to shore up democracy in Afghanistan instead. Imagine if the Taliban, instead of staging a comeback, had instead been eliminated forever. Imagine if Osama bin Laden had been captured or killed, in that first year following the attacks. Imagine how big George W.'s reelection victory would have been in 2004—and how easy it would have been for Jeb to step right up and follow big brother.

But that didn't happen. George W. did attack Iraq—started planning for it, in fact, literally in the hours and days following September 11—and that war, and its conduct and conclusion, could well be the single strongest external event stopping a Jeb Bush presidential run.

Assume, though, that his older brother is smart enough to figure out a "peace with honor" exit strategy from Iraq not just for the sake of his brother, but for his party generally. And further assume that once the troops are home, Americans are willing not to hold it against Jeb that we went to Iraq in the first place.

In those conditions, the GOP nomination would essentially be Jeb's to lose.

WE WENT through earlier the reasons Jeb may not run for president: he needs to replenish his nest egg in the private sector. Columba won't let him. The Bush name continues to poll dismally around the nation.

The flip side of that, of course, is that there are a goodly number of reasons that many Americans, after carefully considering his record, might not *want* him to run for president. Liberals, certainly, moderates, and even conservatives will find plenty of particular positions in his Florida years with which to find fault. But with Jeb, there are even more fundamental questions that participants in a pluralistic republic should be asking about the man.

We take it for granted, most Americans, that all of us who have grown up in this country share basic, democratic values we learned about in civics class. That electing leaders is fundamentally a good thing. That having a king who rules because of a "divine right" or a dictator who rules at the point of a gun is a bad thing.

Maybe it goes too far to suggest that Jeb does not share these values. His own election loss and successes show that he has lived by them. And yet . . .

How much of our internal belief systems are a function of the times we live in? More to the point: how badly would we behave if we lived in times in which we could get away with it? More to the point of this book, how badly would *Jeb* behave, if he thought he could get away with it?

Jeb loves elections, no question about it, both as a candidate and as a strategist. It gets his competitive juices flowing and, given his family name and the campaign money that generated, his side has usually won. Jeb loves to win, and political campaigns have been the perfect sport for him.

Governing, though, was a different matter. Governing meant dealing with other people whom he hadn't hired and couldn't fire—people like state legislators and, even worse, judges.

Bear in mind here that Jeb for his first few years had a more pliant legislature than any previous governor going back decades. For the better part of his first term, with but a few exceptions, whatever Jeb wanted from the Florida legislature, Jeb got. Despite this, he reached a point where lawmakers' unwillingness to do things *exactly* the way he wanted would infuriate him. Just imagine if he had been governor when the legislature was partly or totally controlled by the opposite party, as Democrat Lawton Chiles had to cope with, or Republican Bob Martinez before him.

Clearly, Jeb has some serious issues with dissent. With those in his employ, he rules with an iron fist. Just ask Robert Metty, the whistle-blower within Jeb's education department who tried to warn of fraud and abuse within Jeb's voucher programs who then got pushed aside and ultimately fired for his troubles. Jeb took a similarly blunt approach with lawmakers who dared cross him, axing their pet budget projects and threatening those in his own party with well-funded, primary election opposition.

Playing political hardball, though, is well within the bounds of the acceptable, and a governor probably has the right to expect loyalty from managers in his agencies.

But what about Jeb's efforts to punish others, outside his normal sphere of influence? What about Tammy Jackson, the poor woman who became possibly the only person in Florida to *lose* a school voucher for her son after she criticized the school of one of Jeb's political allies in the "school choice" movement? And, most famously, how about his branding Michael Schiavo a murderer after he thwarted Jeb's efforts to keep his brain-damaged wife alive against her wishes?

What would Jeb have done in analogous circumstances had he been the lord of a medieval manor, or an Italian prince during the Renaissance, or a Communist Party apparatchik under Stalin? How far would his love of "behavior modification" have let him go?

Few of us on this planet are saints, able to turn the other cheek despite our pain and humiliation. But after nearly two decades in the public eye in Florida, it's not clear that Jeb even makes much of an effort.

No question: Jeb would have been much better suited, given his temperament, as a king in earlier times than an elected leader today. Given that, those of us who have been and may again be his subjects are fortunate that we all live today, and not those earlier times.

THAT TENDENCY toward imperiousness may be tough to discern during his campaign, when Jeb decides the time has come to bestow upon all of America the favor of his leadership and he runs for the White House. He is an excellent campaigner, able to say the right things to the right people.

Ironically, the only possible problem he might have, public image wise, is his brains. Because in America, history has shown that we do not like our leaders to be too smart.

It's rather an odd requirement, for office seekers—we don't want to vote for anybody who seems like he or she is smarter than us. Call it a corollary to this nation's long revered tradition of anti-intellectualism, a trend perhaps first noted by Frenchman Alexis de Tocqueville during his travels in this nation when it was still young. It's weird, but it thrives today, starting in elementary schools by the second grade or so, where smarts and academic achievement are qualities to make fun of on the playground, rather than aspire to.

Thus, in a stump speech, it's best not to use correct grammar all the time, best not to be able to rattle off statistics and details about complicated issues—best not to appear *too* educated. Of course, it makes no sense. We don't pick an accountant this way, or a lawyer, or a heart surgeon. Whether we personally like any of these people is way down on the list of important characteristics we consider, well below *is she good with numbers* or *does he practice this kind of law* or *where did she train*.

But when picking a senator or a governor or a president, things like knowledge and intelligence and experience go right out the window, replaced by whether we'd like to have a beer with this particular person. Go look at the regulars at your neighborhood tavern. Any of those guys on the bar stools seem like presidential material?

And yet, the results of recent presidential elections show a strong correlation between the appearance of ignorance and success.

Against Al Gore and John Kerry, but especially Gore, George W. used his apparent intellectual inferiority as a strength. Gore was too much of a smarty-pants. Kerry too aloof and snooty.

When George H.W. Bush ran against Michael Dukakis, he was able to paint his opponent as an elitist Massachusetts intellectual who had gone to Harvard. Never mind that he himself had gone to Yale. In fact, George H.W. took it several steps further, telling America, as we discussed, that his favorite snack was pork rinds, when in fact it was popcorn, and his favorite drink beer, when really it was a vodka martini.

Ronald Reagan's victories over Jimmy Carter and Walter Mondale—same pattern. People never believed Reagan was a rocket scientist (while Carter actually was a nuclear engineer . . . even if he couldn't pronounce it), but they loved him anyway.

The only exception to this general rule was Rhodes scholar Bill Clinton, and the only way he succeeded was by pretending to be Bubba. Snarfing Big Macs, talking Southern—nobody noticed how smart he was.

In this regard, in being dumb enough for voters to like, this could be somewhat of a problem for Jeb, who makes a point both of knowing stuff and of letting everyone know that he knows.

IN ALL LIKELIHOOD, though, none of that will matter—whether Jeb would make a good president, or not, and whether he is someone the country needs in the coming years, or not.

The most frequently given reason that Jeb will not run for president, even by great fans of Jeb and his family, is that America has already had too many Bushes too quickly. That America doesn't like aristocracy. That Americans are wary of family dynasties because they too closely resemble monarchies.

This theory, I will respectfully suggest, is utter hooey. Why, if Americans dislike monarchy, did tens of millions of them get up at oh-dark-thirty to watch Princess Diana's wedding and then, sixteen years later, her funeral? How come, if Americans are wary of electing members of the same family to power, did it take our nation all of six presidencies before electing the son of a president to that top job himself? Bringing things to this century, how come the junior senator from New Hampshire is the son of a former governor and former chief of staff to George H.W.? How come Rockefellers and Kennedys keep getting elected? More to the point, how come the ne'er-do-well, black-sheep son of a former president was given the job himself a mere eight years after the dad was tossed from office after a single term?

Americans like to *think* they don't cotton to kings and barons and dukes. It is part of the nation's great creation myth, that we broke free from England's shackles because of our love of freedom, rather than our dislike of England's taxes. How many Americans know, for example, that citizens of England already *had* most of the freedoms in our Bill of Rights? For that matter, where do we suppose our Founding Fathers got the idea for these freedoms in the first place? How many Americans know that by 1776 England was pretty much a representative democracy, with most of the power resting with Parliament, and not with King George III?

Americans generally are pretty hazy on these sorts of facts, and, as the historical success of the Bushes and other famous families already demonstrates, we really don't have much of a problem with electoral dynasties at all.

It is certainly possible that George W.'s presidency will still be viewed by too many Americans as a dismal failure in the coming years, and the weight of that might be too great for Jeb to overcome. It is possible, but not likely. Popularity goes in cycles, and George W. appeared to have hit rock bottom in 2006. Further, presidents who serve a full two terms historically have enjoyed decent popularity in their final years. Clinton and Reagan both left office with good poll numbers. Nixon and Johnson were forced to abdicate in different ways, but the most recent two-term president before Reagan, Eisenhower, was also well liked as he left.

If George W.'s final years follow that pattern, the much-hypothesized "Bush Fatigue" would likely be a nonissue in the coming election cycles. Certainly, Jeb has enough of his own brand already out there to be an attractive vice presidential candidate in 2008. Such a role would have seemed absurd just several years ago, the idea of Jeb suppressing his own ego and will to be vice anything for anyone. But in 2006, the job seemed more and more of an attractive fit: a relatively nonthreatening way to introduce himself to the nation, prove that he is not his brother, and simultaneously grab the inside track to future presidential elections.

But even if this doesn't pan out, and John McCain or Rudolph Giuliani or whoever is the eventual nominee does not pick Jeb, that is of little long-term consequence. In February 2007, Jeb Bush will have turned fifty-four years old. He has plenty of time. The elections of 2012, 2016 and even 2020 remain in play, and Jeb will be a player. Count on it.

NATIONAL POLITICAL campaigns today are enormous machines that seem to create their own weather. Few people will bother to examine Jeb's real record here in Florida, and so Jeb will likely be able to sell his version of his history to folks in Iowa and New Hampshire, then in South Carolina and so on. Moderate Republicans in these places will believe Jeb dramatically improved Florida schools and created vast numbers of new jobs with his tax cuts. Christian conservatives will know that he created the first statewide voucher program in the nation, and specifically made sure to allow religious schools to participate, while at the same time minimizing government control. Plus they will know that his top education aide for most of those years was a fundamentalist graduate of Bob Jones University.

Jeb is a Bush, and at this moment, the Bushes are the only serious political operation within the Republican Party. That little donor database that started out in Barbara's card boxes is now a sophisticated, well-oiled, and well-used money machine that will give Jeb everything he needs to steamroll his Republican opposition in the primaries. And then, once he has the nomination, he basically has a fifty-fifty chance of winning. His ability on the stump and his relentlessness may give him a few points; a general wariness of the Bush brand might take away a few points.

Given his personality, given his sense of mission, given that his father and his clearly less qualified brother have both accomplished this, it's hard to imagine Jeb *not* running for president. Every step he has taken from moving to Miami forward has built toward this ultimate goal, which, had things gone according to plan, would have been realized in 2000 after a term and a half as Florida governor.

Jeb intensely dislikes quitters, and it stretches credulity that he would accept this label himself. Forget all the flattery he will get from big-money donors who will see him as the best guarantee of continued low capital gains tax rates and generous depreciation allowances. Jeb is shrewd and cynical enough to see their encouragement for what it is, even though he absolutely agrees with their positions.

For Jeb, the biggest factor that will push him into a presidential campaign will be his own boredom.

After having been governor, and having had a well-paid and energetic inner circle quickly carry out his smallest instruction, research his most trivial query, *not* being governor anymore will make him crazy. He won't have a legislature to bully and terrorize. The press corps will rapidly lose interest in him. He suddenly will have all the time in the world, and not a thing to do with it. What's worse, all the statehouse courtiers and professional sycophants who had bowed and scraped to him for eight years will instead be bowing and scraping to the new governor—a man Jeb in his core *knows* is nowhere near worthy to replace him in the Capitol's corner suite. And all he will be able to do from his Coral Gables condo or his real estate office or his think tank is watch as the new governor and the new legislature slowly, bit by bit, start dismantling all his *legacy* achievements.

To do nothing, to merely put together financing deals to pave another few hundred acres of the Everglades or to go around making speeches about education policy to a few dozen think tank wonks—well, for Jeb, this is the surest road to insanity.

REALISTICALLY, the only real question is whether he will make a late entry into the 2008 field or plan instead for a better-grounded attempt in 2012 or 2016.

Yet as speculation started focusing on him in 2005, Jeb's surrogates and allies, including one or two in the Florida political press corps, nonetheless offered a string of reasons why Jeb just could not run for the job himself. His family was a mess. Being governor had left him broke. Columba, who despises publicity, would not let him.

None of these excuses, though, stands up to serious scrutiny. While it is true, and sad, that his daughter continued to have serious drug problems, Jeb's ability to have a positive influence on this issue in 2007 was far less than it might have been in 1993 or in 1997. In both of those earlier instances, Jeb took on an all-consuming governor's race. We do not need to put a value judgment on whether he should have, but the fact was that he did—and he did so because his compulsion to run for office outweighed his need to spend more time with his children.

At least this rationale holds the potential that Jeb could break with his history and trade or put off his political ambition for the sake of his family. The next idea, that he is too poor to run for president, is patently absurd.

It's true that Jeb's net worth dropped during his two terms as governor. He came in with $2.04 million more in assets than liabilities. By the end of 2005, that figure was down to $1.40 million. This is partly because, like everyone else with investments in the stock market, Jeb's portfolio lost value between 2000 and 2003. And this is also partly because Jeb put two children through college in that time period. This is partly because, as governor, his salary was a fraction of what he was making selling real estate in South Florida and water pumps to Nigerians.

Let's concede all that, and grant that he lost 30 percent of his wealth during his time in office. Here's the key question: so what?

He is *still a millionaire.* Not only that, but his children are grown, and he has a new source of retirement income, with a state of Florida pension on top of his other savings plans. Even if you accept the notion that $1.4 million is simply not enough for a fifty-four-year-old man who will share in his parents' wealth and a piece of a seaside Kennebunkport estate—even then, Jeb's earning potential after an unsuccessful presidential run would be every bit as high as it would be as merely a former governor. And should he win? Well, look his at father's moneymaking ability after he left the presidency, just for making speeches and posing for pictures.

Finally, there is the issue of Columba and her dislike of politics. There is no question that Columba is not the politician that Jeb has become. Let's even allow that she dislikes speeches and public appearances and the other things that go along with being the wife of an elected leader.

Given all this, the fact of it is that Columba knew of Jeb's political ambitions when she met him as a schoolgirl in Mexico in 1970. At the time, his father had just lost a Senate race, and was about to become the nation's ambassador to the United Nations. Three years after that, as she prepared to marry Jeb, her father-in-law-to-be was the chairman of the Republican National Committee, defending a Watergate-embattled president.

She kind of knew what she was getting into.

In 1988, Columba became an American citizen so she could vote for her father-in-law that November. During the Republican National Convention that nominated him, Columba gave a seconding speech, in both English and Spanish. And that autumn, she traveled extensively with Jeb, much of it in Hispanic-rich California, in the campaign's attempt to parlay her ethnicity into votes.

Throughout Jeb's tenure in the Governor's Mansion, Columba has participated in public events, both with Jeb and on her own, to promote their goals and interests—just as Rhea Chiles, Mary Jane Martinez, and Adele Graham did in previous administrations. Columba spoke at luncheons involving Hispanic issues, at dinners honoring cultural programs, at antidrug kickoffs. Seemingly every week, Jeb's press office would put out at least one or two news releases telling everyone what luncheon or dinner or ceremony Columba was attending in the days to come.

Maybe she really did hate every second of it, but that invites the obvious question: if she loathed this aspect of first-ladying, why did she continue after Jeb had safely won reelection in 2002? She could have stayed at the Coral Gables condo (where she spent much of her time following an embarrassing 1999 run-in with U.S. Customs when she failed to declare $19,000 worth of clothing and jewelry she had bought in Paris) and no one would have said boo.

No, contrary to the conventional wisdom about Columba and her drag on a potential presidential run, Jeb's wife would be, like most candidate spouses, at worst a nonissue. When people stood in their voting cubicles in November 2004, they didn't agonize over the choice between Teresa Heinz-Kerry and Laura Bush. Likewise, when Jeb takes the presidential plunge, what people think of Columba will pretty much mirror what they think of Jeb. Those who like him will find her down to earth, adorably shy, even courageous. Those who hate Jeb will find reasons to dislike her, too, or, alternatively, praise her as a means of trashing him in comparison.

In fact, the whole *can-Jeb-overcome-the-Columba-problem* analysis is completely upside down. The real question is: can Democrats stop a Republican presidential candidate with a Mexican-born wife? Think back to the last presidential election that the Republicans won with a healthy electoral majority. How did George H.W. Bush do that? He won California.

Imagine Jeb and Columba on a bus tour of California—she speaking the English she learned upon moving to the United States, he slipping into the fluent Spanish he learned courting her. Imagine their sons setting up the *Viva Jeb!* headquarters in Santa Ana.

Imagine the pure terror this would generate at the Democratic National Committee.

Admittedly, California is a completely different state than the one that voted for Ronald Reagan and George Bush in the 1980s. It would be a steep hill for Jeb, even with some traditionally Democratic Mexican-American support, to take California. But the mere possibility of losing that state would drastically alter the Democrats' strategy. They would have to spend a lot of money and waste a lot of their candidate's time defending fifty-five electoral votes that need to be safely in the bank. Combine that danger with the certainty that Jeb would carry Florida, and it becomes clear why Jeb would be the Democrats' nightmare candidate.

It becomes equally clear that Columba Bush is not the terrible burden to a Jeb presidential campaign some would make her out to be. Rather, she could be that campaign's stealth weapon.

FOR HIS PART, Jeb started fielding questions about his intentions even before his brother had secured reelection in 2004. In fact, Jeb used the excuse of the hurricanes that year to skip the Republican National Convention. Too busy helping Florida recover from the storms, was the official line. He was also aware, though, that his presence at an event that was a mere formality in the electoral process would only fuel speculative stories about 2008. Jeb similarly skipped that winter's National Governors Association conference, with its dinner at the White House. On that occasion, at least, Jeb was more forthcoming—he said he did not want to add to the speculation those events always generate about who is and who is not running for president next time around.

For months, the queries continued regularly, and Jeb regularly said the same thing, often with a tone of mock frustration: that was he was not running in 2008. "Why am I not believable on this subject?"

In these exchanges—mainly with reporters, sometimes with audience members at speaking events—two things were notable. First, as he tried to knock down the idea that he might be a candidate for 2008, Jeb made no attempt to diminish the job, or suggest—like he did at the informal chat with the Tallahassee press corps in January 2001—that it held no appeal to him. It was always a plain, quick "I'm not running," and that was that.

The second thing of note was his precise syntax. He never said, "I *will not* seek the 2008 nomination" or "I will not run in 2008." He always used the present tense: "I am not *running.*"

Is that significant? Possibly. Despite the risk of Clintonian parsing, Jeb has sometimes played that sort of word game with the press and public. Compare it to Jeb's definitive "I *will not* run for the Senate" statement in

2006, as Republican candidate Katherine Harris imploded. In contrast, the phrase "I am not running" means exactly that. At the moment he uttered it, he was not running for president. He had no campaign account, no staff, none of those things that politicians acquire when they run for the nation's highest office.

Obviously, there is great strategic value to not announcing your candidacy until you absolutely have to. The more you can accomplish "under the radar"—the nailing down of media and polling, the outline of a national structure, etc.—the better. What's more, if you can choose between having the national political press corps root around your background for three years or for one and a half years, Jeb would obviously prefer one and a half.

Interestingly, Jeb got a little more specific about his reasoning after most reporters stopped asking. It was in response to a question from a gathering in the House chambers of high school student government leaders from around the state.

"I'm not running for president in 2008 for a couple of reasons. The main reason is that I really made a commitment to myself and I think to the people of this state to finish strong," Jeb told the Boys State conference in June 2005. "When I ran for reelection, I wanted this job. I don't want to abandon it. If you're going to run for president, it is something that has to be planned out and worked on long before December 2006, in my opinion. And so I really want to focus on my job, I want to finish strong. I want to finish doing what I said I was going to do."

Got it? By mid-2005—but before his brother's poll numbers took that spectacular tumble—Jeb was saying he couldn't run for president because he didn't want to let Floridians down. But more interesting was his explanation of how two years simply wasn't enough time to organize and field a quality presidential campaign.

Now, this might be true if your name is Smith or Jones . . . or Frist or Pataki or Allen. But if your name is Bush, then two years is plenty of time. For one thing, you're inheriting the biggest, and *only*, serious national political apparatus in the Republican Party. Second, as much as Democratic voters might hate you, and independent voters might be leery of you, the "Pioneers" or "Rangers" or whatever new sports team name Jeb chooses for the rich guys who can sign five- or six-figure checks to your party without blinking—those guys still *love* you.

I think it is safe to say that regardless of who else might get into the Republican race, Jeb Bush would be the prohibitive favorite to win the 2008 nomination should he decide to run. Why? Because that 30 percent of the populous that strongly supports George W. regardless of what the rest of the planet thinks of him? They just happen to be the likely voters in the Republican presidential primaries. That's why.

TRUE, winning the nomination isn't winning the election. Yet, for the purposes of a potential candidate, it may as well be, because predicting the course of what lies beyond that is next to impossible.

In any of the past dozen presidential elections, all of the nominated candidates—with the possible exceptions of Barry Goldwater in 1964 and maybe George McGovern in 1972—had realistic scenarios enabling them to win. Hindsight seems to remove doubt, the further we move from the event, and we tend to forget, for example, what a befuddled old man Reagan seemed after that first debate against Mondale. Which means, in terms of planning, the best anyone who wants to be president can do is map out a strategy to win the nomination. After that, it's essentially a red-black spin of the roulette wheel, which no amount of advance planning can nail down.

Early in 2000, recall, Al Gore looked like he would lose to George W. by double digits. He ended up winning the popular vote. Who would have thought in early 1995 that Bill Clinton would be near invincible by mid-1996? Who could have guessed in mid-1991 that George H.W. would be so vulnerable a year later?

Assessing the lay of the land of a presidential general election more than six months out, then, is little better than guesswork. Just ask all the big-name Democrats who stayed out of the 1992 presidential race because George H.W. was sitting near 90 percent in the polls.

The upshot for Jeb is this: basing a decision two years out on the probability of "Bush fatigue" being an overriding factor is pointless. If he decides to run, and his brother's popularity remains well below 50 percent, he probably will not win. Conversely, if he stays out, and George W. regains respectability in the polls and the Republicans wind up nominating an obviously weaker candidate, his decision will seem foolhardy.

That decision will seem downright nuts, though, if the Republican ends up winning in 2008. That possibility could well rule out any chance Jeb might have for the presidency, ever, because it would mean—presuming whoever it is will want to run for reelection in 2012—that Jeb's next shot will be 2016. He will be sixty-three that February and, although that's not too old by any stretch for a presidential run, age would start becoming a factor then. But even more important is that by 2016, Jeb would have been out of the Governor's Mansion in Florida for a full decade. Could he possibly maintain a national profile over those years? Unless he serves in a Republican administration as vice president or some other high-profile role, not likely. That assumes that Jeb would deign to serve—in the true sense of the word, subordinating his own desires to that of his boss—under another human being, and that's not a given. Some political observers also toss out the idea of the United States Senate, but this is even less likely. First, the idea of Jeb having to work with ninety-nine others who would be his "equal" is at best comical. And second, he would either have to take on Republican Mel Martinez in 2010 or beat incumbent Bill Nelson in 2012.

GIVEN THOSE FACTS, it probably wasn't surprising to see signs of a possible 2008 national run in the latter part of 2005.

Some were subtle—his refusal to postpone a scheduled trip to Washington, D.C., for a meeting and press conference with Health and Human Services secretary Michael Leavitt, even as Hurricane Wilma lurked off the Yucatán, ready to spin toward South Florida with category four winds. Even the mere chance of a hurricane had been enough in 2004 for Jeb to avoid all manner of events. Recall how he was too busy to attend his brother's coronation at the Republican National Convention because of his hurricane duties in Florida. But in 2005, Jeb had important business that would not be put off: the announcement of federal approval of his grand Medicaid privatization scheme. During the conference call with reporters, Leavitt called the plan a national model. The *New York Times* the next day printed an article about it on the front page. Jeb's supposed loathing of the national news media notwithstanding, he went to Washington for the event. Wilma could wait.

Other clues were more like a sledgehammer, in terms of their effect on Florida politics. The most obvious was his reversal on the issue of offshore oil drilling, possibly the one topic that, up until that moment, had united the state's disparate factions.

In 2001, with his brother newly in the White House and Jeb looking at his own reelection the following year, Jeb trumpeted the deal he had won which essentially forced Interior Secretary Gale Norton to back off her plans to permit drilling in the Eastern Gulf. In a press release issued from

Kennebunkport, Jeb touted a new drilling moratorium that he proclaimed would protect Florida's beaches, a major source of the state's top industry, tourism.

"As a result, there will be no new drilling in the Lease Sale 181 Area off the coast of Florida under my watch," Jeb announced. Jeb then went on to trash Democrats Lawton Chiles and Bill Clinton for putting Florida in such imminent jeopardy of offshore drilling in the first place by not aggressively working to stop it.

In 2005, Jeb was ready to deal away half of that protected water. Instead of preventing drilling anywhere in a 200-mile-wide strip around Florida— the entire extent of the United States' economic zone—Jeb was ready to give up the outer seventy-five miles of that in exchange for a permanent 125-mile zone that would be under state control. In other words: that shocking lack of environmental sensitivity exhibited by Chiles and Clinton in the 1990s? Well, Jeb had evidently come around to their way of thinking.

Jeb defended his proposal, arguing that higher oil and gas prices made Florida's outright ban untenable—Jeb suggested acidly that he could take up such an idea with his fairy godmother—and that a permanent ban of any kind was better than a series of moratoria that could eventually end. Jeb's new position split the congressional delegation, with many Republicans, including new senator Mel Martinez, lining up to oppose him. The proposal also enraged environmentalists, who argued that it was insane to accept a 125-mile buffer when a solid political front from a state with twenty-seven swing electoral votes would likely preserve the full, 200-mile limit.

Environmentalists, though, were looking at the issue through the lens of protecting the environment, not national politics. Seen in that context, Jeb's retreat is perfectly sane, even brilliant.

After all, it's one thing to tell Floridians that you've gone to the wall for them to protect their beaches from oil slicks and for them to love you for it. It's quite another to stand in a New Hampshire living room in midwinter, listening to woeful tales of the cost of home heating oil, and explaining why you think oil rigs off the coasts of Texas and Louisiana are perfectly okay but rigs off Florida are wrong. This new, oil-industry friendly approach also sent the message to energy interests that Jeb had not forgotten his Texas roots, should they be wondering whether, after all that time in beach- and swamp-friendly Florida, their boy might have started to go native on them.

The only downside to this would be if this new position so angered Floridians that they would turn against him in a presidential race. This, alas for Democrats, seemed somewhat of a pipedream. Jeb had popularity to burn in Florida, and his new offshore oil stance will not burn much of it.

Finally, and probably most significantly, in the summer of 2005, even as he continued to talk about not running for president, Jeb restarted his dormant Foundation for Florida's Future, putting on its board some of his most reliable political fund-raisers—including Jacksonville insurance executive Tom Petway. By mid-July 2006, Jeb had raised over $1.9 million for it, with little more than e-mail solicitations. Jeb's people assured everyone that this was merely to give him the platform and the money to continue pushing his education reforms after he had left office.

Maybe. But maybe someone from Iowa or New Hampshire or Michigan will decide that Jeb might have an interesting take on education "reform" in that state during a coming conference and Jeb will have a slush fund to travel to that event and, while he's there, maybe roam around to the surrounding counties explaining his views to people.

Maybe.

THERE IS, of course, a purely internal factor in Jeb's decision to run or not to run for the presidency, and that is the one thing that may be more powerful than his ambition: his sibling rivalry with his elder brother.

Regardless of the process and methods of his victory in 2000 and despite his dismal poll numbers in his second term, the indisputable fact of it is that George W. Bush won the presidency not once, but twice. In that regard, in a family that rates and ranks its members' proficiency from tennis to tiddlywinks and everything in between, George W. has now set the high-water mark. A skeptic might wonder whether wrecking the nation's relations with other countries or ballooning the national debt might somehow detract from that. They do not. It's about winning, remember. George W. won the presidency twice.

What would it mean, and how would Jeb deal with it if he were to take a run at the White House and lose? Recall his difficulty handling the election results in 1994, when his brother won and he lost. How much harder would it be with the higher stakes of a presidential race, particularly if Jeb were to fail in a bid to succeed George W.? What if he not only failed, but somehow he failed even to win the nomination?

If avoiding this psychological trauma were at the forefront of Jeb's mind, then the obvious solution would be to completely reject the idea of running for president and embrace a new and different vocation entirely. Remove himself to academia, like so many other Florida politicians have, by grabbing a presidency at one of the state universities. Sure, he has no background and no advanced degree and maybe no interest . . . but on the plus side, he has appointed all the boards of trustees of the schools, and also the members of the Board of Governors. As a candidate, he would be a shoo-in.

Or perhaps he could swallow his pride and take part in the administration of John McCain or Mitt Romney or, just to prove what a devoted public servant he is, Mark Warner or John Kerry. He could be education secretary or, more appropriately, head of FEMA.

Or maybe he could transmogrify his Foundation for Florida's Future into something with a more national-sounding sweep—Foundation for America's Future, say. This would give him the benefit of reusing some of his dad's old stationery from his own Fund for America's Future political action committee from the 1970s and 1980s. He could commission "white papers" on the need for school vouchers and ending teacher tenure and more testing. He could travel on donated corporate jets. He could give speeches.

He could slowly go stark raving bonkers out of sheer boredom.

And that, frankly, is the downside to all of these alternative scenarios. Jeb loves being in charge of stuff, and he loves scheming and campaigning to be in charge of stuff. If he's not doing one or the other, he won't be happy. And like a tiger who has gotten the taste of human flesh and decides that he likes it, so it is with Jeb and power.

Ultimately, if indeed Jeb is hobbled by the myth or reality of Americans' "Bush fatigue," there is one certain cure: Hillary.

Should the senator from New York appear to be the Democratic front-runner, either in 2008 or later, that would immediately provide Jeb a ready answer to those who argue against a Bush dynasty. *We're going to have a dynasty,* he could say. *The question is which one do you want? My family's? Or hers?*

IN THE TINY, walk-in-closet of a room Jeb primarily used rather than his larger, formal office, he kept on the desk behind his laptop computer a small digital countdown clock.

It was a gift from his Department of Environmental Protection secretary partway into his second term, and it provided him a constant reminder of exactly how many days, hours, minutes, and seconds he had left in his reign until noon on January 2, 2007, when he had to step down because of term limits.

In his final year, as the clocked ticked down to the 300-day mark, his imminent departure consumed him. He and his staff schemed up ways to maintain some measure of control from beyond the grave, so to speak, to keep his *bold initiatives* and *sweeping reforms* and other parts of his *legacy* on the books. Like his high-stakes testing plan, and his vouchers, and his various privatization efforts.

Jeb and his people recruited a legislative "farm team"—as can be guessed, it was mainly members of the more impressionable House—to get special briefings and coaching to increase the chances they would preserve his programs. They set up a rapid-response team under the direction of former campaign manager Karen Unger to get favorable coverage of his policies in the media after his departure. They even created a $95,000-a-year position within his education department so that a taxpayer-paid employee could "protect legacy issues." All this on top of the resurrection of his Foundation for Florida's Future slush fund.

It was as if he couldn't quite believe it was happening, that there was going to come a time, exactly *"x"* number of days away and counting, that he was no longer going to be king of Florida, and that he had to rage against that dying of the light.

To his credit, he was not trying to cling to power because the governorship had lined his pockets, or because he was incapable of finding gainful employment outside of government. No, he honestly believed he was a force for positive change, and that his work was unfinished, and that it would tear him up to see his successor start chipping away at all that he had managed to build.

And it was an honest reflection of his certitude in himself and all that he believes that it never really dawned on him that if his duly elected successor and a duly elected legislature were to start undoing some or all of what he had done, that they would do so with *every bit* as much moral authority as he had possessed when he had pushed those things into law. A more self-aware governor might have read that message in all the polling that showed that he personally was always more highly regarded than his policies, be it his education plan or his tax cuts. Alas, Jeb was not that governor. He got his way in so many areas because he understood power, and he was not shy about using it—not because his ideas were necessarily any good.

Truly, he meant well. But it was perhaps the most telling detail of Jeb's rule in Florida that as he watched his days tick away to zero, so many others in the state counted his remaining days, too—not with sadness, but with long anticipated relief.

ACKNOWLEDGMENTS

There are scores of people who contributed to this work, many wittingly, as I sought out their insights and expertise and assistance—but many more unwittingly, by their individually small but cumulatively enormous efforts to tease out some semblance of the truth from a man and a machine generally not eager to release it.

These would include various gadflies and whistle-blowers who, in the course of their own struggles for justice or vindication, helped shine the light of day into the dark corners. Robert Metty, the former Department of Education manager of Jeb's prized voucher programs comes to mind. He, like some others, lost his job because of his actions, and all of Florida is in his debt.

These would also include the many legislators, executive branch staffers, political consultants, and lobbyists who sent tips my way or served as sounding boards for my research. Almost all are Republicans—which is why they were so valuable. All will remain nameless, as per my agreement with them. They provide me with facts that I could confirm with a document or two; I keep their names out of print. It was a quid pro quo that kept me in business for eight years despite my *persona non gratis* status in Jeb's realm—and, I like to believe, it also served the public's right to know about their government.

But mostly I wish to thank the many dozens of my fellow practitioners of daily journalism, whose dutiful scribblings through the years preserved a reliable record of Jeb's activities and ideas from the time of his arrival on the Florida scene for his father's 1980 presidential campaign. It doesn't seem like much, on any given day, to write down a governor's or a candidate's or a businessman's utterings—I know and appreciate this from firsthand experience over two decades. Nevertheless, there is immense value to this thankless chore. Preserving the record is important. What Jeb said about the Nicaraguan contras in 1986 or corporate welfare in 1988 or prison crowding in 1993 matters. And neither I nor the rest of the world could know about these views if the much-derided, much-bullied, ink-stained wretches hadn't been out there doing their jobs.

Along these lines I must thank Kimberly Miller, my *Palm Beach Post* colleague with whom I wrote literally hundreds of articles about Jeb's much-vaunted, and ultimately much-flawed school voucher programs. Without her, the chapter "Voucher Madness," on Jeb's most important priority in office, would have been impossible.

I need to thank my editors at *The Post,* who over the years have stuck by me despite the pressure from Jeb's people to replace me with someone more to their liking. It may seem absurd, for an American politician to believe that he should have the ability to tell an independent news organization who should cover his office—in fact, now that I think about it, it *is* absurd. Still, editors and reporters at other Florida news outlets did allow themselves to be cowed. Not all of them. Not even most of them. But enough of them for Jeb to see this as a winning strategy. The folks at *The Post* deserve kudos for not giving Jeb the time of day in this regard.

(Of course, part of the *The Post*'s disposition toward Jeb, I learned only after I had started my research for this book, may have been based on Jeb's deep-seated antipathy for the paper, based on the editorial board's decision not just to endorse somebody else in his 1994 Republican primary, but to ridicule Jeb's very candidacy. Here is a portion of Jeb's reply in a letter to the editor:

"Putting aside your sophomoric attempts at humor and a quote taken out of context in an attempt to make me look foolish, your objections to my becoming governor seem to be as follows: My last name is Bush; I have no relevant experience; I have not spent enough time on the public payroll to suit you; and my proposals for reform will not work.

"I plead guilty to your first charge; I am the grandson of Sen. Prescott Bush and the son of President George Bush, and I am proud of it. Your attack on my father misses the mark; he is a good man, and he was a good president, as each passing day of the Clinton administration proves. As for me, I cannot help being Jeb Bush; I was born that way. In this context, I have warned my children to keep a

weather eye out for the Editorial Board of The Palm Beach Post *later in their lives since your Bush phobia apparently is indiscriminate and intergenerational.*"

(So there.)

On the business side of things, I must thank my agent, Maria Carvainis, and my editor at Tarcher, Ken Siman, for their enthusiasm for this project. Because of who he is and what he hopes to be, John Ellis Bush is an important man, and Maria and Ken agreed that this should be an important book.

Finally, and once again, I must thank my wife, Mary Beth, and my sons for their patience with yet another book project.

SOURCES

To understand a person fully, you need to understand his family—and in that regard, I was fortunate to have available for my reading pleasure any number of books about Jeb's father, mother, and brother, as well as a couple of books written specifically about the family dynasty.

The life story of George Herbert Walker Bush was probably best told by Herbert Parmet in *George Bush: Life of a Lone Star Yankee* (Scribner's, 1997). Pamela Kilian admirably and evenhandedly told the tale of Jeb's mother in *Barbara Bush: Matriarch of a Dynasty* (Thomas Dunne, 2002). And Bill Minutaglio produced, to the best of my knowledge, the definitive biography to date of George Walker Bush with *First Son: George W. Bush and the Bush Family Dynasty* (Random House, 2001).

The two major books out there about the family dynasty came from two very different directions, but are both helpful in understanding the Bush clan. Peter and Rochelle Schweizer did the authorized version of the family album in *The Bushes: Portrait of a Dynasty* (Doubleday, 2004). It is a sympathetic take, no doubt—to the point of being apologetic. But it provides details that otherwise would never have seen the light of day, and for that I am eternally grateful. In terms of both voluminous and particular research, however, not even the Schweizers with their unparalleled access could match Kitty Kelley's *The Family: The Real Story of the Bush Dynasty* (Doubleday, 2004). This was quite clearly the *unauthorized* version of the Bush story. It is equally clear that Ms. Kelley did her homework. I drew heavily from both works as I pieced together the background of Jeb's provenance and his early years in West Texas.

The vast majority of the available information about Jeb Bush, though, comes from newspaper articles—in particular, newspaper articles written starting with his father's successful run for president in 1988. There is a cadre of Florida government and political journalists who did yeoman's work in documenting his life from that point forward through his successful run for Florida governor in 1998—a group that includes Brian Crowley, Ellen Debenport, Tom Fiedler, Sydney Freedberg, Tim Nickens, and some others. Easily the most entertaining piece, though, and in some ways the most insightful, was a long, rambling first-person account of Jeb's 1994 run by Jim DeFede, who was then a columnist with the alternative *New Times*. Another gem was Joel Achenbach's cover story for *Tropic*, the *Miami Herald*'s now-defunct Sunday magazine, in 1986.

All of the above helped me set the stage for the main topic of this book, which is Jeb's record as governor of the nation's fourth largest state. And in this area, my sources were primarily the people who I spoke to, the original government documents I studied, and the database analyses that I conducted. In those instances when I drew from other articles by other journalists about Jeb's governorship, almost all of them were about events and circumstances that I personally observed, and incorporated reporting whose accuracy I can personally vouch for.

Next is a bibliography of the books I drew from for this volume, followed by a chapter-by-chapter listing of the specific sources used for material that was either historical in nature or the result of enterprise reporting that I did not also replicate. Chapter Eight, "Voucher Madness," has no sources listed, as it is based entirely from my own notes and articles I wrote or cowrote for the *Palm Beach Post*.

Bibliography

Bruni, Frank. *Ambling Into History: The Unlikely Odyssey of George W. Bush*. New York: HarperCollins, 2002.

Bush, Barbara. *Barbara Bush: A Memoir*. New York: Scribner's, 1994.

———. *Barbara Bush: Reflections*. New York: Scribner's, 2003.

Bush, George, and Victor Gold. *Looking Forward: An Autobiography*. New York: Doubleday, 1987.

Bush, George, and Brent Scowcroft. *A World Transformed*. New York: Alfred A. Knopf, 1998.

Bush, George H.W. *All the Best, George Bush: My Life in Letters and Other Writings*. New York: Simon and Schuster, 1999.

Bush, Jeb, and Brian Yablonski. *Profiles in Character.* Miami: Foundation for Florida's Future, 1995.

Cramer, Richard Ben. *What It Takes: The Way to the White House.* New York: Random House, 1992.

Duffy, Michael, and Dan Goodgame. *Marching in Place: The Status Quo Presidency of George Bush.* New York: Simon and Schuster, 1992.

Graham, Bob, and Jeff Nussbaum. *Intelligence Matters: The CIA, the FBI, Saudi Arabia, and Failure of America's War on Terror.* New York: Random House, 2004.

Ivins, Molly, and Lou Dubose. *Shrub: The Short But Happy Political Life of George W. Bush.* New York: Random House, 2000.

Kelley, Kitty. *The Family: The Real Story of the Bush Dynasty.* New York: Doubleday, 2004.

Kilian, Pamela. *Barbara Bush: Matriarch of a Dynasty.* New York: Thomas Dunne, 2002.

Mansfield, Stephen. *The Faith of George W. Bush.* New York: Tarcher, 2003.

Minutaglio, Bill. *First Son: George W. Bush and the Bush Family Dynasty.* New York: Random House, 2001.

Parmet, Herbert. *George Bush: Life of a Lone Star Yankee.* New York: Scribner's, 1997.

Phillips, Kevin. *American Dynasty: Aristocracy, Fortune, and the Politics of Deceit in the House of Bush.* New York: Viking, 2004.

———. *American Theocracy: The Peril and Politics of Radical Religion, Oil, and Borrowed Money in the 21st Century.* New York: Viking, 2006.

Schweizer, Peter, and Rochelle Schweizer. *The Bushes: Portrait of a Dynasty.* New York: Doubleday, 2004.

Suskind, Ron. *The Price of Loyalty: George W. Bush, the White House, and the Education of Paul O'Neill.* New York: Simon and Schuster, 2004.

Chapter One: PRINCE JEB

St. John, Paige. "Challenges from Storm Excite, Define Gov. Bush." *Fort Myers News-Press,* October 3, 2004.

Chapter Two: BORN TO RULE

Blackman, Ann. "Bush Seen as a Driven Man." Associated Press, July 16, 1980.

Bumiller, Elisabeth. "Neighborly Fund-raiser." *Washington Post,* July 13, 1979.

Bush, Barbara. *Barbara Bush: A Memoir.* New York: Scribner's, 1994, pp. 135, 156, 285.

———. *Barbara Bush: Reflections.* New York: Scribner's, 2003, p. 249.

Cramer, Richard Ben. *What It Takes: The Way to the White House.* New York: Random House, 1992, p. 889.

Harrington, Walt. "Born to Run." *Washington Post,* September 28, 1986.

Kelley, Kitty. *The Family: The Real Story of the Bush Dynasty.* New York: Doubleday, 2004, pp. 53, 56, 313.

Kilian, Pamela. *Barbara Bush: Matriarch of a Dynasty.* New York: Thomas Dunne, 2002, pp. 13, 17, 18, 34–36, 40, 152.

Malmgren, Jeanne. "Columba Bush: Shy in the Spotlight." *St. Petersburg Times,* October 28, 1998.

Minutaglio, Bill. *First Son: George W. Bush and the Bush Family Dynasty.* New York: Random House, 2001, pp. 44, 173.

Schweizer, Peter, and Rochelle Schweizer. *The Bushes: Portrait of a Dynasty.* New York: Doubleday, 2004, pp. 7, 63, 132, 409, 497.

"The Men Behind the Masks." *Orlando Sentinel,* October 30, 1994.

Chapter Three: MIAMI

Cole, Richard. "Fugitive at Center of 1980s Political Scandal Arrested." Associated Press, October 6, 1993.

Crowley, Brian E. "The '80s: A Quick Million for Jeb Bush." *Palm Beach Post,* June 26, 1994.

Debenport, Ellen. "Candidate Jeb Bush Talks About His Past." *St. Petersburg Times,* December 19, 1993.

———. "Jeb Bush: His Name Is Scrutiny." *St. Petersburg Times,* December 20, 1993.

Freedberg, Sydney P. "Jeb Bush: The Son Rises Away from Dad's Shadow." *Miami Herald,* August 15, 1994.

Gerth, Jeff. "A Savings and Loan Bailout, and Bush's Son Jeb." *New York Times,* October 14, 1990.

Kelley, Kitty. *The Family: The Real Story of the Bush Dynasty.* New York: Doubleday, 2004, p. 413.

Maraniss, David. "The Bush Bunch." *Washington Post,* January 22, 1989.

Marks, Marilyn. "Governor May Seek State Sales Tax Cut." *St. Petersburg Times,* January 20, 1987.

Minutaglio, Bill. *First Son: George W. Bush and the Bush Family Dynasty.* New York: Random House, 2001, p. 138.

Perkins, Carole. "Jeb Bush a Partner in Renovation of River's Edge." *Business Journal–Jacksonville,* August 28, 1989.

Royce, Knut, and Gaylord Shaw. "The Jeb Connection." *Newsday,* October 3, 1988.

Schweizer, Peter, and Rochelle Schweizer. *The Bushes: Portrait of a Dynasty.* New York: Doubleday, 2004, pp. 270–271.

Singh, John. "Jeb Bush: A Private Son Goes Public." *Chicago Tribune,* June 26, 1992.

Swasy, Alecia, and Robert Trigaux. "Make the Money and Run." *St. Petersburg Times,* September 20, 1998.

"Bush's Son Aided IMC with Feds While Working on Land Deal." Associated Press, March 3, 1988.

Chapter Four: ELECTIONS ARE A CONTACT SPORT

Alterman, Eric. "GOP Chairman Lee Atwater: Playing Hardball." *New York Times,* April 20, 1989.

Crowley, Brian E. "Bush Raises $1 Million for Son's Campaign." *Palm Beach Post,* March 26, 1994.

———. "Jeb Bush Cool to Crenshaw's Call for GOP Debates." *Palm Beach Post,* May 15, 1994.

Davis, Chris, and Matthew Doig. "E-mail on Felon List Contradicts Governor." *Sarasota Herald-Tribune,* October 16, 2004.

———. "Hispanics Missing from Voter Purge List." *Sarasota Herald-Tribune,* July 7, 2004.

Debenport, Ellen. "Bush Banks on National Backing." *St. Petersburg Times,* May 2, 1994.

———. "He Intensifies Bush's Message." *St. Petersburg Times,* August 23, 1994.

Duffy, Michael, and Dan Goodgame. *Marching in Place: The Status Quo Presidency of George Bush.* New York: Simon and Schuster, 1992, pp. 34, 59, 81, 247.

Fiedler, Tom. "Bush Takes 'New Jeb' on Campaign Trail." *Miami Herald,* September 15, 1997.

Kelley, Kitty. *The Family: The Real Story of the Bush Dynasty.* New York: Doubleday, 2004, pp. 115–116, 555.

McCartney, Scott. "Even with Family Aid, Bush Never Made It 'Big Rich' in Oil." Associated Press, June 26, 1988.

Nickens, Tim. "Policy Group Proved Shrewd for Bush." *St. Petersburg Times,* September 13, 1998.

Parmet, Herbert. *George Bush: Life of a Lone Star Yankee.* New York: Scribner's, 1997, p. 298.

Ricker, Daniel. "Bush: Science Comes Before Intelligent Design." *Miami Herald,* December 26, 2005.

Schweizer, Peter, and Rochelle Schweizer. *The Bushes: Portrait of a Dynasty.* New York: Doubleday, 2004, pp. 361, 492.

Chapter Five: THE KING OF FLORIDA

James, Joni. "Bush Counts His What-ifs, Public and Personal." *St. Petersburg Times,* June 15, 2005.

Chapter Six: PRIVATIZE THIS

Cotterell, Bill. "State Audit Hammers Prison Panel." *Tallahassee Democrat,* July 26, 2005.

———. "State 'Efficiency Czar' Resigns in Protest." *Tallahassee Democrat,* May 15, 2001.

Hauserman, Julie. "Bush May Privatize Personnel Operation." *St. Petersburg Times,* September 7, 2001.

Hirth, Diane. "Florida May Go with DCF Privatization." *Tallahassee Democrat,* December 26, 2004.

James, Joni. "Disappointments Wear Away Zest for State Privatization." *St. Petersburg Times,* February 19, 2005.

O'Matz, Megan, Mark Hollis, and Sally Kestin. "3 DCF Staffers Quit After Inquiry." *South Florida Sun-Sentinel,* July 17, 2004.

Chapter Seven: KENDRICK MEEK

Allison, Wes. "Bush, McBride Didn't Draw Black Voters." *St. Petersburg Times,* November 8, 2002.

Cotterell, Bill. "Clergy Leader Sorry for Bush Support." *Tallahassee Democrat,* December 17, 2001.

Kelley, Kitty. *The Family: The Real Story of the Bush Dynasty.* New York: Doubleday, 2004, p. 211.

Kestin, Sally, and Fred Schulte. "How Clout May Count in Florida Health Care." *South Florida Sun-Sentinel,* April 29, 2001.

King, John. "Shadow of Former President Follows Bush Brothers Running for Governor." Associated Press, October 30, 1993.

Kunerth, Jeff. "Think of Me as Your Candidate, Jeb Bush Tells Hispanics." *Orlando Sentinel,* October 14, 1993.

Parmet, Herbert. *George Bush: Life of a Lone Star Yankee.* New York: Scribner's, 1997, pp. 100, 114.

"Bush Targets Hispanic Voters with Texas Ad." Associated Press, October 24, 1988.

"Put Away Those Ribbons." *St. Petersburg Times,* October 7, 1994.

Chapter Nine: WHO WANTS TO KNOW?

Duffy, Michael, and Dan Goodgame. *Marching in Place: The Status Quo Presidency of George Bush.* New York: Simon and Schuster, 1992, pp. 185–187.

Hauserman, Julie. "Plan Would Find Judges Compatible with Bush." *St. Petersburg Times,* October 1, 1999.

Kelley, Kitty. *The Family: The Real Story of the Bush Dynasty.* New York: Doubleday, 2004, pp. 243, 314, 395.

Leonard, Mike. "Bloomington Native Reports the News." *Herald-Times* (Bloomington, Ind.), October 2, 2005.

Schweizer, Peter, and Rochelle Schweizer. *The Bushes: Portrait of a Dynasty.* New York: Doubleday, 2004, p. xiv.

Chapter Ten: LET THEM EAT TAX CUTS

Judd, Alan. "Jeb! Will His Pedigree Carry the Day?" *Gainesville Sun,* November 1, 1994.

Chapter Eleven: IN GOD'S NAME

Decker, Twila. "Bush's Renewed Commitments." *St. Petersburg Times,* June 7, 2005.

Griffin, Michael. "Benefit of Religious Vote in Doubt." *Orlando Sentinel,* July 29, 1994.

Kelley, Kitty. *The Family: The Real Story of the Bush Dynasty.* New York: Doubleday, 2004, p. 371.

Kirkpatrick, David D. "Crisis of the Bush Code." *New York Times,* October 9, 2005.

Mansfield, Stephen. *The Faith of George W. Bush.* New York: Tarcher, 2003, pp. 20, 61–62.

Parmet, Herbert. *George Bush: Life of a Lone Star Yankee.* New York: Scribner's, 1997, pp. 134–135.

Schweizer, Peter, and Rochelle Schweizer. *The Bushes: Portrait of a Dynasty.* New York: Doubleday, 2004, p. 334.

Chapter Twelve: WITH US OR AGAINST US

Bearak, Barry. "U.S. Labels Bosch a Terrorist." *Los Angeles Times,* June 29, 1989.

Boyd, Gerald M. "Bush Aides Assess the Contra Speculation." *New York Times,* October 22, 1986.

Bush, Barbara. *Barbara Bush: A Memoir.* New York: Scribner's, 1994, p. 269.

———. *Barbara Bush: Reflections.* New York: Scribner's, 2003, p. 107

Debenport, Ellen. "Jeb Bush: His Name Is Scrutiny." *St. Petersburg Times,* December 20, 1993.

Kelley, Kitty. *The Family: The Real Story of the Bush Dynasty.* New York: Doubleday, 2004, pp. 286-287, 301, 348, 394.

Minutaglio, Bill. *First Son: George W. Bush and the Bush Family Dynasty.* New York: Random House, 2001, p. 116.

Parmet, Herbert. *George Bush: Life of a Lone Star Yankee.* New York: Scribner's, 1997, pp. 148, 174.

Schweizer, Peter, and Rochelle Schweizer. *The Bushes: Portrait of a Dynasty.* New York: Doubleday, 2004, pp. 81, 190.

Weinraub, Bernard. "Wooing Cuban-Americans in GOP." *New York Times,* May 22, 1987.

Chapter Thirteen: TOO MANY BUSHES?

LaPolt, Alisa, and Paige St. John. "Jeb: Put Class Limits Up to Vote." Gannett News Service, October 4, 2002.

Schweizer, Peter, and Rochelle Schweizer. *The Bushes: Portrait of a Dynasty.* New York: Doubleday, 2004, p. 287.

INDEX